A PRACTICAL APPROACH TO
STRENGTH TRAINING

3rd EDITION

MATT BRZYCKI

**Coordinator of Health Fitness, Strength and Conditioning Programs
Princeton University**

MASTERS PRESS

NTC/Contemporary Publishing Group

Library of Congress Cataloging-in-Publication Data

Brzycki, Matt, 1957–
    A practical approach to strength training / Matt Brzycki.—3rd ed.
       p.   cm.
    Includes bibliographical references and index.
    ISBN 1-57028-018-5
      1. Weight training.   2. Weight training—Equipment and supplies.
  I. Title.
  GV546.B83   1995
  613.7′1—dc20   95-12577
                                              CIP

Front cover design by Phil Velikan
All photographs by Matt Brzycki unless otherwise noted.

Published by Masters Press
A division of NTC/Contemporary Publishing Group, Inc.
4255 West Touhy Avenue, Lincolnwood (Chicago), Illinois 60712-1975
U.S.A.
Printed in the United States of America
International Standard Book Number: 1-57028-018-5

00 01 02 03 04 05 VH 21 20 19 18 17 16 15 14 13 12 11 10 9 8 7

Table of Contents

This book is dedicated in memory of Anna Stanko Balut (1915-1994)

ACKNOWLEDGEMENTS

Books are rarely — if ever — completed by one person single-handedly. Many important people deserve recognition for providing me with timely support, inspiration, information and direction over the course of many years, thereby making this book a reality. In a sense, they're all coauthors.

Family: my wife, Alicia; my mother, Marian Brzycki; my sister, Marlene Brzycki; and my father- and mother-in-law, Lucian and Audrey Grimaldi.

Friends: Tony Alexander, Mark Asanovich, Shaun and Tracey Brown, John Carlson, Robert and Claire Chapman, Paula Contegiacomo, Andy and Terrie Foltiny, Kurt and Dylis Girmen, Dick and Eve Johnson, Joseph Kotch, Kristopher Kotch, Tom and Gail Laputka, Ken and Kathy Leistner, Jim Logue, Ken and Marianne Mannie, Shawn and Kathy McCormick, David and Mimi Metzbower, Tom and Mercy O'Rourke, Jim and Caroline Small, Mike Smith, Ed and Dina Snarski, Peter Soderman, Bill and Helen Tierney, Michael Zerbe and Ray, Jeff and Carole Zirpolo.

Mentors: George Biedenbender, Robert Christina, Robert Corba, Randall Cottrell, John Doolittle, Robert Eisenbraun, Donald Ferrell, Paul Kennedy, Tom Laputka, Robert Moody, Richard Nelson, Dan Riley, Richard Sales, Richard St. Pierre, Karl Stoedefalke, G. Thomas Tait and James Thompson.

Professional Colleagues: Eric Amkraut, Jason Arapoff, Brad Bates, Randy Berning, Joel Blunk, Mike Bradley, Cedric Bryant, Paul Buchkowski, Joey Bullock, Tami Campanella, Rocco Castellano, Ed Cicale, Shawn Cooley, Ed Coviello, Chet Dalgewicz, Mike Fabian, Brandi Feinberg, Jim Flanagan, Jeff Friday, Frank Fugiurele, Chet Fuhrman, John Graham, Jeff Greenburg, Ralph Griesser, Russ Gibson, Chip Harrison, Phil Hartigan, Tom Katenkamp, Hank Kearns, Ted Lambrinides, Jeff Marmelstein, Mickey Marrotti, Karen Mittleman, Steve Murray, Willis Paine, Jim Peterson, Rachael Picone, Jim Plocki, Jim Polli, Frank Pomarico, Robert Spector, Eric Stein, Martin Streight, John Thomas, Kevin Tolbert, Jeff Watson, Doug Werner, Wayne Westcott, Steve Wetzel, Mike Wolf and Ed Zambraski.

Book Models: Marcus Amick, Rich Burton, Christopher Colbeck, Rob Dribbon, Jerry Evans, John Kurelja, Mary Ann McChesney, Pete Ram, Greg Roman, Sasha Ruiz, Ken Samuel, Michele Spreen, Trevor Tierney, Monica Tilton, Paul Vecchione, Greg Williams and Shane Woolf.

Masters Press: Tom Bast (publisher), Holly Kondras (managing editor), Pat Brady (proofreader), Terry Varvel (editorial assistance), Phil Velikan (artist) and other staff members who helped in this project.

Editors: Elmer Blasco (*Athletic Journal*), Lanny Bryant (*Wrestling USA*), Herman Masin (*Scholastic Coach*), Barry Pavelec (*Coaching Clinic*), Amy Stoneman (*Nautilus*) and Amy Wolterstorff (formerly of Masters Press).

I apologize to anyone I may have overlooked. Finally, this book acknowledges all individuals — past, present and future — who thrive on hard work, seek new challenges and always give everything their best effort simply because that's the way it's supposed to be.

Credits:
Front cover design by Phil Velikan
All photos by Matt Brzycki unless otherwise noted.

Part 1

EXPLODING THE MYTHS
AND MISCONCEPTIONS

1

STRENGTH TRAINING: PAST, PRESENT AND FUTURE

Lifting weights wasn't always as popular as it is today. In 1862, Dio Lewis — a well-known physical educator (who practiced medicine without a degree) — wrote "thoughtful physiologists deeply regret the lifting mania" and "lifting is an inferior means of physical training" (Lewis 1862). Lewis wasn't alone in his criticism of weight training. Years ago, a well-developed physique was actually viewed as being somewhat freakish and unnatural. In addition, there were fears that lifting weights would reduce flexibility, dull reactions and ruin skills.

In the late 1800s and early 1900s, lifting weights was done almost exclusively by professional strongmen and amateur competitive weightlifters. Professional strongmen — like the legendary Eugene Sandow and Louis Cyr — performed feats of strength on stage as part of theater and circus acts. After 1910, the professional strongman gradually became a rarity on the performing stage, and the era of the professional stage strongman came to an end with the slow death of vaudeville in the 1930s (Todd 1986). The rise of amateur competitive weightlifting added to the fall of the professional strongman.

Even in the early 1960s lifting weights was rarely done by the average person or, for that matter, by athletes. Needless to say, in those days it was even more unusual for females to lift weights. Prior to this time, almost everything written about athletics or fitness either didn't mention lifting weights or condemned its usage. As some athletes began to experiment with weight training in the early to mid 1960s, the fears concerning lifting weights slowly but gradually subsided. With the realization that weight training could be beneficial, individuals were soon hired by universities and professional sports teams to design and administer programs for the development of muscular strength. These specialists were first referred to as "weight coaches" then later as "strength coaches."

In 1962 — exactly one century after Lewis described lifting weights as an "inferior" form of exercise — Princeton University took a bold step by hiring Dick Landis as its first strength coach (Landis 1983). At that time, there were only a handful of strength coaches in the entire country. In 1963, the San Diego Chargers hired Alvin Roy as the first strength coach in professional football (Leistner 1987b). The Chargers were quite successful, winning the American Football League (AFL) Championship, and much of the team's success was attributed to their organized weight training program. Unfortunately, the 1963 Chargers were also one of the first teams to experiment with anabolic steroids (Gilbert 1969). Nevertheless, the significance of weight training had been firmly established.

By the early 1970s, strength coaching as a profession was still in its infancy. When universities and professional sports teams first began to seek advice, they quickly solicited those individuals who appeared to know something about weight training. The perceived "experts" of that era were the competitive weightlifters. Since Olympic-style weightlifting was more popular in those days than the sport of powerlifting, many of the first strength "authorities" had a background as Olympic-style weightlifters.

To a degree, the strength training specialists in that period of time were chosen almost by default from the ranks of the competitive weightlifters. Back then, there really wasn't any other pool of candidates that could possibly be considered as authorities or advisers on strength training. First of all, relatively few people — other than competitive weightlifters — were involved with lifting weights. Secondly, there wasn't much in the way of specialized or formalized schooling to educate potential strength professionals about weight training. Further, there existed little or no practical knowledge about lifting weights and the only theoretical basis was that handed down from competitive weightlifters. Finally, the selection of competitive weightlifters as consultants in strength training seemed a natural choice since those athletes certainly had above-average levels of strength and muscular development.

The initial practice of hiring competitive weightlifters as strength specialists soon spawned a multitude of growing pains. In most cases, competitive weightlifters knew absolutely nothing about the actual physical demands of other sports — nor were they sensitive to the fitness needs of the general population. A greater problem than that, however, pertained to their weightlifter-inspired methods and mentality. In their new role as strength training consultants, competitive weightlifters advocated programs and routines that were most familiar to them — programs and routines that they themselves used to train with for the sport of competitive weightlifting. Olympic-style weightlifters knew how to get strong in order to perform several specific movements: the overhead press, the snatch and the clean and jerk; with powerlifters, it was the squat, the bench press and the deadlift. In most cases, the protocols that were advocated to others weren't anywhere near being practical. In addition, the movements themselves required a great deal of time, effort and patience simply to learn and perfect the complex, highly specialized skills to the point where they could be performed with any degree of proficiency and safety. To make matters worse, a national organization was formed that glorified, hyped and encouraged methods used by the Eastern European weightlifters — particularly the Soviets, the Bulgarians and the East Germans. As a result, most individuals in the early 1970s were actually using modified competitive weightlifting programs under the guise of strength training programs.

By the mid 1970s, the knowledge and popularity of weight training had increased tremendously and a second school of thought emerged. This particular group realized that the "first generation" of strength specialists was essentially training men and women for competitive weightlifting. As such, this "new breed" of strength professional suggested a much safer and more practical approach to strength training that was based upon scientific investigation and common sense — not anecdotal evidence and wild speculation. Needless to say, the vastly different approaches and perspectives of these two factions sparked bitter and emotional controversies concerning the correct method of lifting weights . . . controversies that still exist to this day. However, virtually every disagreement between the two groups relates to the application of the training information that has been handed down from competitive weightlifters.

WEIGHTLIFTER-INSPIRED PROGRAMMING

The early utilization of competitive weightlifting techniques was a springboard in propagating many myths and misconceptions about proper strength training. The emotional attachments to many of these beliefs has been force-fed to the strength and fitness community with a religious zeal by the "Old Guard." Fortunately, these notions have been questioned and dismantled by logical reasoning and legitimate, unbiased research that has no emotional stake in the results. These are some of the traditional practices and perceptions that have been discredited by the academic community:

Explosive Lifting

Because the Olympic-style lifts are performed in a rapid or explosive manner, it was assumed that doing these lifts and related movements done in preparation for them — such as the power clean and the push press — would develop explosiveness (Leistner 1989a). Lifting a weight in a rapid, explosive fashion is ill-advised for two reasons. First of all, explosive lifting introduces momentum into the movement, which makes the exercise less productive and less efficient. Secondly, explosive lifting can also be danger-

ous. (Explosive lifting is covered in greater detail in Chapter 4.)

Specificity

Another well-intended but misguided practice handed down from competitive weightlifters involves the use of weighted objects —like barbells and medicine balls — to mimic sports skills. The Principle of Specificity states that an activity must be specific to an intended skill in order for maximal improvement, or "carryover," to occur. Specific means exact or identical, not similar or just like. The truth is, there is no exercise done in the weight room — with barbells or machines — that is identical to any athletic skill. (Specificity is discussed further in Chapter 5.)

Periodization

Also referred to as "cycling," periodization is a theoretical training schedule of preplanned workouts that have been popularized by weightlifters to peak for a one-repetition maximum (1-RM) during their competition. The idea is to change or "cycle" the number of sets, repetitions and workload of the exercises performed in the weight room (Matveyev 1981). For example, in its simplest form you might do 3 sets of 10 reps in each exercise with 75 percent of your 1-RM in Week #1, 3 sets of 8 reps with 80 percent of your 1-RM in Week #2 and so on until you are performing a 1-RM.

The concept of periodization is based upon the fact that highly competitive weightlifters peak for only several contests a year. This type of protocol doesn't do much good for someone —such as an athlete — who might have to peak two or three times a week for several months (Leistner 1987a). Indeed, what competitions does an athlete peak for? Aren't they all important? Imagine an athlete saying, "Sorry about my performance tonight, Coach, but I'm not scheduled to peak for 10 more days."

Another problem with periodization is the inflexible nature of preplanned workouts (Lambrinides 1990d). The reality is that people often get sick or injured and are forced to miss workouts. In the event of a missed workout, does the person renew training according to their preplanned schedule? If not, at what point in the preplanned schedule does the person resume? Finally, periodization doesn't consider the fact that individuals progress at varying rates. Some individuals will not be able to proceed as fast as suggested by the preplanned workouts, while the progress of others will be repressed by the restrictiveness.

In short, trying to implement periodization with people other than competitive weightlifters is confusing, impractical and unnecessary. There are more efficient and far less complicated ways of addressing a person's strength training needs.

One-Repetition Maximum Attempts

The most traditional way to assess dynamic strength has been to determine how much weight a person can lift for one repetition (1-RM). Indeed, obtaining a 1-RM is perhaps the most frequently used test for evaluating muscular strength. Such tests are usually performed using three or four exercises that are representative of the body's major muscle groups. For example, a bench press or an incline press is typically used to assess the strength of the chest, shoulders and triceps while a squat or a leg press is often used to measure the strength of the hips and legs.

Obtaining a 1-RM is also an integral aspect of strength programs that are based upon periodized workouts. Success in the sport of competitive weightlifting is determined by the ability of the athlete to lift as much weight as possible one time. However, those who don't participate in weightlifting competitions have no business performing a 1-RM.

Several inherent problems are associated with attempting to lift a maximal weight for one repetition:

- **Orthopedic stress.** A 1-RM is dangerous (Riley 1992; Thomas 1994; Watson 1994) and is often the cause of training injuries (Seminick 1990). Performing a 1-RM with heavy weights can place an inordinate and unreasonable amount of stress on the muscles, bones and connective tissues (Leistner 1987a; LeSuer and McCormick 1993). An injury occurs when the stress exceeds the tensile strength of those structural components.

- **Blood pressure response.** A 1-RM effort tends to increase blood pressure beyond that which is normally encountered when using submaximal weights. These concerns are magnified in certain populations such as younger adolescents and older adults.

- **Skill proficiency.** A 1-RM lift is a highly specialized skill that requires a great deal of technique, practice and patience. Athletes could use this time better by practicing and perfecting sport-specific skills and techniques.

- **Time involvement.** The process of obtaining a 1-RM is time-consuming because of the number of "warm-up sets" preceding the maximum attempt (Riley 1992; LeSuer and McCormick 1993). Again, athletes could spend this valuable time engaged in specific sport-related activities.

- **Muscular inroading.** The amount of muscular fatigue — or "inroading" — that is produced is critical in the development of strength. As the percentage of the weight being used approaches a 1-RM, the degree of muscular inroading becomes less. For instance, reaching muscular failure with a near-maximal weight of 95 percent of a 1-RM indicates that an inroad was made into more than 5 percent of the starting strength level; conversely, reaching muscular failure with a submaximal weight of 75 percent of a 1-RM means that an inroad was made into more than 25 percent of the starting strength level.

In summation, using the 1-RM — either as a testing method or a training protocol — is time-consuming, potentially dangerous and less effective in producing a desirable level of muscular fatigue.

Orthopedically Unsafe Exercises

There's no question that performing the movements practiced by competitive weightlifters can increase strength. Any

The sport of competitive weightlifting carries a certain degree of orthopedic risk. (Photo by Bill Schmidt)

exercise that progressively applies a load on the muscles will stimulate improvements in muscular size and strength. There is, however, a question relating to the inherent risk of injury. Scientific, athletic and rehabilitative professionals have questioned the safety of certain movements done by competitive weightlifters for years (Jesse 1977; Kulund et al. 1978; Reston 1982; Riley 1982c; Leistner 1985; Welday 1986; Vorobyev 1988; Mannie 1993; Friday 1994; Watson 1994). In addition, the American Orthopaedic Society for Sports Medicine — an organization that distinguishes between strength training and weightlifting — contraindicates the Olympic-style lifting movements in training regimens (Mannie 1994). Clearly, the potential for injury from most of these exercises is positively enormous. Young individuals are especially vulnerable (Jesse 1977 and 1979). The American Academy of Pediatrics (1983) recommends that preadolescents should not practice competitive weightlifting movements because of the "high injury rate." Brown and Kimball (1983) questioned 71 competitors entered in the 1981 Michigan Teenage Powerlifting Championship. The population sustained 98 injuries related to powerlifting which caused the 71 individuals to miss 1,126 days of training.

The proper performance of any movement in the weight room requires close supervision. Olympic-style weightlifting movements, however, need the constant, hands-on attention of a qualified individual who teaches proper weightlifting technique (Friday 1994). In many high schools, colleges and fitness centers where a large number of people are participating in a strength program, it's almost impossible for each person to receive adequate instruction and individual attention.

Even if a person has very good technique, various types of injuries can result from the performance of competitive weightlifting movements. Most of the exercises used by competitive weightlifters expose the muscles, joints and connective tissue to excessive biomechanical loading that can immediately result in traumatic injuries (e.g., various sprains and strains) or predispose a person to later injuries (Kennedy 1986a; Leistner 1989b; Brown 1990). Kulund and others (1978) interviewed 80 competitive weightlifters who had 405 years of cumulative experience in competitive weightlifting. The 80 weightlifters reported 111 injuries related to weightlifting. The shoulder, the knee and the wrist accounted for 68 percent of the injuries. Injuries to the elbow have also been noted during the performance of Olympic-style movements (Kulund et al. 1978; Vorobyev 1988).

It's common for competitive weightlifters to suffer lumbar pain (Vorobyev 1988). Brown and Kimball (1983) reported that 50 percent of all injuries sustained by competitive powerlifters were to the low back. Indeed, low back pain is the dominant complaint among former weightlifters (Granhed and Morelli 1988). In most cases, the lumbar pain is caused by compression stress on the spinal column. The intervertebral discs are compressed and the vertebrae are deformed. Ligament pulls and strangulation of nerve roots are sometimes seen (Vorobyev 1988).

Studies have suggested that competitive weightlifters may be prone to developing spondylolysis, which is essentially a vertebral stress fracture (Kulund et al. 1978). The occurrence rate for spondylolysis in the general population has been estimated between 4.2 percent (Rowe and Roche 1953) and 6.0 percent (McCarroll, Miller and Ritter 1986). On the other hand, Kotani and coworkers (1971) reported a 30.7 percent incidence of spondylolysis in a random survey of 26 weightlifters, and Rossi (1978) noted a 36.2 percent occurrence of spondylolysis in 58 weightlifters. A study by Dangles and Spencer (1987) reported spondylolysis in 44 percent of 47 subjects (27 Olympic-style weightlifters and 20 powerlifters). During an interview to discuss his study, Dr. Chris Dangles stated: "We believe that spondylolysis represents a mechanical failure caused by the overload of competitive lifts" (Duda 1987). Rossi and Dragoni (1990) found clinical evidence of spondylolysis in 22.7 percent of 97 weightlifters.

It should be noted that these last four studies, along with that of Kulund and others (1978), investigated seasoned competitive weightlifters who had practiced and perfected their technique far more than the average person. Yet, despite their experience, they exhibited a significantly higher incidence of orthopedic disorder compared to the general population. Although others will not be lifting competitively, they are subject to the same types of injuries if they perform these lifts. And if experienced competitive weightlifters get injured — despite spending several hours each day practicing those movements — imagine the potential for injury in other people who perform those lifts.

The sport of competitive weightlifting carries a certain degree of orthopedic risk. Competitive weightlifters accept those risks as being part of the sport. However, individuals who aren't competitive weightlifters shouldn't have to assume such an unreasonable risk of injury. For reasons of safety, movements done by competitive weightlifters should only be performed by competitive weightlifters — and only because it relates to their sport.

Two specific movements of particular orthopedic concern are power cleans and barbell squats (Riley 1992). Risser, Risser and Preston (1990) examined the incidence of injury related to weight training by surveying 354 junior and senior high school football players. Their study revealed the most common site of injury was the low back. The power clean, the clean and jerk and the barbell squat accounted for the majority of injuries.

Power cleans. This exercise is basically the initial phase of a competitive, Olympic-style lift known as the "clean and jerk" and is one of the most dangerous exercises a person can do (Riley 1982c). Stone and his cohorts (1994) note "It is possible that as the number of clean and jerks [performed] increases in training, so does the number of injuries."

A power clean is inherently dangerous because it is performed explosively (Jacobson 1981; Diange 1984; Welday 1986; Leistner 1987b). Recall that ballistic movements are also inefficient due to the involvement of momentum. Furthermore, "explosive" lifting does not translate into "explosive" athletic skills. (The myth of explosive transfer is discussed further in Chapters 4 and 5.)

Power cleans cause repetitive, forced hyperextension of the lumbar spine. This forced hyperextension can lead to any number of injuries and defects, including lumbar sprain, lumbar strain, disc injury and spondylolysis (Jesse 1977; Mannie 1994). Excessive impact forces as a result of "catching" the bar could also increase the risk of injury (Stone et al. 1994).

Barbell squats. The safety of squatting has been challenged since the early 1960s (Klein 1962). It has also been questioned by researchers (Rasch and Allman 1972) and strength coaches (Andress 1990; Brown 1990; Riley 1992; Thomas 1994). Squatting with a barbell on the shoulders creates excessive shear forces (i.e., side-to-side) in the knee joint. As the length of the legs increase, so does the shearing or "grinding" effect in the knee — someone with long legs is more prone to injury than someone with short legs. In addition, a barbell squat causes compression of the spinal column, which could result in a herniated or ruptured disc. Compression is most evident when the lifter is in the bottom position of the barbell squat, where the anterior aspect of the lumbar vertebrae is compacted and the intervertebral discs are pushed in a posterior direction. Research by Cappozzo and associates (1985) has revealed that when someone squats with as little as .8 to 1.6 times their bodyweight, the force in the low back region is actually 6 to 10 times their bodyweight. That means that if you weigh 180 pounds and do barbell squats with about 144 to 288 pounds, the load on your lumbar area can be anywhere from 1,040 to 1,800 pounds. The exact amount of force is a function of how far the weight is from the low back, so someone with a long torso subjects his or her low back to higher forces than someone with a shorter torso.

There are some people who have the desirable body proportions (i.e., short torsos and legs) necessary to perform barbell squats in a relatively safe fashion. However, someone with a long torso and long legs is not only at a severe biomechanical disadvantage during a barbell squat, but also exposes the joints to unreasonable forces and a higher risk of injury (Leistner 1991; Thomas 1994). Therefore, barbell squats are inappropriate and ill-advised for most of the population, especially those with unfavorable body proportions (i.e., elongated spines and legs). The same muscles used in a barbell squat — namely the hips and the legs — can be exercised in a much safer manner with a movement such as a leg press (Brown 1990; Thomas 1994).

Free Weight Superiority

Another mistaken notion advanced by the competitive weightlifters is that free weights — barbells and dumbbells

The sole factors in determining your response from strength training are your inherited characteristics and your level of intensity — not the equipment that is used. (Photo by Kathy Leistner)

— are superior to machines. Keep in mind that the implement used in competitive weightlifting is a barbell. The first generation of strength coaches, being competitive weightlifters, brought their impassioned devotion in that specific training modality to the strength training arena. The fact is, a person won't develop one way with machines and another way with barbells (assuming that the levels of intensity are similar with both modalities). A 10-week study by Pipes (1978) compared groups training three times per week with either free weights or machines. All groups had significant increases in strength and lean body mass and a decrease in body fat. There were no significant differences between the groups. In another 10-week study, Messier and Dill (1985) found no significant differences in strength increases between a group using machines and a group using free weights.

A muscle must experience an appropriate level of fatigue with a workload that is progressive from one workout to the next in order to increase in size and strength. Since muscles do not have a brain, eyeballs or cognitive ability, they can't possibly "know" the source of the workload. So, it doesn't matter whether the muscles are fatigued with a resistance that comes from a machine, a barbell, a cinder block or a human being (Riley 1982a; Bates, Wolf and Blunk 1990). In short, there's no documented difference in relative strength gains using one form of resistance over another (Lillegard and Terrio 1994). The sole factors in determining your response from strength training are your inherited characteristics and your level of intensity — not the equipment that is used.

If a particular movement should receive more emphasis, it should be primarily because of its role in injury prevention — not because it has been proclaimed somewhere as a core exercise based upon competitive weightlifting-inspired prejudice.

The next time you watch a basketball game, a football game or any other athletic event, see if you can tell which teams used free weights, which teams used machines, which teams used a combination of both and which teams used nothing at all. Obviously, it would be impossible to tell because the source of resistance matters very little, if any, in a person's response to weight training. As such, equipment choices should be based on individual preference — not commercial or personal bias.

Core Exercises

Many of the movements mentioned earlier — such as the bench press, the power clean and the barbell squat — are often referred to as major lifts or "core exercises." Because these exercises generally work a rather large amount of muscle mass, some individuals feel that these movements should comprise the backbone of a strength routine. However, to suggest that there are major lifts is also to suggest that there are minor lifts — or exercises that are somehow less important (Mannie 1988).

Indeed, some movements have been unceremoniously classified as auxiliary or supplemental exercises. But don't all exercises have some importance? For example, is a bench press really more valuable than a lat pulldown? No, not

really. Both movements serve a purpose in strengthening specific muscle groups and, in this case, both exercises are equally important in terms of providing muscular balance between the chest and the upper back, thereby reducing the risk of injury. For those who can perform the movement safely, should a squat be classified as a core exercise and a neck extension be classified as a supplemental exercise? Again, the answer is no. Although a neck extension works considerably less muscle mass than a squat, a neck extension is infinitely more valuable because it protects some athletes — such as football players and wrestlers — from cervical injury. Yet, you'll never see any neck movements recommended as core exercises.

The point is this: All exercises are important in some way and should receive equal emphasis (Riley 1992). If a particular movement should receive more emphasis, it should be primarily because of its role in injury prevention — not because it has been proclaimed somewhere as a core exercise based upon competitive weightlifting-inspired prejudice.

Unnecessary Warm-up Sets

In most workouts, the routine is comprised of numerous warm-up sets — sets that are unproductive because they are submaximal efforts. Warm-up sets are necessary, but only for competitive weightlifters. During their training, competitive weightlifters need those extra sets to practice the specific movement patterns required by their sport; they also require warm-up sets to reduce their risk of sustaining an injury during a 1-RM attempt.

A strength program need not be a marathon session of endless warm-up sets. If a relatively high number of repetitions are performed (i.e., at least 6 repetitions) and the weight is lifted in a controlled fashion, the muscles will "warm-up" as a person does the exercise (Thomas 1994). Keep in mind that performing too many sets can also increase the likelihood of various overuse injuries due to repetitive muscular trauma.

A PRACTICAL APPROACH

Over the years, the popularity of weight training has increased tremendously. Today, strength training has been accepted by mostly everyone as a vital ingredient for achieving physical success.

The strength training profession has matured by leaps and bounds from the early days of weightlifting-inspired programming. Today's strength consultant is now armed with scientifically supported knowledge, research-based information and common sense —factors necessary for a practical approach to strength training.

2
BASIC ANATOMY AND MUSCULAR FUNCTION

Before beginning any detailed discussion about strength training, it's necessary to first explain some basic anatomy and muscular function. The body is basically a system of levers. Movement of these levers — the bones — is produced by the muscles, which are anchored to the bones by tendons.

There are three different types of muscle: cardiac, smooth and skeletal. Cardiac muscle makes up most of the heart wall, smooth muscle is found in the walls of blood vessels and skeletal muscle acts across joints to produce movement.

Muscles are made up of numerous muscle fibers which, in turn, are made up of many myofibrils. (To get an idea of this arrangement, picture a telephone cable containing hundreds of wires.) Myofibrils contain two contractile protein filaments — the thin actin and the thicker myosin — which lie parallel to one another. Muscular contraction occurs at this level.

MUSCLE CONTRACTIONS

Contraction refers to the process of a muscle generating a force. The force exerted by a contracting muscle on an object is known as the muscle tension; the force exerted by the weight of an object on a muscle is known as the load. Therefore, muscle tension and load are opposing forces (Vander, Sherman and Luciano 1975).

There are three types of muscle contractions: concentric, eccentric and isometric. All three types of muscle contractions can be used during the performance of each repetition.

A concentric muscle contraction is one in which a muscle shortens against a load — such as when you raise a weight. In this case, muscular tension is greater than the external load. The mechanical work is positive. As such, raising a weight is sometimes referred to as the positive phase of a movement.

An eccentric muscular contraction occurs when a muscle lengthens against a load — such as when you lower a weight. In this instance, muscular tension is less than the external load. The mechanical work is negative. Therefore, lower-

ing a weight is typically referred to as the negative phase of a movement.

Finally, an isometric (or static) contraction is one in which the contractile component of a muscle shortens while the elastic connective tissue lengthens by the same amount, thereby producing no change in the overall length. An example of an isometric contraction would be exerting tension against an immovable object or holding a weight in a static position. Since no movement takes place during an isometric muscle contraction, the mechanical work is zero. (Of course, energy must be provided for an isometric muscle contraction to occur. Although there is no mechanical work performed, there is metabolic work.)

THE SLIDING FILAMENT THEORY

Initially advanced and later confirmed by Huxley (1958 and 1965), the most widely accepted theory of explaining muscular contraction is the Sliding Filament Theory. As the name of this theory implies, one set of proteinous filaments is thought to slide over the other and overlap (like pistons in a sleeve), thereby shortening the muscle. Here's how: The myosin filaments have tiny protein projections in the shape of globular heads, which extend toward the actin filaments. During a concentric muscular contraction, it's believed that these projections — or "crossbridges" — bind to the actin filament and then swivel in a ratchetlike fashion — much like oars in a boat — in such a way that it pulls the actin over the myosin filament. The crossbridges then uncouple from the actin, pivot, reattach and repeat the cycle. Thus, this process can be summed up as "attach-rotate-detach-rotate." A single myosin crossbridge may attach and detach with an actin filament hundreds of times in the course of a single muscular contraction (i.e., one repetition). This process occurs along the entire myofibril and among all the myofibrils of a muscle fiber. However, the crossbridges do not attach-rotate-detach-rotate at the same time since this would result in a series of jerks rather than a smooth movement.

THE MAJOR MUSCLES

Incredible as it may seem, there are more than 600 muscles in the human body — and about six billion muscle fibers. In fact, each one of the forearms is made up of 19 separate muscles with such exotic-sounding names as "extensor carpi radialis brevis" and "flexor digitorum superficialis." It's well beyond the scope and purpose of this book to discuss the muscles in such great detail. Instead, this chapter will only focus on the major muscle groups —muscles that you should be familiar with.

The major muscle groups described will be the hips, legs, upper torso, arms, neck, abdominals and lower back. These seven major muscle groups are further subdivided into their most important components. Brief notes on each muscle's location and function are given along with anatomical terminology that is generally accepted in weight room parlance.

HIPS

Buttocks. The buttocks muscles are the largest and strongest muscles in the body. The buttocks are composed of three main muscle groups: the gluteus maximus, the gluteus medius and the gluteus minimus. The primary function of the gluteus maximus is hip extension (driving the upper leg backward); the main function of the gluteus medius and the gluteus minimus is hip abduction (spreading the legs apart). The "glutes" are important muscles used in running and jumping.

Adductors. The adductor group is composed of five muscles that are located throughout the inner thigh. The adductor magnus is the largest of these muscles. The muscles of the inner thigh are used during adduction of the hip (bringing the legs together).

Iliopsoas. This is a collective term for the two primary muscles of the front hip area: the iliacus and the psoas. The main function of the iliopsoas is to flex the hip (bring the knee to the chest). The iliopsoas plays a major role in many skills such as lifting your knees as you walk or run. The iliacus and the psoas are sometimes considered with the muscles of the abdomen.

LEGS

Hamstrings. The "hams" are located on the backside of the upper leg and actually include three separate muscles: the semimembranosus, the semitendinosus and the biceps femoris. Together, these muscles are involved in flexing the lower leg around the knee joint (raising the heel toward the hip) and in hip extension. The hamstrings are used during virtually all running and jumping activities. Unfortunately, the muscle is very susceptible to pulls and tears. Strong hamstrings are necessary to balance the effects of the powerful quadricep muscles (Westcott 1983).

Quadriceps. The "quads" are the most important muscles on the front part of the thighs. As the name suggests, the quadriceps are made up of four muscles. The vastus lateralis is located on the outside of the thigh; the vastus medialis resides on the inner (medial) side of the thigh above the patella (the kneecap); between these two thigh muscles is the vastus intermedius; and finally, laying on top of the

vastus intermedius is the rectus femoris. The main function of the quads is extending (or straightening) the lower leg at the knee joint. The quads are involved in all running, kicking and jumping skills.

Calves. Each calf is made up of two important muscles — the gastrocnemius (or "gastroc") and the soleus — which are located on the back side of the lower leg. Sometimes these two muscles are jointly referred to as the "triceps surae" or, more simply, the "gastroc-soleus." The soleus actually resides underneath the gastroc and is used primarily when the knee is bent at 90 degrees or more (e.g., in the seated position). The calves are involved when the foot is extended at the ankle (or when rising up on the toes). The calves play a major role in running and jumping activities.

Dorsi flexors. The front part of the lower leg contains four muscles that are sometimes simply referred to as the "dorsi flexors." The largest of these muscles is the tibialis anterior. The dorsi flexors are primarily used in flexing the foot toward the knee. It is critical to strengthen the dorsi flexors as a safeguard against shin splints.

UPPER TORSO

Chest. The major muscle surrounding the chest area is the pectoralis major. It is thick, flat and fan-shaped and is the most superficial muscle of the chest wall. The pectoralis minor is a thin, flat triangular muscle that is positioned beneath the pectoralis major. The "pecs" pull the upper arm down and across the body. Like most of the upper torso muscles, the pecs are involved in throwing and pushing movements.

Upper back. The latissimus dorsi is the long, broad muscle that comprises most of the upper back. The "lats" are the largest muscles in the upper body. Their primary function is to pull the upper arm backward and downward. The latissmus dorsi is particularly important in pulling movements and climbing skills. In addition, developing the latissimus dorsi is necessary to provide muscular balance between the upper back and the chest areas.

Shoulders. The shoulders are made up of 11 muscles of which the deltoids are the most important. The "delts" are actually composed of three separate parts or heads. The anterior deltoid is found on the front of the shoulder and is used when raising the upper arm forward; the middle deltoid is found on the side of the shoulder and is involved when the upper arm is lifted sideways (away from the body); the posterior deltoid resides on the back of the shoulder and draws the upper arm backward. Several other deep muscles of the shoulder are sometimes referred to as the "internal rotators" (the subscapularis and the teres major) and the "external rotators" (the infraspinatus and the teres minor). In addition to performing rotation, these muscles also prevent shoulder impingement. Along with the muscles of the pectoral region, strong shoulders are a vital part of throwing skills and pushing movements.

ARMS

Biceps. The biceps brachii is the prominent muscle on the front part of the upper arm. It causes the arm to flex (or bend) at the elbow. As the name suggests, the biceps has two separate heads. The separation can sometimes be seen as a groove on a well-developed arm when the biceps are fully flexed. The biceps assist the upper torso muscles — especially the lats — in pulling movements and climbing skills.

Triceps. The triceps brachii is a horseshoe-shaped muscle located on the back of the upper arm. This muscle has three distinct heads — the long, the lateral and the medial. The primary function of the triceps is to extend (or straighten) the arm at the elbow. The triceps assist the upper torso muscles in throwing skills and pushing movements.

Forearms. As stated earlier, the forearm is made up of 19 different muscles. These muscles may be divided into two groups on the basis of their position and functions. The anterior group on the front part of the forearm causes flexion and pronation (turning the palm downward); the posterior group on the back part of the forearm causes extension and supination (turning the palm upward). The forearms effect the wrists and hands, which are important in pulling movements, climbing skills and tasks that involve gripping.

NECK

Sternocleidomastoideus. This muscle has two parts or heads located on each side of the neck, which start behind the ears and run down to the sternum (breastbone) and clavicles (collarbones). When both sides contract at the same time, the sternocleidomastoideus flexes the head toward the chest; when one side acts singly, it brings the head laterally toward the shoulder or rotates the head to the side.

Trapezius. The trapezius is a kite-shaped (or trapezoid-shaped) muscle that covers the uppermost region of the back and the posterior section of the neck. The primary functions of the "traps" are to elevate the shoulders (as in shrugging), to adduct the scapulae (pinch the shoulder blades together) and to extend the head backward. The trapezius is often considered part of the shoulder musculature.

ABDOMINALS

Rectus Abdominis. This long, narrow muscle extends vertically across the front of the abdomen from the lower rim of the rib cage to the pelvis. Its main function is to pull the torso toward the lower body. The fibers of this muscle are interrupted along their course by three horizontal fibrous bands, which give rise to the phrase "washboard abs" when describing an especially well-developed abdomen. The rectus abdominis helps to control your breathing and plays a major role in forced expiration during intense exercise.

Obliques. The external and internal obliques lie on both sides of the waist. The external oblique is a broad muscle whose fibers form a V across the front of the abdominal area, extending diagonally downward from the lower ribs to the pubic bone. The main function of this muscle is to bend the upper torso to the same side and to rotate the torso to the opposite side. The internal obliques lie immediately under the external obliques on both sides of the abdomen. The fibers of the internal obliques form an inverted V along the front of the abdominal wall, extending diagonally upward from the pubic bone to the ribs. The internal obliques bend the upper body to the same side and turn the torso to the same side. The obliques are used in movements in which the upper torso twists or rotates.

Transversus Abdominis. This is the innermost layer of the abdominal musculature. Its fibers run horizontally across the abdomen. The primary function of the transversus abdominis is to constrict the abdomen. This muscle is also involved in forced expiration and in control of your breathing.

LOWER BACK

Erector Spinae. The "spinal erectors" make up the main muscle group in the lower back. Their primary purpose is to extend (or straighten) the upper torso from a bent-over position. Low back pain is one of the most common and costly medical problems today. It has been estimated that 8 out of 10 people will experience low back pain sometime in their lives (Kelsey et al. 1979) with annual costs of more than 50 billion dollars (Frymoyer 1987). Insufficient strength seems to be a factor related to low back pain (Hasue, Masatushi and Kikuch 1980).

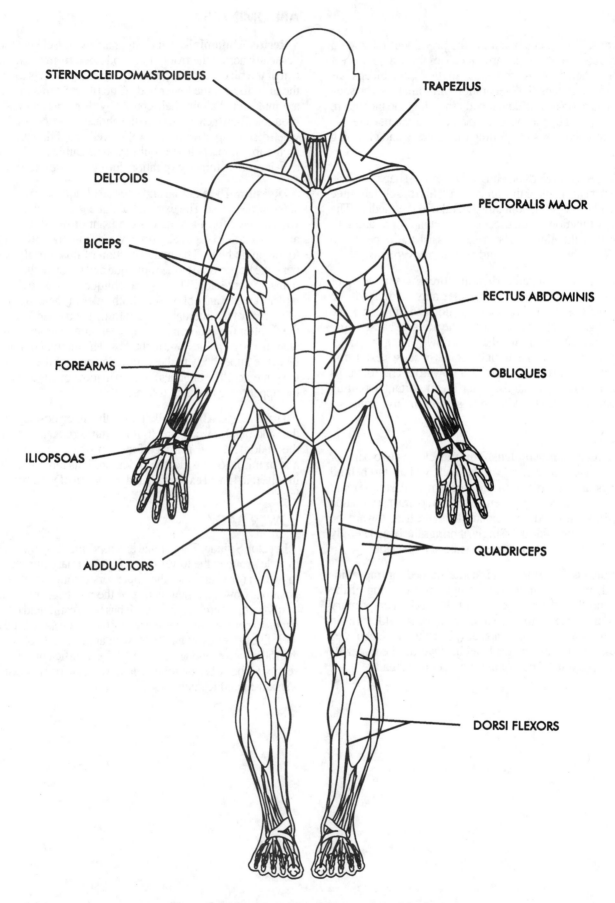

STERNOCLEIDOMASTOIDEUS

TRAPEZIUS

DELTOIDS

PECTORALIS MAJOR

BICEPS

RECTUS ABDOMINIS

FOREARMS

OBLIQUES

ILIOPSOAS

ADDUCTORS

QUADRICEPS

DORSI FLEXORS

Figure 2.1: Anterior view of the muscles of the body

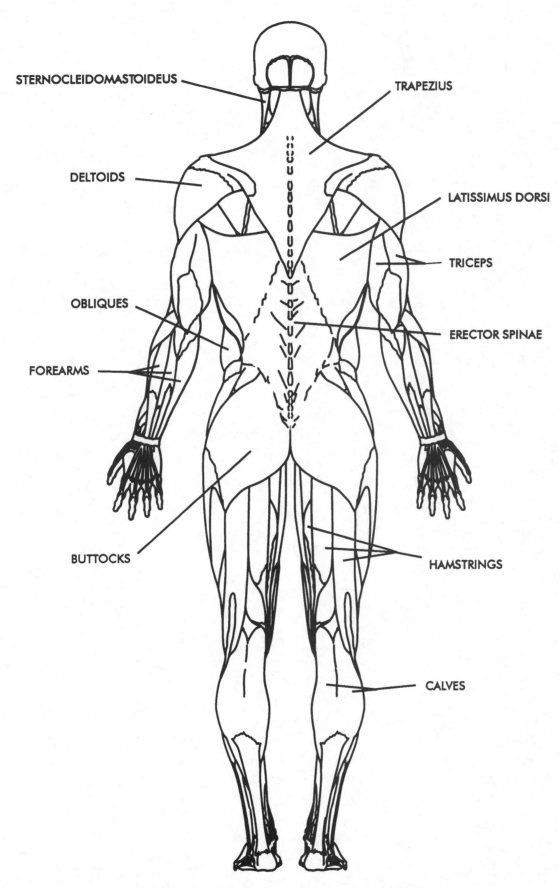

STERNOCLEIDOMASTOIDEUS

TRAPEZIUS

DELTOIDS

LATISSIMUS DORSI

TRICEPS

OBLIQUES

ERECTOR SPINAE

FOREARMS

BUTTOCKS

HAMSTRINGS

CALVES

Figure 2.2: Posterior view of the muscles Fuction of the body

3
THE ROLE OF GENETICS IN STRENGTH TRAINING

Have you ever noticed that some people make striking gains in muscular size and strength while others make only modest ones — even though all of them may be performing the identical weight training program (i.e., the same exercises using the same number of sets and repetitions)? In some cases, a different training response may be the result of exercising with different levels of intensity. However, most of the variations in the response to strength training are primarily the result of a person's inherited characteristics or genetics. Quite simply, except for identical twins, each individual has a different genetic potential for achieving size and strength.

GENETIC FACTORS

Your genetic makeup is the single most important ingredient in determining your potential for improving your muscular size and physical strength. A number of specific genetic traits influence your response to strength training.

Predominant Muscle Fiber Type

A person's predominant muscle fiber type plays a major role in determining his or her potential for attaining muscular size and strength (Graves and Pollock 1992). Muscle fiber composition also determines the ultimate potential of the neuromuscular system to produce fast speeds of movement (Hakkinen, Komi and Alen 1985). Fiber types may be grouped into two major categories: slow twitch (ST) or Type I and fast twitch (FT) or Type II (Close 1972; Piehl 1974; Lamb 1984a; Graves and Pollock 1992). These two major fiber types differ in several areas including speed of contraction, force of contraction and endurance capacity. FT fibers can contract quickly and generate large amounts of force, but they fatigue rather easily. Relative to FT muscle fibers, ST fibers contract slower and produce less force, but they have greater endurance. Because of their fatigue characteristics, FT fibers are often referred to as being "gly-colytic" and ST fibers as "oxidative." (Some researchers also recognize one or more intermediate fiber types that possess characteristics of both FT and ST fibers.)

Each person's muscles are composed of both fiber types, and the different types are intermingled throughout each muscle (Fox and Mathews 1981). However, the distribution of FT and ST fibers within each muscle is genetically determined (Komi et al. 1977; Komi and Karlsson 1979; Fox 1984). Some individuals have inherited a predominant fiber type that allows them to be successful in certain activities. For example, an accomplished sprinter is capable of generating tremendous amounts of force in a rather short period of time. A high percentage of FT fibers would be revealed in a microscopic analysis of a muscle tissue sample taken from a sprinter's lower body musculature. The same holds true for highly competitive shot putters, football players, competitive weightlifters and any other athletes whose success is predicated upon rapid, powerful movements (Gollnick et al. 1972b; Costill et al. 1976; Saltin et al. 1977). On the other hand, a successful long-distance runner has a high capacity for endurance. A high distribution of ST fibers would be disclosed in a microscopic analysis of a muscle tissue sample taken from the lower body of a distance runner or any other individual who excels in events that require large amounts of muscular endurance (Gollnick et al. 1972a; Costill et al. 1976). It should also be noted that an individual's fiber type mixture may differ from one muscle to another and may even vary from one side of the body to the other (Dintiman 1984).

Implications. The technical term for an increase in muscular size is hypertrophy. (Its inverse — a decrease in muscular size — is called atrophy.) Both FT and ST muscle fibers have the potential for hypertrophy. However, FT fibers display a much greater capacity for hypertrophy than ST fibers (Sharkey 1975; Thorstensson 1976; MacDougall et al. 1980; Komi 1986; Graves and Pollock 1992). This indicates that people who have a high percentage of FT fibers have a greater potential to increase the size of their muscles. Because FT fibers can produce greater force than ST fibers, these individuals also display a higher potential for strength gains (Sharkey 1975; Fox and Mathews 1981; Westcott 1983). It is interesting to note that FT fibers not only hypertrophy faster and to a greater degree than ST fibers but also atrophy faster and to a greater extent (MacDougall et al. 1980; Jones 1993).

Fiber conversion. No conclusive evidence exists to suggest that strength training will change ST fibers to FT fibers or vice versa (Gollnick et al. 1973b; McCafferty and Horvath 1977; Costill et al. 1979; Dons et al. 1979; Hatfield 1981; Wilmore 1982; Lamb 1984a; McDonagh and Davies

1984; Sharkey 1984; Howley and Franks 1992; Pipes 1994). Though one type of muscle fiber may take on certain metabolic characteristics of the other type of fiber, actual conversion appears to be impossible. In other words, you cannot convert one fiber type into another any more than you can make a racehorse out of a mule. The lack of effects of strength training on muscle fiber composition is not surprising considering a study on monozygous and dizygous twins by Karlsson, Komi and Viitasalo (1979). Their work indicates that hereditary factors determine almost solely the variance in skeletal muscle fiber composition.

Hyperplasia. There's no definitive proof that strength training increases the number of muscle fibers in humans (Jones 1971a; MacDougall et al. 1984; Komi 1986; Graves and Pollock 1992). An increase in the number of muscle fibers — known as hyperplasia — has been demonstrated in animals (Gonyea 1980) but not in humans (MacDougall et al. 1976). The effect of strength training would likely be the addition of contractile protein (i.e., actin and myosin) and not the growth of new fibers (Sharkey 1975; Westcott 1983; MacDougall 1986; Graves and Pollock 1992).

Individuals who excel in events that require large amounts of muscular endurance posess a high percentage of slow twitch muscle fibers. (Photo by C.W. Pack Sports)

Muscular endurance. At one time or another, almost everyone involved in strength training has seen a chart listing "percentage of maximum" along with guidelines that explain how many repetitions should be done with a given percentage of a maximum lift. The truth is that each individual has a different capacity for muscular endurance based upon his or her inherited fiber type mixture. For example, an individual with a high percentage of FT fibers may not be able to achieve as many repetitions in an exercise as a person with a high percentage of ST fibers — despite the fact that both used the same percentage of their maximum strength. Jones and his associates (1988) tested an individual who could only perform one repetition with 80 percent of his maximum strength. Another person was able to execute 34 repetitions with 83 percent of her maximum strength before reaching muscular failure. She had an identical twin sister who also performed 34 repetitions with 83 percent of her maximum strength. Interestingly, neither woman was present while the other was being tested, and neither knew the results until after both had been tested.

Therefore, percentage charts and their accompanying training schedules are worthless to everyone except that relatively small segment of the population that happens to have inherited a specific mixture of fiber types that corresponds to a prescribed number of repetitions.

Muscle-to-Tendon Ratio

The muscle organ consists of two parts: the belly (which is predominantly muscle fibers) and the tendon (the fibrous connective tissue). Another factor that determines a person's potential for increasing muscular size and strength is the relationship between the muscle belly length and the tendon length (Riley 1982b; Westcott 1983; Jones 1993). Figure 3.1 depicts two anatomical examples labeled as A and B. Both examples are identical except for one feature. Note that A illustrates a relatively long muscle belly and a short tendinous attachment. By comparison, B has a shorter muscle belly and a longer tendon. The potential for muscular growth is directly related to muscle length (Riley 1982b; Westcott 1983; Jones 1993). Everything else being equal, a person with a muscle-to-tendon ratio depicted by A would have a greater genetic potential for achieving muscular size than a person having a muscle-to-tendon ratio shown by B.

A bigger muscle has a larger cross-sectional area. A larger cross-sectional area contains a greater number of protein filaments and crossbridges, thereby increasing its force-generating capacity. Therefore, a bigger muscle — in terms of its cross-sectional area — is also a stronger muscle (Ikai and Fukunaga 1970; Jones 1971a; Sharkey 1975; Frankel and Nordin 1980; Young et al. 1983; Wirhed 1984; Enoka 1988a). This means that an individual with long muscle bellies tends to be exceptionally strong.

A small variation in muscle length can make a considerable difference in the potential for size and strength. In theory, the potential cross-sectional area of a muscle is equal

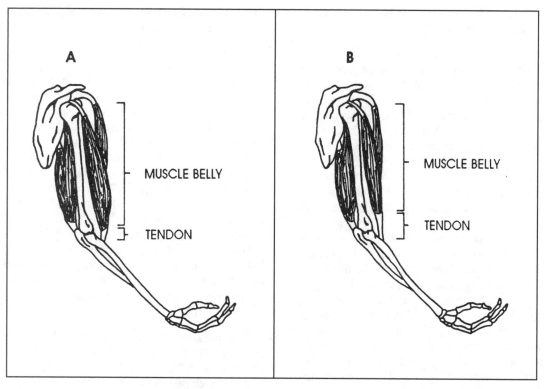

Figure 3.1: Muscle-to-tendon ratio

to the length of the muscle squared and the potential volume of a muscle is equal to the length of the muscle cubed (Asmussen and Heeboll-Nielson 1955). For example, a muscle that is 3 inches long would have a potential cross-sectional area of 9 square inches [3 inches x 3 inches] and a potential volume of 27 cubic inches [3 inches x 3 inches x 3 inches]. On the other hand, a muscle that is 4 inches long would have a potential cross-sectional area of 16 square inches [4 inches x 4 inches] and a potential volume of 64 cubic inches [4 inches x 4 inches x 4 inches].

As with muscle fiber type, a person's muscle-to-tendon ratio may vary from one muscle to another. It's difficult to determine the actual length of a muscle belly because the muscle may be hidden by subcutaneous fat or lie beneath other muscles. However, the length of a muscle belly is usually most obvious in the triceps, the forearms and especially the calves. The length of a muscle belly is not subject to change (Riley 1982b; Westcott 1983).

Testosterone Levels

Although it is a male sex hormone, testosterone is also found in the blood of perfectly normal women. In males, testosterone is secreted by the testes, while in females it is produced primarily by the adrenal gland. Its secretion is regulated by pituitary hormones. Testosterone encourages protein synthesis and influences the secondary sexual characteristics. For example, in men it lowers the pitch of the voice and is associated with the growth of facial hair and, inexplicably, male pattern baldness. Additionally, testosterone stimulates skeletal growth and the development of the male body structure. In short, its major action is to pro-

mote growth. Because of this, individuals who inherit above-average levels of testosterone have a greater potential for accelerated growth and maturation.

Lever Lengths

Some people inherit short levers (i.e., bones) and other bodily proportions that give them a significant advantage in biomechanical leverage (Boileau and Lohman 1977). For example, if you could line up the best bench pressers in the world, you would notice that they tend to have similar bodily dimensions — namely, relatively short arms and thick chests. People with short arms are at a distinct advantage in most pushing and pulling movements because they don't have to move the weight as far as someone with longer arms. Likewise, the best squatters in the world generally have short torsos, thick abdomens, wide hips and short legs. Again, this biomechanical advantage in leverage allows these athletes to lift extraordinarily heavy weights.

Interestingly, an individual with longer arms may actually be doing more work than someone with shorter arms — even when using less weight. How is this possible? Consider two individuals: The first person has arms that are 20 inches long and can bench press 200 pounds; the second person has arms that are 24 inches long and can bench press 180 pounds. Because work is defined as "weight times distance," the 200-pound bench presser has done 4,000 inch-pounds of work [20 inches x 200 pounds] and the 180-pound bench presser has done 4,320 inch-pounds of work [24 x 180 pounds]. Therefore, even though the second person cannot bench press as much weight as the other, the effort of the second person is actually greater because the weight is moved a greater distance.

Poundage Clubs. The ubiquitous 300-Pound and 400-Pound Club listings that adorn many weight room walls tend to glorify a person's ability to demonstrate strength due to favorable body proportions. What's really being measured is anatomical leverage. Membership into the "club" is based more on uncontrollable genetic factors than on actual strength. Understandably, it's motivating for a person to walk into a weight room and see their name and maximum poundages posted on a wall in full view of everyone. However, those who are able to lift heavy weights aren't the ones who need to be motivated — no one would ever have any difficulty convincing those individuals to strength train. But what about the average person who may never make the 300-Pound Club because they happen to have inherited elongated limbs? Seeing the listings on the wall would certainly be frustrating and could possibly be intimidating or embarrassing. Some individuals may even decide that weight training isn't for them. It would be wise to remove these Poundage Club listings from weight room walls and post something that everyone has an equal chance of attaining — like Most Dedicated Lifter. Surely a much more enthusiastic response would be received from those individuals who are at a mechanical disadvantage in terms of demonstrating strength.

Somatotypes

Also playing a critical role in strength and muscular development is a person's inherited body type or somatotype. There are three main terms used to describe a person's body type: endomorph, mesomorph and ectomorph. An endomorph is characterized by softness and round features. Endomorphs have a high percentage of body fat and very little muscle tone. A sumo wrestler would be an example of an extreme endomorph. A mesomorph is typified by a heavily muscled physique. Mesomorphs have athletic builds with broad shoulders, large chests and slender waists. Most competitive bodybuilders have a high degree of mesomorphy. Finally, an ectomorph is characterized by long limbs, leanness and a slender physique. Ectomorphs have little body fat but also little in the way of muscular development. Successful long-distance runners are usually ectomorphic.

Since almost everyone has some degree of each component, a rating system was developed in which a person is given a "score" in each of the three areas. The original system developed by Sheldon (1954) used a scale of from 1

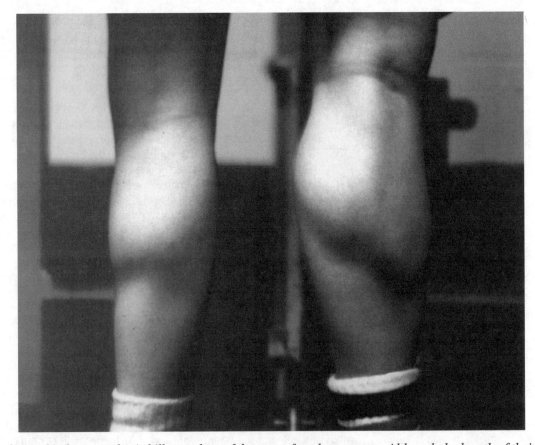

Note the relationship between the Achilles tendons of these two female gymnasts. Although the length of their lower legs is approximately the same, the woman on the right has a much longer muscle belly than the woman on the left. The potential for muscular growth is directly related to muscle length. Therefore, the woman on the right has a greater potential for muscular growth than the woman on the left. (At the time this photo was taken, both women had been strength training exactly the same way for nearly eight months.)

to 7 to designate the degree of each of the three components. Numeral one represents the least amount of the component, while numeral seven indicates the greatest. Therefore, a somatotype of 7-1-1 would indicate extreme endomorphy (fatness), 1-7-1 extreme mesomorphy (muscularity) and 1-1-7 extreme ectomorphy (leanness).

However, there are relatively few people who can be classified as being purely one type or another. Although people have a tendency toward one body type, most individuals are a combination of types. For example, a somatotype of 2-6-3 (endomorphy-mesomorphy-ectomorphy) would describe an individual who has very little body fat, high muscular development and a slender frame. So, this "ecto-mesomorph" would exhibit both ectomorphic and mesomorphic tendencies.

A number of studies have related body type to physical performance (Correnti and Zauli 1964; Tanner 1964; Carter 1970 and 1974; Malina et al. 1971; Jokl 1973; deGaray, Levine and Carter 1974; Borms et al. 1986). As you might suspect, the somatotype that has the greatest genetic potential for developing muscular size and strength is the mesomorph. In fact, a study by Borms and others (1986) concluded that world class bodybuilders were the "prototype of pure extreme mesomorphs."

Tendon Insertion Points

At one time or another, most of us have encountered an individual who was far stronger than he or she appeared to be. In fact, the person may have been incredibly strong despite not being very muscularly developed. How is this possible if strength is directly related to muscle size (i.e., cross-sectional area)? One possible reason is that the person may have favorable points of tendon insertions. In Figure 3.2, note that A and B are holding the same resistance in their hands [100 pounds], which is applied the same distance from their elbows [12 inches]. The only difference is in their bicep tendons' point of insertion. A has a bicep tendon that inserts on the forearm 1.2 inches from the elbow, whereas B has a bicep tendon that inserts on the forearm 1.0 inches from the elbow.

The fact of the matter is that the farther away a tendon inserts from the axis of rotation the greater the biomechanical advantage (Jones 1972; Riley 1982b; Westcott 1983; Wirhed 1984; Thompson 1985; Stamford 1986). In this example, the force necessary to maintain the resistance in a static position can be calculated using the formula "force times force arm equals resistance times resistance arm" or, more simply, "F x FA = R x RA" (Nelson 1979; Westcott 1983; Wirhed 1984; Thompson 1985). The force arm is

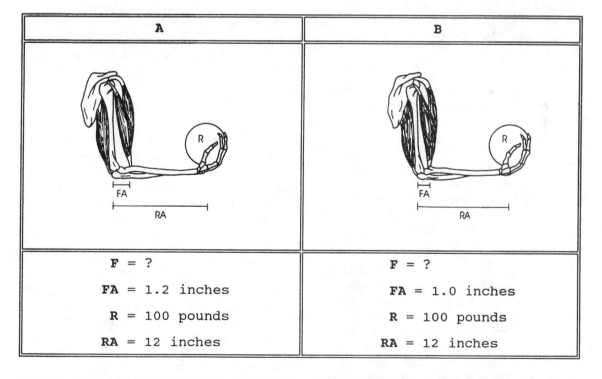

A	B
F = ?	F = ?
FA = 1.2 inches	FA = 1.0 inches
R = 100 pounds	R = 100 pounds
RA = 12 inches	RA = 12 inches

Force x Force Arm = Resistance x Resistance Arm	
(F)(1.2") = (100 lbs)(12")	(F)(1.0") = (100 lbs)(12")
F = 1,000 pounds	F = 1,200 pounds

Figure 3.2: Tendon insertion points

defined as the distance from the axis of rotation (in this case, the elbow) to the point where the force is applied (the insertion point of the tendon); the resistance arm is defined as the distance from the axis of rotation to the point where the resistance is applied. Inserting the previously given numbers into the formula reveals that A must generate 1,000 pounds of force to hold the resistance in a static position. On the other hand, B must produce 1,200 pounds of force to accomplish the same task. In other words, B must work 20 percent harder than A. A would have greater leverage than B and, everything else being equal, would have a much greater potential for demonstrating strength. Indeed, Roberts (1984) has reported that the insertions of muscles have considerable effects on their muscular efficiency.

This depiction of static forces is somewhat simplified. However, it still illustrates the fact that a very small difference in a tendon's point of insertion can make a considerable amount of variation in leverage (Dyson 1973; Thompson 1985; Kennedy 1986c; Stamford 1986). X rays and magnetic resonance imaging (MRI) can be used to accurately determine points of tendon insertion.

Neurological Efficiency

One final genetic factor deals with the nervous system and has been termed neurological (or neuromuscular) efficiency. This refers to a person's inherited proficiency at innervating muscle fibers. The role of neurological efficiency has been noted by several authors (Jones 1975b and 1977a; Darden 1982; Riley 1982b; Kennedy 1986c; Hutchins 1992).

It has been suggested that some people can recruit a higher percentage of their available muscle fibers than other people, which gives them a decided advantage in terms of strength potential. For example, suppose A can recruit 40 percent of his or her available muscle fibers, whereas B can only contract 30 percent. Assuming that both individuals have the same amount of muscle mass, A would have a greater potential for strength because he or she is able to recruit a higher percentage of his or her muscle fibers. This is another reason that someone may be far stronger than he or she appears.

Jones (1977a) has proposed that neurological efficiency is inversely proportional to anaerobic muscular endurance. In simple terms, this means that if you have a high level of muscular endurance, you are probably not very efficient neurologically; likewise, if you have a low level of muscular endurance, you are more likely to possess an efficient neurological system. Using the previous example, if A can recruit more muscle fibers than B, it follows that B will have more fibers in reserve. Everything else being equal, A would exhibit a greater capacity for strength and B would have greater muscular endurance. (Keep in mind that this refers to muscular endurance, not cardiovascular endurance.)

HERITABILITY VERSUS TRAINABILITY

In terms of results from a weight training program, all individuals are not created equal. If you perform the exact strength program as someone else for a period of time, the odds are that you won't end up looking like physical clones of each other. Each person responds differently because each person is a unique genetic entity with a different genetic potential for achieving muscular size and strength. Some people are predisposed toward developing large, heavily muscled physiques, while others are predisposed more toward a defined physique. Therefore, the belief that performing low repetitions with heavy weights will accelerate muscular size and doing high repetitions with light weights will enhance muscular definition is entirely anecdotal with no factual basis whatsoever. Whether your sets consist of low repetitions, high repetitions or intermediate repetitions you're still going to develop according to your inherited characteristics — provided that the sets are done with similar levels of intensity.

Those who have a genetic tendency for both muscular size and definition are the people who are glamorized in the so-called "muscle mags." If all you had to do to develop huge muscles was to follow the program of the latest bodybuilding champion, then millions of men and women would certainly look like Mr. or Ms. Olympia. Likewise, following the routine of a world weightlifting champion doesn't mean you'll develop the same level of physical strength. Unfortunately, millions of men and women make a terrible mistake by trying to heroically follow the programs of the current physique stars and strength athletes — programs that are usually impractical, inefficient and, in some cases, dangerous for the majority of the population.

An individual's response isn't necessarily due to a particular program or routine. The next time you're in the weight room, take a look at the assorted pairs of training partners. You'll see that people who work out together usually have different builds — despite training with the same exercises using the same number of sets and repetitions.

The truth is that heritability dictates trainability. The main determinant for a person's response to strength training is genetics. The cumulative effect of your inherited muscular, mechanical, hormonal and neural qualities is what determines your physical potential. A person who possesses a high percentage of FT fibers, long muscle bellies, high levels of testosterone, favorable lever lengths, mesomorphic tendencies, low points of tendon insertions and an efficient neurological system would prove to be incredibly strong as well as physically impressive. Compared to the average person, this genetic marvel would be capable of almost unbelievable feats of strength. There are a few individuals like that, but most of us are not so fortunate. However, that doesn't mean that you can't get stronger or improve your physique. Indeed, you should be encouraged and challenged to become as strong as possible within your genetic profile.

4
SPEED OF MOVEMENT: AN EXPLOSIVE ISSUE

Individuals are continually looking for ways to increase their speed, power and explosiveness. The search for these elusive athletic ingredients has led to one of the most heavily debated subjects in the field of strength and fitness. The dispute concerns the speed at which an exercise or movement should be performed. Essentially, there are two schools of thought among strength and fitness professionals. One group advocates high velocity, explosive movements that are ballistic in nature whereas the other group recommends deliberate movements that are performed in a controlled manner.

THE BIRTH OF A CONTROVERSY

In 1970, Nautilus Sports Medical Industries began offering comprehensive guidelines for strength training to fitness enthusiasts. In retrospect this was a critical time to disseminate training advice since the strength coaching profession was going through a period of growing pains, and, at about the same time, the so-called "fitness boom" was just entering its embryonic stage. Included among these guidelines was the suggestion that each repetition should be performed in a deliberate, controlled fashion. (The recommended speed of movement was later quantified as raising a weight in two seconds and lowering a weight in four seconds. This was sometimes referred to as simply "up two, down four" or "2/4.")

Recall from Chapter 1 that during that era of resistance exercise, protocols were heavily influenced by the opinions and training methods of the competitive Olympic-style weightlifters who perform their repetitions in a rapid, explosive fashion. The advancement of the idea that weights should be lifted with a controlled speed of movement went against the prevailing train of thought, thereby sparking a fiery controversy that continues to rage with heated passion.

The associations and individuals that promote explosive lifting would have you believe that their philosophy represents the best approach and that anyone who believes otherwise is either misinformed, misguided or else not very knowledgeable about strength training. Those with different views are quickly and feverishly attacked for their non-acceptance of the traditional "party line" thinking. In reality, there are rather large numbers of highly qualified and completely competent strength and fitness professionals and rehabilitative specialists who do not recommend explosive movements or techniques (Jones 1970; Darden 1975; Allman 1976; Pipes 1979; Riley 1979; Wolf 1982; Bryant 1988; Dunn 1989a; Leistner 1989a; Andress 1990; Bates, Wolf and Blunk 1990; Morton 1990; Peterson and Westcott 1990; Hutchins 1992; Asanovich 1993; Ash 1993; Mentzer 1993; Bradley 1994; Bullock 1994; Friday 1994; Mannie 1994; Thomas 1994; Watson 1994).

SCIENTIFIC LEGITIMACY

The debate over the appropriate speed of movement for a repetition has stimulated quite a number of research studies. Unfortunately, some of the studies have left much to be desired in terms of providing definitive conclusions and establishing scientific legitimacy. The unyielding, sentimental attachment to certain explosive movements — including the so-called "quick lifts" and plyometrics — has been supported with various articles, research studies and position papers overflowing with biased, sketchy protocols and other design flaws that make their results scientifically unacceptable.

For example, one of the most frequently cited studies used by advocates of explosive training is the research performed by Moffroid and Whipple (1970). Their research has been referenced hundreds of times as evidence that weight training should occur at high speeds. However, the authors violated a basic principle of statistical analysis and experimental design (Wolf 1982). As a result, their conclusions were unsupported by their data. In reality, their study actually indicated that slow training speeds increased strength at both slow and fast lifting speeds (Hutchins 1992).

Research has shown that slow movement speeds can be at least as effective as fast movement speeds in improving strength and power. For instance, a study by Van Oteghen (1975) showed significant gains in the vertical jump that resulted from slow isokinetic leg press training. Her study also found no significant differences in strength improvement between a "slow speed" group and a "fast speed" group. A study by Rosentswieg, Hinson and Ridgway (1975) noted that "slower speeds appear to develop strength quicker than [muscular] contractions using faster speeds." In a study by Kanehisa and Miyashita (1983), a group using low velocity repetitions demonstrated significant increases in power at all velocities tested. Adeyanju, Crews and Meadors (1983) and Vitti (1984) reported no significant difference between slow training speeds and fast training speeds on strength and power production. Studies by Palmieri (1987) and Wenzel and Perfetto (1992) found that the use of fast movement speeds while strength training does not develop power any more than slower lifting speeds. In a study that involved the use of free weights, Kasper (1990) reported greater strength increases from slower movement speeds. A study by Behm and Sale (1993) concluded that "an actual high velocity movement in training exercises is not necessary to produce a high velocity specific training response." Finally, slow velocity resistance training has demonstrated that improvements in knee extension torque (i.e., force acting about an axis of rotation) and power are greatest at slow angular velocities (Caizzo, Perrine and Edgerton 1981; Nobbs and Rhodes 1986; Petersen 1988; Colliander and Tesch 1990b).

FIBER RECRUITMENT

Proponents of high-speed movements argue that in order to become "explosive" you must train "explosive." Their assumption is that by lifting explosively in the weight room, the fast speed of movement will somehow change the chemical composition of the slow twitch (ST) fibers and/or preferentially recruit the fast twitch (FT) fibers.

Clearly, muscle fiber composition determines the ultimate potential of the neuromuscular system to produce fast speeds of movement (Hakkinen, Komi and Alen 1985). As noted in Chapter 3, however, there's no conclusive evidence in the scientific literature to firmly support the notion that muscle fibers can be converted from one type to another. Training may alter the metabolic characteristics of the fiber types, but it does not alter the basic contraction speed of the fibers (Lamb 1984a).

Furthermore, the selective recruitment of muscle fibers is physiologically impossible. Muscle fibers are recruited by the nervous system in an orderly fashion according to the intensity or force requirements and not by the speed of movement (Henneman, Somjen and Carpenter 1965; Desmedt and Godaux 1977a and 1977b; Vrbova 1979; Skinner and McLellan 1980; Wolf 1982; Wirhed 1984; Sale 1987; Enoka 1988a; Howley and Franks 1992). Demands of low muscular intensity are met by the ST fiber population. Intermediate fibers are recruited once the ST fibers are no longer able to continue the task. The FT fibers are finally recruited only when the other fatigue-resistant fibers have severely depleted their energy stores and cannot meet the force requirements (Gollnick et al. 1973a). All fibers are working when the FT fibers are being used. The orderly recruitment pattern remains the same regardless of whether the movement speed was fast or slow (Desmedt and Godaux 1977a and 1978; Lesmes et al. 1983; Enoka 1988b; Bell and Wenger 1992).

Muscle fibers are recruited by the nervous system in an orderly fashion according to the intensity or force requirements and not by the speed of movement.

This orderly recruitment pattern is consistent with the "size principle" of recruitment advanced by Henneman (1957). He suggested that motoneurons are recruited according to increasing size: The motor unit with the smallest motoneuron is recruited first, and the motor unit with the largest motoneuron is recruited last. (A motor unit consists of a motoneuron and all the muscle fibers it innervates.) In general, the smallest motoneurons innervate ST fibers, and the largest motoneurons innervate FT fibers (Wolf 1982; Enoka 1988a; Salmons 1994). Therefore, ST fibers are recruited first and FT fibers are recruited last.

Lifting weights at rapid speeds does not necessarily mean that the muscular intensity is high. Pipes (1979) notes "Speed of limb movement has little to do with intensity. If anything, there is an inverse relationship. You can have speed or you can have intensity; you cannot have both." In short, there is absolutely no definitive proof that movements performed in an explosive or ballistic manner will bypass the ST and intermediate fibers in order to specifically recruit the FT fibers (Wolf 1982; Palmieri 1983). In a nutshell, muscle fibers are recruited according to their increasing size — which translates into "need not speed."

This sequential recruitment of muscle fibers is actually ideal in terms of physiological efficiency. The ST fibers — which generate less force than FT fibers — are recruited early when the force demands are low. In addition, their resistance to fatigue is advantageous in generating a sustained force output over a series of muscular contractions (i.e., a set of an exercise). It would not be economical for the nervous system to recruit the quicker-to-fatigue FT fibers in the early stages of an exercise. This orderly innervation of muscle fibers minimizes the energy cost of motor activities.

"EXPLOSIVE" SPECIFICITY

It's also believed that lifting weights explosively will "carry over" to explosive movements performed in the athletic arena. In particular, the Olympic-style movements and related "quick lifts" have been glorified as exercises which — when performed at rapid speeds of movement — supposedly transfer this explosiveness to other sports skills (Stone et al. 1994).

There's simply no evidence in the motor learning literature to support the notion that specific explosive movements done in the weight room will contribute to improving explosiveness on the athletic field. According to Schmidt (1991), the practice of giving athletes various "quickening" exercises, with the hope that these exercises will train some fundamental ability to be quick, thereby allowing quicker responses in their particular sport, simply does not work. In other words, the explosiveness demonstrated during a movement such as a power clean is only specific to a power clean. Likewise the explosive power demonstrated in an athletic skill such as a vertical jump is only specific to a vertical jump. Doing power cleans will not help your explosiveness in a vertical jump any more than doing vertical jumps will improve your explosiveness in a power clean. (The myth of "quickening" exercises is presented in greater detail in Chapter 5.)

MOMENTUM

Aside from all of the scientific facts concerning muscle fiber recruitment and explosive specificity, lifting weights in a rapid, explosive fashion is not recommended for two reasons — both of which relate to the effects of momentum.

Reduced Efficiency

Explosive lifting introduces momentum into the movement, which makes the exercise less productive and less efficient (Jones 1977c; Pipes 1979; Rasch 1979; Riley 1979; Jacobson 1981; Reston 1982; Andress 1990; Bates, Wolf and Blunk 1990; Peterson and Westcott 1990; Mentzer 1993; Pollock et al. 1993b; Bradley 1994). After the initial explosive movement, little or no resistance is encountered by the muscles throughout the remaining range of motion (Allman 1976; Bryant 1988). In simple terms, the weight is practically moving under its own power.

According to Hill (1922), in order to obtain the maximum work from a contracting muscle it is necessary to oppose its contraction at every stage by a force which it is just able to overcome. To illustrate the effects of momentum on muscular tension, imagine that you pushed a 100-pound cart a distance of 50 yards at a steady, deliberate pace. In this instance, your muscles produced a constant tension for the entire 50 yards. Now, suppose that you were to push that same cart another 50 yards. This time, however, you accelerated your pace to the point where you were running as fast as you possibly could. If you were to stop pushing the cart after 35 yards, the cart would continue to move by itself because you gave it momentum. So, your muscles had resistance for the first 35 yards . . . but not for the final 15 yards. The same effect occurs in the weight room. When weights are lifted explosively, a load is placed on the muscles during the initial part of the movement . . . but not during the last part. In effect, the requirement for muscular tension is lessened. Since increases in size and strength are related to the amount of tension developed by the muscle (Goldberg et al. 1975), the potential improvements are reduced accordingly.

In the early 1920s Hill (1922) was the first to note an inverse relationship existed between velocity and the production of muscular tension. Huxley (1958) states that "[muscular] tension decreases as the speed of shortening increases." Stated otherwise, as the velocity of muscular contraction increases, the tension that can be exerted by a muscle decreases. Rosentswieg, Hinson and Ridgway (1975) demonstrated greater electromyographic (EMG) activity in the target muscles of the group using the slowest isokinetic speed of three groups. Greater EMG activity indicates a greater muscular response due to maximum resistance throughout the range of motion. Therefore, maximal tension is developed by a muscle at slower velocities. This has been supported by numerous authors and researchers (Thorstensson, Grimby and Karlsson 1976; Costill et al. 1979; Coyle, Costill and Lesmes 1979; Pipes 1979; Riley 1982b; Lesmes et al. 1983; Westcott 1983; Enoka 1988b; Winter 1990; Bell and Wenger 1992; Kraemer 1992). Low velocity movements produce longer periods of continuous muscle tension during both the concentric and the eccentric phases, thereby placing heavier demands on the target muscles. As such, high velocity movements are less productive with respect to producing maximal tension within a muscle.

Why does a muscle produce less tension at faster speeds of movement? As the speed of movement increases so does the speed of muscular contraction and the rate of crossbridge attachment-detachment (Huxley 1958). As a muscle contracts more quickly, the average tension exerted by each crossbridge decreases, and there may even be fewer crossbridges formed. Therefore, increased velocities reduce the force-development capabilities of a muscle (Gulch 1994). Furthermore, during fast speeds of movement the energy used by a muscle increases (due to increased crossbridge detachment). As a result, there is decreasing muscular tension and increasing energy demands. As the gap between work output and energy input becomes greater, a muscle becomes less efficient (Enoka 1988a).

It's also been suggested that the greatest power outputs are yielded during high-speed movements. If anything, the opposite may be true. Studies by Kaneko and coworkers (1983) and Duchateau and Hainaut (1984) found that gains in maximal power production were greater with isometric training (i.e., high tension but essentially zero velocity) than with dynamic training. This suggests the greatest increases in power output are obtained with high tension/low velocity training and not low tension/high velocity training (Enoka 1988a).

Injury Potential

Explosive lifting can also be dangerous (Allman 1976; Jones 1977c; Pipes 1979; Riley 1982c; Diange 1984; Kennedy 1986a; Welday 1986; Leistner 1989a; Andress 1990; Bates, Wolf and Blunk 1990; Peterson and Westcott 1990; Asanovich 1993; Behm and Sale 1993; Pollock et al. 1993b; Bradley 1994; Friday 1994; Mannie 1994; Watson 1994). Wilmore (1982) notes that "actual structural damage is a possible outcome of certain types of explosive exercise." Dr. Lyle J. Micheli, a past president of the American College of Sports Medicine, stated that a study by Dangles and Spencer (1987) suggests "ballistic weight training contributes to the occurrence of spondylolysis" (Duda 1987). Dr. Fred Allman, a past president of both the

It's much safer and more efficient to lift weights in a deliberate, controlled manner.

American Orthopaedic Society for Sports Medicine and the American College of Sports Medicine, states: "It is even possible that many injuries . . . may be the result of weakened connective tissue caused by explosive training in the weight room" (Reston 1982).

Here's why: Using momentum to lift a weight increases the internal forces encountered by a given joint; the faster a weight is lifted, the greater these forces are amplified — especially at the point of explosion. An injury occurs when the forces exceed the structural limits of a muscle, a bone or connective tissue. During explosive movements, these forces are far in excess of the weight lifted (Friday 1994). For example, it was reported that the load on the patellar ligament at rupture during a jerk attempt was 17.5 times the athlete's bodyweight (Garhammer 1989).

No one knows what the exact tensile strength of muscles, bones and connective tissue are at any given moment. The only way to ascertain tensile strength is when the structural capacity is surpassed. Then, of course, it's too late. Therefore, an exercise's speed of movement is a critical concern because the precise structural limitations of the human body's various connective tissues are unknown.

Research findings. In a study by Andrews, Hay and Vaughan (1983), a subject squatting with 80 percent of his 4-RM incurred a 225-pound peak shearing force during a repetition that took 4.5 seconds to complete and a 270-pound peak shearing force during a repetition that took 2.1 seconds to complete — clear evidence that slower speeds of movement reduce the shearing forces on joints. Hall (1985) examined the clean and jerk movement and reported that when the lifting speed is fast, dramatic increases occur in compressive force, shear force and torque in the lumbar region. Additional damning evidence was offered by Reid, Yeater and Ullrich (1987). Their study noted that a group who trained explosively had the highest injury rate, and the authors recommended against this type of training. Hattin, Pierrynowski and Ball (1989) noted increased compressive force and shear force in the knee joint as the speed of movement increased. A study by Wenzel and Perfetto (1992) reported that 25 percent of the "speed training" group did not complete the program due to "varying illness and injuries." Behm and Sale (1993) concluded that "training contractions characterized by rapid force development to relatively high peak force may be more likely to cause muscle injuries such as strains and tears."

The high risk of injury incurred during explosive weight training has also been noted by the American Academy of Pediatrics (1983 and 1990) and has been reported by numerous other researchers and authors (Kotani et al. 1971; Jesse 1977; Brady, Cahill and Bodnar 1982; Westcott 1983; Alexander 1985; Duda 1987; Brown, Yost and McCarron 1990; Risser 1991; Mazur, Yetman and Risser 1993; Friday 1994; Mannie 1994).

Fundamental physics. The potentially damaging effects of high-speed movements can be demonstrated rather easily using an ordinary 16-ounce hammer. Suppose you were to take the hammer and lay it across your hand. This action wouldn't elicit any feelings of pain or cause any tissue damage. However, what if you were to lift the hammer and drop it on your hand from a height of about two feet? Certainly, this action would be more painful and would likely even injure tissue. But why would dropping a hammer on your hand cause significantly more pain and traumatic injury than just resting a hammer on your hand? After all, in both cases the weight of the hammer remains unchanged. The answer has to do with velocity. A hammer resting on your hand has a velocity of zero; by dropping that same hammer, you would increase its velocity and, in effect, magnify its force.

Assuming that an object's mass (or weight) does not change, the amount of potential force is then directly related to its acceleration. In other words, as the speed of movement increases so does its potential force. This isn't merely an opinion or an observation — it's a fundamental law of physics. Something new? No. In fact, it was first proposed about 300 years ago by Isaac Newton and is known as his Second Law of Motion. If slower speeds of movement are safer, it follows that faster speeds of movement are more dangerous.

Proponents of explosive training sometimes counter these facts by saying, "So what? Sports are dangerous — just look at football and wrestling. Maybe we should stop playing sports." Arguments like this miss the point entirely. It's true that sports are inherently dangerous. However, using potentially dangerous techniques in the weight room to prepare for potentially dangerous activities is like banging your head against the wall to prepare for a concussion (Mannie 1994). Clearly, encouraging anyone to explode with a weight is suggesting musculoskeletal trauma. The only thing that might explode is a tendon from its point of insertion.

UNDERSTANDING EXPLOSIVENESS

When someone is described as being "explosive" on an athletic field, essentially what is being said is that the athlete performs, moves or reacts quickly and forcefully. This is primarily due to the fact that the athlete's movement patterns for a particular skill are so firmly ingrained in his or her "motor memory" that there is little or no wasted effort. In other words, it's because the athlete is highly efficient at performing the intended sports skill — not because he or she practiced explosive movements with barbells, medicine balls or other implements in search of a nebulous concept such as "explosiveness" or "speed-strength."

A SAFER WAY

To ignore, discredit or criticize the opinions of anyone who suggests that there might be a safer and more practical method of training represents a rather narrow-minded and self-centered viewpoint that smacks of state-controlled thought. Such condemnation also creates an enormous injustice for the millions of individuals who are searching for the appropriate answers to their difficult questions.

Absolutely no one really knows exactly how fast a repetition should be performed for safe, efficient strength training — nor is it likely that anyone will ever know. Appropriate speeds of movement must certainly differ from one individual to another and probably even vary within the same person from time to time depending upon that person's current level of strength. At any rate, one thing is certain: It's much safer and more efficient to lift weights in a deliberate, controlled manner. Regardless of whether you're using machines or barbells, the weight should be raised without any jerking or explosive movements and then lowered under control. Raising the weight in about 1-2 seconds and lowering it in about 3-4 seconds will ensure that speeds of movement are not ballistic in nature and that momentum does not play a significant role in the efficiency of the exercise.

5
DEVELOPING ATHLETIC SKILLS

The science of motor learning is the study of muscular movement or, simply, "motor skills." Research in this discipline promotes an understanding of how motor skills are learned, applied and refined. The intent to expedite the acquisition of skills has given rise to a number of practices that are well-meaning but are generally unsupported by the motor learning literature.

SKILLS AND ABILITIES

Though the terms are often used interchangeably and are somewhat related, skills are vastly different from abilities (Sage 1977; Schmidt 1991). A skill refers to the level of performance in one specific action. Skills can be modified and improved through practice. On the other hand, an ability refers to a general trait. This includes dynamic strength, static strength, explosive strength, speed of limb movement, quickness, coordination, dynamic balance, static balance and stamina. Abilities are thought to be genetically determined and, unlike skills, cannot be changed by practice or experience (Schmidt 1991). Abilities are not specific skills in themselves. However, abilities are factors that determine performance potential and form the foundation of a number of specific skills. For example, performing a distinct skill such as a handstand requires the general underlying abilities of static strength and static balance.

Henry (1968) hypothesized that a very large number of abilities underlie a motor response. Each of these abilities is responsible for only a very limited number of movements — and even slightly different movements require that different abilities come into play. For instance, throwing two balls of different size and/or weight would involve different motor abilities. Further, these abilities are thought to be independent of each other — the quality of any one ability is not dependent upon the quality of another. Stated otherwise, individuals who perform well in one task do not necessarily perform well in another.

Quickness and Balance Exercises

General "quickening" and "balancing" drills are frequently used with the expectation that the movement patterns learned in those exercises will transfer to specific sports skills and thus improve performance. Numerous studies have investigated the possibility of transferring quickness and bal-

ance to other skills. According to Schmidt (1975), there is little evidence that practicing a skill that requires a certain ability — such as quickness or balance — will improve another skill that requires the same abilities.

Being "quick" is advantageous in just about any sport or activity. Schmidt (1991) suggests that there are at least three separate abilities that are used to act quickly: (1) reaction time (the interval of time between an unanticipated stimulus and the start of the response); (2) response orientation (where one of many stimuli is presented, each of which requires its own response); and (3) speed of movement (the interval of time between the start of a movement and its completion). Each of these three abilities involves quickness. However, these abilities are separate and independent of each other. Studies by Lindeburg (1949) and Blankenship (1952) reported no transfer effect from quickening exercises to a motor task requiring quickness. Henry (1961) has shown that reaction time and speed of movement have essentially no correlation — that is, the abilities have very little in common. Therefore, being "quick" depends on the circumstances under which speedy responses are required.

Balance is an ability that is important for the performance of a wide range of skills in sports such as football, basketball, gymnastics and hockey. As with quickness, the balance required for one activity is not related to the balance needed in another. A study by Bachman (1961) involving 320 subjects found no underlying ability for balance and noted that two balance tasks were dependent upon separate and independent abilities. The author concluded that the correlation between the two balance tasks was "little more than zero." Drowatzky and Zuccato (1967) examined six tests of static and dynamic balance and found that the abilities supporting one test of balance were separate from those supporting another. Their study suggests that there is no general ability for balance and that even skills that appear quite similar usually correlate poorly.

Similar findings were reported by a number of other researchers (Lotter 1960 and 1961; Henry and Smith 1961; Oxendine 1967; Marteniuk 1969). With very few exceptions, the correlations among motor tasks are very low (Schmidt 1975). In short, there is no general ability for quickness, balance or anything else (Schmidt 1991). It would

27

not be expected that an ability such as quickness or balance could be improved by practice anyway.

Open and Closed Skills

Poulton (1957) suggested that sport skills can be classified as either "open" or "closed." Both types of skills differ in several areas and demand entirely different learning strategies. Designations of "open" and "closed" actually mark the extreme points of a spectrum, with skills lying between having varying degrees of environmental variability and predictability (Schmidt 1991).

Open skills are performed in an environment that is variable and unpredictable. The performer must react to a situation and produce a response that can match the constantly changing environmental conditions. Since environmental conditions may vary from one response to another, the performer must have a variety of responses available to accomplish the skill. Examples of open skills are returning a tennis serve and reacting to an opponent's movement. Basketball, soccer and baseball are sports in which open skills dominate.

The balance required for an activity such as gymnastic handstand is not related to the balance needed in another sport or activity.

Conversely, a closed skill occurs in an environment that is stable and predictable. Because the environment does not fluctuate, the performer can plan or predict a response well in advance. Mannie (1992a) notes that in a closed skill, an object waits to be acted upon by the performer. Further, the performer is not required to begin action until ready to do so. Closed skills depend upon strength, endurance, power and technique for performance. Weightlifting — whether it be competitive or recreational — is an excellent example of an activity in which closed skills dominate. Other examples of closed skills are gymnastics, diving and putting the shot.

THE TRANSFER OF LEARNING

The transfer of learning refers to the effects of past learning upon the acquisition of a new skill. Many individuals take the transfer of learning for granted. They assume that movements for the execution of one skill always and automatically transfer or "carry over" to the learning of another.

Types of Transfer

The truth of the matter is that the acquisition of skills can be enhanced or impaired depending upon the correct use of the transfer of learning principles. The transfer of learning from one skill to another may be positive, negative or absent altogether (Sage 1977).

Positive transfer occurs when the influence of prior learning facilitates the learning of a new skill. Learning to position yourself to field a baseball would probably facilitate learning to position yourself to field a softball.

Negative transfer happens when the learning of a new skill inhibits the learning of a second skill. For instance, after hitting a baseball or a softball, running the bases clockwise (i.e., running from home plate to third base) instead of the traditional counterclockwise (i.e., running from home plate to first base) will likely create initial motor confusion.

No transfer occurs if the learning of one skill has a negligible influence on the learning of a second skill. As an example, learning to swim would have no effect on learning to accurately tap a volleyball (Nelson 1957).

THE USE OF WEIGHTED OBJECTS

It's widely believed that using weighted implements contributes to the learning of specific motor patterns and sports skills. This has led to the practice of trying to simulate sports skills in the weight room using a variety of weighted objects. In the motor learning literature, practicing a particular motor skill with weighted implements is known as "overload training." Barbells, dumbbells, medicine balls and other weighted objects are used during overload training with the expectation of improving performance.

The basis for mimicking sports skills with weighted implements is entirely anecdotal, having very little support from the motor learning literature. There is no research evidence suggesting that basic movement patterns can be transferred from task to task. Yet, many individuals still insist that the use of certain weightlifting movements encourages a positive transfer of motor ability to the athletic arena. If there were a correlation between weightlifting skills and other sports skills, then highly successful weightlifters would excel at literally every sports-related movement that they attempted. For instance, if eight elite weightlifters were placed in a rowing shell, they should easily win every regatta. Of course, this wouldn't happen because there is absolutely no positive transfer between weightlifting skills and other athletic skills (Jacobson 1981; Riley 1982c; Welday 1986).

The Kinesthetic Aftereffect

Motor learning research refers to a "kinesthetic aftereffect," which is defined by Sage (1977) as a "perceived modification in the shape, size or weight of an object . . . as a result of experience with a previous object." Athletes experience the kinesthetic aftereffect during overload training. This phenomenon is exemplified by the baseball batter who swings several bats in the on-deck circle so that the bat which is eventually used at the plate will seem lighter. Of course, the bat isn't really lighter but it creates a perceptual illusion that makes the batter feel he or she can swing faster. In a sense, the neurological pathways are fooled into believing the bat is lighter. Another example is the person who runs with a weighted vest, followed by the perceived ability to run faster after the vest is removed. Essentially, the kinesthetic aftereffect is nothing more than a sensory illusion.

Research findings. The research indicates that the kinesthetic aftereffect is not accompanied by a measurable improvement in performance in the skills that have been practiced using weighted objects. Investigations into the effects of using weighted basketball shoes (Gallon 1962) and ankle weights (Winningham 1966) found that the control groups who practiced without the weighted devices actually improved more on speed run tests than did the experimental groups who practiced with the weighted devices. Nelson and Nofsinger (1965) reported no significant changes in the speed of movement during elbow flexion immediately following the application of overload. A study by Stockholm and Nelson (1965) had subjects perform vertical jumps with a weighted vest, followed by jumps without the weight. They found no improvements in vertical jump performance after the overload practices. Nearly identical results were reported by Boyd (1969). Brose and Hanson (1967) reported no significant differences in throwing speed among a group who threw weighted baseballs, a group who used a pulley device to resist the mechanics of throwing and a control group who threw regulation baseballs. Also, neither of the training groups improved significantly in accuracy. The authors concluded that throwing weighted baseballs or using added resistance from a wall pulley does not significantly alter throwing velocity or accuracy. Hopek (1967) found no significant difference in accuracy between groups who trained with a regulation football and those who trained with a weighted football. Straub (1968) had subjects use weighted baseballs and reported that the use of these balls resulted in no immediate or long-range improvement in throwing speed or throwing accuracy. Unfortunately, research pertaining to the transfer of learning "dropped from sight" during the 1960s (Adams 1987).

Sage (1977) suggests that "any attempt to improve performance by utilizing objects that are slightly heavier than normal while practicing gross motor skills that will be later used in sports competition seems to be hardly worth the time spent and the money paid for the weighted objects." Schmidt (1991) adds, "Teaching a particular Skill A simply because you would like it to transfer to Skill B, which is of major interest, is not very effective, especially if you consider the time spent on Skill A that could have been spent on Skill B instead."

Problems with Using Weighted Objects

Westcott (1983) cites four problems that occur when practicing sports skills with weighted objects. The problem areas relate to neuromuscular confusion, incorrect movement speed, orthopedic stress and insufficient workload.

Neuromuscular confusion. Attempting to duplicate a sports skill with a weight or a weighted implement is a gigantic step in the wrong direction (Bryant 1988). Each time an athlete performs a given sports skill, there is a specific neuromuscular pattern involved that is unique to that movement alone. Introducing anything foreign to the "pattern" — such as weighted footballs, weighted vests, ankle weights, barbells or medicine balls — will only serve to confuse the original neuromuscular pathways, actually creating a negative transfer and a resultant decrease in performance (Westcott 1983; Thomas 1994).

Incorrect movement speed. If a skill is to be performed at a given speed, it should be practiced at that speed in order to facilitate the learning of the skill. Practicing a skill at a slower or a faster speed than actually would be used in the performance of the skill will cause a momentary negative transfer (Sage 1977). Pipes (1979) suggests that running with ankle weights will train the neuromuscular system at slower speeds and can cause a person to actually run slower. The same negative effects are produced when running with a parachute or while pulling a sled (Thomas 1994). A 6-week study by Hollering and Simpson (1977) had a group of ice hockey players perform a skating movement with resistance by pushing a partner across the ice. The group actually skated at slower speeds after the 6 weeks of resistive speed training (as determined by pre-testing and post-testing).

Consider a quarterback who practices his throwing motion with a weighted football. Will his movement pattern with the weighted object be faster, slower or the same as his usual throwing motion? Obviously, it must be slower. Therefore, it follows that the use of weighted implements actually impairs the learning of sports skills. Watch someone swing a weighted tennis racquet or shoot a weighted basketball and you'll quickly notice that the effort used to direct the unfamiliar weight results in a different movement pattern that is labored and awkward. In reality, it is a very different motion altogether.

Orthopedic stress. Another problem associated with practicing an athletic skill with a weighted object pertains to the stresses that are placed on the joints. Practicing with implements that are heavier than usual can place considerable orthopedic stress on the bodyparts involved (Westcott 1983; Bryant 1988) and is dangerous (Thomas 1994). Structural stress is most evident in the shoulder, elbow and wrist (Westcott 1983).

Insufficient workload. Another reason why weighted objects do not enhance performance is that they do not increase strength in the involved musculature. The added resistance provided by a weighted object is not sufficient enough to surpass the "threshold" for strength development. (This threshold is detailed in Chapter 6.) The added resistance is a mere fraction of what is necessary to overload the muscles.

SPECIFICITY VERSUS GENERALITY

In the early part of the twentieth century, Thorndike (1903) proposed his "identical elements" theory of transfer. Later, Henry (1968) advanced his "specificity hypothesis."

Both theories are forerunners of what is frequently referred to as the Principle of Specificity. The underlying fundamentals of this principle are well-documented in the motor learning literature. Nevertheless, the Principle of Specificity continues to be misinterpreted and misused almost as often as it is referenced. The principle states that activities must be specific to an intended skill in order for a maximal transfer of learning — or carryover — to occur. Specific means exact or identical, not similar or just like. Indeed, Lindeburg (1949) states that "transfer is highly specific and occurs only when the practiced movements are identical."

Movement patterns for different skills are never executed exactly alike. According to Henry (1968), very similar-appearing motor skills are based on very different patterns of muscular activity. Some movement patterns — although they outwardly appear to use the same muscular actions — are actually quite different and require learning and practice on each task separately (Schmidt 1975). So, learning a tennis skill would not transfer to a badminton skill. Similarly, learning to throw a football would not transfer to throwing a baseball.

Power Cleans Revisited

Power cleans have long been touted as being specific to an incredibly wide range of skills, from the breast stroke to the golf swing to the shot put. How is it possible that any one movement could be identical to such a broad group of differing skills? Answer: It can't.

A study by Rasch and Morehouse (1957) had subjects perform elbow flexion (i.e., a bicep curl) in the standing position. After training, elbow flexion strength had increased considerably when measured in the standing position. However, similar movements in an unfamiliar position (supine) revealed only a slight increase in strength. In other words, a standing bicep curl isn't even specific to a nearly identical exercise such as a supine bicep curl. Likewise, a power clean isn't specific to any other similar lifting movement — such as an upright row. A power clean is even less similar to athletic skills and, therefore, is not specific to any athletic skill (Thomas 1994). In terms of a power clean being specific to another athletic skill, Jesse (1979) asks, "What other activity requires lifting a heavy weight to the shoulders?" The answer is none.

So, performing power cleans may be similar to driving off the line of scrimmage, and doing lunges may be just like driving toward the basket, but the truth is power cleans will only help you get better at doing power cleans, and lunges will only help you get better at doing lunges. Similarly, heaving medicine balls around is great for improving your skill at heaving medicine balls around and nothing else. Also, jumping off of boxes will only perfect your skill at jumping off of boxes. There is no exercise done in the weight room — with barbells or machines — that will expedite the learning of sports skills (Wood 1991). Allman (1976) and Jesse (1979) have stated that the performance of Olympic-style weightlifting movements provide little benefit to athletes in training programs other than the sport of Olympic-style weightlifting.

In addition, a power clean is an extremely complex motor skill. Like any other motor skill, it takes a lot of time and patience to master its specific neuromuscular pattern. This valuable time and energy could be used more effectively elsewhere — such as perfecting specific sports techniques and skills that will actually be used in competition.

Elements of Specificity

According to Freedman (1990), there are four elements of specificity. These four components define the rules for determining whether two movements are specific or not:

- **Muscle specificity.** The exact muscle(s) used in the exercise must also be used in the athletic skill.

- **Movement specificity.** The exact movement pattern used in the exercise must be the same as the athletic skill.

- **Speed specificity.** The speed of movement used in the exercise must be identical to the athletic skill.

- **Resistance specificity.** The precise resistance used in the exercise must be identical to the external resistance encountered in the athletic skill.

In order for a weight training exercise to be specific to an athletic skill, all four of these elements would have to be true. One skill may resemble another in terms of identical muscle(s), movement pattern, speed of movement and resistance used. However, at best a weight training exercise can only approximate an athletic skill . . . it cannot duplicate it.

THE STAGES OF MOTOR LEARNING

The development of motor skills is accomplished in stages or phases of learning. It is important to understand that skill learning is a continuous process. Therefore, these stages do not have a distinct beginning or ending and should not be viewed as being separate or unconnected elements.

Fitts (1964) identified three phases of motor learning: an early or cognitive phase, an intermediate or associative phase and a final or autonomous phase.

The Cognitive Phase

In this first phase of motor learning, the skill is completely new to the performer. The performer seeks an understanding of the skill and its demands. During this phase, the attention requirements are high and movements are jerky and fragmented. Performance is usually very inconsistent, but gains in proficiency are very rapid. Good strategies are retained, and inappropriate ones are discarded. The cognitive phase may last anywhere from several moments to several weeks depending upon the complexity of the skill, the frequency of practice and so on.

The Associative Phase

During this second phase of motor learning, the performer organizes more effective and efficient movement patterns that are more coordinated and consistent. The enhanced movement efficiency reduces the energy costs of the skill. Performance improvements are rapid — although not as fast as in the cognitive phase. The length of this phase varies considerably and may last several weeks or months.

The Autonomous Phase

After many months and possibly years of painstaking practice, the skill becomes highly organized and well-developed. In this final phase of motor learning, the movement patterns are performed with little or no conscious attention. In other words, the movement becomes automatic. In the final stage of learning a closed skill, the emphasis is on refinement of technique; for open skills, the emphasis is on adaptation of the movement to various environmental conditions and possibilities. Because of the high degree of skill, performance improvements are slower in the autonomous phase.

IMPROVING ATHLETIC SKILLS

The acquisition and improvement of athletic skills is a process in which the performer develops a set of responses into an integrated and organized movement pattern. A study by Bobbert and van Soest (1994) implies two requirements that are necessary in order to increase efficiency at performing athletic skills: practicing the skill and strengthening the muscles. These two requirements have also been noted by Bryant (1988).

An athletic skill must be practiced perfectly and exactly as it would be used in competition.

Skill training is specific to a sport but strength training is general.

Practicing the Skill

The first requirement for improving athletic skills is to literally practice the intended skill for thousands and thousands of task-specific repetitions. Each repetition must be done with perfect technique so that its specific movement pattern becomes firmly ingrained in your "motor memory." The skill must be practiced perfectly and exactly as it would be used in competition. Further, the skill should be practiced with regulation equipment, not weighted implements.

Strengthening the Muscles

The second requirement for improving athletic skills is to strengthen the major muscle groups that are used during the performance of a particular skill. Strength training should not be done in a manner that mimics or apes a particular sports skill so as not to confuse or impair the intended movement pattern. A stronger muscle can produce more force; if you can produce more force, you'll require less effort and be able to perform the skill more quickly, more accurately and more efficiently. But again, this is provided that you've practiced enough in a correct manner so that you'll be more skillful in applying that force. Remember, practice makes perfect . . . but only if you practice perfect.

SPORT-SPECIFIC EXERCISES

Are there sport-specific or even position-specific exercises? Should a basketball player perform different exercises than a football player or a swimmer? Or, should a pitcher perform a strength workout that differs from that of a catcher or an outfielder?

Each person has the same muscles that function in the same manner as any other person. For example, your bicep muscle flexes your lower arm around your elbow joint. The same is true for a diver, a shot putter, a quarterback, a lacrosse player and a defensive lineman. It follows then that there is no such thing as a sport-specific or a position-specific exercise (Mannie 1990; Riley 1992; Thomas 1994; Wetzel 1994). For that matter, there aren't any gender-specific exercises, either. Some athletes might perform certain movements as a precaution to prevent an injury to a joint that receives a lot of stress in their particular sport, such as a wrestler using neck exercises. Athletes might also perform a movement to focus on a particular muscle group that is absolutely critical to their sport. For instance, a golfer who relies on grip strength might exercise his or her forearms, while a soccer player would not. Other than that, people should select movements that exercise their muscles in the safest and most efficient way possible — regardless of their sport or activity. Remember, skill training is specific to a sport but strength training is general (Allman 1976; Jones 1977b; Hewgley 1984; Leistner 1986b; Wood 1991). In other words, the development of strength is general but the application of strength is specific.

Part 2

ORGANIZING THE STRENGTH PROGRAM

6
THE PRINCIPLES OF STRENGTH DEVELOPMENT

Asanovich (1992) has defined strength as "the ability of the musculoskeletal system to produce force." It follows that strength training is the process of improving or increasing this ability.

The primary purpose of strength training is to decrease your injury potential and its second purpose is to increase your performance potential (Riley 1982c; Mannie 1989; Thomas 1994). Make no mistake about it — strength training is primarily a mechanism to prevent injury (Brown 1990). Increasing the strength of your muscles, bones and connective tissue will reduce the likelihood that you will incur an injury (Fahey 1989; Bates, Wolf and Blunk 1990; Graves and Pollock 1992). That doesn't mean that a person will never get hurt . . . sometimes injuries are a matter of being in the wrong spot at the wrong time. However, strength training will reduce that risk considerably. And, improving your functional strength will be an important step in realizing your physical potential. Strength training doesn't guarantee that you will improve your performance (Rutherford and Jones 1986; Bates, Wolf and Blunk 1990). Nevertheless, strength training will enhance your potential to become as successful as you possibly can.

STRENGTH TRAINING GUIDELINES

Science has been unable to discover one strength training method that is superior to another. Research has only shown that there are a variety of training methods that increase strength. For instance, Berger (1962) noted significant strength increases in all nine training groups who used different combinations of one, two and three sets and two, six and ten repetitions. Westcott (1989) found no statistically significant differences in the strength increases produced by nine different training routines consisting of various combinations of sets and repetitions.

Increases in strength can also be produced by a variety of equipment (Riley 1982b; Gittleson 1984; Fuhrman 1987; Peterson and Horodyski 1988; Brown 1989; Bates, Wolf and Blunk 1990; Mannie 1992b). Studies have demonstrated no significant differences in strength improvement between groups using free weights and groups using machines (Pipes 1978; Messier and Dill 1985). Since just about any type of program or equipment will yield favor-

able results, you must decide what is most practical for you based upon safety and time considerations.

A safe, efficient, productive, comprehensive and practical workout can be performed with virtually any type of equipment by using the following ten principles of strength development:

1. Train with a high level of intensity.

Other than genetics, the intensity of effort is the most important factor in determining the response from strength training. Intensity has been defined as "a percentage of momentary ability" (Jones 1973). In other words, intensity relates to the degree of the "inroads" — or amount of fatigue — made into the muscle at any given instant. When the muscles are fresh at the beginning of an exercise, the percentage of momentary ability is high . . . and the intensity (or effort) is obviously low. When the muscles are fatigued at the end of an exercise, the percentage of momentary ability is low . . . but now the intensity is high. (A percentage of momentary ability or intensity should not be confused with a percentage of maximum weight.)

As early as 1945, a high level of effort was identified as being the most important factor in determining favorable results from strength training (DeLorme 1945) and has been noted by numerous authors since (Hellebrandt and Houtz 1956; Jones 1970; Pipes 1979; Rasch 1979; Westcott 1983; Diange 1984; Kennedy 1986b; MacDougall 1986; McArdle, Katch and Katch 1986; Bryant 1988; Mannie 1988; Dunn 1989a; Andress 1990; Bates, Wolf and Blunk 1990; Verkhoshansky 1991; Wood 1991; Pollock et al. 1993b; Bullock 1994; Thomas 1994; Wetzel 1994). Essentially, the harder you train, the better your response. In the weight room, a high level of intensity is characterized by performing each exercise to the point of concentric muscular failure: when the muscles have been exhausted to the extent that the weight literally cannot be raised for any more repetitions (Jones 1970; Riley 1982b; Gittleson 1984; Hewgley 1984; Bryant 1988; Brown 1989; Bates, Wolf and Blunk 1990; Verkhoshansky 1991; Thomas 1994). Failure to reach a desirable level of intensity — or muscular fatigue — will result in little or no gains in muscular size or strength (DeLorme 1945; Jones 1970; Wilmore 1982; Graves and Pollock 1992).

The Overload Principle

Evidence for this "threshold" is suggested in the literature by the "Overload Principle" — a term first coined by Dr. Arthur Steinhaus in 1933 (Arendt 1984). One of the earliest experimental demonstrations of this principle was made by Hellebrandt and Houtz (1956). The Overload Principle states that in order to increase muscular size and strength, a muscle must be stressed — or "overloaded" — with a workload that is beyond its present capacity (DeLateur, Lehmann and Giaconi 1976; Darden 1977; Fox and Mathews 1981; Wilmore 1982; Fuhrman 1987; Enoka 1988a; Bates, Wolf and Blunk 1990). The intensity of effort must be great enough to exceed this threshold level so that a sufficient amount of muscular fatigue is produced to trigger an adaptive response: muscular growth. Given proper nourishment and an adequate amount of recovery between workouts, a muscle will adapt to these demands by increasing in size and strength. The extent to which this "compensatory adaptation" occurs then becomes a function of a person's inherited characteristics. (Chapter 3 contains detailed information on the role of genetics in strength training.)

Post-fatigue Repetitions

After reaching concentric muscular failure, the intensity of the exercise can be increased even further by performing 3-5 additional post-fatigue repetitions. These intensification repetitions may be either negatives or regressions and will allow the muscles to be overloaded in a safe, efficient manner.

Negatives. After reaching concentric muscular failure, one method of increasing the intensity of the exercise is through the performance of "negatives." Recall from Chapter 2 that raising a weight is sometimes referred to as the positive phase of a movement and involves a concentric muscular contraction; lowering a weight is typically referred to as the negative phase of a movement and involves an eccentric muscular contraction. Your eccentric strength is always greater than your concentric and isometric strength (Enoka 1988a; Jones et al. 1988; Jones 1993). This means that when you reach a point where you are unable to raise the weight concentrically, you still have the ability to lower the weight eccentrically. Herein lies the reasoning and the value behind performing "negatives" after reaching concentric muscular failure at the end of a set. In a negative repetition, a training partner raises the weight concentrically and the lifter lowers the weight eccentrically (Dunn 1989a). This is repeated for 3-5 repetitions. Brown (1989) recommends that each negative repetition should last 6-8 seconds.

As an example, suppose that you reached concentric muscular failure on a barbell bench press. Your partner would help you raise the weight off your chest until your arms are extended. Then, you lower the weight under control back to your chest. Your partner can even add a little extra resistance by pushing down on the bar as you lower it. This variation of a negative repetition using added pressure during the lowering phase is known as a "forced rep" (Mannie 1989).

In effect, these post-fatigue repetitions are positive-assisted and negative-resisted. Performing a few negative

Other than genetics, the intensity of effort is the most important factor in determining the response from strength training. (Photo by Kathy Leistner)

repetitions at the end of an exercise will allow you to reach eccentric muscular failure — when your muscles have fatigued to the point where you can't even lower the weight. That's why a set-to-failure followed immediately by several negatives is so brutally effective: you've managed to exhaust the muscle completely — both concentrically and eccentrically. (Protocols for negative-only and negative-accentuated exercise are described in Chapter 7.)

Regressions. Another way of achieving a greater level of intensity and concomitant muscular overload is to perform regressions — also called "breakdowns" or "burnouts" — after reaching concentric muscular exhaustion (Brown 1989; Verkhoshansky 1991). When you reach concentric muscular failure, your muscles are still capable of producing force. However, their force-producing capacity is not enough to move that level of resistance. After reaching muscular failure, you (or your training partner) quickly reduce the starting weight by about 25-30 percent and the lifter does 3-5 post-fatigue repetitions with the lighter resistance. Let's say you did 14 repetitions with 100 pounds on the calf raise before reaching concentric muscular failure. You (or your partner) would immediately reduce the weight to about 70-75 pounds and you would then attempt to perform 3-5 repetitions with the lighter weight. If desired, a second series of 3-5 regressions may be performed

When performing negatives on the barbell bench press, a training partner raises the weight concentrically and the lifter lowers the weight eccentrically.

immediately after the first series by reducing the lightened load by 25-30 percent. (In this example, the 70-75 pounds would be quickly reduced to about 50-55 pounds.)

This method of using regressions is actually a variation of the Oxford Technique proposed by Zinovieff (1951). The idea is to use the heaviest possible weight during a set and then systematically reduce the weight for subsequent repetitions to offset the fatigue that was developed during the first effort.

Some strength and fitness professionals consider the performance of post-fatigue repetitions (i.e., negatives or regressions) as a second (or third) "set." Since they've come immediately after reaching muscular failure with little or no recovery, others view the additional post-fatigue repetitions as simply an extension of the first set. Regardless of how post-fatigue repetitions are perceived, they should be used carefully and — in the case of individuals who do not tolerate physiological stress well — infrequently.

The General Adaptation Syndrome

The amount of fatigue produced by exercise determines the training effect (Rasch 1979). Exercise that does not produce enough stress (i.e., fatigue) will not stimulate muscular growth (Hellebrandt and Houtz 1956); exercise that produces too much stress will not permit muscular growth either — and may even produce a loss in muscle size and strength. The General Adaptation Syndrome (GAS) is a three-stage process proposed by Selye (1956) to explain the physical effects of stress. The GAS may be applied to the stress placed upon the muscles during strength training activities. In the first stage of the GAS, the physiological stress or demands applied on the muscle cause damage or microtrauma. This is followed by the second stage during which the body defends itself against the stress-induced damage by compensatory adaptation (i.e., an increase in size and strength). However, stress that is prolonged or too severe induces a third stage in which the demands on the muscles exceed their ability to recover and adapt.

The Intensity Continuum

Failure to reach a certain level of intensity will result in submaximal improvements. Unfortunately, no one knows precisely the minimum level of intensity necessary to surpass the "threshold" and stimulate muscular growth. However, even if the minimum level is unknown, the most productive level of intensity can be determined by deductive reasoning. For the moment, let's suppose that a 90 percent level of intensity is the threshold for achieving maximal results. If so, how do we pinpoint 90 percent intensity . . . or 95 percent intensity . . . or any other level of intensity for that matter? Answer: You can't. (Again, a percentage of intensity should not be confused with a percentage of maximum weight.)

There are exactly two levels of intensity that can be determined easily and accurately. One level is 0 percent intensity or complete inactivity. Obviously, no intensity creates no stimulus and therefore produces no effect. The only other identifiable level is at the opposite end of the intensity continuum. That level is 100 percent intensity, which is characterized by a total, all-out effort for a prescribed amount of time. It is literally impossible to determine any other levels of intensity. Therefore, the only level of effort that is both productive and measurable is 100 percent intensity.

Time and Intensity

It is also important to understand that an inverse relationship exists between time and intensity: As the time or the length of an activity increases, the level of intensity decreases (Matveyev 1981). Stated otherwise, a person cannot train at a high level of intensity for long periods of time (Mentzer 1993).

For example, suppose you had to sprint as fast as you possibly could for as long as you could. If you're in reasonably good condition, you wouldn't be able to run more than about 300 yards at an absolute breakneck speed before stopping due to total exhaustion. Your time would probably be in the neighborhood of 40-50 seconds. In this

When performing regressions on the calf raise, the lifter (or the training partner) quickly reduces the starting weight by about 25-30 percent and the lifter does 3-5 post-fatigue repetitions with the lighter resistance.

case, your level of effort was extremely high but your time of activity was somewhat low. On the other hand, imagine that you were asked to run that same distance in three minutes. Relative to the first example, your level of intensity was rather low and your duration of activity was high.

The fact is a person can exercise for a short period of time with a high level of intensity or a long period of time with a low level of intensity. However, a person cannot possibly train at a high level of intensity for a long period of time. In order to train with a fairly high level of intensity, a person must train for a relatively brief period of time. It is important to understand that increasing the number of sets or exercises performed will increase the length of time a person is exercising and decrease the level of intensity.

Favorable Results

Simply, a submaximal effort will yield submaximal results. The fact that your results are directly related to your level of effort shouldn't come as much of a surprise. It's like anything else in life: How hard you work at your studies, your practice sessions, your job and even your relationships will largely determine your success at those endeavors. This also applies to your strength training. Clearly, a high level of intensity is an absolute requirement for achieving optimal gains in muscular size and strength.

Mannie (1990) has stated that high intensity strength training is "the most productive, most efficient and without a doubt, the most demanding form of strength training known." When you perform an exercise to the point of muscular failure and follow it by immediately performing a few negative or regressive repetitions, you'll quickly realize why it's called "high intensity training."

2. Attempt to increase the resistance used or the repetitions performed every work out.

In the late 1940s, the term "Progressive Resistance Exercise" was coined by Dr. Thomas L. DeLorme (DeLorme and Watkins 1948). In fact, DeLorme is often referred to as the father of progressive resistance exercise. DeLorme started lifting weights in 1932 at the age of 16 in an attempt to increase his size and strength. During World War II, he applied the lessons he had learned from his own experience to the rehabilitation of large numbers of wounded soldiers.

Unfortunately, little of what is done in most weight rooms can be characterized as being "progressive." It's not uncommon to hear of someone who performs the same number of repetitions with the same amount of weight over and over again, workout after workout. Suppose that today you did a set of leg curls for 10 repetitions with 100 pounds and a month later you're still doing 10 repetitions with 100 pounds. Did you increase your strength? Probably not. On the other hand, what if you were able to do 11 repetitions with 120 pounds a month later? In this case, you were able to perform 10 percent more repetitions with 20 percent more weight — excellent progress over a period of one month.

Changes in the functional and structural abilities of a muscle depend upon the continued use of the Overload Principle (Enoka 1988a). Therefore, if a muscle is to continually increase in size and strength it must be forced to do progressively harder work (Lange 1919; Jones 1971a; Westcott 1983; Fuhrman 1987; Pollock et al. 1993b). The muscles must be overloaded with a workload that is increased steadily and systematically throughout the course of a strength training program. This is often referred to as "progressive overload." Legend has it that Milo of Crotona, an Olympic athlete in ancient Greece, periodically lifted a baby bull on his shoulders. Milo's strength increased as the bull increased in size and weight. This crude method of progression was responsible for Milo's legendary strength gains.

In order to overload your muscles, every time you work out you must attempt to increase either the weight you use or the repetitions you perform in relation to your previous workout (Jones et al. 1988; Brown 1989; Bates, Wolf and Blunk 1990; Lambrinides 1990c). This can be viewed as a "double progressive" technique (resistance and repetitions). Challenging the muscles in this manner will stimulate compensatory adaptation in response to the imposed demands (or stress) placed upon them.

Each time the maximum number of repetitions are attained, the resistance should be increased for the next workout. Progressions need not be in Herculean leaps and bounds . . . but the weight must always be challenging. The resistance should be increased in an amount that a person is comfortable with. Fortunately, this may be accomplished much more systematically than the method used by Milo and his growing bull. The muscles will respond better if the progressions in resistance are five percent or less. But again, remember that the resistance must always be challenging. If a person is just beginning a strength training program, or the exercises are changed in a routine, it may take several workouts before a challenging weight is found. That's okay — the person should simply continue to make progressions in the resistance as needed.

Recall from Chapter 3 that everyone has a different genetic potential for developing strength. As such, you shouldn't really be concerned with what you can lift relative to another person. However, you should be concerned with what you can lift relative to your previous performances. In other words, don't compare your strength to anyone else — just make sure that you are as strong as you can be.

3. Perform one set of each exercise to the point of muscular exhaustion.

Another controversial area in strength training pertains to the number of sets of an exercise that are required to increase muscular size and strength. If performed properly, traditional multiple-set routines (i.e., more than one set) can be effective in "overloading" a muscle. They've been used successfully by competitive weightlifters and bodybuilders for decades. And, since many strength and fitness professionals have competed in weightlifting meets and bodybuilding events, it's no surprise that most athletic and recreational programs incorporate a traditional multiple-set program.

Few strength and fitness professionals ever recommend performing more than three sets per exercise. Anything more than about three sets is generally considered to be an unproductive form of manual labor. Performing too many sets can also create a catabolic effect in which the muscles are broken down in such an extreme manner that the body is unable to regenerate muscle tissue (essentially the resynthesis of myofibrillar proteins).

In seeking the most practical and time-efficient strength training method possible, a necessary question is: Can performing one set of each exercise with a high level of intensity give an individual the same results as performing two or three sets? The answer is a resounding yes. Recall that in order for a muscle to increase in size and strength, it must be fatigued or overloaded. It's that simple. It really doesn't matter whether the muscles are fatigued in one set or several sets — as long as the muscles experience a certain level of exhaustion. When performing multiple sets, the cumulative effect of each successive set makes deeper inroads into the muscle thereby creating muscular fatigue; when performing a single-set-to-failure, the cumulative effect of each successive repetition makes deeper inroads into the muscle thereby creating muscular fatigue. An overwhelming amount of research has shown that one set of an exercise can produce significant strength improvements. Other studies have demonstrated that there are no significant differences between either one, two or three sets of an exercise. Of course, if a single set of an exercise is to be productive, the set must be done with an appropriate level of intensity (i.e., to the point of concentric muscular failure). The muscle(s) must be completely fatigued at the end of each exercise. Following concentric muscular failure, the muscle(s) can be overloaded further by incorporating a few post-fatigue repetitions (either negatives or regressions).

Both a single-set-to-failure and multiple sets produce muscular fatigue. However, multiple sets do not necessarily guarantee that the muscles have received a sufficient level of muscular fatigue. Indeed, a large amount of low-intensity exercise will do very little in the way of increasing strength. But, performing one set of an exercise to the point where a person cannot do any more repetitions always achieves a desirable level of muscular exhaustion.

Efficient Inroads

How is a favorable level of muscular exhaustion produced by performing only one set? Suppose that you are to perform a set of leg extensions with 100 pounds. In order to overcome inertia and give movement to the 100 pounds of resistance, your quadriceps must exert slightly more than

100 pounds of force. The weight will not move if a force less than or equal to 100 pounds is applied. During the first repetition, your intensity is low. At this point, only a small percentage of your available muscle fibers is being used — just enough to move the weight. As you perform each repetition, your intensity increases progressively and you'll make deeper inroads into your muscle. Some of your muscle fibers will fatigue and will no longer be able to keep up with the increasing metabolic demands. Fresh fibers are simultaneously recruited to assist the fatigued fibers in generating ample force. This process continues until the last repetition, when concentric muscular failure is finally reached and your intensity is at its highest. Now, your remaining fibers cannot collectively produce enough force to raise the weight. During this final repetition, the cumulative effect of each preceding repetition has fatigued the muscle thereby providing a sufficient — and efficient — stimulus for muscular growth. It should be noted that your first few repetitions are the least productive because your intensity is low. On the other hand, your very last repetition is the most productive because your intensity is very high. Truly, one set done with a maximal level of effort is the metabolic equivalent of several sets done with a submaximal level of effort. (Recall, too, the "size principle" of muscle fiber recruitment discussed in Chapter 4.)

Utilization

According to Stone and Kroll (1978), "one set of an exercise can produce significant strength improvement." Graves and his colleagues (1990) also noted that performing one set to fatigue is a popular and very effective method of strength training. Indeed, doing a single set to exhaustion has been advocated by numerous strength and fitness authorities (Jones 1971b; Darden 1975; Pipes 1989; Kotch 1990; Peterson and Westcott 1990; Hutchins 1992; Mentzer 1993). In addition, a protocol of one-set-to-failure has been endorsed by strength coaches for collegiate teams (Riley 1982b; Diange 1984; Gittleson 1984; Kennedy 1986b; Andress 1990; Brown 1990; Thomas 1994; Watson 1994) and professional teams (Riley 1982f and 1992; Dunn 1989a; Wood 1991; Reinebold 1993; Wetzel 1994).

Research Findings

Performing one-set-to-fatigue has been shown to be effective and comparable to doing multiple sets in a convincing number of research studies. In a 12-week study involving 177 subjects, Berger (1962) reported significant strength increases in a group who used one set of 6 repetitions and another group who used one set of 10 repetitions. More-

A protocol of one-set-to-failure has been endorsed by strength coaches for collegiate teams and professional teams. (Photo by Rick Phelps)

over, he noted that the rates of strength improvement in groups using one, two or three sets of an exercise "were practically the same" during the last three weeks of training. Peterson (1975) reported an average overall strength increase of 58.54 percent and a vertical jump improvement of 6.49 percent in 18 varsity football players who performed a single set of each exercise to muscle exhaustion. In this six-week study, the total training time per person was less than 8.5 hours in 17 workouts (i.e., less than 30 minutes per workout). Since early increases in strength are mainly associated with neural adaptation (Komi 1986; Rutherford and Jones 1986; Enoka 1988b), it should also be noted that the subjects performed two weeks of workouts preceding this study to minimize the influence of this so-called "learning effect."

Silvester and others (1982) found little difference when single-set training protocols were compared to training with two sets. Stower and coworkers (1983) reported no significant differences in upper body strength increases when comparing one-set and multiple-set programs. A 16-week study by Hurley and others (1984) demonstrated a 50 percent increase in upper body strength and a 33 percent increase in lower body strength from a single set to volitional fatigue. A 10-week study by Messier and Dill (1985) found no significant differences in strength increases between groups using one set of an exercise (with machines) and three sets of an exercise (with free weights). The group performing one-set-to-failure demonstrated a 30 percent increase in upper body strength and a 46 percent increase in lower body strength. In an 8-week study that involved 100 untrained females, Terbizan and Bartels (1985) found no differences between four groups using protocols of one set of 6-9 repetitions, one set of 10-15 repetitions, three sets of 6-9 repetitions and three sets of 10-15 repetitions. Jacobson (1986) concluded that performing one intense set yielded "nearly identical" results as performing three sets.

Studies have also examined the effects of a single set on an isolated muscle. In a study by Braith and others (1989), two groups using different repetition schemes showed significant strength gains from performing a single set of leg extensions. A study by Graves and his colleagues (1991) compared the effect of doing one versus two sets of an exercise and found one set to be equally effective for the development of isolated lumbar extension strength. Leggett and his coworkers (1991) reported significant increases in neck extension strength at 6 of 8 angles evaluated following 10 weeks of training that was conducted one time per week using a single set of dynamic variable resistance exercise. A study by Pollock and his associates (1993b) concluded that only a single set of neck extension exercise performed to exhaustion is required to attain a full range of motion increase in strength, provided the training frequency is at least two times per week. Starkey and others (1994) concluded that doing one set of high intensity resistance training is as effective as three sets for increasing knee flex-

ion/extension strength and muscle thickness and also represents a more efficient use of time. Many additional studies have found significant gains in strength in response to a single set of an exercise performed to muscle fatigue (Gettman, Ward and Hagman 1982; Graves et al. 1988; Graves et al. 1989; Pollock et al. 1989; Graves et al. 1990; Leggett et al. 1991; Risch et al. 1993).

Practical and Purposeful

If doing one set of an exercise produces the same results as two or three sets, then a one-set protocol represents a more efficient and practical means of strength training. After all, why should a person perform several sets when similar results can be obtained from one set in a fraction of the time? Again, this is not to say that traditional multiple-set programs are unproductive. It's just that multiple sets are extremely inefficient in terms of time and, therefore, are undesirable for much of the population. If you're like most people, time is a precious commodity — most people simply do not have much free time. Recall that performing too many sets can also retard muscular growth. Finally, doing multiple sets can significantly increase the risk of incurring an overuse injury — such as tendinitis — due to repetitive muscular trauma.

Everything done in the weight room should have a purpose. That purpose is to reduce your risk of injury and to realize your performance potential. You should emphasize the quality of work done in the weight room rather than the quantity of work. Don't do meaningless sets in the weight room — make every single exercise count. The most efficient program is one that produces the maximum possible results in the least amount of time.

4. Reach concentric muscular failure within a prescribed number of repetitions or amount of time.

The question "How many repetitions should be performed?" can have virtually an infinite number of answers. However, recall from Chapter 3 that there's no conclusive scientific evidence to suggest that low repetitions will "bulk up" muscles and high repetitions will "tone" muscles. The number of repetitions that are performed depends on at least four factors: (1) the duration of each repetition; (2) individual genetic influences; (3) the range of motion of the exercise; and (4) any orthopedic or health concerns.

Repetition Duration

A muscle must be exercised for a certain amount of time in order to increase in size and strength. Optimal time frames are about 90-120 seconds for the buttocks, 60-90 seconds for the rest of the lower body and 40-70 seconds for the upper torso (Riley 1980; Verkhoshansky 1991). The muscles of the lower body should be exercised for a slightly longer amount of time because of their greater size and work capacity (Andress 1990).

It's usually not practical to perform a set for a precise amount of time. However, this information can be used to formulate something more convenient: repetition ranges. For example, if a weight is to be raised in about 2 seconds and lowered in about 4 seconds, each repetition would be about 6 seconds long. Based upon the optimal time frames and using a 6-second repetition, the buttocks need to be exercised for 15-20 reps, the lower body for 10-15 reps and the upper torso for about 6-12 reps. On the other hand, the so-called Super Slow Protocol advanced by Hutchins (1992) recommends that a weight be raised in 10 seconds and lowered in about 5 seconds (provided that the exercise does not have a significant amount of mechanical friction). As such, each repetition is about 15 seconds long. Based upon the optimal time frames and using a 15-second repetition, the buttocks should be exercised for about 6-8 reps, the lower body for about 4-6 reps and the upper torso for about 3-5 reps.

As you can see, repetition ranges are not as important as the length of time that a muscle is exercised. However, it's usually much more practical to count repetitions during a workout than to be followed around by someone with a stopwatch. In general, assuming a traditional 6-second repetition concentric muscular failure should be reached within 15-20 reps for exercises involving the buttocks, 10-15 reps for the legs and 6-12 reps for the upper torso.

If concentric muscular failure occurs before the lower level of the repetition range is reached, the weight is too heavy and should be reduced for the next workout. If the upper level of the repetition range is exceeded before muscular exhaustion is experienced, the weight is too light and should be increased for the next workout by five percent or less.

It should be noted that attempting a one-repetition maximum (1-RM) or performing low-repetition movements that are considerably less than the optimal time frames will increase the risk of injury. (The dangers of 1-RMs are discussed in Chapter 1.) Likewise, as an exercise exceeds the recommended time frames, it becomes a greater test of aerobic endurance rather than muscular strength.

Genetic Influences

Some people, because of their genetic makeup, may require a slightly lower or a slightly higher repetition range in order to maximize their response to strength training. For example, some individuals inherit a higher percentage of fast twitch (FT) muscle fibers than the average person.

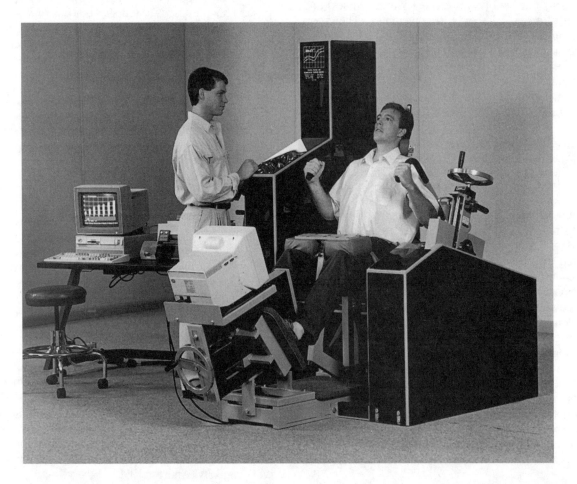

MedX Corporation offers elaborate testing devices that are safe and accurate for conducting tests of muscular endurance to evaluate muscle fiber type. (Photo by MedX Corporation)

These individuals would probably benefit more from strength training by using a slightly lower repetition range because their high percentage of FT fibers tend to limit their muscular endurance. Slightly lower ranges of perhaps 10-15 for the buttocks, 9-12 for the rest of the lower body and 6-10 for the upper torso would probably yield better results for someone with a predominance of FT fibers in those bodyparts. Conversely, some individuals inherit a high percentage of slow twitch (ST) fibers. Slightly higher ranges of perhaps 20-25 for the buttocks, 15-20 for the rest of the lower body and 10-15 for the upper body would probably produce a better response for someone with a predominance of ST fibers in those bodyparts. A study by Westcott (1987) had sprinters train with low repetitions, middle-distance runners with medium repetitions and long-distance runners with high repetitions. The study revealed excellent and equal strength gains in all three groups. (Recall that successful sprinters likely inherit a high percentage of FT fibers and successful distance runners likely inherit a high percentage of ST fibers.)

The only way to positively determine a person's fiber type distribution is by removing a small section of muscle by way of a biopsy and analyzing the tissue sample under a microscope. (The sample from a muscle biopsy weighs about 15-45 milligrams. The muscle sample is frozen, thinly sliced and stained with chemicals which show enzyme activity — an indicator of fiber type — when the tissue slices are observed under a microscope.) Most people are understandably reluctant to part with samples of their muscle tissue. However, a logical guesstimate of someone's fiber type makeup can sometimes be made based upon certain metabolic and physical characteristics. Those who are reasonably successful at sports that require them to generate a lot of strength in a short period of time probably have a high percentage of FT fibers and should use slightly lower repetitions; those who seem to be more successful at endurance activities probably possess a high percentage of ST fibers and should use slightly higher repetitions.

Another way of making a reasonable assessment of a person's predominant fiber type is by examining the extent of muscular development. Because FT fibers have a much greater capacity for hypertrophy than ST fibers, it's likely that a muscle that is heavily developed contains a high percentage of FT fibers. Likewise, a muscle that has slight development will probably be composed of mostly ST fibers.

An endurance test is a crude, albeit reasonably effective, way of assessing muscle fiber types in a noninvasive manner based upon fatigue characteristics. Because an endurance test involves determining a 1-RM, this test is not recommended for use with conventional equipment. Nevertheless, endurance testing is still quite interesting and deserves special note. Suppose your 1-RM in the leg extension is 200 pounds. An endurance test is performed with 80 percent of maximal strength or, in this case, 160 pounds. If you can do a relatively high number of repetitions with 160 pounds (more than about 15), you can assume that

your quadriceps are composed primarily of ST fibers; if you perform a rather low number of repetitions with 160 pounds (less than about 5), it's likely that your quadriceps have a high percentage of FT fibers. Because the distribution of fiber types varies from muscle to muscle, an endurance test would have to be performed for each muscle group. Again, this test is not recommended for use with conventional equipment because it involves obtaining a potentially dangerous 1-RM. At least one company offers much more elaborate testing devices that are infinitely safer and far more accurate for conducting tests of muscular endurance to evaluate fiber type.

Another consideration for repetition ranges that deals specifically with genetic influences is lever arm length. Suppose two individuals each used 100 pounds on the bench press, but one person's arms were 24 inches long and the other's were 20 inches long. This means that the longer-armed individual must maintain muscular tension over a greater distance than the shorter-armed individual. Everything else being equal, the longer-armed individual would probably fatigue more quickly after a lower number of repetitions than the shorter-armed individual. In the case of elongated limbs, the use of slightly lower repetitions will prevent muscle fatigue from occurring beyond the recommended "window" of time. As such, someone with extremely long arms or legs may actually benefit more from a slightly lower repetition range — especially in multiple-joint exercises (e.g., leg press, bench press, lat pulldown).

This really isn't a factor during single-joint movements performed on machines with fixed movement arms, since the length of a machine's movement arm is the same for everyone regardless of limb length. This would be a factor, however, when using free weights to perform certain single-joint movements that have fairly large ranges of motion such as the bicep curl and the tricep extension.

For those in doubt regarding the number of repetitions they should perform, and for those who feel they are normal in terms of their genetics, the repetition ranges that were initially suggested will serve as excellent guidelines. In fact, those ranges are correct for most of the general population. (The role of genetics is detailed fully in Chapter 3.)

Range of Motion

Another factor in determining appropriate repetition ranges pertains to the range of motion involved in some exercises. Earlier it was noted that upper body exercises should be performed for 6-12 repetitions (assuming a 6-second repetition). Some movements have relatively short ranges of motion and require a minor adjustment in the minimum number of repetitions to ensure that the muscles produce tension for an adequate amount of time. Generally, these are single-joint movements that have a range of motion of about 90 degrees or less. Therefore, shoulder shrugs and internal/external rotation along with exercises for the forearms, abdominals and neck should be done for

8-12 repetitions to guarantee a desirable amount of contraction time.

Orthopedic or Health Concerns

It's safer for certain populations to perform more repetitions than previously suggested in order to reduce orthopedic stress. For example, younger teenagers should use slightly higher repetition ranges — such as 20-25 reps for exercises involving the buttocks, 15-20 reps for the legs and 10-15 reps for the upper torso. The higher repetition ranges will necessitate using somewhat lighter weights, which will in turn reduce the stress placed upon their bones and joints. Similar repetition ranges should also be used by older adults — particularly those with hypertension (high blood pressure). Finally, females experience an increased laxity in their ligaments and joints during pregnancy. As such, pregnant females should also use slightly higher repetitions in order to reduce the orthopedic stress placed upon their vulnerable joint structures.

5. Perform each repetition with proper technique.

A quality program begins with a quality repetition. Indeed, the repetition is the most basic and integral aspect of a strength training program. A repetition consists of raising the weight to the mid-range position, pausing briefly and then returning the weight to the starting/stretched posi-

Exercising throughout a full range of motion allows you to maintain (or perhaps increase) your flexibility.

tion. A repetition is also performed over the greatest possible range-of-motion that safety permits.

Raising the Weight

A quality repetition starts with the raising of the weight or resistance. The weight should be lifted concentrically in a deliberate, controlled manner without any jerking movements (Westcott 1983; Hewgley 1984; Riley 1992; Bradley 1994). As noted in Chapter 4, lifting a weight in a rapid, explosive fashion is ill-advised for two reasons: (1) it introduces momentum into the movement which makes the exercise less productive and less efficient and (2) it exposes the muscles, joint structures and connective tissue to potentially dangerous forces which magnify the likelihood of incurring an injury while strength training. Lifting a weight in about 1-2 seconds guarantees that a person is exercising in a safe, efficient manner (Riley 1982c; Gittleson 1984; Leistner 1986a; Peterson and Horodyski 1988; Bradley 1994).

Pausing in the Mid-range

After raising the weight, you should pause briefly in the position of full muscle contraction or the "mid-range" position (Gittleson 1984; Leistner 1986a; Jones et al. 1988; Mannie 1989a; Dunn 1989a; Kearns 1990; Riley 1992; Mentzer 1993; Bradley 1994). Most people are very weak in the mid-range of exercises because they rarely, if ever, emphasize that position. Pausing momentarily in this position allows you to focus attention on your muscles when they are fully contracted. Further, a brief pause in the mid-range position permits a smooth transition between the concentric and eccentric phases of the repetition (Mannie 1989a) and helps eliminate the effects of momentum (Dunn 1989a; Bradley 1994). If an individual cannot pause momentarily in the mid-range position, then the weight was moved too quickly (Jones et al. 1988) and thrown into position (Bradley 1994).

Lowering the Weight

Colliander and Tesch (1990a) compared one group who performed only concentric contractions and another group who performed both concentric and eccentric contractions. The researchers reported greater increases in peak torque, vertical jump height and a 3-repetition maximum by the group doing both concentric and eccentric contractions. Exercise involving both concentric and eccentric contractions produced greater increases in strength than exercise involving just concentric contractions in other studies (Hakkinen and Komi 1981; Dudley et al. 1991). A study by Hather and co-workers (1991) suggested that optimal muscular hypertrophy is not attained with resistance training unless eccentric muscle contractions are involved. The importance of involving eccentric contractions in resistance training has also been noted by other authors (Komi and Buskirk 1972; Kennedy 1986b; Kraemer 1992).

Research by Jones (1993) and his associates indicates that a "strength ratio" exists between your concentric, isometric and eccentric strength levels. For a fresh muscle, that ratio appears to be about 1: 1.2: 1.4. In other words, you can hold isometrically about 20 percent more than you can raise concentrically and you can lower eccentrically about 40 percent more than you can raise concentrically. So, if you can raise 100 pounds concentrically, you can hold about 120 pounds statically and you can lower about 140 pounds eccentrically.

Jones (1976) proposed that the differences in these strength levels are due to the effects of internal muscular friction ... friction that is produced when a muscle contracts. During a concentric muscle contraction, friction is created by the contact between the myosin crossbridges and the surfaces of the actin filaments as the two filaments slide past each other. Friction is also produced during an eccentric muscle contraction as the two filaments slide past each other — this time in the opposite direction. When you raise a weight, the friction works against you — you are lifting the weight plus internal muscular friction; when you lower a weight, the friction works for you — you are lowering the weight minus internal muscular friction. That's why it takes more effort to raise a weight than it does to lower it.

The fact that you can lower more weight than you can raise can be used to your advantage. In order to make deeper inroads into your eccentric strength, the lowering portion of the movement should be emphasized for a longer time. It should take about 3-4 seconds to lower the weight back to the starting/stretched position (Peterson and Horodyski 1988; Kearns 1990; Thomas 1994). The lowering of the weight should also be emphasized because it makes the exercise more efficient: The same muscles that are used to raise the weight concentrically are also used to lower it eccentrically. The only difference is that when a weight is raised, the muscles are shortening against a load, and when a weight is lowered, the muscles are lengthening against a load. So, by emphasizing the lowering of a weight, each repetition becomes more efficient and each set becomes more productive. Because a "loaded" muscle lengthens as it is lowered, lowering the weight in a controlled manner also ensures that the exercised muscle is being stretched properly and safely.

In effect, each repetition would be roughly 4-6 seconds in length. Most strength coaches who are opposed to explosive, ballistic movements in the weight room consider a 4-6 second repetition as a general guideline for lifting "under control" or "without momentum." A 16-week study by Hurley and others (1984) demonstrated a 50 percent increase in upper body strength and a 33 percent increase in lower body strength in a group that performed each repetition by raising the weight in 2 seconds and lowering the weight in 4 seconds.

Full Range of Motion

Finally, a quality repetition is done throughout the greatest possible range of motion that safety allows — from a position of full stretch to a position of full muscular con-

traction and back to a position of full stretch. Exercising throughout a full range of motion allows you to maintain (or perhaps increase) your flexibility (Riley 1982c; Thrash and Kelly 1987; Bryant 1988; Fahey 1989; Lillegard and Terrio 1994), which reduces the potential for injury. Furthermore, it ensures that the entire muscle is being exercised — not just a portion of it — thereby making the movement more efficient (Riley 1982c; Fahey 1989; Lillegard and Terrio 1994).

Research has shown that strength training is very angular-specific (Sale and MacDougall 1981). When a muscle is trained at a specific angle, its strength increases are limited to about 15 to 20 degrees on either side of that point (Gardner 1963; Lindh 1979; Knapik, Mawdsley and Ramos 1983; Graves et al. 1989) In other words, full-range exercise is necessary for a full-range effect. This does not imply that limited range movements should be avoided altogether. During rehabilitation, for example, a person can exercise throughout a pain-free range and still manage to stimulate some gains in strength. However, full range movements are more productive and should be performed whenever possible.

Remember, how you lift a weight is more important than how much weight you lift (Brown 1990; Riley 1992). Strength training will be safer and more efficient by performing each repetition with proper technique. The most efficient muscular stimulus is one which involves a combination of concentric, isometric and eccentric workloads.

6. Strength train for no more than one hour per workout.

More may be better when it comes to knowledge and happiness, but more isn't necessarily better when it comes to strength training. Recall that if you are training with a high level of intensity, you literally cannot exercise for a long period of time.

It is important to note that carbohydrates are the body's preferred fuel during intense exercise. Carbohydrates are stored in the liver and the bloodstream as glucose and in the muscles as glycogen. Most people exhaust their carbohydrate stores after about one hour of intense exercise (Pipes 1989). Therefore, strength workouts should be completed in one hour or less (Allman 1976; Pipes 1989 and 1992; Spassov 1989; Wetzel 1994). Under normal circumstances, if you are spending much more than one hour in the weight room then you are probably not training with a desirable level of intensity. This one-hour window of time also dictates the number of sets that can be performed for each exercise.

The exact duration of a workout depends on several factors, such as the size of the facility, the amount of equipment, the preparation for each exercise (i.e., changing plates, moving pins, etc.), the number of people in the facility, the transition time between each set, the availability of supervisory personnel and the managerial ability of that personnel.

Muscles must receive an adequate amount of recovery between intense strength workouts in order to adapt to the imposed demands.

The transition time between one exercise and another will vary with your level of conditioning. You should proceed from one exercise to the next as soon as you "catch your breath" or feel that you can produce a maximal level of effort (Dunn 1989a). After an initial period of adjustment, a person should be able to recover adequately within 1-3 minutes. Training with a minimal amount of recovery time between exercises will elicit a metabolic conditioning effect that cannot be approached by traditional multiple-set programs. Anyone who has been through a rigorous session of high intensity training knows exactly what this means. Indeed, the effects of such workouts must be experienced to be fully appreciated.

7. Perform no more than about 14 exercises each workout.

For most people, a comprehensive strength training program can be performed using 14 exercises or less during each workout. The focal point for most of these exercises should be the major muscle groups (i.e., the hips, the legs and the upper torso). Include one exercise for the hips, hamstrings, quadriceps, calves/dorsi flexors, biceps, triceps, abdominals and lower back. Because the shoulder joint allows movement at many different angles, two exercises should be selected for the chest, the upper back (the "lats") and the shoulders. A person should select any exercises that are preferred in order to train those bodyparts.

For some individuals, a thorough workout may require slightly more than 14 movements. For instance, a comprehensive workout for a person who is involved in a combative sport — such as football, rugby, wrestling, boxing or judo — must include an additional 2-4 neck exercises to strengthen and protect the cervical area against possible traumatic injury. Additionally, anyone involved in a sport or activity that requires grip strength — such as baseball, tennis or golf — should perform one forearm exercise.

Once again, more isn't necessarily better when it comes to strength training. Performing too many movements may produce too much stress, which will retard muscular growth. A workout consisting of 20 movements could be metabolically devastating to an individual with a low tolerance level for exercise. In addition, the more exercises that are performed, the harder it will be to maintain a desirable level of intensity. Occasionally, an extra movement may be performed to emphasize a particular bodypart. As long as improvements in strength continue, a person isn't performing too many exercises. If a person starts to level off or "plateau" in one or more exercises, it's probably due to the catabolic effect from doing too many movements.

8. Whenever possible, the muscles should be exercised from largest to smallest.

A strength training program should begin with exercises that influence the largest muscles and proceed to those that involve the smallest muscles (Jones 1970; Westcott 1983; Gittleson 1984; Bryant 1988; Peterson and Horodyski 1988; Pipes 1989; Bates, Wolf and Blunk 1990; Lillegard and Terrio 1994). Exercises for the hips should be performed first, followed by the upper legs (hamstrings and quadriceps), the lower legs (calves or dorsi flexors), the upper torso (chest, upper back and shoulders), the arms (biceps, triceps and forearms), the abdominals and finally the lower back.

It is important to note that the mid-section should not be fatigued early in the workout. The abdominals stabilize the rib cage and aid in forced expiration. Therefore, early fatigue of the abdominals would detract from the performance of the other exercises that involve larger, more powerful muscles. The low back should be the very last muscle to be exercised. Fatiguing the low back earlier in the workout will also hinder the performance of other movements.

Riley (1982d), Thomas (1994) and Wetzel (1994) suggest exercising the neck at the beginning of the workout or just after the lower body (prior to beginning the upper body movements). This would seem to violate the "largest to smallest" rule. However, people are fatigued both physically and mentally at the end of a workout. Because of this, they're less likely to train the all-important neck area with a desirable level of effort or enthusiasm. Exercising the neck earlier in a workout when a person is not fatigued elicits a more favorable response.

It is especially important not to exercise the arms before exercising the upper torso. Multiple-joint movements done for the upper body require the use of the arms to assist the movement. The arms are the "weak link" in the exercise because they are smaller. So, fatiguing the arms first will weaken an already weak link, thereby limiting the workload placed on the larger and stronger muscles of the upper torso. Likewise, the legs are the weak link when performing exercises for the hips and buttocks. Therefore, avoid training the legs — especially the hamstrings and quadriceps — before performing an exercise for the hips, such as the leg press.

9. Strength train 2-3 times per week on non-consecutive days.

Intense strength training places great demands and stress on the muscles. The muscles must receive an adequate amount of recovery between strength workouts in order to adapt to those demands.

Adaptation to the stress occurs during the recovery process (McCafferty and Horvath 1977). In other words, muscles do not get stronger during a workout — muscles get stronger during the recovery from a workout (Riley 1992). When weights are lifted, muscle tissue is broken down and the recovery process allows the muscle time to rebuild itself. Think of this as allowing a wound to heal. If you had a scab and picked at it every day, you would delay the healing process, but if you left it alone you would permit the damaged tissue time to heal. There are individual variations in recovery ability — everyone has different levels of tolerance for exercise. However, a period of about 48-72 hours is usually necessary for muscle tissue to recover sufficiently from a strength workout (Jacobson 1981; Riley 1982c; Verkhoshansky 1991).

A period of about 48 hours is also required to replenish the depleted carbohydrate (or glycogen) stores (Pipes 1989). The resynthesis of muscle glycogen is biphasic. Following an exercise session and with adequate carbohydrate consumption, muscle glycogen is rapidly replenished almost to the pre-exercise level within 24 hours. Thereafter, however, muscle glycogen increases very slowly to above-normal levels (Ivy 1991). Research by Piehl (1974) demonstrated that almost 46 hours were needed to reach pre-exercise glycogen levels — despite a carbohydrate enriched diet and without physical activity for as long as possible. As such, it is suggested that strength training be performed on nonconsecutive days — such as on Monday, Wednesday and Friday (Mannie 1988; Pipes 1989; Thomas 1994).

Some individuals respond well to three weekly workouts; others react more favorably to two sessions per week. (In rare circumstances, an individual may respond better from one workout per week.) In general, significant improvements in strength can occur from as little as two weekly workouts. Braith and coworkers (1989) reported that a group training two times per week showed approximately 80 percent of the gains of the three times per week group after 10 and 18 weeks. The American College of Sports Medicine (1991) recommends that strength training be performed 2-3 times per week. Performing any more than three sessions a week can gradually become counterproductive due to a catabolic effect. This occurs when the demands placed on the muscles have exceeded the recovery ability.

A muscle will begin to progressively lose size and strength if it isn't exercised within about 96 hours of its previous workout. That's why it's important for an athlete to continue strength training even while in-season or while competing. However, the workouts should be reduced to twice a week due to the increased activity level of practices and games. One session should be done as soon as possible following a game and another no later than 48 hours before the next game. So, an athlete who plays on Saturdays and Tuesdays should strength train on Sundays and Wednesdays (or Thursdays — providing that it's not within 48 hours of the next game). From time to time, an athlete may only be able to strength train once a week because of a particularly heavy schedule (e.g., playing three games in one week, participating in a holiday or post-season tournament, etc.).

How do you know if a person has had sufficient recovery time? There should be a gradual improvement in the amount of weight and/or the number of repetitions that a person is able to do over the course of several weeks. If not, then the person is probably not getting enough of a recovery between workouts.

Split Routines

Exercising different bodyparts on alternating days is known as a "split routine." This has been a popular training method of bodybuilders and recreational lifters for many years. In this type of routine, a person works out on consecutive days but exercises different muscles. For example, the muscle groups might be "split" such that the lower body is exercised on Mondays and Thursdays and the upper body is trained on Tuesdays and Fridays.

It's certainly true that a person using a split routine doesn't usually exercise the same muscles two days in a row. Recall, however, that it takes a minimum of 48 hours in order for the body to replenish its stockpiles of carbohydrates following an intense workout. (Again, carbohydrates are the principal fuel during intense exercise.) So, if the lower body was worked out on Monday, the body's carbohydrate stores were depleted. Even if different muscles are trained on Tuesday, the body hasn't had the necessary 48 hours to fully recover those carbohydrate stores.

There are individual variations in recovery ability, but split routines are generally inappropriate, inefficient and unreasonable for the majority of the population. Remember, the most efficient program is one that produces the maximum possible results in the least amount of time.

	EXERCISE	Rep Range	Seat Adj	WT / REP	WT / REP	WT / REP	WT / REP	WT / REP	WT / REP	WT / REP	WT / REP	WT / REP
HIPS (1)	Leg Press	15-20										
		15-20										
LEGS (2)	Leg Extension	10-15										
	Leg Curl	10-15										
LEGS (1)	Calf Raise	10-15										
	Dorsi Flexion	10-15										
CHEST (2)	Bench Press	6-12										
	Arm Cross	6-12										
BACK (2)	Pullover	6-12										
	Seated Row	6-12										
SHOULDER (2)	Seated Press	6-12										
	Lateral Raise	6-12										
ARMS (2-3)	Bicep Curl	6-12										
	Tricep Extension	6-12										
	Wrist Flexion	8-12										
NECK (2-4)	Neck Extension	8-12										
	Neck Flexion	8-12										
	Lateral Flexion/R	8-12										
	Lateral Flexion/L	8-12										
ABS (1)	Situp	8-12										
		8-12										
BACK (1)	Back Extension	10-15										

DATE: BODYWEIGHT: NAME:

Figure 6.1: Sample workout card

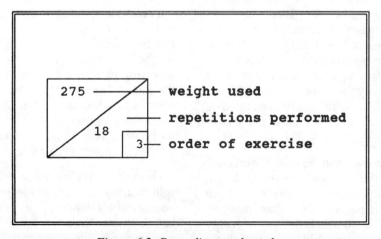

275 — weight used
18 — repetitions performed
3 — order of exercise

Figure 6.2: Recording workout data

10. Keep accurate records of performance.

The importance of accurate record keeping cannot be overemphasized (Jones 1970; Jacobson 1981; Mannie 1988; Dunn 1989a; Andress 1990; Bates, Wolf and Blunk 1990; Riley 1992; Mentzer 1993; Thomas 1994; Wetzel 1994). Records are a log of what a person has accomplished during each and every exercise of each and every strength session. In a sense, a workout card is a history of the activities in the weight room.

A workout card can be an extremely valuable tool to monitor progress and make workouts more meaningful. It can also be used to identify exercises in which a plateau has been reached. In the unfortunate event of an injury, the effectiveness of the rehabilitative process can be gauged if there is a record of the pre-injury strength levels,

A workout card can take an infinite number of appearances. However, individuals should be able to record their bodyweight, the date of each workout, the weight used for each exercise, the number of repetitions performed for each exercise, the order in which the exercises were completed and any necessary seat adjustments.

In addition, it's helpful to separate the exercises according to bodyparts along with the suggested number of exercises that are to be performed for each bodypart. The card can list specific exercises and the more common movements (e.g., leg curl, leg extension, bench press) and/or may contain blank spaces that individuals can use to fill in their own menu of exercises. The recommended repetition ranges should also be given for each exercise along with spaces to record any seat adjustments. A sample workout card is shown in Figure 6.1.

The area to the immediate right of this information is where the data can be recorded from the strength training sessions. Figure 6.2 details how to record the weight used, the repetitions performed and the order in which the exercises were completed.

7
DESIGNING AND REVISING THE STRENGTH TRAINING PROGRAM

A strength training program should be geared toward personal likes and dislikes in terms of exercise selection and equipment preference. This chapter will describe how to effectively structure and fine-tune a personalized program using the ten strength training principles detailed in Chapter 6 in conjunction with the exercises that will be detailed in Chapters 8 through 11.

PROGRAM OVERVIEW

Recall that one movement should be performed for the hips, hamstrings, quadriceps, calves/dorsi flexors, biceps, triceps, abdominals and lower back. Because the shoulder joint allows freedom of movement in a variety of directions, two exercises should be selected for the chest, upper

Individuals who participate in combative sports should perform 2-4 neck exercises as a safeguard against injury. (Photo by The Daily Targum)

back (the "lats") and shoulders. Therefore, a practical, time-efficient and comprehensive program can be performed using no more than about 14 exercises during each strength workout. Individuals who participate in combative sports should perform an additional 2-4 neck exercises as a safeguard against cervical injury; others should do one forearm movement if increased grip strength is desired for a sport or activity.

Additional movements may be performed to emphasize a particular bodypart as long as strength gains continue. If strength levels begin to plateau in an exercise, it's probably due to a catabolic effect from performing too many exercises. In addition, too much emphasis on one bodypart may eventually produce abnormal development (Riley 1982b) or create a muscle imbalance, which can predispose an individual to injury (Riley 1982b; Bryant 1988; Mannie 1988; Peterson and Horodyski 1988). For instance, too many chest exercises may lead to a round-shouldered appearance; too much work on the quadriceps may make a person susceptible to a hamstring pull.

Antagonistic Muscles

How do you know if too much work is being done for one bodypart and not enough for another? Muscles are arranged in the body in opposing positions, such as flexors-extensors, abductors-adductors and so on. As an example, the biceps flex (or bend) the arm at the elbow and the triceps extend (or straighten) the arm at the elbow. When one muscle acts in opposition to another, it is referred to as an antagonist. In addition to the biceps-triceps pairing, other antagonistic partnerships include the hip abductors-hip adductors, hamstrings-quadriceps, calves-dorsi flexors, chest-upper back, anterior deltoid-posterior deltoid, forearm flexors-forearm extensors and abdominals-lower back. In short, a strength training program should not emphasize certain muscle groups without also addressing their antagonistic counterparts in some fashion (Lillegard and Terrio 1994).

Types of Movements

Essentially, there are two types of exercise movements: single-joint and multiple-joint. A single-joint movement (also known as a simple or a primary movement) involves a range of motion around only one joint. The advantage of a single-joint movement is that it usually provides muscle isolation. A good example is a pullover, in which the upper arm rotates around the shoulder joint thereby isolating the upper back muscles.

A multiple-joint movement (also known as a compound or a secondary movement) involves ranges of motion around more than one joint. For instance, during a lat pulldown, there is rotation around both the shoulder and the elbow joints — the upper back pulls the upper arm backward around the shoulder joint and the bicep bends the arm at the elbow joint. There's even some work being done at the wrist joint by the forearm flexors to maintain a grip on the bar. Multiple-joint exercises are advantageous because relatively large amounts of muscle mass can be worked in one movement.

Whenever two exercises are done for a particular bodypart (i.e., the chest, upper back and shoulders), one of the selections should be a multiple-joint movement and the other should be a single-joint movement. Why one of each?

Multiple-joint movements have a distinct disadvantage because they generally have a "weak link." When a person fatigues in a multiple-joint exercise it's because the resistance has been filtered through a smaller, weaker muscle that exhausts well before the larger and stronger muscle has received a sufficient workload. In an exercise such as the aforementioned lat pulldown, the biceps are the smaller muscle and, therefore, will fatigue long before the upper back. In fact, the forearm muscles may fatigue even earlier than the biceps. So, the biceps and the forearms get an adequate workload but the upper back — which is really the target of the exercise — gets very little stimulus. Therefore, if two multiple-joint movements have been selected as the two exercise options for a particular bodypart, the smaller muscle structures would receive much of the workload and the larger muscles would receive very little.

On the one hand, a single-joint movement is superior to a multiple-joint movement because it allows a person to isolate a large muscle without being impaired by the limited strength capacity of a small muscle. On the other hand, a multiple-joint movement is superior to a single-joint movement because it exercises a larger amount of muscle mass. Therefore, both single-joint and multiple-joint movements have advantages and disadvantages. This doesn't mean that it would be totally wrong to do two multiple-joint movements for the same bodypart. However, a strength training routine will be more efficient and productive if a single-joint movement is selected to offset the limitations of a multiple-joint movement.

Sequence

Recall that the muscles should be exercised from largest to smallest: hips, upper legs (hamstrings and quadriceps), lower legs (calves or dorsi flexors), upper torso (chest, up-

Dumbells can be used to provide variety to a workout.

BODYPART	SELECTIONS	EXERCISE	REPS	EQUIPMENT
HIPS	1	Deadlift Leg Press Hip Abduction Hip Adduction	15-20 15-20 10-15 10-15	BD NU MN MN
UPPER LEG	2	Leg Curl Leg Extension	10-15 10-15	MNU MNU
LOWER LEG	1	Calf Raise Dorsi Flexion	10-15 10-15	DNU M
CHEST	2	Arm Cross Bench Press Bent Arm Fly Decline Press Dip Incline Press Pushup	6-12 6-12 6-12 6-12 6-12 6-12 6-12	N BDU DM N UW BD MW
UPPER BACK	2	Bent Over Row Chin Lat Pulldown Pullover Seated Row Torso Arm	6-12 6-12 6-12 6-12 6-12 6-12	DM NW MU N MU N
SHOULDERS	2	External Rotation Front Raise Internal Rotation Lateral Raise Overhead Press Seated Press Shoulder Shrug Upright Row	8-12 6-12 8-12 6-12 6-12 6-12 8-12 6-12	DM DM DM DMN N BDMU BDNU BDU
ARMS	2	Bicep Curl Tricep Extension	6-12 6-12	BDMNU BDMNU
FOREARMS	1	Wrist Extension Wrist Flexion	8-12 8-12	D BDNU
ABDOMINALS	1	Knee-up Side Bend Situp	8-12 8-12 8-12	UW DN MUW
LOWER BACK	1	Back Extension	10-15	NUW
NECK	2 - 4	Lateral Flexion/L Lateral Flexion/R Neck Extension Neck Flexion	8-12 8-12 8-12 8-12	N N MN MN

EQUIPMENT CODES:

B - Barbell, D - Dumbbell, M - Manual Resistance,
N - Nautilus, U - Universal, W - Body Weight

Figure 7.1: Composite list of exercise selections

SAMPLE ROUTINE #1	SAMPLE ROUTINE #2
Neck Flexion (M)	Lateral Flexion/L (N)
Neck Extension (M)	Lateral Flexion/R (N)
Leg Press (U)	Deadlift (B)
Leg Curl (N)	Leg Curl (U)
Leg Extension (N)	Leg Extension (U)
Calf Raise (D)	Dorsi Flexion (M)
Bench Press (B)	Arm Cross (N)
Bent Arm Fly (M)	Dip (W)
Chin/Negative Only (W)	Pullover (N)
Pullover (N)	Seated Row (U)
Seated Press (D)	Shoulder Shrug (D)
Lateral Raise (M)	Upright Row (B)
Bicep Curl (B)	Bicep Curl (M)
Tricep Extension (M)	Tricep Extension (U)
Wrist Flexion (N)	Wrist Extension (D)
Knee-up (U)	Situp (M)
Back Extension (N)	Back Extension (W)

EQUIPMENT CODES:

B – Barbell, **D** – Dumbbell, **M** – Manual Resistance,
N – Nautilus, **U** – Universal, **W** – Body Weight

Figure 7.2: Two sample routines

per back and shoulders), arms (biceps, triceps and forearms), abdominals and lower back.

It is especially important not to exercise the arms before exercising the upper torso or to exercise the legs before exercising the hips. It was noted earlier that multiple-joint movements require the use of smaller, weaker muscles to assist in the exercise. (As a rule of thumb, the arms are the weak link when performing multiple-joint movements for the upper body and the legs are the weak link when performing multiple-joint movements for the hips.) If the smaller muscles are fatigued first, an already weak link will be weakened further, thereby limiting the workload placed on the larger, more powerful muscles and will restrict the potential for their development. As such, the smaller muscles should not be exercised before the larger muscles.

Exercise Options

A composite list of the exercises detailed in Chapters 8 through 11 appears in Figure 7.1. Free weights (i.e., barbells and dumbbells), machines (Nautilus and Universal) and manual resistance are the featured exercises in these chapters. Naturally, a person's options will differ based upon the available equipment. It would be next to impossible to list exercises for every manufacturer's equipment. However, many companies market products that are quite similar to Nautilus and Universal equipment in terms of design and function; barbells and dumbbells are fairly standard and are usually available at most high schools, uni-

versities and fitness centers. Finally, manual resistance exercises are always an option, provided that a partner is available.

Based on the information contained in this and the previous chapter, two sample workouts have been constructed and are shown in Figure 7.2. Note that the design of a strength training routine can have almost an infinite number of possibilities. The only limits are your available equipment and your imagination.

OVERCOMING THE STRENGTH "PLATEAU"

Periodically, a point will be reached in training where strength gains level off or "plateau." Quite often, this is a result of overtraining — a person is performing entirely too much work, which causes the muscular system to be overstressed. In effect, the demands of the activity have exceeded the recovery ability of the person. In this case, the volume of work being done in the weight room simply needs to be reduced.

It is important to understand that an athlete's strength gains will be minimal during the season, especially as practices become more intense. Although this isn't necessarily cause for alarm, the workout frequency and the total number of exercises that are performed in the weight room may need to be reduced to allow for adequate recovery. In any event, the added activity of practices, games and sometimes even traveling will make strength gains difficult to accomplish during the season.

Sometimes, however, a person's strength will plateau as a result of performing the same routines over and over again during each session for lengthy periods of time. In these instances, the workout has become a form of unproductive manual labor that is monotonous, dull and unchallenging.

Monotony can be prevented by revising or varying the strength training workouts. As an example, a person can do an entirely different workout during each of the three weekly sessions, such as Workout A on Monday, Workout B on Wednesday and Workout C on Friday. Another possibility is to perform the same workout one week and a different one the next. Or, one or two aspects of the workout can simply be changed as needed in order to inject a little enthusiasm back into the strength training program.

Simply checking the workout card will reveal if a person has begun to level off. The workout card should be reviewed carefully, however. If someone appears to have plateaued in a certain movement, the performance in earlier exercises of that workout must be considered. For instance, suppose you did 10 repetitions with 120 pounds on the leg extension for five consecutive workouts. At first glance, it may not seem as if your quadriceps have gotten any stronger. However, what if your leg press increased from 250 pounds to 275 pounds during those same five workouts? That means the load on your hips, hamstrings and quadriceps increased by 10 percent, or an average of 2 percent per workout. In other words, your quadriceps were increasingly more pre-fatigued each time prior to performing your leg extensions. In this case, there's little doubt that your quadriceps did get stronger. In fact, simply being able to duplicate your past performances on the leg extensions would actually be quite a feat, although that would not be readily apparent. Similarly, if the weight used in the bicep curl levels off, it's possible that increasingly heavier weights are being used by the biceps earlier in the workout — perhaps during lat pulldowns, seated rows or upright rows. So, the entire workout must be considered when determining whether someone has indeed reached a plateau.

Individuals won't be able to improve their performance in every exercise from one workout to the next. However, gradual strength gains should be observed in all exercises over the course of about four or five workouts. Failure to make a progression in an exercise (in resistance or in repetitions) by this time is a signal to change some aspect of the routine. There are several ways that this may be accomplished.

Rearrange the Order

One of the easiest ways to modify a workout is to rearrange the order in which the exercises for a particular bodypart are performed. Suppose, for example, your shoulder strength seems to have reached a plateau. If you've been doing an upright row followed by a seated press, you can simply switch these two movements, performing the seated press first and the upright row next.

Whenever the order of exercises is varied, the weights that are used must be adjusted accordingly. Using the previous example, let's say you normally use 90 pounds in the upright row, followed quickly by a seated press using 100 pounds. If the order of the exercises is changed (i.e., the seated press is done first), your shoulder musculature will be relatively fresh for the seated press and, therefore, you would now be able to handle more resistance in that movement. However, you must reduce the weight usually used in the upright row since your deltoids will be more fatigued when the seated press is performed first.

An additional possibility is to exercise the muscle groups in a different sequence. Instead of going from chest to upper back to shoulders, a person might start with the upper back exercises, proceed to the shoulder movements and then finish with the chest area. So, an upper torso routine of bench press, bent arm fly, lat pulldown, pullover, seated press and lateral raise could be changed to pullover, lat pulldown, lateral raise, seated press, bent arm fly and bench press. In fact, these six exercises alone could be rearranged for 720 different routines. [These six exercises can be placed in six different ordered positions. The first exercise chosen can be placed in six possible spots. After choosing the first exercise, a second exercise can be put in one of the five remaining spots, a third exercise can be put in one of the four remaining spots and so on. Therefore, the total number of possible arrangements for six exercises is 6 x 5 x 4 x 3 x 2 x 1 = 720 (Mendenhall 1979).] Once again, any time the sequence of exercises is rearranged, the levels of resistance will need to be adjusted accordingly.

Change the Modality

Another way to vary a workout is to change the modality or the equipment used. For instance, if you plateau on the bench press, you can perform a similar movement using different equipment. Chapters 8 through 11 describe several different ways of doing a bench press using a barbell, dumbbells, manual resistance (i.e., partner-resisted push-ups) and two of the more popular machines that are commercially available. Obviously, the extent to which the modality can be changed depends upon the equipment that is on hand.

Alternate the Exercises

A third means of varying a workout is to alternate the exercises that involve the same muscle group(s). For example, the bench press, incline press, decline press and dip are all multiple-joint chest movements that also exercise the shoulders and the triceps. If someone peaks in one of these exercises, another movement can simply be substituted that employs the same musculature. Once again, the availability of equipment will determine how much the exercises may be alternated.

Vary the Repetition

A final option is to vary the manner in which the repetitions are done. Repetitions are ordinarily performed in a bilateral manner — that is, with both limbs at the same time. Repetitions can be done at least five other ways: negative-only, negative-accentuated, unilateral, modified cadence and extended pause.

Negative-only repetitions. Eccentric contractions have been shown to produce the greatest amount of muscular tension (Ashton and Singh 1975; Seliger, Dolejs and Karas 1980). Numerous authors have reported that increases in strength can be produced by negative-only or pure eccentric exercise (Mannheimer 1969; Laycoe and Marteniuk 1971; Jones 1973). It has also been demonstrated that, on the average, eccentric training causes a greater improvement in muscle strength than concentric training (Komi and Buskirk 1972).

It is also interesting to note that oxygen consumption (Asmussen 1952) and energy expenditure (Seliger, Dolejs and Karas 1980) are much lower during eccentric exercise

Negative-only chins can be done by stepping or climbing up to the mid-range postition of the movement (i.e., with your chin over the bar) and slowly lowering yourself under control to the stretched position (i.e., with your arms extended).

than in comparable concentric exercise. In fact, the mechanical efficiency of eccentric exercise may be several times higher than that of pure concentric exercise (Kaneko, Komi and Aura 1984). As an example, climbing stairs (which primarily involves concentric muscle contractions) will quickly elevate the heart rate and the rate of breathing while going downstairs (which mainly involves eccentric muscle contractions) will have a much lower effect.

An entire set of repetitions may be performed in a negative-only manner by having a training partner (or partners) raise the weight while the lifter lowers the weight. Essentially, the positive work is done by the helper(s) and the negative work is done by the lifter. For instance, in a negative-only barbell bench press, two helpers (one at each end of the bar) would raise the weight into a position where the lifter's arms are fully extended (with no help from the lifter). The helpers would then release the bar at the arms-extended position and the lifter slowly lowers the bar until it touches the chest. This procedure is repeated until muscular failure occurs. (Recall that the same muscles used to raise a weight concentrically are also used to lower a weight eccentrically.)

To benefit from negative-only exercise, each repetition must be done slowly (Enoka 1988b). Brown (1989) recommends that a negative repetition be performed in 6-8 seconds. Chapter 6 noted optimal time frames for exercising the muscles. For most of the population, the ranges of time are 90-120 seconds for the buttocks, 60-90 seconds for the rest of the lower body and 40-70 seconds for the upper torso. Therefore, an 8-second negative-only repetition would translate into repetition ranges of about 11-15 for the buttocks, 8-11 for the rest of the lower body and 5-9 for the upper body.

Recall that your eccentric strength is always greater than your concentric strength. This means that a person is able to use more resistance in a negative-only exercise than in the same exercise performed in the traditional manner. Jones (1993) and his associates have reported that eccentric strength is approximatley 40 percent more than concentric strength in a fresh, unfatigued muscle. However, someone doing negative-only exercise for the first time should begin with a weight that is only slightly more than he or she is capable of using in the customary fashion. For instance, someone who most recently used 150 pounds in the bench press done in the traditional manner for a prescribed number of repetitions should use about 10 percent more weight (i.e., an additional 15 pounds) when performing a set of negative-only bench press for the first time. Thereafter, the resistance should be increased for the next workout whenever the maximum number of negative-only repetitions are attained.

The major disadvantage with negative-only exercise is that it almost always requires one or more helpers to lift the weight. Chins and dips are two common exercises that can be performed in a negative-only fashion without assistance. Negative-only chins can be done by stepping or climbing up to the mid-range position of the movement (i.e., with your chin over the bar) and slowly lowering yourself under control to the stretched position (i.e., with your arms extended). Stated otherwise, the lower body does the positive work and the upper body does the negative work. Negative-only dips can be done in a similar fashion.

Negative-accentuated repetitions. The value of negative-accentuated repetitions is that they emphasize the eccentric component of an exercise, yet they can be performed without assistance from helpers. When performing negative-accentuated exercise, the positive work is shared by both limbs but the negative work is done by only one limb. In other words, the weight is raised with both arms or legs and then lowered with only one arm or leg. Therefore, the resistance is literally twice as high during the negative phase as it is during the positive phase.

For example, in negative-accentuated repetitions on a leg extension, a person would raise the weight to the extended position with both legs and pause momentarily in that position. One leg would be moved carefully away from the resistance pad so that the weight is being held briefly in the fully extended position by only one leg. The weight should then be lowered slowly and steadily using only one leg. To summarize negative-accentuated repetitions: Raise the weight with both limbs, lower the weight with one limb, raise the weight with both limbs and lower the weight with the other limb (Jones 1993).

Jones (1975a) suggests that the weight should be raised with both limbs in about 1-2 seconds and then lowered with one limb in about 8 seconds. In addition, he recommends using 70 percent of the weight normally used in the traditional fashion. So, if you last used 100 pounds on the leg extension in a traditional manner, you would use 70 pounds as a starting point for a set of negative-accentuated repetitions in that movement. In the case of negative-accentuated exercise, muscular exhaustion should be reached within repetition ranges of about 15-20 for the buttocks, 10-15 for the rest of the lower body and 6-12 for the upper body.

It is literally impossible to perform negative-accentuated exercise with a barbell. However, most machines permit a person to do repetitions in a negative-accentuated fashion.

Unilateral repetitions. As a variation in the repetition style, many exercises may also be done unilaterally — that is, with one limb at a time. Leistner (1986a) notes that "one limb work is effective because, in almost all cases, it is more intense than the same exercise done with two limbs working simultaneously." Exercising with unilateral movements would be especially recommended for someone with a strength imbalance between one side of the body and the other. Unilateral movements are also advised for individuals who experience an exaggerated rise in their blood pressure while strength training (Bryant and Peterson 1994).

Modified cadence repetitions. The cadence of a repetition may be varied from the usual "up two, down four" (or simply 2/4) speed of movement. For example, the Super Slow protocol advocated by Hutchins (1992) calls for each

repetition to be raised in 10 seconds and lowered in 5 seconds (or 10/5). Leistner (1986a) suggests a 4/4 speed of movement as a variation of the traditional 2/4 speed and also a single set consisting of one 30/30 repetition.

Extended pause repetitions. The importance of including a momentary pause in the mid-range position was noted in Chapter 6. Most people are usually quite weak in the mid-range position of an exercise because it is rarely emphasized. As a repetition variation, the normally brief pause in the mid-range position can be done for a slightly longer duration — perhaps in 3-4 seconds. Using an extended pause is also an excellent tool to incorporate when first teaching someone the idea of pausing in the mid-range position. However, an extended pause in the mid-range position essentially involves a mild isometric muscular contraction that tends to elevate blood pressure. As such, this technique should not be used by individuals who suffer from hypertension.

REHABILITATIVE STRENGTH TRAINING

As much as a person prepares for the rigors of athletics, injuries sustained during practices and competition are still an unforeseen and inevitable occurrence. An individual may also have various "noncontact" injuries such as tendinitis, bursitis, general muscular soreness or other nagging afflictions. Once a person is injured, the injured area should be treated by qualified sportsmedicine personnel (i.e., sport physicians, athletic trainers, physical therapists, etc.). However, it's very important to continue some type of strength training whenever possible — even in the event of an injury. This will prevent a significant loss in muscular size and strength that would otherwise result in the injured bodypart (Jones et al. 1988; Lambrinides 1989). Recall that a muscle begins to lose size and strength if it isn't exercised within about 48-96 hours of its previous workout. Moreover, the rate of strength loss is most rapid during the first few weeks.

There are several different revisions and adjustments that can be made in the basic program design that would enable a person to continue strength training an injured area or bodypart in a safe, prudent and pain-free manner. It should be noted that these methods are intended for injuries that aren't viewed as being very serious or extremely painful. Therefore, a person should receive approval from a certified sportsmedical authority before initiating any rehabilitative strength training.

Lighten the Resistance

To continue strength training an injured bodypart, the first step is to reduce the amount of weight being used. Let's suppose that your patellar tendon hurts when you do leg extensions with your normal training weight. Reducing the amount of weight will produce less stress on your tendon and perhaps allow you to perform the exercise in a pain-free manner. The amount that the weight is reduced will depend upon the extent and the nature of the injury.

Reduce the Speed of Movement

If pain-free exercise is still not possible even after reducing the amount of weight, the next maneuver would be to slow down the speed of movement. This may involve raising the weight in about 4-8 seconds instead of the traditional 1-2 seconds. Reducing the speed of movement will decrease the amount of stress placed on a given joint. Slowing down the speed of movement will also necessitate using a reduced amount of weight, thereby lowering the stress even further.

Change the Exercise Angle

If pain persists during certain exercises involving an injured bodypart, the angle at which the movement is normally performed can be changed. This option can be used with many exercises for the upper body — especially those that involve the shoulder joint. Let's say that someone has slight shoulder pain when doing a bench press in the supine position (i.e., the torso is positioned level with the ground). In many cases, if the angle of the bench is changed to either an incline or to a decline, there will be less stress on the shoulder joint. Likewise, some people experience pain when performing a seated press with the bar positioned behind the head. The pain is usually alleviated when performing a seated press with the bar positioned in front of the head.

Another exercise that may exacerbate shoulder pain is a behind-the-neck lat pulldown with an overhand grip. Often, the pain is characterized as a tightness or a pinching in the shoulder joint. Generally, the discomfort can be lessened by changing the angle of the pull. This is accomplished by grasping the bar underhanded with the palms facing the torso and pulling the bar to the upper chest instead of behind the neck.

Use a Different Grip

In the case of the shoulder joint, many times there is less stress if a different grip is used. Again, let's say that a person has slight pain when doing an exercise such as a bench press. It is quite possible that there will be a significant reduction in pain by simply changing the grip from that used with a barbell to a parallel grip using dumbbells. It should be noted that any exercise that can be performed with a barbell can also be performed with dumbbells. As such, there is an option for varying the grip used in movements for every major muscle group in the upper torso.

Perform Different Exercises

Another option is to perform different exercises that use the same muscle groups. For instance, if a person simply cannot perform a lat pulldown without experiencing pain or discomfort, then perhaps a different exercise can be used that works the same muscles in a pain-free manner. In this case, a seated row or a bent over row can be substituted to involve the same muscles as a lat pulldown, namely the upper back, biceps and forearms.

Limit the Range of Motion

There's a possibility that pain occurs only at certain points in the range of motion such as the starting or the mid-range position of the movement. In either case, the range of movement for the exercise can be restricted. For example, if pain occurs at the starting position of a movement, a person should stop short of a full stretch; similarly, if pain occurs at the mid-range position of an exercise, a person should stop short of a full muscular contraction. As the injured area heals over a period of time, the range of motion can be gradually increased until a full, pain-free range of movement is obtained.

Exercise the Good Limb

If all else fails, the unaffected limb can still be exercised. For example, suppose you had knee surgery and, as a result, your left leg was placed in a cast from your mid-thigh to your ankle. Obviously, you would not be able to perform any exercises below your left hip joint. However, you can still strength train the muscles on the right side of your lower body.

Interestingly, research has shown that training a limb on one side of the body will actually increase the strength of the untrained limb on the other side of the body. This phenomenon of "bilateral transfer" has been described a number of different ways including cross transfer, cross education, cross exercise and cross training. Perhaps the first to

In the event of an injury, the unaffected limb can still be exercised.

demonstrate the effects of a bilateral transfer of strength were Scripture, Smith and Brown (1894). Since then, a number of other researchers have confirmed their findings (Hellebrandt, Parrish and Houtz 1947; Slater-Hammel 1950; Mathews et al. 1956; Rasch and Morehouse 1957; Ikai and Fukunaga 1970; Komi et al. 1978; Moritani and deVries 1979; Yasuda and Miyamura 1983; Cannon and Cafarelli 1987; Jones et al. 1988). The transfer of strength is usually small, but Moritani and deVries (1979) reported a strength increase of 36.4 percent in the trained limb and a 24.7 percent increase in the untrained contralateral limb. Hellbrandt, Parrish and Houtz (1947) proposed that there is a strong association between training intensity and the magnitude of the bilateral transfer effect. In other words, the greater the intensity of the exercise, the greater the degree of transfer. This is corroborated by Enoka (1988b) in his review of the relevant literature.

The increase in strength in the untrained limb has been attributed to neural adaptation (Enoka 1988b). Support for neural adaption comes from studies that have demonstrated increases in strength without an accompanying increase in muscular hypertrophy (Ikai and Fukunaga 1970; Krotkiewski et al. 1979; Moritani and deVries 1979). It has also been theorized that the muscles on the untrained side of the body experience slight isometric contractions while the muscles on the side of the body being trained are contracting through a range of motion (Davis 1898; Rasch and Morehouse 1957; Lambrinides 1989).

Several studies have also shown that performing a movement pattern with one limb produces an improvement in performance in the contralateral limb (Swift 1903; Munn 1932; Cook 1933). This bilateral transfer of skill has been reported as occurring from hand to foot as well as from hand to hand. Sage (1977) notes that the greatest bilateral transfer of skill is in the symmetrical muscle group on the opposite side of the body.

The literature also reports a "bilateral deficit." Oddly enough, the force produced in bilateral contractions is less than the sum of the forces produced by the right and left limbs contracting singly (Henry and Smith 1961; Ohtsuki 1981; Vandervoort, Sale and Moroz 1987).

Exercise Unaffected Bodyparts

Even though a person may not be able to exercise an injured area due to an unreasonable amount of pain or discomfort, movements can still be performed for the uninjured bodyparts. If a person has a knee injury, exercises can still be done for the entire upper torso — assuming, of course, that the exercises are done while sitting or laying down and not while standing. Likewise, a person with a shoulder injury can still train the muscles of the lower body.

An "indirect effect" has been suggested by several authors (Jones et al. 1988; Lambrinides 1989). It is believed that exercising the larger muscles of the body will produce at least some degree of size and strength increases in other, smaller muscles even when no exercise is performed for the smaller muscles.

8

FREE WEIGHT EXERCISES

In 1902, the Milo Barbell Company — founded by Alvin Calvert — manufactured and sold the first adjustable, plate-loading barbell in the United States (Darden 1982; Pearl and Moran 1986). The plate-loading barbell — patterned after the Berg-Hantel barbell from Germany — was a revolutionary step forward in weight training. For the first time, a barbell could be loaded quickly with any amount of weight desired. Previously, a different barbell was necessary for a different weight.

Today, free weights are extremely popular pieces of equipment that are inexpensive and can last for years with little or no maintenance. Most universities, high schools, YMCAs and commercial fitness centers outfit their weight training areas with at least some free weight equipment.

THE USE OF DUMBBELLS

A dumbbell is essentially a shorter version of a barbell that is intended for use with one hand. There are several advantages in using dumbbells (DBs). First of all, DBs can provide variety to a routine. Variety can be furnished in at least two ways. For one thing, every exercise that can be performed with a barbell can also be performed with DBs. This means that every barbell exercise has a DB counterpart that can be used as an alternative movement. Secondly, the lifter has the added option of being able to use a different grip with DBs. For example, a DB bench press can be done with a "parallel grip" (i.e., the palms facing each other) as well as the traditional bench press grip.

Perhaps the biggest advantage in using DBs, however, is that each of the limbs must work independently of the other. Since most people have a dominant side of the body, they're often stronger (and more flexible) on one side of the body than the other. Usually, this isn't a significant difference. But, the use of DBs is highly recommended when there is a gross difference in the strength between limbs. This is also an important consideration for rehabilitative strength training. In this case, an individual may have to work one limb at a time while using a lighter weight for the weaker limb. In short, the advantages of DBs are pure and simple: variety and an independent workload.

THE EXERCISES

This chapter will describe and illustrate the safest and most productive exercises that can be performed with free weights. Included in the descriptions for each exercise are the muscles used (if more than one muscle is involved, the first muscle listed is the prime mover), the suggested repetitions, the type of movement and performance points for making the exercise safer and more productive. The exercises described in this chapter are:

Deadlift

Calf Raise

Bench Press

Incline Press

Bent Arm Fly

Bent Over Row

Seated Press

Lateral Raise

Front Raise

Internal Rotation

External Rotation

Shoulder Shrug

Upright Row

Bicep Curl

Tricep Extension

Wrist Flexion

Wrist Extension

Side Bend

DEADLIFT

Start/Finish Position

Mid-Range Position

Muscles used: buttocks, quadriceps, hamstrings, erector spinae

Suggested repetitions: 15-20

Type of movement: multiple-joint

Starting position: The feet should be spread slightly wider than shoulder width apart. Reach down and grasp a bar on the outside of the legs with an alternating grip (dominant palm forward, nondominant palm backward). Lower the hips until the upper legs are almost parallel to the floor. Flatten the lower back and look up slightly. Most of the bodyweight should be centered on the heels, not on the toes.

Description: Stand upright by straightening the legs and the upper torso. Pause briefly in the mid-range position and then lower the weight under control to the starting position.

Performance points:

- The hips should not be lifted up too early during the execution of this movement. Raising the hips up too soon negates their effectiveness and causes the movement to be performed entirely with the lower back. Ideally, the hips, the legs and the lower back should work together. However, most of the work should be done by the hips and the legs.

- The knees should not lock or "snap" in the mid-range of a repetition. This takes the tension off the target muscles and may hyperextend the knees. Also, there should not be an excessive backward lean in the mid-range position.

- Keep the arms straight, the head up and the back relatively flat throughout the performance of this exercise.

- The weight should not be bounced off the floor between repetitions.

- This movement can also be done with dumbbells.

- Wrist straps can be used if there is difficulty in maintaining a grip on the bar (or the dumbbells).

- This exercise may be contraindicated for individuals with low back pain or an exceptionally long torso and/or legs.

CALF RAISE

Start/Finish Position

Mid-Range Position

Muscles used: calves

Suggested repetitions: 10-15

Type of movement: single-joint

Starting position: Hold a dumbbell in the right hand and stand on a small block of wood. Hold onto a machine with the left hand to maintain balance and position the body so that the ball of the right foot is on the edge of the block and the right heel extends over the edge. Cross the left foot behind the right ankle.

Description: Keeping the right leg straight, rise up onto the toes as high as possible. Pause briefly in the mid-range position and then lower the weight under control to the starting position (heel near the floor) to ensure a proper stretch. After performing a set with the right leg, repeat the exercise with the left leg (with the dumbbell in the left hand).

Performance points:

• The block of wood is used to obtain a better stretch. Another person can stand on the side of a block that is especially high so that it doesn't tip over.

• Keep the exercising leg straight while performing this movement.

• Traditionally, this exercise is done with a weight placed on the shoulders — either a barbell or a machine's movement arm. However, this should not be done because it involves spinal compression.

• Wrist straps can be used if there is difficulty in maintaining a grip on the dumbbell.

• This exercise may be contraindicated for individuals with shin splints.

BENCH PRESS

Start/Finish Position   *Mid-Range Position*

Muscles used: chest, anterior deltoid, triceps

Suggested repetitions: 6-12

Type of movement: multiple-joint

Starting position: Lay down on a bench and place the feet flat on the floor. Grasp a bar and spread the hands slightly wider than shoulder width apart. Lift the bar out of the uprights or have a spotter provide assistance.

Description: Lower the bar under control until it touches the middle part of the chest. Without bouncing the weight off the chest, push the bar back to the starting position.

Performance points:

• For safety reasons, this exercise should always be performed with a spotter.

• An excessively wide grip should not be used since this will reduce the range of motion.

• The buttocks should remain flat on the bench and the feet kept flat on the floor throughout the performance of this exercise. In the event of low back pain, the feet may be placed on the bench or a stool. This will flatten the lumbar area against the bench and reduce the stress in the lower back region.

• The elbows should not lock or "snap" in the mid-range of a repetition. This takes the tension off the target muscles and may hyperextend the elbows.

• The bar should move upward and backward as the weight is pressed.

• This exercise can also be performed with dumbbells.

INCLINE PRESS

Start/Finish Position

Mid-Range Position

Muscles used: chest (upper portion), anterior deltoid, triceps

Suggested repetitions: 6-12

Type of movement: multiple-joint

Starting position: Lay down on a bench and place the feet flat on the floor (or against a footrest, if provided). Grasp a bar and space the hands slightly wider than shoulder width apart. Lift the bar out of the uprights or have a spotter provide assistance.

Description: Lower the bar under control until it touches the upper part of the chest (i.e., near the collarbones). Without bouncing the weight off the chest, push the bar back to the starting position.

Performance points:

• For safety reasons, this exercise should always be performed with a spotter.

• An excessively wide grip should not be used since this will reduce the range of motion.

• The buttocks should remain flat on the bench and the feet kept flat on the floor (or footrest) throughout the performance of this exercise. In the event of low back pain, the feet may be placed on a stool (if a footrest is not provided). This will flatten the lumbar area against the bench and reduce the stress in the lower back region.

• The elbows should not lock or "snap" in the mid-range of a repetition. This takes the tension off the target muscles and may hyperextend the elbows.

• The bar should move upward and backward as the weight is pressed.

• This exercise can also be performed with dumbbells.

BENT ARM FLY

Start/Finish Position   *Mid-Range Position*

Muscles used: chest, anterior deltoid

Suggested repetitions: 6-12

Type of movement: single-joint

Starting position: Sit down on the end of a bench, bend over and grasp two dumbbells. Lay down on the bench, lift up the dumbbells and position them on both sides of the torso so that they are even with the chest. One or two spotters can assist in positioning heavy dumbbells. Point the palms toward the knees and move the dumbbells up and away from the chest until the angle between the upper and the lower arms is about 90 degrees.

Description: Without significantly changing the angle between the upper and lower arms, bring the dumbbells together. Pause briefly in the mid-range position and then return the weights under control to the starting position (arms apart) to obtain a sufficient stretch.

Performance points:

• Maintain about a 90 degree angle between the upper and lower arms as the dumbbells are raised and lowered. (Imagine hugging a tree.) Extending the arms as the dumbbells are raised will turn the bent arm fly into a dumbbell bench press.

• The buttocks should remain flat on the bench and the feet kept flat on the floor throughout the performance of this exercise. In the event of low back pain, the feet may be placed on the bench or a stool. This will flatten the lumbar area against the bench and reduce the stress in the lower back region.

BENT OVER ROW

Start/Finish Position

Mid-Range Position

Muscles used: upper back (lats), biceps, forearms

Suggested repetitions: 6-12

Type of movement: multiple-joint

Starting position: Place the left hand and the left knee on a bench and position the right foot on the floor at a comfortable distance from the bench. Reach down with the right hand and grasp a dumbbell. Lift the dumbbell slightly off the floor and keep the right arm straight. The right palm should be facing the bench.

Description: Keeping the upper arm near the torso, pull the dumbbell up to the right shoulder. Pause briefly in the mid-range position and then return the dumbbell under control to the starting position (arm fully extended) to ensure an adequate stretch. After performing a set with the right arm, repeat the exercise with the left arm (with the right hand and the right knee on the bench for support).

Performance points:

- It's natural for the shoulder to change its position as this exercise is performed. However, the movement of the shoulder should not be excessive or used to throw the dumbbell — movement should only occur around the shoulder and the elbow joints.

- This exercise can also be done with the upper arm farther away from the torso. This will involve the posterior deltoid and the trapezius to a greater degree. In this case, the upper arm would be almost perpendicular to the torso in the mid-range position and the palm would be facing backward slightly.

- Wrist straps can be used if there is difficulty in maintaining a grip on the dumbbell.

SEATED PRESS

Start/Finish Position

Mid-Range Position

Muscles used: anterior deltoid, triceps

Suggested repetitions: 6-12

Type of movement: multiple-joint

Starting position: Sit down and place the feet flat on the floor. Grasp a bar and spread the hands slightly wider than shoulder width apart. Have a spotter provide assistance in getting the bar out of the uprights. The bar should be placed behind the neck on the upper part of the trapezius. If uprights are unavailable, two spotters can place the bar in the same position.

Description: Push the bar straight up until the arms are just short of full extension. Pause briefly in the mid-range position and then return the weight under control to the starting position (bar on the trapezius) to provide a proper stretch.

Performance points:

• For safety reasons, this exercise should always be performed with a spotter.

• An excessively wide grip should not be used since this will reduce the range of motion.

• The buttocks should remain flat on the seat, the feet kept flat on the floor and the torso kept against the back pad throughout the performance of this exercise. In the event of low back pain, the feet may be placed on a stool. This will flatten the lumbar area against the bench and reduce the stress in the lower back region.

• The elbows should not lock or "snap" in the mid-range of a repetition. This takes the tension off the target muscles and may hyperextend the elbows.

• This exercise can also be performed with dumbbells.

• This exercise may be contraindicated for individuals with shoulder impingement syndrome. In this case, however, lowering the bar in front of the head rather than behind the head will reduce the stress on an impinged shoulder.

LATERAL RAISE

Start/Finish Position   *Mid-Range Position*

Muscles used: middle deltoid, trapezius

Suggested repetitions: 6-12

Type of movement: single-joint

Starting position: Hold a dumbbell in each hand at the sides of the body with the palms facing the legs. Spread the feet apart a comfortable distance.

Description: Keeping the arms fairly straight, raise the dumbbells away from the sides of the body until the arms are parallel to the floor. Pause briefly in the mid-range position and then lower the dumbbells under control to the starting position (arms at the sides) to ensure an adequate stretch.

Performance points:

• The arms should not be lifted beyond a point that is parallel to the floor.

• The palms should be facing down in the mid-range position (arms parallel to the floor).

• Avoid throwing the dumbbells by using the legs or by swinging the upper torso back and forth — movement should only occur around the shoulder joint.

FRONT RAISE

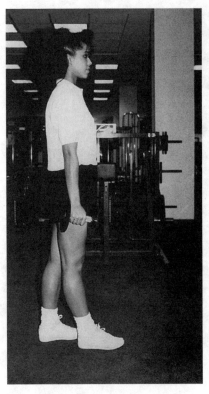

Start/Finish Position

Mid-Range Position

Muscle used: anterior deltoid

Suggested repetitions: 6-12

Type of movement: single-joint

Starting position: Hold a dumbbell in each hand at the sides of the body with the palms facing the legs. Spread the feet apart a comfortable distance with one foot slightly in front of the other.

Description: Keeping the arms fairly straight, raise the dumbbells in front of the body until the arms are parallel to the floor. Pause briefly in the mid-range position and then return the dumbbells under control to the starting position (arms at the sides) to obtain a proper stretch.

Performance points:

- The arms should not be lifted beyond a point that is parallel to the floor.

- The palms should be facing each other in the mid-range position (arms parallel to the floor).

- Avoid throwing the dumbbells by using the legs or by swinging the upper torso back and forth — movement should only occur around the shoulder joint.

INTERNAL ROTATION

Start/Finish Position

Mid-Range Position

Muscles used: internal rotators

Suggested repetitions: 8-12

Type of movement: single-joint

Starting position: Grasp a dumbbell with the right hand, lay down on the right side and draw the knees toward the upper torso. Position the right elbow slightly in front of the body and bend the right arm so that the angle between the upper and the lower arms is about 90 degrees. Point the right palm upward.

Description: Without moving the right elbow or changing the angle of the right arm, pull the dumbbell up to the left shoulder. Pause briefly in the mid-range position and then lower the dumbbell under control to the starting position to ensure a sufficient stretch. After performing a set with the right arm, turn to the left side and repeat the exercise with the left arm.

Performance points:

• The torso should not lay directly on the upper arm as this movement is performed.

• Doing this exercise on a bench (instead of the floor) will increase the range of motion and permit a greater stretch.

• This movement can also be performed with surgical tubing or elastic cord as the resistance. The tubing is secured to an object that will not move such as a machine. Simply grasp the free end of the tubing and pull it horizontally across the body in the fashion described above. In this case, the movement can be done while standing.

EXTERNAL ROTATION

Start/Finish Position

Mid-Range Position

Muscles used: external rotators

Suggested repetitions: 8-12

Type of movement: single-joint

Starting position: Grasp a dumbbell with the right hand, lay down on the left side and draw the knees toward the upper torso. Extend the left arm across the floor and lean back slightly. Keep the right elbow against the side and bend the right arm so that the angle between the upper and the lower arms is about 90 degrees. Point the right palm downward.

Description: Without moving the right elbow away from the side or changing the angle of the right arm, raise the dumbbell up as high as possible. Pause briefly in the mid-range position and then lower the dumbbell under control to the starting position to obtain a proper stretch. After performing a set with the right arm, turn to the right side and repeat the exercise with the left arm.

Performance points:

• Doing this exercise on a bench (instead of the floor) will increase the range of motion and permit a greater stretch.

• This movement can also be performed with surgical tubing or elastic cord as the resistance. The tubing is secured to an object that will not move such as a machine. Simply grasp the free end of the tubing and pull it horizontally across the body in the fashion described above. In this case, the movement can be done while standing.

SHOULDER SHRUG

Start/Finish Position

Mid-Range Position

Muscle used: trapezius

Suggested repetitions: 8-12

Type of movement: single-joint

Starting position: Spread the feet approximately shoulder width apart. Reach down and grasp a bar on the outside of the legs with the palms facing backward. Stand upright by straightening the legs and the upper torso (as if performing a deadlift). Two spotters can also place the bar in this position.

Description: Keeping the arms and the legs straight, pull the bar up as high as possible trying to touch the shoulders to the ears (as if to say, "I don't know"). Pause briefly in the mid-range position and then lower the weight under control to the starting position to obtain an adequate stretch.

Performance points:

• It's not necessary or advisable to "roll" the shoulders during the performance of this exercise.

• For better biomechanical leverage, the bar should be kept close to the body as this movement is performed.

• Avoid throwing the weight by using the legs or by swinging the upper torso back and forth — movement should only occur around the shoulder joints.

• This exercise can also be performed with dumbbells. In this case, a dumbbell would be held in each hand at the sides with the palms facing the legs.

• Wrist straps can be used if there is difficulty in maintaining a grip on the bar (or the dumbbells).

• This exercise may be contraindicated for individuals with low back pain.

UPRIGHT ROW

Start/Finish Position

Mid-Range Position

Muscles used: trapezius, biceps, forearms

Suggested repetitions: 6-12

Type of movement: multiple-joint

Starting position: Spread the feet approximately shoulder width apart. Reach down and grasp a bar with the hands spaced apart about 8-10 inches and the palms facing the thighs. Stand upright by straightening the legs and the upper torso (as if performing a deadlift).

Description: Pull the bar up until the hands are approximately level with the shoulders. The elbows should be slightly higher than the hands in this position. Pause briefly in the mid-range position and then return the bar under control to the starting position (arms fully extended) to ensure a proper stretch.

Performance points:

• For better biomechanical leverage, the bar should be kept close to the body as this movement is performed.

• Avoid throwing the weight by using the legs or by swinging the upper torso back and forth — movement should only occur around the shoulder and the elbow joints.

• This exercise can also be performed with dumbbells. In this case, a dumbbell would be held in each hand at the front of the thighs with the palms facing the legs.

• Wrist straps can be used if there is difficulty in maintaining a grip on the bar (or the dumbbells).

• This exercise may be contraindicated for individuals with shoulder impingement syndrome. In this case, however, pulling the bar to the lower portion of the chest rather than to the upper portion of the chest will reduce the stress on an impinged shoulder. This exercise may also be contraindicated for individuals with low back pain.

BICEP CURL

Start/Finish Position   *Mid-Range Position*

Muscles used: biceps, forearms

Suggested repetitions: 6-12

Type of movement: single-joint

Starting position: Spread the feet approximately shoulder width apart. Reach down and grasp a bar with the palms facing forward. Stand upright by straightening the legs and the upper torso.

Description: Keeping the elbows against the sides of the body, pull the bar below the chin by bending the arms. Pause briefly in the mid-range position and then lower the weight under control to the starting position (arms fully extended) to provide a sufficient stretch.

Performance points:

• Avoid throwing the weight by using the legs or by swinging the upper torso back and forth — movement should only occur around the elbow joints.

• This exercise can also be performed with dumbbells or the so-called E-Z curl bar.

• This exercise may be contraindicated for individuals with hyperextended elbows.

TRICEP EXTENSION

 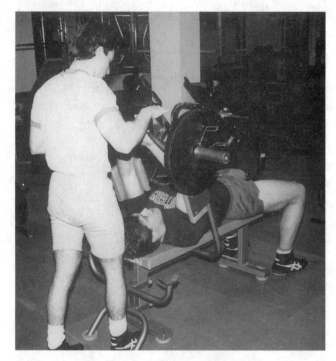

Start/Finish Position   *Mid-Range Position*

Muscle used: triceps

Suggested repetitions: 6-12

Type of movement: single-joint

Starting position: Lay down on a bench and place the feet flat on the floor. Place the backs of the upper arms against the elbow pads. Position the upper arms so that they are roughly perpendicular to the floor. One or two spotters can assist in positioning a bar. Grasp the bar with the palms facing upward and spread the hands apart about 4-6 inches. The bar should be near the forehead. (How close the bar is to the forehead depends on the length of the lower arms).

Description: Keeping the elbows against the pads, push the bar up by straightening the arms. Pause briefly in the mid-range position and then return the weight under control to the starting position (arms bent) to obtain a proper stretch.

Performance points:

• If a bench with a tricep attachment is unavailable, the movement can still be performed. However, the upper arms should remain perpendicular to the floor and the elbows should be pointed toward the knees. Movement should only occur around the elbow joints.

• The buttocks should remain flat on the bench and the feet kept flat on the floor throughout the performance of this exercise. In the event of low back pain, the feet may be placed on the bench or a stool. This will flatten the lumbar area against the bench and reduce the stress in the lower back region.

• This exercise can also be performed sitting upright or standing upright.

• This movement can also be done with dumbbells.

• This exercise may be contraindicated for individuals with shoulder impingement syndrome.

WRIST FLEXION

Start/Finish Position   *Mid-Range Position*

Muscles used: wrist flexors

Suggested repetitions: 8-12

Type of movement: single-joint

Starting position: Reach down and grasp a bar with the palms facing upward. Place the thumbs underneath the bar alongside the fingers and spread the hands apart about 4-6 inches. Lift up the bar, sit down on a bench and place the backs of the forearms directly over the upper legs. (The forearms can also be placed between the legs flat on the bench.) In this position, the forearms should be approximately parallel to the floor. (This may require placing a pad underneath the feet.) Lean forward slightly so that the angle between the upper and the lower arms is 90 degrees or less. The wrists should be over the kneecaps (or over the edge of the bench if the forearms are placed on the bench).

Description: Pull the bar up as high as possible by bending the wrists. Pause briefly in the mid-range position and then lower the weight under control to the starting position (wrists extended) to provide a sufficient stretch.

Performance points:

• The forearms should remain directly over the upper legs throughout the performance of this exercise. The elbows should not flare out to the sides.

• Placing the thumbs underneath the bar alongside the fingers will permit a greater range of motion.

• Avoid throwing the weight by using the legs or by swinging the upper torso back and forth — movement should only occur around the wrist joints.

• This movement can also be done with dumbbells.

WRIST EXTENSION

Start/Finish Position

Mid-Range Position

Muscles used: wrist extensors

Suggested repetitions: 8-12

Type of movement: single-joint

Starting position: Reach down and grasp a dumbbell with the right hand. Lift up the dumbbell, sit down on a bench and place the front of the right forearm directly over the right upper leg so that the palm is facing down. (The right forearm can also be placed between the legs flat on the bench.) In this position, the forearm should be approximately parallel to the floor. (This may require placing a pad underneath the feet.) Lean forward slightly so that the angle between the upper and the lower arm is 90 degrees or less. The right wrist should be over the right kneecap (or over the edge of the bench if the forearm is placed on the bench).

Description: Pull the dumbbell up as high as possible by bending the wrist. Pause briefly in the mid-range position and then lower the weight under control to the starting position to obtain an adequate stretch. After performing a set for the right forearm, repeat the exercise for the left forearm.

Performance points:

• The forearm should remain directly over the upper leg throughout the performance of this exercise. The elbow should not flare out to the side.

• Avoid throwing the weight by using the legs or by swinging the upper torso back and forth — movement should only occur around the wrist joint.

• This exercise is more comfortable when it is performed one limb at a time with a dumbbell rather than both limbs at a time with a barbell.

SIDE BEND

Start/Finish Position

Mid-Range Position

Muscles used: obliques

Suggested repetitions: 8-12

Type of movement: single-joint

Starting position: Hold a dumbbell in the right hand with the palm facing the right side of the leg. The feet should be spread about shoulder width apart. Place the left palm against the left side of the head. Without moving the hips, bend the upper torso to the right as far as possible.

Description: Without moving the hips, pull the upper torso to the left as far as possible. Pause briefly in the mid-range position and then lower the dumbbell under control to the starting position to ensure a sufficient stretch. After performing a set for the left side of the mid-section, repeat the exercise for the right side of the mid-section.

Performance points:

• It's natural for the hips to change their position as this exercise is performed. However, the movement of the hips should not be excessive or used to throw the dumbbell — movement should only occur around the waist.

• Avoid bending forward at the waist while performing this exercise.

• The feet should remain flat on the floor throughout the performance of this movement.

• This exercise may be contraindicated for individuals with low back pain.

9

NAUTILUS EXERCISES

Legend has it that the first Nautilus machine (a prototype pullover model) was built on a front porch in Tulsa, Oklahoma by Arthur Jones in 1948. Over the next 20 years, 27 different prototypes of the pullover machine were built and tested. It wasn't until late November 1970 that the first Nautilus machine was actually sold and delivered to a customer — an attorney from Miami.

However, it was the original 1948 prototype that provided the initial spark for a revolution — not only in the design and function of future equipment for resistance exercise but also in the way in which equipment was used for strength training. Previously, all conventional forms of exercise for the upper back mainly consisted of chinning, rowing and various pulling movements. When doing these movements, the resistance was applied to the hands and was filtered through the weaker muscles of the arms. The development of the Nautilus pullover machine overcame the shortcomings of conventional exercises because it applied the resistance directly to the backs of the upper arms — not the hands — thereby allowing the lifter to isolate the upper back throughout a very large range of motion. For the first time, a lifter could train the muscles of the upper back without being limited by the strength of the biceps and forearms.

Over the years, the name "Nautilus" has become synonymous with fitness and exercise equipment. Today, Nautilus continues to manufacture productive equipment that remains a popular choice among fitness enthusiasts. Nautilus equipment is used in fitness centers in more than 25 countries around the world. The machines are also used at government and military installations, hospitals, sportsmedicine clinics, universities and high schools.

THE NAUTILUS CAM

The heart of a Nautilus machine is an asymmetrical pulley known as a cam. As an exercise is performed, the biomechanical leverage of the skeletal system changes — which makes the movement feel easier in some positions and harder in others. As the cam rotates around its axis, it automatically varies the resistance to match the changes in biomechanical leverage. In positions of inferior leverage (and inferior strength), the length of the cam's effective radius (i.e., the resistance arm) is relatively small. This creates a

mechanical advantage and a lower level of resistance. As the skeletal system moves into a position of superior leverage (and superior strength), the length of the cam's effective radius becomes larger. This creates a mechanical disadvantage and a higher level of resistance. The end result is greater muscular effort throughout the range of motion.

Figure 9.1 is a simplified illustration of the dynamics of the Nautilus cam. The force necessary to maintain the 100-pound resistance in Position #1 and Position #2 can be calculated using the formula "force times force arm equals resistance times resistance arm" or, more simply, "F x FA = R x RA." The force arm (FA) is defined as the distance from the axis of rotation (i.e., the fulcrum) to the point where the force is applied or exerted. In this example, the FA is 10 inches and is the same length in both positions. The resistance arm (RA) is defined as the distance from the axis of rotation to the point where the resistance is applied. Note that as the cam rotates from Position #1 to Position #2, the length of the RA (i.e., the effective radius) changes from 8 inches to 9 inches. Inserting the values of the FA, the RA and the resistance into the previously mentioned formula reveals that a force of 80 pounds is required to hold the resistance in Position #1 and a force of 90 pounds is necessary to hold the resistance in Position #2. In other words, the shorter RA in Position #1 produces a mechanical advantage and a lower level of resistance to coincide with a person's inferior biomechanical leverage in that position. The longer RA in Position #2 produces a mechanical disadvantage and a higher level of resistance to correspond with a person's superior biomechanical leverage in that position.

Plotting the variation in biomechanical leverage on a graph reveals what is known as a "strength curve." The elliptical dimensions of each Nautilus cam are derived through a sampling of the strength curves of many individuals. The final cam design for each machine is based upon an approximation of the typical strength curve exhibited during the performance of the exercise.

THE EXERCISES

This chapter will focus on the most common and most productive exercises that can be performed using Nautilus equipment. Included in the descriptions are the muscles used (if more than one muscle is involved, the first muscle listed is the prime mover), the suggested repetitions, the type of movement and performance points for making the exercise safer and more productive. The exercises described in this chapter are:

Leg Press

Hip Abduction

Hip Adduction

Leg Curl

Leg Extension

Calf Raise

Arm Cross

Decline Press

Pullover

Torso Arm

Chin

Overhead Press

Lateral Raise

Shoulder Shrug

Bicep Curl

Tricep Extension

Wrist Flexion

Neck Flexion

Neck Extension

Lateral Flexion

Side Bend

Back Extension

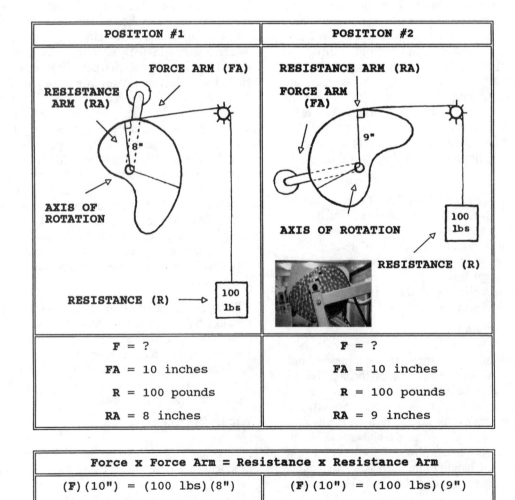

POSITION #1	POSITION #2
F = ?	F = ?
FA = 10 inches	FA = 10 inches
R = 100 pounds	R = 100 pounds
RA = 8 inches	RA = 9 inches

Force x Force Arm = Resistance x Resistance Arm	
(F)(10") = (100 lbs)(8")	(F)(10") = (100 lbs)(9")
F = 80 pounds	F = 90 pounds

Figure 9.1: Nautilus cam action

LEG PRESS

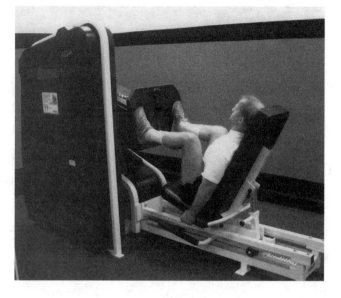 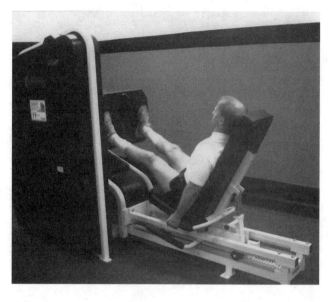

Start/Finish Position   *Mid-Range Position*

Muscle used: buttocks, quadriceps, hamstrings

Suggested repetitions: 15-20

Type of movement: multiple-joint

Starting position: Adjust the seat position so that the angle between the upper and the lower legs is about 90 degrees. Sit down and place the feet on the foot pedal so that they are slightly wider than shoulder width apart. Position the lower legs so that they are roughly perpendicular to the floor. Lightly grasp the handles located on the sides of the seat pad.

Description: Push the foot pedal forward until the legs are just short of full extension. Pause briefly in the mid-range position and then return the weight under control to the starting position to provide a proper stretch.

Performance points:

• The back pad on this machine has five different settings. As the back pad is positioned more parallel to the floor (i.e., less upright), there is more emphasis on the buttocks. In the less upright positions, the seat must be moved closer to the foot pedal to maintain the same range of motion as the more upright positions.

• Force should be exerted through the heels, not through the balls of the feet.

• The knees should not lock or "snap" in the mid-range of a repetition. This takes the tension off the target muscles and may hyperextend the knees.

• The portion of the weight stack being lifted should not bounce off or slam against the remainder of the weight stack between repetitions.

• This movement may be done unilaterally (one limb at a time) in the event of a knee injury or a gross strength imbalance. It may also be done in this fashion if a training variation is desired.

• This exercise may be contraindicated for individuals with hyperextended knees.

HIP ABDUCTION

Start/Finish Position   *Mid-Range Position*

Muscle used: gluteus medius

Suggested repetitions: 10-15

Type of movement: single-joint

Starting position: Adjust the lever on the side of the machine so that the movement arms are together. Rotate the thigh pads to the outside, sit down, place the legs on top of the leg pads and lay against the back pad. Secure the seat belt and lightly grasp the handles located on the sides of the seat pad.

Description: Spread the legs apart as far as possible by pushing against the thigh pads. Pause briefly in the mid-range position and then lower the weight under control to the starting position (legs together) to obtain a proper stretch.

Performance points:

• Individuals with relatively short legs may require an additional back elevation pad.

• To ensure a maximum possible muscular contraction during every repetition, aim the feet toward a reference point on the floor or wall in the mid-range position (legs apart).

• The body should not bend forward as this exercise is performed.

• The portion of the weight stack being lifted should not bounce off or slam against the remainder of the weight stack between repetitions.

HIP ADDUCTION

Start/Finish Position   *Mid-Range Position*

Muscle used: hip adductors (inner thigh)

Suggested repetitions: 10-15

Type of movement: single-joint

Starting position: Adjust the side lever of the machine so that the movement arms are spaced as far apart as possible. Rotate the thigh pads to the inside, sit down, place the legs on top of the leg pads and lay against the back pad. A spotter can assist in pushing the movement arms together so that the legs can be placed on the leg pads. Secure the seat belt and lightly grasp the handles located on the sides of the seat pad.

Description: Bring the legs as close together as possible by pushing against the thigh pads. Pause briefly in the mid-range position and then return the weight under control to the starting position (legs apart) to provide an adequate stretch.

Performance points:

• Individuals with relatively short legs may require an additional back elevation pad.

• To ensure a maximum possible muscular contraction during every repetition, attempt to bring the movement arms together in the mid-range position (legs together).

LEG CURL

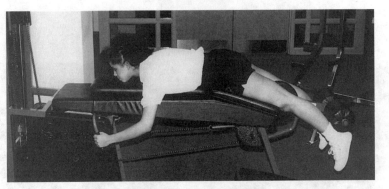

Start/Finish Position

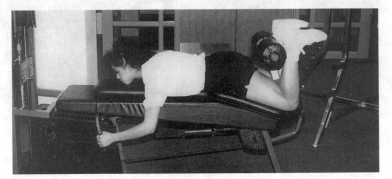

Mid-Range Position

Muscle used: hamstrings

Suggested repetitions: 10-15

Type of movement: single-joint

Starting position: Lay face down on the bench pad and place the lower legs underneath the roller pads. The tops of the kneecaps should be positioned just over the edge of the bench pad, not on the pad. Lightly grasp the handles located on the sides of the bench pad.

Description: Pull the heels up as close to the buttocks as possible. Pause briefly in the mid-range position and then lower the weight under control to the starting position (legs fully extended) to ensure a sufficient stretch.

Performance points:

• The angle between the upper and the lower legs should be 90 degrees or less in the mid-range position (heels near the buttocks). This could be deceiving if the pad is humped or angled rather than flat.

• Raising the hips during the performance of this movement is acceptable since this action actually increases the range of motion.

• The portion of the weight stack being lifted should not bounce off or slam against the remainder of the weight stack between repetitions.

• This movement may be done unilaterally (one limb at a time) in the event of a knee injury or a gross strength imbalance. It may also be done in this fashion if a training variation is desired.

• This exercise may be contraindicated for individuals with low back pain or hyperextended knees.

LEG EXTENSION

Start/Finish Position

Mid-Range Position

Muscle used: quadriceps

Suggested repetitions: 10-15

Type of movement: single-joint

Starting position: Sit down, place the backs of the knees against the end of the seat pad and position the feet behind the roller pad(s). There should be little or no space between the buttocks and the back pad. Secure the seat belt and lightly grasp the handles located on the sides of the seat pad.

Description: Extend the lower legs as high as possible by pushing against the roller pad(s). Pause briefly in the mid-range position and then return the weight under control to the starting position to obtain a proper stretch.

Performance points:

• Individuals with relatively short legs may require an additional back elevation pad (if the back pad on the machine does not adjust).

• The upper torso should remain against the back pad as this exercise is performed — movement should only occur around the knee joints.

• The portion of the weight stack being lifted should not bounce off or slam against the remainder of the weight stack between repetitions.

• This movement may be done unilaterally (one limb at a time) in the event of a knee injury or a gross strength imbalance. It may also be done in this fashion if a training variation is desired.

CALF RAISE

Start/Finish Position

Mid-Range Position

Muscles used: calves

Suggested repetitions: 10-15

Type of movement: single-joint

Starting position: Step into the belt and place it around the waist. Twist the end of the waist belt once or twice (near the D-ring) so that it fits more snugly. Bend down and snap the metal D-ring onto the hook at the end of the movement arm on the Multi-Exercise machine. Stand upright and reposition the belt so that it is not too high on the waist. Stand on the bottom step so that the balls of the feet are on the edge of the step and the heels extend over the edge. Hold onto the horizontal bar to maintain balance.

Description: Keeping the legs straight, rise up onto the toes as high as possible. Pause briefly in the mid-range position and then lower the weight under control to the starting position (heels near the floor) to provide a proper stretch.

Performance points:

• The belt should not be positioned too high on the waist so that the resistance doesn't tug the lower back forward.

• Individuals with relatively short legs may have to stand on the middle step in order to obtain an adequate stretch.

• Keep the legs straight while performing this movement.

• This movement may be done unilaterally (one limb at a time) in the event of an ankle injury or a gross strength imbalance. It may also be done in this fashion if a training variation is desired.

• This exercise may be contraindicated for individuals with shin splints.

ARM CROSS

Start/Finish Position

Mid-Range Position

Muscles used: chest, anterior deltoid

Suggested repetitions: 6-12

Type of movement: single-joint

Starting position: Adjust the seat height so that the front part of the shoulder is directly below the axis of rotation. Sit down and secure the seat belt. Place the forearms against the arm pads and grasp the upper handles. (Smaller proportioned individuals should use the lower handles.) The elbows should be slightly higher than the shoulders.

Description: Without moving the upper torso or the head away from the back pad, bring the elbows as close together as possible by pushing against the arm pads. Pause briefly in the mid-range position and then lower the weight under control to the starting position (arms apart) to provide an adequate stretch.

Performance points:

• Individuals with relatively short torsos may require an additional seat elevation pad and/or back elevation pad.

• The elbows should not come off the arm pads as the weight is raised. Force should be exerted against the arm pads rather than the handles.

• The upper torso and the head should remain against the back pad and the buttocks should be kept against the seat pad as this exercise is performed — movement should only occur around the shoulder joints.

• The portion of the weight stack being lifted should not bounce off or slam against the remainder of the weight stack between repetitions.

• This movement may be done unilaterally (one limb at a time) in the event of a shoulder injury or a gross strength imbalance. It may also be done in this fashion if a training variation is desired.

• The arm cross is similar to the bent arm fly performed with dumbbells.

• This exercise may be contraindicated for individuals with shoulder impingement syndrome.

DECLINE PRESS

Start/Finish Position   *Mid-Range Position*

Muscles used: chest (lower portion), anterior deltoid, triceps

Suggested repetitions: 6-12

Type of movement: multiple-joint

Starting position: Use the same seat adjustment as the arm cross (page 89). Sit down and secure the seat belt. Lay back and place the feet on the foot pedal. Push the foot pedal forward with the legs and grasp the top of the movement arms with the palms facing forward (i.e., knuckles facing up). Remove the feet from the foot pedal, place the lower legs on the leg rest and position the hands near the chest.

Description: Push the movement arm forward until the arms are just short of full extension. Pause briefly in the mid-range position and then lower the weight under control to the starting position (hands near the chest) to obtain a sufficient stretch. After completing the exercise, place the feet on the foot pedal, remove the hands from the handles and use the legs to return the resistance to the rest of the weight stack.

Performance points:

• This exercise may be performed with a "parallel grip" in which the palms face each other. However, using a palms forward grip at the top of the movement arms permits a better stretch.

• The buttocks should remain on the seat pad throughout the performance of this exercise.

• The elbows should not lock or "snap" in the mid-range of a repetition. This takes the tension off the target muscles and may hyperextend the elbows.

• After reaching concentric muscular failure, the muscles can be overloaded further by pushing the foot pedal forward with the feet and lowering the weight under control to the starting position for 3-5 additional "negative" repetitions.

PULLOVER

Start/Finish Position

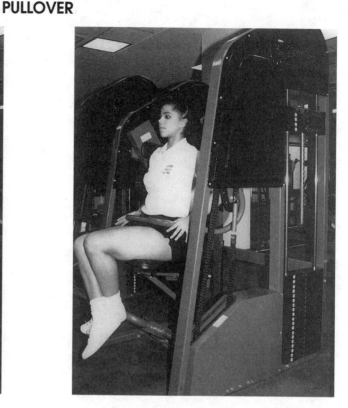

Mid-Range Position

Muscles used: upper back (lats)

Suggested repetitions: 6-12

Type of movement: single-joint

Starting position: Adjust the seat height so that the shoulders are slightly below the axis of rotation when sitting upright with the arms hanging straight down. Secure the seat belt, position the upper torso against the back pad and place the feet on the foot bar. Push the foot bar forward with the legs and place the backs of the upper arms against the elbow pads. Position the hands on the movement arm so that the palms are facing the bar and the hands are open (i.e., the fingers are extended). Remove the feet from the foot bar and position the movement arm near or slightly behind the head.

Description: Pull the movement arm down to the mid-section by exerting force against the elbow pads. Pause briefly in the mid-range position and then lower the weight under control to the starting position (elbows near or slightly past the head) to ensure a sufficient stretch. After completing the exercise, place the feet back on the foot bar, remove the arms from the elbow pads and use the legs to return the resistance to the rest of the weight stack.

Performance points:

• Individuals with relatively short arms may require an additional back elevation pad. If there is still difficulty in keeping the elbows against the pads, the bar can be grasped with an underhand grip and pulled with the hands.

• Keep the palms open and the fingers extended so that force is exerted against the movement arm with the elbows, not the hands.

• The upper torso and the head should remain against the back pad as this exercise is performed — movement should only occur around the shoulder joints.

• The portion of the weight stack being lifted should not bounce off or slam against the remainder of the weight stack between repetitions.

• This movement may be done unilaterally (one limb at a time) in the event of a shoulder injury or a gross strength imbalance. It may also be done in this fashion if a training variation is desired.

• This exercise may be contraindicated for individuals with low back pain or shoulder impingement syndrome.

TORSO ARM

Start/Finish Position

Mid-Range Position

Muscles used: upper back (lats), biceps, forearms

Suggested repetitions: 6-12

Type of movement: multiple-joint

Starting position: Adjust the seat height so that the movement arm is slightly out of reach. Sit down and secure the seat belt. A spotter can assist in pulling the movement arm down. Grasp the handles with the palms facing each other (i.e., a "parallel grip"). Bend forward at the waist, bring the knees together and cross the ankles.

Description: Pull the bar behind the head to the base of the neck. Pause briefly in the mid-range position and then lower the weight under control to the starting position (arms fully extended) to provide a proper stretch.

Performance points:

• Avoid swinging the upper torso back and forth as this exercise is performed — movement should only occur around the shoulder and the elbow joints.

• Wrist straps can be used if there is difficulty in maintaining a grip on the bar.

• The torso arm is similar to the overhand lat pulldown exercise in Chapter 10 (page 114).

• This exercise may be contraindicated for individuals with shoulder impingement syndrome.

CHIN

Start/Finish Position

Mid-Range Position

Muscles used: upper back (lats), biceps, forearms

Suggested repetitions: 6-12

Type of movement: multiple-joint

Starting position: Reach up, grasp the chin bar of the Multi-Exercise machine with the palms facing toward the body and space the hands approximately shoulder width apart. Lift the feet off the floor and cross the ankles.

Description: Pull the body up, touch the upper chest to the bar and rotate the elbows backward. Pause briefly in the mid-range position and then lower the body under control to the starting position (arms fully extended) to obtain a proper stretch.

Performance points:

- Touching the upper chest to the bar rather the chin will permit a greater range of motion. Rotating the elbows backward in the mid-range position will increase the workload performed by the upper back muscles.

- Individuals who are unable to do 6 repetitions in strict form using the bodyweight can exercise the same muscles by performing the underhand lat pulldown exercise in Chapter 10 (page 113).

- Individuals who are able to do 12 repetitions or more in strict form using the bodyweight can increase the resistance by attaching the waist belt to the end of the movement arm on the Multi-Exercise machine (thereby engaging the weight stack), by performing the exercise at a slower speed of movement or by having a spotter apply manual resistance to the waist.

- After reaching concentric muscular failure, the muscles can be overloaded further by climbing up the steps to the mid-range position and lowering the bodyweight under control to the starting position for 3-5 additional "negative" repetitions.

- Wrist straps can be used if there is difficulty in maintaining a grip on the chin bar.

- This movement can also be performed by spacing the hands several inches wider than shoulder width apart with the palms facing away from the body. (This is typically referred to as a "pullup.") However, doing this movement with an overhand grip (palms facing away from the body) is not as biomechanically efficient as performing it with an underhand grip (palms facing toward the body) for the same reason as described in the underhand lat pulldown exercise in Chapter 10.

- Pullups (palms facing away from the body) may be contraindicated for individuals with shoulder impingement syndrome.

OVERHEAD PRESS

Start/Finish Position

Mid-Range Position

Muscles used: anterior deltoid, triceps

Suggested repetitions: 6-12

Type of movement: multiple-joint

Starting position: Adjust the seat height so that the tops of the shoulders are near the handles of the movement arm. Sit down and secure the seat belt. Reach up and grasp the handles with the palms facing each other.

Description: Push the handles straight up until the arms are just short of full extension. Pause briefly in the mid-range position and then lower the weight under control to the starting position (hands near the shoulders) to ensure a proper stretch.

Performance points:

• The buttocks should remain flat on the seat and the upper torso kept against the back pad throughout the performance of this exercise. In the event of low back pain, the feet may be placed on a stool. This will flatten the lumbar area against the back pad and reduce the stress in the lower back region.

• The elbows should not lock or "snap" in the mid-range of a repetition. This takes the tension off the target muscles and may hyperextend the elbows.

• The portion of the weight stack being lifted should not bounce off or slam against the remainder of the weight stack between repetitions.

• This exercise may be contraindicated for individuals with low back pain or shoulder impingement syndrome.

LATERAL RAISE

Start/Finish Position

Mid-Range Position

Muscles used: middle deltoid, trapezius

Suggested repetitions: 6-12

Type of movement: single-joint

Starting position: Adjust the seat height so that the back of the shoulder is aligned with the axis of rotation. Sit down and secure the seat belt. Position the upper arms against the arm pads and lay the upper torso against the back pad. The arms should extend straight down and the palms should be facing each other. Bring the knees together and cross the ankles.

Description: Keeping the arms fairly straight, raise them away from the sides of the body until they are parallel to the floor. Pause briefly in the mid-range position and then lower the weight under control to the starting position (arms at the sides) to provide a proper stretch.

Performance points:

• The arms should not be lifted beyond a point that is parallel to the floor.

• The palms should be facing down in the mid-range position (arms parallel to the floor).

• The upper torso and the head should remain against the back pad as this exercise is performed — movement should only occur around the shoulder joints.

• The portion of the weight stack being lifted should not bounce off or slam against the remainder of the weight stack between repetitions.

• This movement may be done unilaterally (one limb at a time) in the event of a shoulder injury or a gross strength imbalance. It may also be done in this fashion if a training variation is desired.

SHOULDER SHRUG

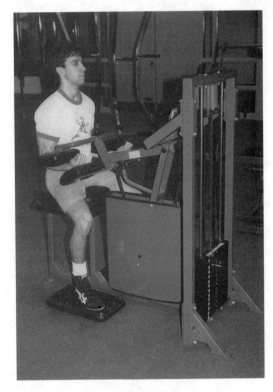

Start/Finish Position

Mid-Range Position

Muscles used: trapezius

Suggested repetitions: 8-12

Type of movement: single-joint

Starting position: Sit down and place the feet flat on the floor. Insert the lower arms between the arm pads all the way up to the biceps with the palms facing upward. Sit upright so that the selected portion of the weight stack is not touching the remainder of the weight stack.

Description: Raise the weight up as high as possible trying to touch the shoulders to the ears (as if to say, "I don't know"). Pause briefly in the mid-range position and then lower the weight under control to the starting position to ensure an adequate stretch.

Performance points:

• Individuals with relatively short upper torsos may require one or two additional seat elevation pads; individuals with relatively short lower legs may require additional seat elevation pads beneath the feet.

• It's not necessary or advisable to "roll" the shoulders during the performance of this exercise.

• The buttocks should remain on the seat pad and the feet kept flat on the floor as this exercise is performed — movement should only occur around the shoulder joints.

• This movement can also be performed on the Multi-Exercise machine using the shrug bar attachment.

• This exercise may be contraindicated for individuals with low back pain.

BICEP CURL

Start/Finish Position

Mid-Point Position

Muscles used: biceps, forearms

Suggested repetitions: 6-12

Type of movement: single-joint

Starting position: Sit down and place the feet flat on the floor (or on the bottom portion of the frame). Reach across the elbow pad and grasp the handles with the palms facing upward. The elbows should be placed on the elbow pad in alignment with the axis of rotation. The shoulders should be slightly lower than the elbows in this position.

Description: Without moving the elbows or bending backward at the waist, pull the handles up until they are alongside the head. Pause briefly in the mid-range position and then return the weight under control to the starting position (arms fully extended) to obtain a sufficient stretch.

Performance points:

• Individuals with relatively short upper torsos may require an additional seat elevation pad.

• Performing this exercise with the hands open (i.e., with the fingers extended) will place more of the workload on the biceps rather than the forearms.

• Avoid swinging the upper torso back and forth as this exercise is performed — movement should only occur around the elbow joints.

• The portion of the weight stack being lifted should not bounce off or slam against the remainder of the weight stack between repetitions.

• This movement may be done unilaterally (one limb at a time) in the event of an elbow injury or a gross strength imbalance. It may also be done in this fashion if a training variation is desired.

• This exercise may be contraindicated for individuals with hyperextended elbows. In this case, however, raising the seat to a higher position than that recommended will reduce the stress on a hyperextended elbow.

TRICEP EXTENSION

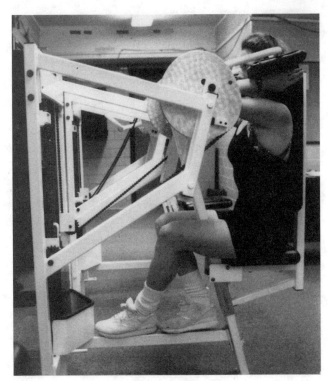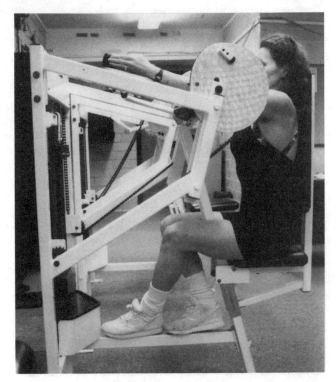

Start/Finish Position   *Mid-Range Position*

Muscle used: triceps

Suggested repetitions: 6-12

Type of movement: single-joint

Starting position: Push forward one of the movement arms and step across the seat pad. Sit down and place the feet flat on the floor (or on the bottom portion of the frame). Position the hands on the wrist pads so that the palms are facing each other and the hands are open (i.e., the fingers are extended). The elbows should be placed on the elbow pad in alignment with the axis of rotation. The shoulders should be slightly lower than the elbows in this position.

Description: Keeping the elbows against the elbow pad, push the movement arms forward by straightening the lower arms. Pause briefly in the mid-range position and then lower the weight under control to the starting position (arms bent) to ensure a sufficient stretch.

Performance points:

• Individuals with relatively short arms may require an additional back elevation pad.

• The elbows should remain in contact with the elbow pad as this exercise is performed.

• The upper torso and the head should remain against the back pad and the buttocks should be kept against the seat pad as this exercise is performed — movement should only occur around the elbow joints.

• The portion of the weight stack being lifted should not bounce off or slam against the remainder of the weight stack between repetitions.

• This movement may be done unilaterally (one limb at a time) in the event of an elbow injury or a gross strength imbalance. It may also be done in this fashion if a training variation is desired.

• This exercise may be contraindicated for individuals with shoulder impingement syndrome. In this case, however, raising the seat to a higher position than that recommended will reduce the stress on an impinged shoulder.

WRIST FLEXION

Start/Finish Position

Mid-Range Position

Muscles used: wrist flexors

Suggested repetitions: 8-12

Type of movement: single-joint

Starting position: Sit down on a bench or a stool facing the Multi-Exercise machine and place the feet on the bottom step. Reach down and grasp the wrist curl bar attachment with the palms facing upward. Place the thumbs underneath the bar alongside the fingers and spread the hands apart about 4-6 inches. Lift up the bar and place the backs of the forearms directly over the upper legs. (The forearms can also be placed between the legs flat on a bench.) In this position, the forearms should be approximately parallel to the floor. Lean forward slightly so that the angle between the upper and the lower arms is 90 degrees or less. The wrists should be over the kneecaps (or over the edge of the bench if the forearms are placed on the bench).

Description: Pull the bar up as high as possible by bending the wrists. Pause briefly in the mid-range position and then lower the weight under control to the starting position (wrists fully extended) to provide a sufficient stretch.

Performance points:

• The forearms should remain directly over the upper legs throughout the performance of this exercise. The elbows should not flare out to the sides.

• Placing the thumbs underneath the bar alongside the fingers will permit a greater range of motion.

• Avoid throwing the weight by using the legs or by swinging the upper torso back and forth — movement should only occur around the wrist joints.

NECK FLEXION

Start/Finish Position

Mid-Range Position

Muscle used: sternocleidomastoideus (both sides acting together)

Suggested repetitions: 8-12

Type of movement: single-joint

Starting position: Adjust the seat height so that the front of the head is centered on the face pads when sitting upright. Place the feet flat on the floor, grasp the handles and bring the head forward so that it is perpendicular to the floor.

Description: Without moving the upper torso, bring the head forward as far as possible by pushing against the face pads. Pause briefly in the mid-range position and then lower the weight under control to the starting position (head perpendicular to the floor) to provide an adequate stretch.

Performance points:

• The head should not extend backward beyond a point that is perpendicular to the floor.

• It's natural for the upper torso to change its position as this exercise is performed. However, the movement of the upper torso should not be excessive or used to throw the weight — movement should only occur around the neck. Crossing the arms (right hand on the left handle and left hand on the right handle) is a way of stabilizing the shoulders to limit excessive movement.

• The buttocks should be kept on the seat pad as this movement is performed.

• The portion of the weight stack being lifted should not bounce off or slam against the remainder of the weight stack between repetitions.

NECK EXTENSION

Start/Finish Position

Mid-Range Position

Muscles used: neck extensors, trapezius

Suggested repetitions: 8-12

Type of movement: single-joint

Starting position: Adjust the seat height so that the back of the head is centered on the face pads when sitting upright. Place the feet flat on the floor, grasp the handles and tilt the head forward.

Description: Without moving the upper torso, extend the head backward as far as possible by pushing against the face pads. Pause briefly in the mid-range position and then return the weight under control to the starting position (head forward) to ensure an adequate stretch.

Performance points:

- It's natural for the upper torso to change its position as this exercise is performed. However, the movement of the upper torso should not be excessive or used to throw the weight — movement should only occur around the neck.

- The buttocks should be kept on the seat pad as this movement is performed.

- The portion of the weight stack being lifted should not bounce off or slam against the remainder of the weight stack between repetitions.

LATERAL FLEXION

Start/Finish Position

Mid-Range Position

Muscle used: sternocleidomastoideus (one side acting singly)

Suggested repetitions: 8-12

Type of movement: single-joint

Starting position: Adjust the seat height so that the left side of the head is centered on the face pads when sitting upright. Place the feet flat on the floor and tilt the head toward the right shoulder. Cross the left arm over the right arm and grasp the handles.

Description: Without moving the upper torso, bring the head to the left shoulder by pushing against the face pads. Pause briefly in the mid-range position and then return the weight under control to the starting position (head against the right shoulder) to provide a proper stretch. After performing a set for the left side of the neck, repeat the exercise for the right side of the neck (by turning around on the seat 180 degrees and crossing the right arm over the left arm).

Performance points:

• It's natural for the upper torso to change its position as this exercise is performed. However, the movement of the upper torso should not be excessive or used to throw the weight — movement should only occur around the neck.

• The buttocks should be kept on the seat pad as this movement is performed.

• The portion of the weight stack being lifted should not bounce off or slam against the remainder of the weight stack between repetitions.

SIDE BEND

Start/Finish Position

Mid-Range Position

Muscles used: obliques

Suggested repetitions: 8-12

Type of movement: single-joint

Starting position: Bend down and snap the metal D-ring of the wrist strap attachment onto the hook at the end of the movement arm on the Multi-Exercise machine. Place the right wrist through the strap. Twist the hand once around the strap and grasp it above the D-ring. Stand upright and spread the feet about shoulder width apart. Place the left palm against the left side of the head. Without moving the hips, bend the upper torso to the right as far as possible.

Description: Without moving the hips, pull the upper torso to the left as far as possible. Pause briefly in the mid-range position and then lower the weight under control to the starting position to ensure a sufficient stretch. After performing a set for the left side of the mid-section, repeat the exercise for the right side of the mid-section.

Performance points:

• It's natural for the hips to change their position as this exercise is performed. However, the movement of the hips should not be excessive or used to throw the weight — movement should only occur around the waist.

• Avoid bending forward at the waist while performing this exercise.

• The feet should remain flat on the floor throughout the performance of this movement.

• This exercise may be contraindicated for individuals with low back pain.

BACK EXTENSION

Start/Finish Position   *Mid-Range Position*

Muscles used: erector spinae (lower back)

Suggested repetitions: 10-15

Type of movement: single-joint

Starting position: Sit down on the seat pad, place the legs underneath the leg roller pads and position the upper back against the back roller pad. Place the feet flat on the platform and rotate the leg roller pads so that they fit snugly against the upper legs. Secure the seat belt across the upper legs. Interlock the fingers and place the palms against the mid-section.

Description: Extend the upper torso backward by pushing against the back roller pad. Pause briefly in the mid-range position and then lower the weight under control to the starting position (torso bent forward) to ensure a sufficient stretch.

Performance points:

• Individuals with relatively short legs may have to place the feet on the upper foot pedal to obtain a proper fit.

• The upper torso should be in alignment with the upper legs in the mid-range position.

• Avoid throwing the upper torso backward or snapping the head backward as this exercise is performed — movement should only occur around the hip joint.

• The portion of the weight stack being lifted should not bounce off or slam against the remainder of the weight stack between repetitions.

• This exercise may be contraindicated for individuals with low back pain.

10

UNIVERSAL GYM EXERCISES

In 1957, the original Universal Gym Company developed the first multi-station selectorized weight training machine. Invented by Harold Zinkin, this revolutionary machine featured several exercise stations with separate stacks of flat weight plates that traveled up and down solid steel guide rods. Adjustments in weight were made quickly and easily through the use of a selector pin or key.

A Universal Multi-Gym has various stations that can accommodate many individuals at one time. The Multi-Gym is exceptionally versatile and has gained widespread acceptance at universities, YMCAs and especially at high schools. Universal equipment can also be found at government and military installations, hotels, resorts, hospitals and sportsmedicine clinics.

DYNAMIC VARIABLE RESISTANCE

Chapter 9 noted that movements feel easier in some positions and harder in others due to the changing biomechanical leverage of the skeletal system. In a typical pressing movement, for example, biomechanical leverage increases as the limbs are extended away from the body and decreases as the limbs near the body. In other words, the weight feels heavier near the body and lighter away from the body. Patented in 1974, Universal's Dynamic Variable Resistance (DVR) consistently varies the resistance to match the natural biomechanical advantages and disadvantages of the skeletal system. As a pressing movement is performed, the resistance slides up and down the movement arm on rollers thereby changing the length of the resistance arm (RA). In positions of inferior leverage (and inferior strength), the length of the RA is relatively short. This creates a mechanical advantage and a lower level of resistance. As the skeletal system moves into a position of superior leverage (and superior strength), the length of the RA becomes longer.

This creates a mechanical disadvantage and a higher level of resistance. The end result is greater muscular effort throughout the range of motion.

Figure 10.1 illustrates the dynamics of the Universal DVR in simplified terms. The force necessary to maintain the 135-pound resistance in Position #1 and Position #2 can be calculated using the formula "force times force arm equals resistance times resistance arm" or, more simply, "F x FA = R x RA." The force arm (FA) is defined as the distance from the axis of rotation (i.e., the fulcrum) to the point where the force is applied or exerted. In this example, the FA is 54 inches and is the same length in both positions. The resistance arm is defined as the distance from the axis of rotation to the point where the resistance is applied. Note that as the resistance moves from Position #1 to Position #2, the length of the RA changes from 34 inches to 39 inches. Inserting the values of the FA, the RA and the resistance into the previously mentioned formula reveals that a force of 85 pounds is required to hold the resistance in Position #1 and a force of 97.5 pounds is necessary to hold the resistance in Position #2. In other words, the shorter RA in Position #1 produces a mechanical advantage and a lower level of resistance to coincide with a person's inferior biomechanical leverage in that position. The longer RA in Position #2 produces a mechanical disadvantage and a higher level of resistance to coincide with a person's superior biomechanical leverage in that position.

The effects of DVR on leverage is reflected by the two numbers that appear on each weight plate. On the movements incorporating DVR, the lower number indicates the approximate resistance in the starting position and the higher number denotes the approximate resistance in the mid-range position.

THE EXERCISES

This chapter will detail the most common and most productive exercises that can be performed on Universal equipment. Included in the descriptions for each exercise are the muscles used (if more than one muscle is involved, the first muscle listed is the prime mover), the suggested repetitions, the type of movement and performance points for making the exercise safer and more productive. The exercises described in this chapter are:

Leg Press

Leg Curl

Leg Extension

Calf Raise

Bench Press

Dip

Underhand Lat Pulldown

Overhand Lat Pulldown

Seated Row

Seated Press

Shoulder Shrug

Upright Row

Bicep Curl

Tricep Extension

Wrist Flexion

Sit-up

Knee-up

Back Extension

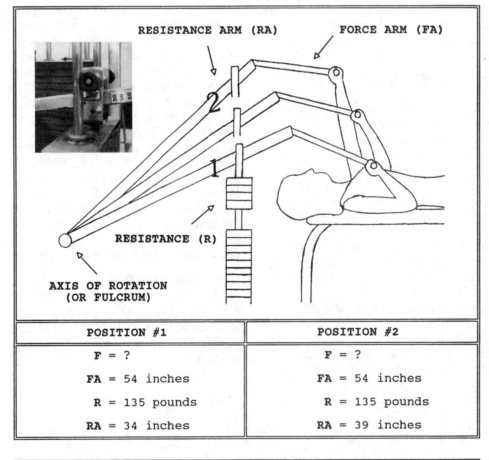

POSITION #1	POSITION #2
F = ?	F = ?
FA = 54 inches	FA = 54 inches
R = 135 pounds	R = 135 pounds
RA = 34 inches	RA = 39 inches

Force x Force Arm = Resistance x Resistance Arm	
(F)(54") = (135 lbs)(34")	(F)(54") = (135 lbs)(39")
F = 85 pounds	F = 97.5 pounds

Figure 10.1: Universal's Dynamic Variable Resistance (DVR)

LEG PRESS

Start/Finish Position   *Mid-Range Position*

Muscles used: buttocks, quadriceps, hamstrings

Suggested repetitions: 15-20

Type of movement: multiple-joint

Starting position: Adjust the seat position so that the angle between the upper and the lower legs is about 90 degrees. Sit down and place the feet on the upper foot pedals. Lightly grasp the handles located on the sides of the seat pad.

Description: Push the foot pedal forward until the legs are just short of full extension. Pause briefly in the mid-range position and then lower the weight under control to the starting position to provide a proper stretch.

Performance points:

- The upper foot pedals should be used if available. Use of the lower foot pedals tends to create excessive shear forces in the knee joint.

- Force should be exerted through the bottom portion of the feet, not through the upper portion of the feet.

- The knees should not lock or "snap" in the mid-range of a repetition. This takes the tension off the target muscles and may hyperextend the knees.

- The portion of the weight stack being lifted should not bounce off or slam against the remainder of the weight stack between repetitions.

- This movement may be done unilaterally (one limb at a time) in the event of a knee injury or a gross strength imbalance. It may also be done in this fashion if a training variation is desired.

- This exercise may be contraindicated for individuals with hyperextended knees.

LEG CURL

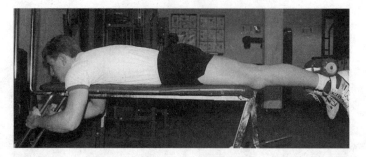

Start/Finish Position

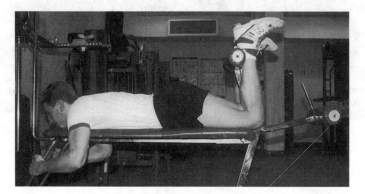

Mid-Range Position

Muscles used: hamstrings

Suggested repetitions: 10-15

Type of movement: single-joint

Starting position: Lay face down on the bench pad and place the lower legs underneath the roller pads. The tops of the kneecaps should be positioned just over the edge of the bench pad, not on the pad. Lightly grasp the support bars located on the sides of the bench pad.

Description: Pull the heels up as close to the buttocks as possible. Pause briefly in the mid-range position and then lower the weight under control to the starting position (legs fully extended) to ensure a sufficient stretch.

Performance points:

• The angle between the upper and the lower legs should be 90 degrees or less in the mid-range position (heels near the buttocks). This could be deceiving if the pad is humped or angled rather than flat.

• Raising the hips during the performance of this movement is acceptable since this action actually increases the range of motion.

• The portion of the weight stack being lifted should not bounce off or slam against the remainder of the weight stack between repetitions.

• This movement may be done unilaterally (one limb at a time) in the event of a knee injury or a gross strength imbalance. It may also be done in this fashion if a training variation is desired.

• This exercise may be contraindicated for individuals with low back pain or hyperextended knees.

LEG EXTENSION

Start/Finish Position

Mid-Range Position

Muscle used: quadriceps

Suggested repetitions: 10-15

Type of movement: single-joint

Starting position: Sit down, place the backs of the knees against the end of the bench pad and position the feet behind the roller pads. Lightly grasp the sides of the bench pad and lean back slightly.

Description: Extend the lower legs as high as possible by pushing against the roller pad. Pause briefly in the mid-range position and then return the weight under control to the starting position to obtain a proper stretch.

Performance points:

- Avoid swinging the upper torso back and forth as this exercise is performed — movement should only occur around the knee joints.

- The portion of the weight stack being lifted should not bounce off or slam against the remainder of the weight stack between repetitions.

- This movement may be done unilaterally (one limb at a time) in the event of a knee injury or a gross strength imbalance. It may also be done in this fashion if a training variation is desired.

CALF RAISE

Start/Finish Position

Mid-Range Position

Muscles used: calves

Suggested repetitions: 10-15

Type of movement: single-joint

Starting position: This exercise can be performed at the bench press station. Stand on a small block of wood, reach down and grasp the handles of the movement arm about shoulder width apart with the palms facing backward. Stand upright by straightening the legs and the upper torso (as if performing a deadlift). Position the body so that the balls of the feet are on the edge of the block and the heels extend over the edge.

Description: Keeping the legs straight, rise up onto the toes as high as possible. Pause briefly in the mid-range position and then lower the weight under control to the starting position (heels near the floor) to provide a proper stretch.

Performance points:

• The block of wood is used to obtain a better stretch. Another person can stand on the side of a block that is especially high so that it doesn't tip over.

• Keep the arms and the legs straight while performing this movement.

• Wrist straps can be used if there is difficulty in maintaining a grip on the handles.

• This exercise may be contraindicated for individuals with low back pain or shin splints.

BENCH PRESS

Start/Finish Position   *Mid-Range Position*

Muscles used: chest, anterior deltoid, triceps

Suggested repetitions: 6-12

Type of movement: multiple-joint

Starting position: Lay down on the bench and place the feet flat on the floor. Grasp the handles and spread the hands slightly wider than shoulder width apart. Position the upper torso so that the handles are approximately even with the shoulders.

Description: Push the movement arm straight up until the arms are just short of full extension. Pause briefly in the mid-range position and then lower the weight under control to the starting position (hands near the chest) to obtain a sufficient stretch.

Performance points:

- The buttocks should remain flat on the bench and the feet kept flat on the floor throughout the performance of this exercise. In the event of low back pain, the feet may be placed on the bench or a stool. This will flatten the lumbar area against the bench and reduce the stress in the lower back region.

- The elbows should not lock or "snap" in the mid-range of a repetition. This takes the tension off the target muscles and may hyperextend the elbows.

- An excessively wide grip should not be used since this will reduce the range of motion.

- The portion of the weight stack being lifted should not bounce off or slam against the remainder of the weight stack between repetitions.

DIP

Start/Finish Position   *Mid-Range Position*

Muscles used: chest (lower portion), anterior deltoid, triceps

Suggested repetitions: 6-12

Type of movement: multiple-joint

Starting position: Grasp the handles with a "parallel grip" (i.e., the palms facing each other). Lift the feet off the floor, bend the knees and cross the ankles.

Description: Push the body straight up until the arms are just short of full extension. Pause briefly in the mid-range position and then lower the body under control to the starting position (hands near the chest) to obtain a sufficient stretch.

Performance points:

- The elbows should not lock or "snap" in the mid-range of a repetition. This takes the tension off the target muscles and may hyperextend the elbows.

- Individuals who are able to do 12 repetitions or more in strict form using the bodyweight can increase the resistance by attaching extra weight to the waist, by performing the exercise at a slower speed of movement or by having a spotter apply manual resistance to the waist.

- After reaching concentric muscular failure, the muscles can be overloaded further by stepping up to the mid-range position and lowering the bodyweight under control to the starting position for 3-5 additional "negative" repetitions.

UNDERHAND LAT PULLDOWN

Start/Finish Position

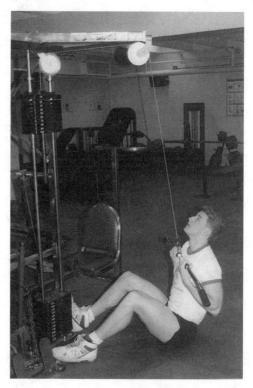

Mid-Range Position

Muscles used: upper back (lats), biceps, forearms

Suggested repetitions: 6-12

Type of movement: multiple-joint

Starting position: Grasp the bar with the palms facing toward the body and space the hands approximately shoulder width apart. Sit down on the floor directly below the high pulley and lean back slightly.

Description: Pull the bar to the upper chest and rotate the elbows backward. Pause briefly in the mid-range position and then return the weight under control to the starting position (arms fully extended) to obtain a proper stretch.

Performance points:

• A spotter can assist in holding the shoulders down if the weight being lifted is close to or greater than the bodyweight.

• Avoid swinging the upper torso back and forth as this exercise is performed — movement should only occur around the shoulder and the elbow joints.

• Touching the bar to the upper chest rather than just below the chin will permit a greater range of motion. Rotating the elbows backward in the mid-range position will increase the workload performed by the upper back muscles.

• Regardless of hand positioning, just about any type of pulling movement — whether it be rowing, chinning or any pulldown variation — exercises the upper back, the biceps and the forearms. However, there are differences in the leverage received from these muscles based upon the grip used. Performing a lat pulldown with an underhand grip (palms facing toward the body) is more biomechanically efficient than doing it with an overhand grip (palms facing away from the body). With an underhand grip, the forearm bones (the radius and the ulna) run parallel to one another; with an overhand grip, the radius pivots near the elbow and crosses over the ulna forming an "X". When this happens, the bicep tendon wraps around the radius, creating a biomechanical disadvantage and a loss in leverage. This is also true when using these grips during rowing and chinning movements — the same muscles are used but with varying degrees of leverage.

• Wrist straps can be used if there is difficulty in maintaining a grip on the bar.

• This exercise may be contraindicated for individuals with shoulder impingement syndrome.

OVERHAND LAT PULLDOWN

Start/Finish Position

Mid-Range Position

Muscles used: upper back (lats), biceps, forearms

Suggested repetitions: 6-12

Type of movement: multiple-joint

Starting position: Grab the bar with the palms facing away from the body and space the hands several inches wider than shoulder width apart. Sit down on the floor directly below the high pulley.

Description: Pull the bar behind the head to the base of the neck. Pause briefly in the mid-range position and then lower the weight under control to the starting position (arms fully extended) to obtain an adequate stretch.

Performance points:

- A spotter can assist in holding the shoulders down if the weight being lifted is close to or greater than the bodyweight.

- Avoid swinging the upper torso back and forth as this exercise is performed — movement should only occur around the shoulder and the elbow joints.

- An excessively wide grip should not be used since this will reduce the range of motion.

- Performing this movement with an overhand grip (palms facing away from the body) is not as biomechanically efficient as doing it with an underhand grip (palms facing toward the body). However, this movement is still productive when performed with an overhand grip in the manner described above.

- Wrist straps can be used if there is difficulty in maintaining a grip on the bar.

- This exercise may be contraindicated for individuals with shoulder impingement syndrome.

SEATED ROW

Start/Finish Position

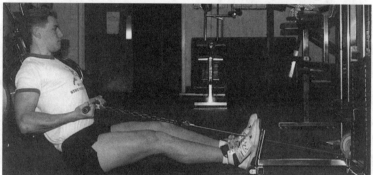

Mid-Range Position

Muscles used: upper back (lats), biceps, forearms

Suggested repetitions: 6-12

Type of movement: multiple-joint

Starting position: This exercise can be performed by using the low pulley. Sit down and place the feet against the foot pedals (a wooden board can be used if foot pedals aren't available). Grasp the bar with the palms facing upward, spread the hands approximately shoulder width apart and lean back slightly.

Description: Pull the bar to the mid-section. Pause briefly in the mid-range position and then lower the weight under control to the starting position (arms fully extended) to ensure a sufficient stretch.

Performance points:

• Performing this movement with an underhand grip (palms facing upward) is more biomechanically efficient than doing it with an overhand grip (palms facing downward) for the same reason as described in the underhand lat pulldown exercise on page 113. However, this movement is still productive when performed with an overhand grip in the manner described above.

• It's natural for the upper torso to change its position as this exercise is performed. However, avoid swinging the upper torso back and forth as this exercise is performed — movement should only occur around the shoulder and the elbow joints.

• The portion of the weight stack being lifted should not bounce off or slam against the remainder of the weight stack between repetitions.

• Wrist straps can be used if there is difficulty in maintaining a grip on the bar.

SEATED PRESS

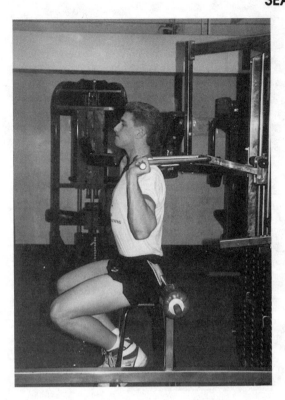

Start/Finish Position   *Mid-Range Position*

Muscles used: anterior deltoid, triceps

Suggested repetitions: 6-12

Type of movement: multiple-joint

Starting position: Sit down on the stool facing away from the machine. Grasp the handles, spread the hands slightly wider than shoulder width apart and sit up straight.

Description: Push the movement arm straight up until the arms are just short of full extension. Pause briefly in the mid-range position and then return the weight under control to the starting position (hands near the shoulders) to ensure a proper stretch.

Performance points:

- Avoid leaning backward during this exercise so as not to stress the lumbar area. Facing away from the machine reduces this possibility.

- The buttocks should remain flat on the stool throughout the performance of this exercise.

- The elbows should not lock or "snap" in the mid-range of a repetition. This takes the tension off the target muscles and may hyperextend the elbows.

- The portion of the weight stack being lifted should not bounce off or slam against the remainder of the weight stack between repetitions.

- This exercise may be contraindicated for individuals with low back pain or shoulder impingement syndrome.

SHOULDER SHRUG

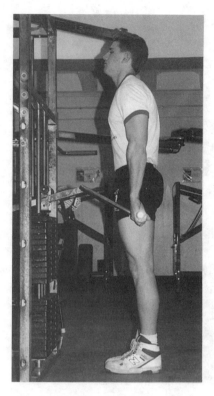

Start/Finish Position

Mid-Range Position

Muscle used: trapezius

Suggested repetitions: 8-12

Type of movement: single-joint

Starting position: This exercise can be performed at the bench press station. Spread the feet approximately shoulder width apart. Reach down and grasp the handles of the movement arm with the palms facing backward. Stand upright by straightening the legs and the upper torso (as if performing a deadlift).

Description: Keeping the arms and the legs straight, pull the movement arm up as high as possible trying to touch the shoulders to the ears (as if to say, "I don't know"). Pause briefly in the mid-range position and then lower the weight under control to the starting position to ensure an adequate stretch.

Performance points:

- It's not necessary or advisable to "roll" the shoulders during the performance of this exercise.

- Avoid throwing the weight by using the legs or by swinging the upper torso back and forth — movement should only occur around the shoulder joint.

- Wrist straps can be used if there is difficulty in maintaining a grip on the bar.

- This exercise may be contraindicated for individuals with low back pain.

UPRIGHT ROW

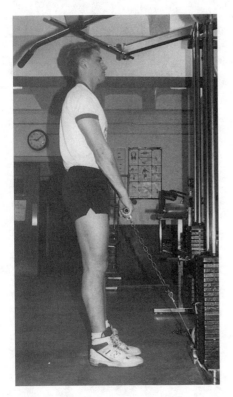

Start/Finish Position

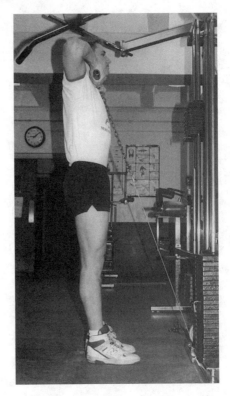

Mid-Range Position

Muscles used: trapezius, biceps, forearms

Suggested repetitions: 6-12

Type of movement: multiple-joint

Starting position: This exercise can be performed by using the low pulley. Spread the feet approximately shoulder width apart. Reach down and grasp the bar with the hands spaced apart about 8-10 inches and the palms facing the thighs. Stand upright by straightening the legs and the upper torso.

Description: Pull the bar up until the hands are approximately level with the shoulders. The elbows should be slightly higher than the hands in this position. Pause briefly in the mid-range position and then return the weight under control to the starting position (arms fully extended) to ensure a proper stretch.

Performance points:

• Avoid throwing the weight by using the legs or by swinging the upper torso back and forth — movement should only occur around the shoulder and the elbow joints.

• Wrist straps can be used if there is difficulty in maintaining a grip on the bar.

• This exercise may be contraindicated for individuals with shoulder impingement syndrome. In this case, however, pulling the bar to the lower portion of the chest rather than to the upper portion of the chest will reduce the stress on an impinged shoulder. This exercise may also be contraindicated for individuals with low back pain.

BICEP CURL

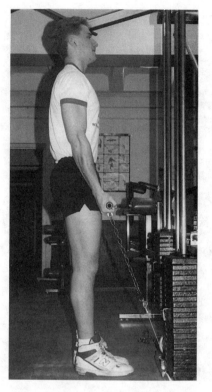

Start/Finish Position

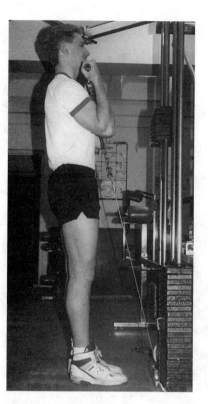

Mid-Range Position

Muscles used: biceps, forearms

Suggested repetitions: 6-12

Type of movement: single-joint

Starting position: This exercise can be performed by using the low pulley. Spread the feet approximately shoulder width apart. Reach down and grasp the bar with the hands spaced slightly less than shoulder width apart and the palms facing forward. Stand upright by straightening the legs and the upper torso.

Description: Keeping the elbows against the sides of the body, pull the bar below the chin by bending the arms. Pause briefly in the mid-range position and then return the weight under control to the starting position (arms fully extended) to provide an adequate stretch.

Performance points:

- It's natural for the elbows to change their position as this exercise is performed. However, the movement of the elbows should not be excessive.

- Avoid swinging the upper torso back and forth as this exercise is performed — movement should only occur around the elbow joints.

- This exercise may be contraindicated for individuals with hyperextended elbows.

TRICEP EXTENSION

Start/Finish Position

Mid-Range Position

Muscle used: triceps

Suggested repetitions: 6-12

Type of movement: single-joint

Starting position: This exercise can be performed by using the high pulley. Grasp the bar with the hands spaced apart about 4-6 inches and the palms facing downward. Place one foot slightly in front of the other and pull the bar down until the elbows are against the sides.

Description: Keeping the elbows against the sides of the body, push the bar down by straightening the arms. Pause briefly in the mid-range position and then return the weight under control to the starting position (arms bent) to ensure a proper stretch.

Performance points:

• The elbows should remain in contact with the sides of the body as this exercise is performed. The elbows should not flare out to the sides.

• Avoid swinging the upper torso back and forth as this exercise is performed — movement should only occur around the elbow joints.

WRIST FLEXION

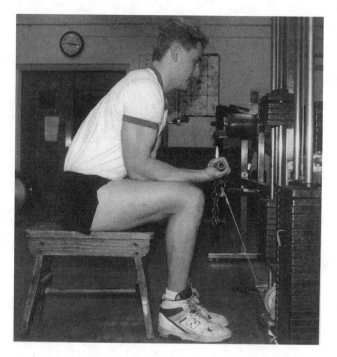

Start/Finish Position

Mid-Range Position

Muscles used: wrist flexors

Suggested repetitions: 8-12

Type of movement: single-joint

Starting position: This exercise can be performed by using the low pulley. Sit down on a bench or stool facing the machine. Reach down and grasp the bar with the palms facing upward. Place the thumbs underneath the bar alongside the fingers and spread the hands apart about 4-6 inches. Lift up the bar and place the backs of the forearms directly over the upper legs. (The forearms can also be placed between the legs flat on a bench.) In this position, the forearms should be approximately parallel to the floor. Lean forward slightly so that the angle between the upper and the lower arms is 90 degrees or less. The wrists should be over the kneecaps (or over the edge of the bench if the forearms are placed on the bench).

Description: Pull the bar up as high as possible by bending the wrists. Pause briefly in the mid-range position and then lower the weight under control to the starting position (wrists fully extended) to provide a sufficient stretch.

Performance points:

- The forearms should remain directly over the upper legs throughout the performance of this exercise. The elbows should not flare out to the sides.

- Placing the thumbs underneath the bar alongside the fingers will permit a greater range of motion.

- Avoid throwing the weight by using the legs or by swinging the upper torso back and forth — movement should only occur around the wrist joints.

SIT-UP

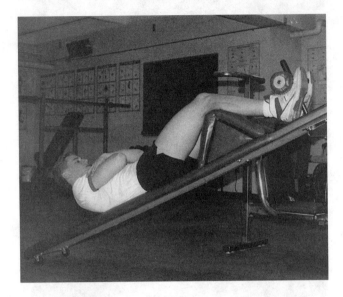 

Start/Finish Position   *Mid-Range Position*

Muscles used: rectus abdominis, iliopsoas

Suggested repetitions: 8-12

Type of movement: single-joint

Starting position: Lay down on the sit-up board and place the feet under the roller pads. The angle between the upper and the lower legs should be about 90 degrees. Fold the arms across the chest and lift the head off the board. The upper portion of the shoulder blades should not be touching the board.

Description: Bring the upper torso forward until it is just short of being perpendicular to the floor. Pause briefly in the mid-range position and then lower the upper torso under control to the starting position to obtain a proper stretch.

Performance points:

• The abdominals are used during the first 30 degrees of this movement, so it's not necessary to bring the upper torso all the way up to the legs. Movement should stop, however, before reaching a point where the upper torso is perpendicular to the floor.

• The knees should always be bent when performing sit-ups to reduce the strain on the lower back.

• Avoid throwing the upper torso forward by swinging the arms back and forth or by snapping the head forward — movement should only occur around the hip joint.

• Individuals who are able to do 12 repetitions or more in strict form using the bodyweight can increase the workload by holding on to a weight, by increasing the incline of the board, by performing the exercise with a slower speed of movement or by having a spotter apply manual resistance to the shoulders.

• This exercise may be contraindicated for individuals with low back pain.

KNEE-UP

Start/Finish Position

Mid-Range Position

Muscles used: iliopsoas, rectus abdominis (lower portion)

Suggested repetitions: 8-12

Type of movement: single-joint

Starting position: Reach up and grasp the handles with the palms facing away from the body. Lift the feet off the floor and cross the ankles.

Description: Pull the knees up as close to the chest as possible. Pause briefly in the mid-range position and then lower the legs under control to the starting position (legs extended) to ensure a proper stretch.

Performance points:

• Avoid throwing the knees up by swinging the body back and forth — movement should only occur around the hip and the knee joints.

• Individuals who are able to do 12 repetitions or more in strict form using the bodyweight can increase the workload by performing the exercise at a slower speed of movement or by having a spotter apply manual resistance to the upper legs.

BACK EXTENSION

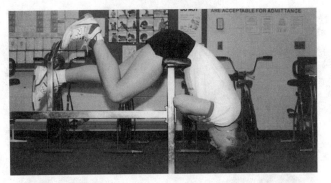

Start/Finish Position

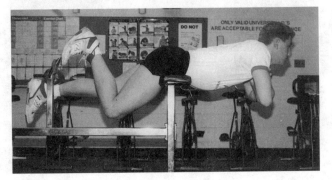

Mid-Range Position

Muscles used: erector spinae (lower back)

Suggested repetitions: 10-15

Type of movement: single-joint

Starting position: Straddle the support bar with the body facing away from the machine and place the pelvis on top of the rectangular hip pad. Position the left foot underneath the roller pad and the right foot against the foot pedal. Allow the upper torso to hang straight down over the edge of the hip pad and fold the arms across the chest.

Description: Raise the upper torso until it is approximately parallel to the floor. Pause briefly in the mid-range position and then lower the upper torso under control to the starting position (torso positioned straight down) to obtain a sufficient stretch.

Performance points:

• The upper torso should not be lifted beyond a point that is parallel to the floor.

• Avoid throwing the upper torso backward or snapping the head backward as this exercise is performed — movement should only occur around the hip joint.

• Individuals who are able to do 15 repetitions or more in strict form using the bodyweight can increase the workload by holding on to a weight, by performing the exercise at a slower speed of movement or by having a spotter apply manual resistance to the upper back.

• This exercise may be contraindicated for individuals with low back pain.

11

MANUAL RESISTANCE EXERCISES

Manual resistance (MR) has been referred to as a "productive alternative" for developing strength when equipment isn't available (Riley 1981a). It is an extremely effective way of strength training in which another person supplies the resistance. Surprisingly, MR has actually been around for quite a long time. One of the earliest accounts of partner-resisted exercise was by Lewis (1862). He described several exercises in which an individual pulled one or two wooden gymnastic rings that were held by another person who offered resistance. In support of these movements, Lewis wrote, "In most exercises there must be some resistance. How much better that this should be another human being, rather than a pole, ladder or bar!"

In the 1920s, Angelo Siciliano was awarded the title as "The World's Most Perfectly Developed Man" after winning a physique contest. Although Siciliano developed his award-winning physique using barbells and dumbbells (Hoffman 1939; Todd 1986), he claimed to have used his body to provide its own resistance. Siciliano called his system "Dynamic Tension" and began a lucrative mail-order service to market these self-resistive exercises under the more recognizable name of Charles Atlas.

During the late 1970s, MR was refined and popularized by Dan Riley. Partner-resisted exercises have been used as a productive alternative by athletes at numerous universities (Jacobson 1981; Riley 1981a; Gittleson 1984; Brown 1989; Mannie 1989a; Bates, Wolf and Blunk 1990; Thomas 1994) and professional sports teams (Riley 1982e; Simmons 1994). MR has also been adopted by many personal trainers for use with their clients.

ADVANTAGES AND DISADVANTAGES

There are many advantages to using MR. First of all, little or no equipment is required. In addition, the exercises can be done just about anywhere — even on an athletic field after practice — without having to go to the weightroom. MR is also extremely time-efficient. A coach can train a large number of athletes in a relatively short period of time. (One half of the team can perform the exercises while the other half of the team can act as spotters.) The major disadvantage of MR is that the resistance cannot be quantified, thereby making it impossible to monitor progress. Another drawback is that MR requires a competent spotter.

GENERAL TECHNIQUE

In order for MR to be productive, the exercises must be performed with proper technique. The following are general guidelines for the lifter and the spotter:

The Lifter

As in lifting any weight, the lifter should raise the resistance in a deliberate, controlled manner throughout the greatest possible range of motion that safety allows. The resistance (applied by the spotter) should be raised in about 1-2 seconds and lowered in about 3-4 seconds. As an alternative to counting repetitions, the exercises can be performed for a prescribed amount of time. In this case, the lifter should generally reach concentric muscular failure within about 60-90 seconds for the lower body and about 40-70 seconds for the upper torso. If it is more preferable to count repetitions, muscular failure should be attained in 10-15 repetitions for the lower body and 6-12 repetitions for the upper torso. (Muscular failure should occur with 8-12 repetitions — or about 50-70 seconds — for exercises involving the rotator cuff, the neck and the mid-section.) It should be noted that these repetition ranges are based upon a 6-second repetition. Finally, the lifter must keep tension on the muscles throughout the entire exercise.

The Spotter

Because an individual is naturally stronger in some positions than others due to the changing biomechanical leverage of the skeletal system, the spotter is responsible for varying the resistance throughout the lifter's entire range of motion. Since individuals are considerably stronger eccentrically, the spotter must apply more resistance during the lowering phase of the exercise. The spotter must also regulate the resistance in accordance with the lifter's momentary level of strength. In other words, the spotter must furnish less resistance as the lifter fatigues during each repetition. The spotter must regulate the speed of movement (up in 1-2 seconds and down in 3-4 seconds). Communication between the partners is extremely important so that the spotter knows when the resistance is too much or not enough.Finally, the spotter must encourage and motivate the lifter.

THE EXERCISES

This chapter will focus on the most productive exercises that can be performed using manual resistance. Included in the descriptions for each exercise are the muscles used (if more than one muscle is involved, the first muscle listed is the prime mover), the suggested repetitions and time frames, the type of movement and performance points for making the exercise safer and more efficient. (In the accompanying photographs, the lifter is wearing the darker shirt.) The exercises described in this chapter are:

Hip Abduction

Hip Adduction

Leg Curl

Leg Extension

Dorsi Flexion

Push-up

Bent Arm Fly

Bent Over Row

Seated Row

Lat Pulldown

Seated Press

Lateral Raise

Front Raise

Internal Rotation

External Rotation

Bicep Curl

Tricep Extension

Neck Flexion

Neck Extension

Sit-up

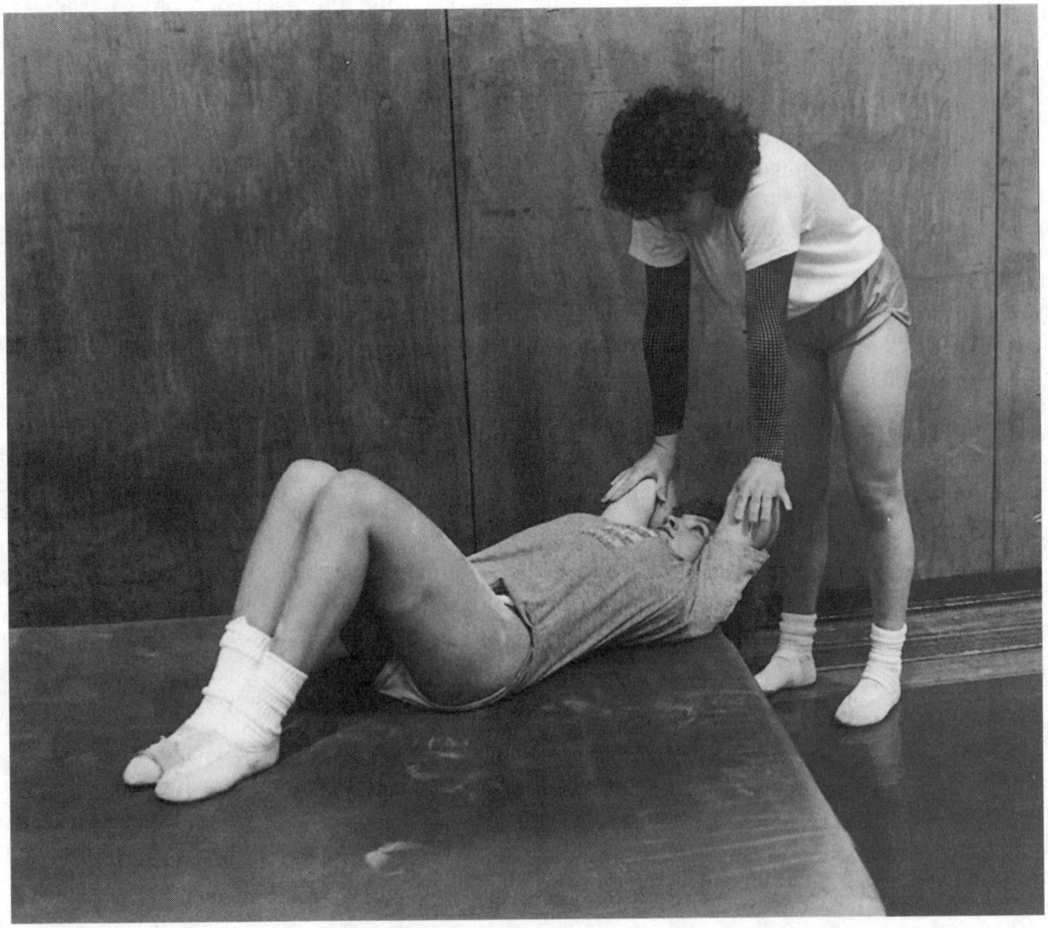

An advantage of manual resistance is that the exercises can be done just about anywhere — without having to go to the weightroom. (Photo by Al Gomez)

HIP ABDUCTION

Start/Finish Position   *Mid-Range Position*

Muscle used: gluteus medius

Suggested repetitions: 10-15 (or 60-90 seconds)

Type of movement: single-joint

Starting position: Lay on the left side of the body with the legs straight and the toes pointed toward the knees. Extend the left arm across the floor. The spotter should kneel behind the lifter and apply resistance against the lifter's right ankle.

Description: Raise the right leg up as high as possible as the spotter provides resistance evenly throughout the full range of movement. Pause briefly in the mid-range position and then resist as the spotter pushes the leg back to the starting position (legs together) to obtain a proper stretch. After performing a set with the right leg, turn to the right side of the body and repeat the exercise with the left leg.

Performance points:

• The spotter should apply resistance above the knees if the lifter suffers from hyperextended knees or other joint pain.

• The lifter should avoid bending the body forward at the waist as this exercise is performed.

• The lifter should reach a point where the leg cannot be lifted. At this time, the spotter can assist the lifter in the performance of 3-5 post-fatigue repetitions by lifting the leg to the mid-range position and then pushing it back to the starting position as the lifter resists.

HIP ADDUCTION

Start/Finish Position   *Mid-Range Position*

Muscles used: hip adductors (inner thigh)

Suggested repetitions: 10-15 (or 60-90 seconds)

Type of movement: single-joint

Starting position: Sit upright on the floor with the legs bent, the soles of the feet together and the knees spread apart. Place the hands alongside the hips and lean back slightly. The spotter should kneel in front of the lifter and apply resistance against the insides of the lifter's knees.

Description: Raise the knees as close together as possible as the spotter provides resistance evenly throughout the full range of movement. Pause briefly in the mid-range position and then resist as the spotter pushes the legs back to the starting position (knees apart) to provide an adequate stretch.

Performance points:

- The lifter should reach a point where the knees cannot be brought together. At this time, the spotter can assist the lifter in the performance of 3-5 post-fatigue repetitions by lifting the knees to the mid-range position and then pushing them back to the starting position as the lifter resists.

LEG CURL

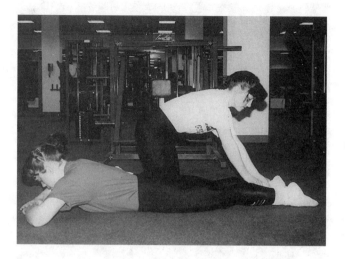

Start/Finish Position   *Mid-Range Position*

Muscles used: hamstrings

Suggested repetitions: 10-15 (or 60-90 seconds)

Type of movement: single-joint

Starting position: Because the muscles of the upper legs are relatively strong, this movement will probably need to be done with one leg at a time. Lay face down on the floor (or a bench if one is available) with the legs straight and the toes pointed. The spotter should kneel alongside the lifter and apply resistance against the lifter's right heel.

Description: Keeping the right upper leg flat on the ground (or the bench), pull the right heel as close to the buttocks as possible as the spotter provides resistance evenly throughout the full range of movement. Pause briefly in the mid-range position and then resist as the spotter pushes the lower leg back to the starting position (leg fully extended) to ensure a sufficient stretch. After performing a set with the right leg, repeat the exercise with the left leg.

Performance points:

- The angle between the upper and the lower leg should be 90 degrees or less in the mid-range position (heel near the buttocks).

- Raising the hips during the performance of this movement is acceptable since this action actually increases the range of motion.

- The lifter should reach a point where the lower leg cannot be lifted. At this time, the spotter can assist the lifter in the performance of 3-5 post-fatigue repetitions by lifting the lower leg to the mid-range position and then pushing it back to the starting position as the lifter resists.

- This exercise may be contraindicated for individuals with low back pain or hyperextended knees.

LEG EXTENSION

Start/Finish Position

Mid-Range Position

Muscle used: quadriceps

Suggested repetitions: 10-15 (or 60-90 seconds)

Type of movement: single-joint

Starting position: Because the muscles of the upper legs are relatively strong, this movement will probably need to be done with one leg at a time. Sit on a bench, a table or a chair that is high enough so that the feet do not touch the floor. The spotter should kneel in front of the lifter and apply resistance against the upper part of the lifter's right instep.

Description: Extend the right lower leg as high as possible as the spotter provides resistance evenly throughout the full range of movement. Pause briefly in the mid-range position and then resist as the spotter pushes the lower leg back to the starting position (leg bent) to obtain a proper stretch. After performing a set with the right leg, repeat the exercise with the left leg.

Performance points:

- Avoid swinging the upper torso back and forth as this exercise is performed — movement should only occur around the knee joint.

- The lifter should reach a point where the lower leg cannot be lifted. At this time, the spotter can assist the lifter in the performance of 3-5 post-fatigue repetitions by lifting the lower leg to the mid-range position and then pushing it back to the starting position as the lifter resists.

DORSI FLEXION

Start/Finish Position *Mid-Range Position*

Muscles used: dorsi flexors

Suggested repetitions: 10-15 (or 60-90 seconds)

Type of movement: single-joint

Starting position: Because the muscles of the legs are relatively strong, this movement will probably need to be done with one leg at a time. Sit down on a bench and lay the right leg across the length of the bench. The right heel should hang slightly over the edge of the bench and the toes should be pointed away from the body. The spotter should sit or kneel in front of the lifter and apply resistance against the lower part of the lifter's right foot.

Description: Keeping the right leg flat on the bench, pull the right foot toward the body as the spotter provides resistance evenly throughout the full range of movement. Pause briefly in the mid-range position and then resist as the spotter pulls the foot back to the starting position (foot fully extended) to ensure a sufficient stretch. After performing a set with the right leg, repeat the exercise with the left leg.

Performance points:

- The lifter should reach a point where the foot cannot be brought toward the body. At this time, the spotter can assist the lifter in the performance of 3-5 post-fatigue repetitions by bringing the foot to the mid-range position and then pulling it back to the starting position as the lifter resists.

PUSH-UP

Start/Finish Position   *Mid-Range Position*

Muscles used: chest, anterior deltoid, triceps

Suggested repetitions: 6-12 (or 40-70 seconds)

Type of movement: multiple-joint

Starting position: Lay face down on the floor with the legs straight and the toes curled under the feet. Place the palms on the floor and spread the hands approximately shoulder width apart. The spotter should straddle the lifter's body and apply resistance against the lifter's upper back.

Description: Push the body straight up until the arms are just short of full extension as the spotter provides resistance evenly throughout the full range of movement. Pause briefly in the mid-range position and then resist as the spotter pushes the body back to the starting position (chest touching the floor) to obtain a sufficient stretch.

Performance points:

- An excessively wide hand position should not be used since this will reduce the range of motion.

- Placing the hands on elevation pads or wooden blocks permits a better stretch.

- Avoid arching the lower back during this movement — the upper torso should remain in alignment with the lower body throughout the performance of this movement.

- The elbows should not lock or "snap" in the mid-range of a repetition. This takes the tension off the target muscles and may hyperextend the elbows.

- Individuals who are unable to do 6 repetitions in strict form using the bodyweight can obtain better leverage by performing this movement in the kneeling position.

- The lifter should reach a point where the body cannot be lifted. At this time, the spotter can assist the lifter in the performance of 3-5 post-fatigue repetitions by raising the body to the mid-range position and then pushing it back to the starting position as the lifter resists.

BENT ARM FLY

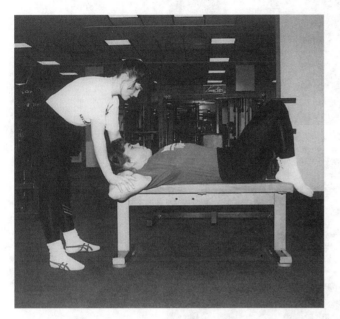 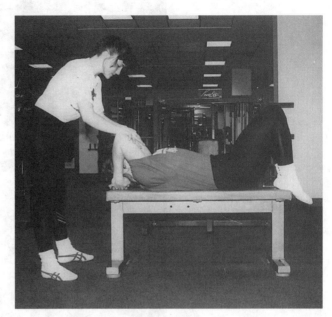

Start/Finish Position   *Mid-Range Position*

Muscles used: chest, anterior deltoid

Suggested repetitions: 6-12 (or 40-70 seconds)

Type of movement: single-joint

Starting position: Lay down on a bench and interlock the fingers behind the head. The spotter should stand directly behind the lifter's head and apply resistance against the insides of the lifter's elbows.

Description: Keeping the head against the bench, bring the elbows as close together as possible as the spotter provides resistance evenly throughout the full range of movement. Pause briefly in the mid-range position and then resist as the spotter pushes the arms back to the starting position (arms apart) to obtain a sufficient stretch.

Performance points:

- The head and the buttocks should remain flat on the bench and the feet kept flat on the floor throughout the performance of this exercise — movement should only occur around the shoulder joints.

- In the event of low back pain, the feet may be placed on the end of the bench. This will flatten the lumbar area against the bench and reduce the stress in the lower back region.

- The lifter should reach a point where the elbows cannot be brought together. At this time, the spotter can assist the lifter in the performance of 3-5 post-fatigue repetitions by lifting the elbows to the mid-range position and then pushing them back to the starting position as the lifter resists.

BENT OVER ROW

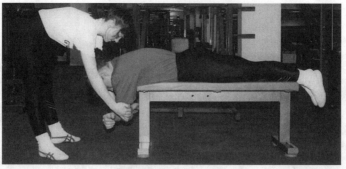

Start/Finish Position

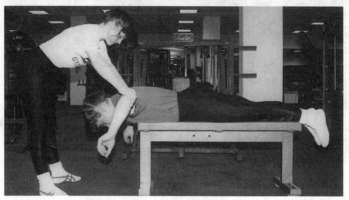

Mid-Range Position

Muscles used: upper back (lats), posterior deltoid, trapezius

Suggested repetitions: 6-12 (or 40-70 seconds)

Type of movement: single-joint

Starting position: Lay face down on a bench so that the shoulders extend slightly past the end of the bench. The upper arms should be almost perpendicular to the upper torso and the forearms should be crossed. The spotter should stand near the lifter's head and apply resistance against the backs of the lifter's upper arms near the elbows.

Description: Keeping the upper arms almost perpendicular to the upper torso, lift the elbows upward as high as possible as the spotter provides resistance evenly throughout the full range of movement. Pause briefly in the mid-range position and then resist as the spotter pushes the arms back to the starting position (forearms crossed) to provide a proper stretch.

Performance points:

• The hands should remain open (i.e., the fingers extended) throughout the performance of this movement.

• This exercise can also be done with the upper arm closer to the upper torso. This will involve the upper back to a greater degree. However, this also dramatically increases the leverage of the lifter thereby making it extremely difficult for the spotter to apply adequate resistance.

• This exercise is a multiple-joint movement when performed with dumbbells, but it becomes a single-joint movement when using manual resistance because the resistance is applied above the elbows instead of to the hands.

• The lifter should reach a point where the arms cannot be lifted. At this time, the spotter can assist the lifter in the performance of 3-5 post-fatigue repetitions by lifting the elbows to the mid-range position and then pushing them back to the starting position as the lifter resists.

SEATED ROW

Start/Finish Position   *Mid-Range Position*

Muscles used: upper back (lats), biceps, forearms

Suggested repetitions: 6-12 (or 40-70 seconds)

Type of movement: multiple-joint

Starting position: Sit down on the floor with the legs extended toward the spotter. Grasp a stick or a bar with the palms facing upward and spread the hands approximately shoulder width apart. The spotter should sit down on the floor between the lifter's legs. The spotter should grasp the stick on the outside of the lifter's grip with the palms facing downward. The lifter should extend the arms fully and lean back slightly.

Description: Pull the stick to the mid-section as the spotter provides resistance evenly throughout the full range of movement. Pause briefly in the mid-range position and then resist as the spotter pulls the arms back to the starting position (arms fully extended) to ensure a sufficient stretch.

Performance points:

• If a stick or a similar item isn't available, the lifter and the spotter can interlock each other's hands.

• An excessively wide grip should not be used since this will reduce the range of motion.

• The spotter should maintain straight arms and supply resistance by bending forward and backward at the waist to involve the larger, more powerful muscles of the lower back.

• It's natural for the lifter's upper torso to change its position as this exercise is performed. However, the lifter should avoid swinging the upper torso back and forth as this exercise is performed — movement should only occur around the shoulder and the elbow joints.

• Performing this movement with an underhand grip (palms facing upward) is more biomechanically efficient than doing it with an overhand grip (palms facing downward) for the same reason as described in the underhand lat pulldown exercise on page 113. However, this movement is still productive when performed using an overhand grip in the manner described above.

• Wrist straps can be used if there is difficulty in maintaining a grip on the stick.

• The lifter should reach a point where the stick cannot be pulled to the mid-section. At this time, the spotter can assist the lifter in the performance of 3-5 post-fatigue repetitions by positioning the stick in the mid-range position and then pulling it back to the starting position as the lifter resists.

LAT PULLDOWN

Start/Finish Position

Mid-Range Position

Muscles used: upper back (lats)

Suggested repetitions: 6-12 (or 40-70 seconds)

Type of movement: single-joint

Starting position: Sit down on a bench or a stool, place the upper arms against the sides of the head and cross the forearms behind the head. The spotter should stand behind the lifter and apply resistance against the backs of the lifter's upper arms near the elbows.

Description: Keeping the upper arms aligned with the upper torso, pull the elbows down toward the sides of the body as the spotter provides resistance evenly throughout the full range of movement. Pause briefly in the mid-range position and then resist as the spotter pulls the arms back to the starting position (upper arms against the sides of the head) to obtain a sufficient stretch.

Performance points:

• The hands should remain open (i.e., the fingers extended) throughout the performance of this movement.

• The hands should not move in front of the face as this movement is performed — the hands should remain out of sight.

• This exercise is a multiple-joint movement when performed on a pulldown device, but it becomes a single-joint movement when using manual resistance because the resistance is applied above the elbows instead of to the hands.

• The lifter should reach a point where additional repetitions cannot be performed. At this time, the spotter can assist the lifter in the performance of 3-5 post-fatigue repetitions by positioning the elbows in the mid-range position and then pulling them back to the starting position as the lifter resists.

• This exercise may be contraindicated for individuals with shoulder impingement syndrome.

SEATED PRESS

Start/Finish Position

Mid-Range Position

Muscles used: anterior deltoid, triceps

Suggested repetitions: 6-12 (or 40-70 seconds)

Type of movement: multiple-joint

Starting position: Sit down on the floor, bend the knees and lean back against the spotter's leg. Grasp a stick or a bar with the palms facing upward and spread the hands slightly wider than shoulder width apart. Position the stick behind the neck on the upper part of the trapezius. The spotter should grasp the stick on the inside of the lifter's grip with the palms facing downward.

Description: Push the stick straight up until the arms are just short of full extension as the spotter provides resistance evenly throughout the full range of movement. Pause briefly in the mid-range position and then resist as the spotter pushes the stick back to the starting position (stick on the trapezius) to provide a proper stretch.

Performance points:

• If a stick or a similar item isn't available, the lifter and the spotter can place their palms together.

• An excessively wide grip should not be used since this will reduce the range of motion.

• The elbows should not lock or "snap" in the mid-range of a repetition. This takes the tension off the target muscles and may hyperextend the elbows.

• The lifter should reach a point where the stick cannot be lifted. At this time, the spotter can assist the lifter in the performance of 3-5 post-fatigue repetitions by lifting the stick to the mid-range position and then pushing it back to the starting position as the lifter resists.

• This exercise may be contraindicated for individuals with shoulder impingement syndrome. In this case, however, lowering the stick in front of the head rather than behind the head will reduce the stress on an impinged shoulder.

LATERAL RAISE

Start/Finish Position

Mid-Range Position

Muscles used: middle deltoid, trapezius

Suggested repetitions: 6-12 (or 40-70 seconds)

Type of movement: single-joint

Starting position: Stand upright with the arms hanging straight down and the palms facing the legs. Spread the feet apart a comfortable distance. The spotter should stand behind the lifter and apply resistance against the lifter's lower arms.

Description: Keeping the arms fairly straight, raise them away from the sides of the body until they are parallel to the floor as the spotter provides resistance evenly throughout the full range of movement. Pause briefly in the mid-range position and then resist as the spotter pushes the arms back to the starting position (arms at the sides) to ensure an adequate stretch.

Performance points:

• The spotter should apply resistance above the elbows if the lifter suffers from hyperextended elbows or other joint pain.

• The hands should remain open (i.e., the fingers extended) throughout the performance of this movement.

• The arms should not be lifted beyond a point that is parallel to the floor.

• The palms should be facing down in the mid-range position (arms parallel to the floor).

• Avoid throwing the arms upward by using the legs or by swinging the upper torso back and forth — movement should only occur around the shoulder joints.

• The lifter should reach a point where the arms cannot be lifted. At this time, the spotter can assist the lifter in the performance of 3-5 post-fatigue repetitions by lifting the arms to the mid-range position and then pushing them back to the starting position as the lifter resists.

FRONT RAISE

Start/Finish Position

Mid-Range Position

Muscle used: anterior deltoid

Suggested repetitions: 6-12 (or 40-70 seconds)

Type of movement: single-joint

Starting position: Stand upright with the hands slightly beyond the hips and the palms facing each other. Spread the feet apart a comfortable distance with one foot in front of the other. The spotter should stand in front of the lifter, place one foot to the inside of the lifter's forward foot and apply resistance against the lifter's wrists.

Description: Keeping the arms fairly straight, raise them in front of the body until they are parallel to the floor as the spotter applies resistance evenly throughout the full range of movement. Pause briefly in the mid-range position and then resist as the spotter pushes the arms back to the starting position (hands beyond the hips) to obtain a proper stretch.

Performance points:

- The spotters' front foot should slide backward as the lifter's arms are raised up to the mid-range position and forward as the arms are lowered to the starting position.

- The spotter should apply resistance above the elbows if the lifter suffers from hyperextended elbows or other joint pain.

- The hands should remain open (i.e., the fingers extended) throughout the performance of this movement.

- The arms should not be lifted beyond a point that is parallel to the floor.

- The palms should be facing each other in the mid-range position (arms parallel to the floor).

- Avoid throwing the arms upward by using the legs or by swinging the upper torso back and forth — movement should only occur around the shoulder joints.

- The lifter should reach a point where the arms cannot be lifted. At this time, the spotter can assist the lifter in the performance of 3-5 post-fatigue repetitions by lifting the arms to the mid-range position and then pushing them back to the starting position as the lifter resists.

INTERNAL ROTATION

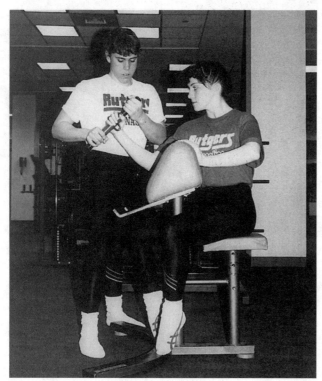 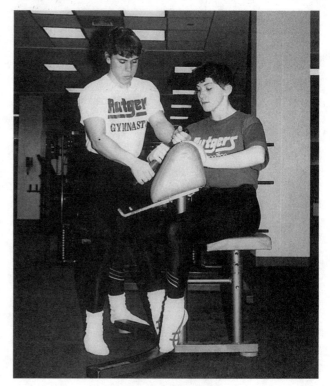

Start/Finish Position   *Mid-Range Position*

Muscles used: internal rotators

Suggested repetitions: 8-12 (or 50-70 seconds)

Type of movement: single-joint

Starting position: Sit down on a preacher bench and position the right arm against the pad. Grasp a short stick or a bar with the right hand and bend the right arm so that the angle between the upper and the lower arms is about 90 degrees. The right forearm should be pointed directly ahead. The spotter should stand alongside the lifter and grasp the stick above and below the lifter's right hand.

Description: Without moving the right elbow or changing the angle of the right arm, pull the stick toward the bench as the spotter applies resistance evenly throughout the full range of movement. Pause briefly in the mid-range position and then resist as the spotter pulls the stick back to the starting position to provide a proper stretch. After performing a set with the right arm, repeat the exercise with the left arm.

Performance points:

- The lifter should reach a point where the stick cannot be pulled toward the bench. At this time, the spotter can assist the lifter in the performance of 3-5 post-fatigue repetitions by positioning the stick in the mid-range position and then pulling it back to the starting position as the lifter resists.

EXTERNAL ROTATION

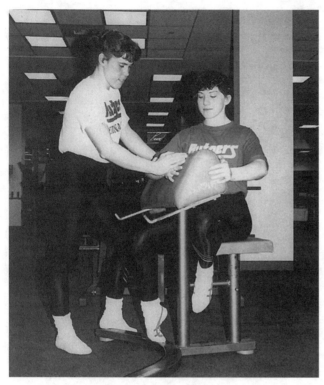

Start/Finish Position

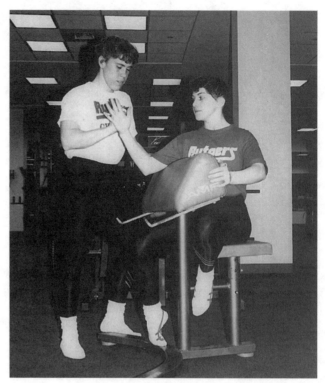

Mid-Range Position

Muscles used: external rotators

Suggested repetitions: 8-12 (or 50-70 seconds)

Type of movement: single-joint

Starting position: Sit down on a preacher bench and position the right arm against the pad. Bend the right arm so that the angle between the upper and the lower arms is about 90 degrees. Place the right forearm against the bench and open the right hand (i.e., fingers extended). The spotter should stand alongside the lifter and apply resistance near the lifter's right wrist.

Description: Without moving the right elbow or changing the angle of the right arm, push the hand away from the bench as the spotter applies resistance evenly throughout the full range of movement. Pause briefly in the mid-range position and then resist as the spotter pushes the hand back to the starting position to obtain a proper stretch. After performing a set with the right arm, repeat the exercise with the left arm.

Performance points:

• The hand should remain open (i.e., the fingers extended) throughout the performance of this movement.

• The lifter should reach a point where the hand cannot be pushed away from the bench. At this time, the spotter can assist the lifter in the performance of 3-5 post-fatigue repetitions by positioning the hand in the mid-range position and then pushing it back to the starting position as the lifter resists.

BICEP CURL

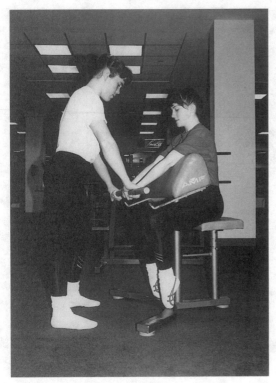

Start/Finish Position

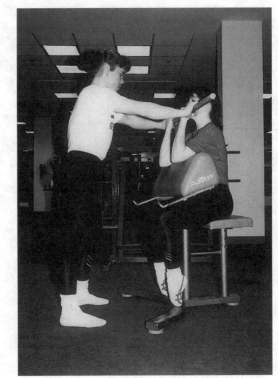

Mid-Range Position

Muscles used: biceps, forearms

Suggested repetitions: 6-12 (or 40-70 seconds)

Type of movement: single-joint

Starting position: Sit down on a preacher bench and position the backs of the arms against the pad. Grasp a stick with the palms facing upward and spread the hands slightly less than shoulder width apart. The spotter should stand in front of the lifter and grasp the stick on the outside of the lifter's grip with the palms facing downward.

Description: Without moving the elbows or bending backward at the waist, pull the stick up below the chin as the spotter applies resistance evenly throughout the full range of movement. Pause briefly in the mid-range position and then resist as the spotter pulls the stick back to the starting position (arms fully extended) to obtain a sufficient stretch.

Performance points:

- Performing this exercise with the hands open (i.e., the fingers extended) will place more of the workload on the biceps rather than the forearms.

- Avoid swinging the upper torso back and forth as this exercise is performed — movement should only occur around the elbow joints.

- The lifter should reach a point where the stick cannot be lifted. At this time, the spotter can assist the lifter in the performance of 3-5 post-fatigue repetitions by lifting the stick to the mid-range position and then pulling it back to the starting position as the lifter resists.

- This exercise may be contraindicated for individuals with hyperextended elbows.

TRICEP EXTENSION

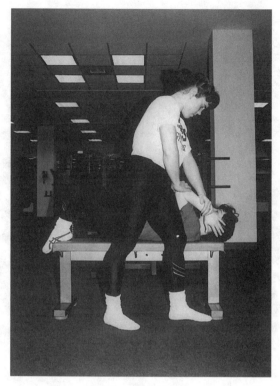

Start/Finish Position

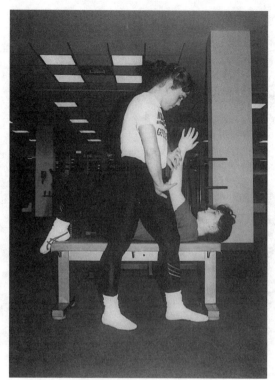

Mid-Range Position

Muscle used: triceps

Suggested repetitions: 6-12 (or 40-70 seconds)

Type of movement: single-joint

Starting position: Lay down on a bench and place the feet flat on the floor. Place the back of the left upper arm against the spotter's left thigh. Position the left upper arm so that it is roughly perpendicular to the floor. The left hand should be near the left side of the head with the hand open (i.e., the fingers extended) and facing the head. The spotter should apply resistance near the lifter's left wrist.

Description: Without moving the upper arm, extend the lower arm as the spotter applies resistance evenly throughout the full range of movement. Pause briefly in the mid-range position and then resist as the spotter pushes the lower arm back to the starting position (arm bent) to obtain an adequate stretch. After performing a set with the left arm, repeat the exercise with the right arm.

Performance points:

• The upper arm should remain perpendicular to the floor and in contact with the spotter's thigh as this exercise is performed.

• In the event of low back pain, the feet may be placed on the bench or a stool. This will flatten the lumbar area against the bench and reduce the stress in the lower back region.

• This exercise can also be performed sitting upright.

• The lifter should reach a point where the arm cannot be lifted. At this time, the spotter can assist the lifter in the performance of 3-5 post-fatigue repetitions by lifting the arm to the mid-range position and then pushing it back to the starting position as the lifter resists.

• This exercise may be contraindicated for individuals with shoulder impingement syndrome.

NECK FLEXION

Start/Finish Position　　　　　　　　　　　　*Mid-Range Position*

Muscle used: sternocleidomastoideus (both sides acting together)

Suggested repetitions: 8-12 (or 50-70 seconds)

Type of movement: single-joint

Starting position: Lay face up on a bench, place the feet flat on the floor and hang the head over the end of the bench. Interlock the fingers and place them across the chest. The spotter should stand alongside the lifter's head and apply resistance against the chin with one hand and the forehead with the other hand.

Description: Pull the head as close to the chest as possible as the spotter applies resistance evenly throughout the full range of movement. Pause briefly in the mid-range position and then resist as the spotter pushes the head back to the starting position (head hanging down) to provide an adequate stretch.

Performance points:

- The spotter must be especially careful when applying resistance since the cervical area is involved during this exercise.

- The lifter should reach a point where the head cannot be lifted. At this time, the spotter can assist the lifter in the performance of 3-5 post-fatigue repetitions by lifting the head to the mid-range position and then pushing it back to the starting position as the lifter resists.

NECK EXTENSION

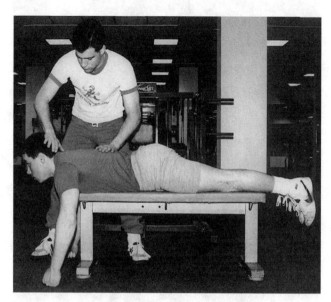

Start/Finish Position   *Mid-Range Position*

Muscles used: neck extensors, trapezius

Suggested repetitions: 8-12 (or 50-70 seconds)

Type of movement: single-joint

Starting position: Lay face down on a bench so that the head hangs over the end of the bench. Place the hands and the feet on the floor (or position the legs across the bench). The spotter should stand alongside the lifter's head and apply resistance against the back of the head.

Description: Extend the head backward as far as possible as the spotter applies resistance evenly throughout the full range of movement. Pause briefly in the mid-range position and then resist as the spotter pushes the head back to the starting position (head hanging down) to ensure an adequate stretch.

Performance points:

- The spotter must be especially careful when applying resistance since the cervical area is involved during this exercise.

- The lifter should reach a point where the head cannot be lifted. At this time, the spotter can assist the lifter in the performance of 3-5 post-fatigue repetitions by lifting the head to the mid-range position and then pushing it back to the starting position as the lifter resists.

SIT-UP

Start/Finish Position

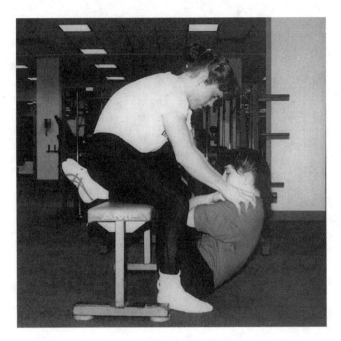

Mid-Range Position

Muscle used: rectus abdominis

Suggested repetitions: 8-12 (or 50-70 seconds)

Type of movement: single-joint

Starting position: Lay down on the floor and place the backs of the lower legs on a bench or stool. The angle between the upper and the lower legs should be about 90 degrees. Fold the arms across the chest and lift the head off the floor. The upper portion of the shoulder blades should not be touching the floor. The spotter should sit on the lifter's lower legs and apply resistance against the front part of the shoulders.

Description: Bring the upper torso forward until it is almost to the legs as the spotter applies resistance evenly throughout the full range of movement. Pause briefly in the mid-range position and then resist as the spotter pushes the upper torso back to the starting position to obtain a proper stretch.

Performance points:

• The abdominals are used during the first 30 degrees of this movement, so it's not necessary to bring the upper torso all the way up to the legs. Movement should stop, however, before reaching a point where the upper torso is perpendicular to the floor.

• Placing the lower legs on a bench or stool in the manner described above will relax the iliopsoas muscle, thereby reducing its "tugging" effects on the lumbar spine.

• Avoid throwing the upper torso forward by swinging the arms back and forth or by snapping the head forward — movement should only occur around the hip joint.

• The lifter should reach a point where the upper torso cannot be lifted. At this time, the spotter can assist the lifter in the performance of 3-5 post-fatigue repetitions by lifting the upper torso to the mid-range position and then pushing it back to the starting position as the lifter resists.

• This exercise may be contraindicated for individuals with low back pain.

Part 3

EXAMING OTHER ISSUES

12
STRENGTHENING THE HEART

Strength training is an excellent tool to decrease injury potential and to increase performance potential. However, most sports and activities require a combination of not only strength but also cardiovascular or aerobic conditioning. An individual who is highly conditioned will have a lower resting heart rate (Clausen 1977; Stromme and Skard 1980) and lower blood pressure (ACSM 1991). In addition, a highly conditioned person will be able to work at higher levels of intensity for longer periods of time at a lower heart rate than someone who is less conditioned. This "conditioning advantage" means that a person won't have to expend as much energy as an opponent and will be able to perform activities with less visible effort. As conditioning improves, the heart rate will recover faster from exercise and return to its resting level more quickly (Astrand and Rodahl 1977). Finally, aerobic training — performed in conjunction with wise nutritional planning — will help decrease the percentage of body fat and maintain it at an acceptable level.

THE ULTIMATE "PUMP"

Aerobic conditioning can be improved by targeting the most important muscle in the body: the heart. Located just behind the sternum (or breastbone), the heart is the focal point of the cardiovascular system. It is a cone-shaped organ about 5 inches long and 3-1/2 inches wide — roughly the size of a fist. The average adult male heart weighs about 10 ounces while its female counterpart weighs about 8 ounces.

The heart is the ultimate endurance muscle or "pump" — it contracts about 100,000 times each day, pausing only briefly after a contraction to fill with more blood for its next contraction. Each half of the heart consists of two chambers: an atrium and a ventricle. The left half of the heart pumps blood to the body tissues, such as the skeletal muscles; the right half of the heart sends blood to the lungs. During each beat, the heart pumps about 130 cubic centimeters of blood or roughly 5 liters per minute. That's about 1,900 gallons of blood each day. As the blood surges out of the ventricle, it pounds the arterial wall. This impact is transmitted along the length of the artery and can be felt as a throb or a "pulse" at those points where an artery lies just under the skin. The beat of the pulse is synchronous with the beat of the heart.

To a degree, the rate of the heartbeat is dependent upon the size of the organism. In general, the smaller the size the faster the heartbeat. A normal resting heart rate for humans is about 60-80 beats per minute (bpm). Women's hearts beat 6-8 times per minute faster than those of men. Children's hearts beat even more rapidly — as high as 130 bpm at birth. Animals larger than man have slower heart rates — an elephant has one of only 20 bpm. On the other hand, a shrew's heart beats 1,000 times per minute.

Most sports and activities require a combination of not only strength but also cardiovascular or aerobic conditioning. (Photo by David Coyle)

149

THE TRAINING EFFECT

Like other muscle tissue, the heart will hypertrophy with training (Wilmore 1982). Specifically, its ventricular wall becomes thicker from anaerobic training (e.g., strength training) and its ventricular cavity becomes larger from aerobic training (Fox and Mathews 1981). This permits the heart to accept more blood and expel it more powerfully. As the heart becomes a better conditioned muscle, its ability to circulate blood also improves. In particular, the amount of blood pumped by the heart during each beat increases. As noted previously, the resting heart rate decreases as a direct result of aerobic conditioning. A slower heart rate coupled with the ejection of a larger volume of blood per beat indicates an efficient circulatory system. This is because the heart won't beat as often for a given cardiac output.

Because of this training effect, athletes usually have a lower resting heart rate than sedentary individuals; in fact, some highly conditioned athletes have resting heart rates of less than 40 bpm (Fox and Mathews 1981). A lower resting heart rate may be especially important if the heart is limited to a certain number of beats over the course of a lifetime. For example, suppose that the human heart is confined to about 2.5 million beats before it simply wears out from the labors of continual usage. In this scenario, a person with an average resting heart rate of 60 bpm could expect to live a little more than 79 years; on the other hand, a person with an average resting heart rate of 70 bpm could expect to live a little less than 68 years. If this concept were true, a decrease in the resting heart rate of just 10 bpm would translate into more than 11 additional years of life. While this notion is intriguing, it has yet to have been proven scientifically. Nevertheless, it does generate the possibility of added importance in having a lower resting heart rate.

AEROBIC GUIDELINES

Most sedentary individuals can safely begin an exercise program of moderate intensity. However, the American College of Sports Medicine (ACSM) recommends that males at or above the age of 40 and females at or above the age of 50 receive a medical examination before beginning a vigorous exercise program. Once approval is received, cardiovascular fitness may be developed and improved by using several easy-to-follow guidelines. These guidelines have been developed by the ACSM (1990) based upon the existing scientific evidence concerning exercise prescription for healthy adults and can be organized under the acronym FITT, which stands for Frequency, Intensity, Time and Type.

Frequency

In order to improve aerobic fitness, most authorities suggest that a selected activity should be performed 3-5 days per week. Exercising less than two days per week does not appear adequate enough to promote any meaningful changes in aerobic capacity (Pollock 1973; Gettman et al. 1976; Wenger and Bell 1986). The amount of aerobic improvement from exercising more than five days per week is neg-

The heart rate is commonly used as an estimate of aerobic intensity.

ligible (Pollock 1973; Hickson et al. 1982). However, training more frequently is beneficial when weight reduction is a goal. Beginning with too much exercise too soon may very well lead to an overuse injury.

Intensity

It was noted in Chapter 6 that the level of intensity (or effort) is the most critical factor — other than genetics — in determining the response from strength training. The most important component of a cardiovascular conditioning program is also the level of intensity (McArdle, Katch and Katch 1986).

The heart rate increases in direct proportion to the intensity of the exercise. As such, the heart rate is commonly used as an estimate of aerobic intensity (Pollock and Wilmore 1990). The ACSM (1990) suggests that a level of 60-90 percent of the age-predicted maximum heart rate must be maintained to receive a desirable training effect. (Previously, the ACSM recommended exercising at 70-85 percent of the age-predicted maximum heart rate. In 1990, the ACSM expanded their guideline presumably to encompass extremes in the population — the poorly conditioned and the highly conditioned.) Because of potential health risks and possible compliance problems, the ACSM (1991) recommends activity of low to moderate intensity of longer duration for the nonathletic adult in the early stages of a conditioning program.

Since there is a slight but steady decrease in the maximal heart rate with aging, estimates of the maximal heart rate are made on the basis of age. To find a rough estimate of the age-predicted maximum heart rate, simply subtract the age from 220 (Stromme and Skard 1980; Wilmore 1982; Bryant and Peterson 1992; Riley 1992; Skinner 1992). For example, the age-predicted maximum heart rate of a 30-year-old individual is 190 bpm [220 - 30 = 190]. To find the recommended heart rate training zone, multiply 190 bpm by .60 and .90. This means that a 30-year-old individual needs to maintain an exercise heart rate between about 114-171 bpm to elicit an aerobic conditioning effect [190 bpm x .60 = 114 bpm; 190 bpm x .90 = 171 bpm]. Individuals having a relatively low level of fitness should exercise closer to 60 percent of their age-predicted maximum or perhaps slightly lower; those with above-average fitness levels will need to exercise at higher heart rates to receive a sufficient workload.

In the case of maximal heart rate, it should be noted that the equation "220 minus age" has a standard deviation of about 11 bpm (Londeree and Moeschberger 1982). Considering all 30-year-old individuals, this means that about 68.26 percent of them will have maximal heart rates between 179-201 bpm, 95.44 percent between 168-212 bpm and 99.73 percent between 157-223 bpm.

The heart rate can be easily measured at several different sites on the body. There are numerous heart rate monitors that are available commercially that will give a reasonably accurate reading of the heart rate. However, the easiest and least expensive way is for people to measure their own heart rate. This can be done by locating the pulse at either the carotid artery (in the neck) or the radial artery (in the wrist). Simply place the tips of the index and middle fingers over one of these sites. (During intense exercise, the carotid and the radial arteries will be easy to find.) Counting the pulse for 10 (or 15) seconds immediately after a conditioning session and multiplying that number by 6 (or 4) gives a good estimate of the exercise heart rate for one minute.

Time

The ACSM (1990) recommends that a person should exercise continuously for 20-60 minutes in order to receive an aerobic training response. A review of the literature by the ACSM (1990) suggests that an aerobic training effect may be obtained by exercising for a duration of as little as 10-15 minutes. However, exercising for such a short period of time won't use up many calories. Since the duration of the activity is dependent on the intensity of the activity, such a brief workout would also have to be extremely intense. If weight loss is a priority, it is suggested that aerobic-type activities be performed for 30-60 minutes. Recall that the ACSM (1990) recommends activity of low to moderate intensity of longer duration for the nonathletic adult in the early stages of a conditioning program. Activities involving a lower intensity should be conducted over a longer period of time.

Type

If the frequency, the intensity and the duration of the cardiovascular conditioning program are similar (i.e., in terms of total caloric expenditure), training adaptations appear to be independent of the mode of aerobic activity (Pollock et al. 1975; Lieber, Lieber and Adams 1989). Therefore a variety of endurance activities may be used to obtain an aerobic conditioning effect.

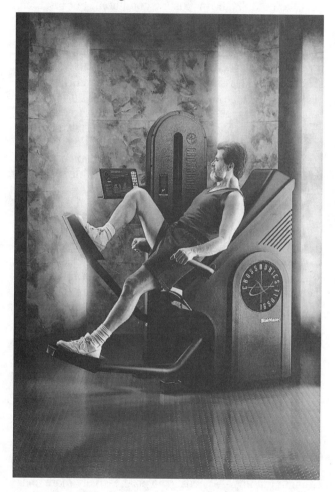

A variety of endurance activities may be used to obtain an aerobic conditioning effect. (Photo by StairMaster Sports/ Medical Products, Inc.)

The preferred types of aerobic activities are those that require a continuous effort, are rhythmic in nature and involve large amounts of muscle mass. Traditional outdoor aerobic activities that can be used to meet these criteria include hiking, walking, jogging, running, cycling, cross country skiing, roller/in-line skating and rowing; popular indoor activities are aerobic dancing, swimming, ice skating, rope jumping and stationary exercises on specialized equipment such as rowers, cycles (upright or recumbent), steppers/stairclimbers and motorized treadmills.

Each aerobic modality has its strong and weak points. An activity like swimming is desirable because it's non-weightbearing — there's no stress on the body's joint structures. On the other hand, swimming requires a certain degree of proficiency. The exercising heart rate of individuals with poor swimming skills may exceed their recommended training zone in a struggle just to stay afloat. Therefore, swimming would not be a good aerobic choice for anyone with poor swimming fundamentals. However, swimming is an excellent choice when skills are adequate.

In addition, some activities are not prudent for certain individuals who may be prone to injury or those who are likely to complicate an existing condition. For instance, rope jumping is a high impact activity associated with significantly more debilitating injuries than low impact and non-weightbearing activities. As such, rope jumping would not be recommended for overweight individuals because of the excessive stress on the ankles, the knees and the lower back. Likewise, a woman who jumps rope during pregnancy may endanger the fetus. Furthermore, someone with chronic low back pain would be more comfortable cycling in a recumbent position instead of in the traditional upright position to decrease the stress on the lumbar spine. So, the best advice is for individuals to select suitable activities that are enjoyable, compatible with their skill levels and orthopedically safe.

To avoid boredom, it's important to change modalities from time to time. Fortunately, aerobic training permits a large amount of variety in terms of exercise selection. As long as it's appropriate, the modality chosen to strengthen the heart is not as critical as the intensity and the duration of the activity. The heart doesn't know if a recumbent bike was used one day and a stairclimber the next.

MEANINGFUL EXERCISE

Throughout the course of an aerobic conditioning program, the heart will gradually adapt to the demands placed on it. Over a period of time, a person will find that the same workout — which was originally difficult — can be performed at a lower exercising heart rate. Also, the ability to maintain a higher training heart rate will become easier. As such, it's important to note that aerobic training — like strength training — needs to be progressively more challenging in order for a person to make further improvements. For this reason, it's meaningful to keep accurate records of conditioning workouts in order to monitor the key program components — such as the duration of the workouts, the frequency of the training and the intensity levels (i.e., the exercise heart rate).

In a nutshell, a person must train 3-5 times per week [frequency] at 60-90 percent of the age-predicted maximum heart rate [intensity] for 20-60 consecutive minutes [time] using appropriate activities that require a sustained effort [type]. Remember, all of these guidelines must be included in a program in order to strengthen the heart and improve aerobic conditioning.

SCHEDULING TRAINING SESSIONS

Essentially, there are two options for scheduling strength training and aerobic conditioning sessions: Both sessions can be performed on the same day or the sessions can be performed on alternate days. The advantage of doing both activities on the same day is that it permits a more complete recovery. If strength training is performed on one day and conditioning the next, the muscles will be constantly stressed and the body may not have adequate time to recover properly. After a while, it may also be very difficult for someone to perform intensive training sessions several days in a row without a break with a high degree of enthusiasm. Therefore, the recommended way of scheduling strength training and conditioning sessions is to do both activities on the same day (Westcott 1986). However, the activities may be done on alternating days if enough time is not available to perform both activities on the same day.

SEQUENCE OF ACTIVITIES

If skill work, conditioning and strength training are performed on the same day, better results will be obtained if the skill work is done first. Of all three activities, the one that is most important to a sport is skill development. If individuals are exhausted after conditioning and strength training, they'll be drained both physically and mentally. Therefore, they won't practice very hard or work on their technique very well. In fact, they're sure to be inattentive and their performance will probably be quite careless, labored and awkward. This is supported by Barnett and her associates (1973) who reported that practicing under nonfatigued conditions was more effective than practicing under fatigued conditions. Furthermore, an individual is more prone to injury when practicing in a pre-fatigued state. Because of this, it's best not to practice athletic skills after intense strength training and/or conditioning activities.

Whether strength training or conditioning follows skill training depends upon the nature of the sport. If a sport or activity has a greater strength component (e.g., shot putting and high jumping), then the strength training workout should come before the conditioning workout. On the other hand, if a sport or activity has a greater endurance component (e.g., basketball and soccer), then the conditioning workout should precede the strength workout.

Research by Westcott (1986) also indicates that better overall results are obtained when aerobic conditioning activities are performed before strength training activities. In his study, the subjects performed a strength training workout, rested for 5 minutes and then cycled for 20 minutes of aerobic activity. During a subsequent session, the same subjects cycled for 20 minutes of aerobic activity, rested for 5 minutes and then performed a strength training workout. Performing the strength training workout before the conditioning workout resulted in a 1 percent improvement in strength performance compared to performing the strength training workout after the conditioning workout; performing the conditioning workout before the strength training workout resulted in an 8 percent improvement in conditioning performance compared to performing the conditioning workout after the strength training workout. The study also suggested that strength training has a greater impact on aerobic conditioning performance than aerobic conditioning has on strength performance.

PREDICTING OXYGEN UPTAKE

Oxygen uptake — or how much oxygen is consumed — is a very reliable indicator of a person's level of cardiovascular conditioning. There are a number of ways to accurately measure oxygen uptake in a laboratory. One way is to step up and down from a bench of a standard height at a fixed rate of stepping. Another way is to pedal a bicycle ergometer in an upright or a recumbent position using the legs and/or the arms. Perhaps the most widely used laboratory device is the motor-driven treadmill. Each of these devices makes it possible for an individual to exercise at different levels of intensity while maintaining the body in a relatively stable position. This allows a person to be instrumented to measure various physiological responses. For example, expired air can be collected to determine the exact amount of oxygen being consumed as well as the response of the heart rate, the blood pressure and the body temperature.

Laboratory testing is an excellent means of providing accurate and valid data. However, such tests can be expensive, time-consuming and impractical for the average person. A much more practical way of assessing oxygen uptake is to have a person run 1.5 miles as fast as possible on a level surface. (Ben-Ezra 1992; Bryant and Peterson 1992). This type of test can be given on an indoor track or an outdoor track. The results of a 1.5 mile run are an excellent predictor of oxygen uptake. (A 1.0 mile run is more appropriate for adolescents and the elderly.)

Table 12.1 lists predicted values of oxygen uptake for various running times between 8:00-15:55. These values are an absolute measure of how much oxygen was consumed in milliliters per kilogram of bodyweight per minute (or ml/kg•min). Table 12.2 shows norms for oxygen consumption in absolute terms based upon age and gender.

TIME	VALUE	TIME	VALUE	TIME	VALUE	TIME	VALUE
8:00	63.84	10:00	51.77	12:00	43.73	14:00	37.98
8:05	63.22	10:05	51.37	12:05	43.45	14:05	37.77
8:10	62.61	10:10	50.98	12:10	43.17	14:10	37.57
8:15	62.01	10:15	50.59	12:15	42.90	14:15	37.37
8:20	61.42	10:20	50.21	12:20	42.64	14:20	37.18
8:25	60.85	10:25	49.84	12:25	42.38	14:25	36.98
8:30	60.29	10:30	49.47	12:30	42.12	14:30	36.79
8:35	59.74	10:35	49.11	12:35	41.86	14:35	36.60
8:40	59.20	10:40	48.75	12:40	41.61	14:40	36.41
8:45	58.67	10:45	48.40	12:45	41.36	14:45	36.23
8:50	58.15	10:50	48.06	12:50	41.11	14:50	36.04
8:55	57.63	10:55	47.72	12:55	40.87	14:55	35.86
9:00	57.13	11:00	47.38	13:00	40.63	15:00	35.68
9:05	56.64	11:05	47.05	13:05	40.39	15:05	35.50
9:10	56.16	11:10	46.73	13:10	40.16	15:10	35.33
9:15	55.68	11:15	46.41	13:15	39.93	15:15	35.15
9:20	55.21	11:20	46.09	13:20	39.70	15:20	34.98
9:25	54.76	11:25	45.78	13:25	39.48	15:25	34.81
9:30	54.31	11:30	45.47	13:30	39.26	15:30	34.64
9:35	53.87	11:35	45.17	13:35	39.04	15:35	34.48
9:40	53.43	11:40	44.87	13:40	38.82	15:40	34.31
9:45	53.01	11:45	44.58	13:45	38.61	15:45	34.15
9:50	52.59	11:50	44.29	13:50	38.39	15:50	33.99
9:55	52.18	11:55	44.01	13:55	38.19	15:55	33.83

Table 12.1: Predicted values of oxygen uptake based upon the time to complete a 1.5 mile run

WOMEN					
Age	**Low**	**Fair**	**Average**	**Good**	**High**
20-29	<28	29-34	35-43	44-48	49+
30-39	<27	28-33	34-41	42-47	48+
40-49	<25	26-31	32-40	41-45	46+
50-65	<21	22-28	29-36	37-41	42+

MEN					
Age	**Low**	**Fair**	**Average**	**Good**	**High**
20-29	<38	39-43	44-51	52-56	57+
30-39	<34	35-39	40-47	48-51	52+
40-49	<30	31-35	36-43	44-47	48+
50-59	<25	26-31	32-39	40-43	44+
60-69	<21	22-26	27-35	36-39	40+

Table 12.2: Norms for oxygen uptake in absolute terms (from Astrand 1960)

WOMEN					
Age	**Low**	**Fair**	**Average**	**Good**	**High**
20-29	<1.69	1.70-1.99	2.00-2.49	2.50-2.79	2.80+
30-39	<1.59	1.60-1.89	1.90-2.39	2.40-2.69	2.70+
40-49	<1.49	1.50-1.79	1.80-2.29	2.30-2.59	2.60+
50-65	<1.29	1.30-1.59	1.60-2.09	2.10-2.39	2.40+

MEN					
Age	**Low**	**Fair**	**Average**	**Good**	**High**
20-29	<2.79	2.80-3.09	3.10-3.69	3.70-3.99	4.00+
30-39	<2.49	2.50-2.79	2.80-3.39	3.40-3.69	3.70+
40-49	<2.19	2.20-2.49	2.50-3.09	3.10-3.39	3.40+
50-59	<1.89	1.90-2.19	2.20-2.79	2.80-3.09	3.10+
60-69	<1.59	1.60-1.89	1.90-2.49	2.50-2.79	2.80+

Table 12.3: Norms for oxygen uptake in relative terms

Finally, Table 12.3 lists norms for oxygen consumption in relative terms based upon age, gender and bodyweight.

Oxygen Consumption: Absolute

Let's suppose that a 30-year-old man weighs 198 pounds and can run 1.5 miles in 12:30. Note in Table 12.1 that his oxygen uptake for this particular running time is 42.12 ml/kg•min — or simply 42.12. In other words, he consumed about 42.12 milliliters of oxygen for every kilogram that he weighed during each minute of his 1.5 mile run. Referring to Table 12.2 (under 30-39-year-old males), note that this value [42.12] falls between the range of 40-47. This indicates that his level of aerobic fitness would be considered average.

Table 12.1 is only valid for determining oxygen uptake during a 1.5 mile run. The ACSM offers this formula for determining oxygen uptake in ml/kg•min for a run of any known distance and duration:

$$\text{oxygen uptake} = (\text{speed in m/min}) \times (.2 \text{ ml/kg•min per m/min}) + 3.5 \text{ ml/kg•min}$$

As an example, suppose a woman just completed a 5,000-meter race in 20:00. In this case, her running speed was 250 meters per minute [5,000 meters divided by 20 minutes]. Next, multiply her speed [250 m/min] by the oxygen cost of horizontal running [.2 ml/kg•min per m/min] and add the oxygen cost at rest [3.5 ml/kg•min]. This calculation yields a value of 53.5 ml/kg•min [250 m/min x .2 ml/kg•min per m/min + 3.5 ml/kg•min = 53.5 ml/kg•min]. For this formula to be accurate, a person must run at a speed of at least 5 miles per hour (mph) — or 134 m/min — and it must be on a level surface.

A similar formula is used to determine oxygen uptake for walking speeds between 1.9-3.7 mph. At lower speeds, walking is generally a more efficient process than running. In fact, the oxygen cost of horizontal walking at a given speed is about one-half that for running. Therefore, the only difference in the previously mentioned formula is that the walking speed is multiplied by .1 ml/kg•min per m/min (the oxygen cost of horizontal walking) and then added to 3.5 ml/kg•min (the oxygen cost at rest).

Oxygen Consumption: Relative

Oxygen uptake can also be expressed in relative terms in liters per minute (or L/min). Determining oxygen uptake in relative terms is usually a better indicator of aerobic fitness because the value takes into account differences in bodyweight. For instance, if two people ran the same distance in the same time, they would consume the same amount of oxygen per unit of bodyweight in absolute terms. In relative terms, however, a larger individual would actually consume more oxygen than a smaller individual because a greater body mass was displaced over a given distance.

To determine oxygen uptake in L/min, the person's bodyweight must first be converted to kilograms. To do this, divide the bodyweight (in pounds) by 2.2. Using the earlier example of the 30-year-old male, 198 pounds is equal to 90 kilograms [198 divided by 2.2 = 90]. Next, multiply his bodyweight (in kilograms) by his oxygen uptake (in ml/kg•min) and divide by 1,000 (to convert to liters). Staying with the same example as before, his bodyweight [90 kg] multiplied by his oxygen uptake [42.12 ml/kg•min] is 3,790.8 ml/min. To divide by 1,000, simply move the decimal point three places to the left. This means that a 198-pound individual who ran 1.5 miles in 12:30 would consume about 3.79 liters of oxygen during every minute of his run. Referring to Table 12.3 (again under 30-39-year-old males), you'll find that this value [3.79 L/min] is considered to be an excellent level of fitness for males of his age relative to his bodyweight. Recall that when his bodyweight wasn't considered, his level of aerobic fitness was considered "average." As such, oxygen uptake gives a truer indication of fitness levels when it is expressed relative to bodyweight in L/min.

Oxygen Consumption Expectations

According to the ACSM (1991), the following regression equations can be used to predict the expected oxygen uptake of an individual based upon activity level, age and gender:

Active men:	69.7 - (.612 x age)
Active women:	42.9 - (.312 x age)
Sedentary men:	57.8 - (.445 x age)
Sedentary women:	42.3 - (.356 x age)

For example, a sedentary 40-year-old woman would be expected to have an oxygen uptake of about 28.06 ml/kg•min [42.3 minus the value of .356 x 40]. Comparing the expected oxygen uptake to the actual oxygen uptake is helpful in determining whether a person has any Functional Aerobic Impairment (FAI). The FAI may be found by subtracting the actual oxygen uptake from the expected oxygen uptake. This value is divided by the expected oxygen uptake and then multiplied by 100 (to convert to a percentage). If the 40-year-old woman in this example was found to have an actual oxygen uptake of 22.45 ml/kg•min, she would have an FAI of about 20 percent [the expected oxygen uptake of 28.06 ml/kg•min minus the actual oxygen uptake of 22.45ml/kg•min divided by the expected oxygen uptake of 28.06 ml/kg•min times 100 equals 19.99 percent]. A negative percentage indicates that the person's actual oxygen uptake is better than expected. It should be noted that heredity plays an important role in determining a person's level of aerobic fitness (Klissouras 1971).

ESTIMATING CALORIC EXPENDITURE

The caloric equivalent of one liter of oxygen ranges from 4.7 calories when fats are used as the sole source of energy to 5.0 calories when carbohydrates are used as the only source of energy. (The caloric equivalent of one liter of oxygen is 4.4 calories when proteins are used as the single source of energy. Under most circumstances, however,

Exercising at a high level of intensity results in a greater total caloric expenditure than exercising at a low level of intensity and also uses a greater number of calories from fat.

protein utilization during exercise is negligible in terms of energy production and is usually disregarded.) For all practical purposes — with little loss in precision — a person uses about 5 calories for every liter of oxygen that is consumed (Howley and Franks 1992). To determine the rate of caloric expenditure, simply take the oxygen uptake value in L/min and multiply it by 5 calories per liter (cal/L). Recall the earlier example of the 198-pound male whose oxygen uptake was 3.79 L/min. In this case, his rate of caloric expenditure would be almost 19 calories per minute [3.79 L/min x 5 cal/L = 18.95 cal/min].

To determine the total number of calories that were used during the run, multiply the rate of caloric expenditure (in cal/min) by the running time. In this case, multiplying 18.95 cal/min by 12.5 minutes (12:30 in decimal form) indicates that he used about 237 calories during his run [18.95 cal/min x 12.5 min = 237 calories].

EXERCISE: HIGH INTENSITY VERSUS LOW INTENSITY

A greater percentage of carbohydrates are used as an energy source during exercise of higher intensity. Conversely, a greater percentage of fats are used as an energy source during exercise of lower intensity. (Carbohydrates are a more efficient source of energy. However, fats are used as an energy source because the body doesn't need to be efficient at lower levels of intensity.) These physiological facts have led to the mistaken belief that "fat-burning" (or low intensity) exercise is better than "carbohydrate-burn-

ing" (or high intensity) exercise when it comes to losing weight, "burning" fat and expending calories. This misconception continues to be endorsed by many fitness professionals — particularly aerobic instructors.

According to Porcari (1994), the concept of keeping the exercise intensity low in order to mobilize and selectively utilize a higher percentage of fat may sound logical, but it doesn't hold up mathematically and has never been verified in the laboratory. In truth, even though the percentage of calories used from fats are greater during low intensity exercise, the total number of calories expended during high intensity exercise is greater (Bryant, Peterson and Hagen 1994).

During any activity, the rate of caloric expenditure is directly related to the intensity of effort — the higher the intensity, the greater the rate of caloric expenditure. In the case of running, for example, the intensity is directly associated with the speed — the faster the running speed, the greater the rate of caloric utilization. The time of activity is also a factor — the longer that a person performs a given activity, the greater the total caloric expenditure.

Based upon the ACSM formulas for determining oxygen uptake and caloric expenditure during walking and running, a 165-pound man who walks 3 miles in 60 minutes will utilize roughly 4.33 cal/min. Over the course of his 60-minute walk, his total caloric usage would be about 260 calories. If that same individual ran those 3 miles in 30 minutes, he would use about 13.38 cal/min. (Note the higher rate of caloric utilization.) In this case, he would have expended about 401 total calories during his 30-minute run. So, exercising at a higher level of intensity used up significantly more calories than exercising at a lower level of intensity [401 calories compared to 260 calories]. This is true despite the fact that the activity of lower intensity was performed for twice as long as the activity of higher intensity.

These calculations have been corroborated by research performed in the laboratory. Porcari (1994) notes a study in which a group of subjects walked on a treadmill at an average speed of 3.8 mph for 30 minutes. In this instance, the subjects used about 8 cal/min for a total caloric expenditure of 240 calories. Of these 240 calories, 59 percent [144 calories] were from carbohydrates and 41 percent [96 calories] were from fats. As part of the study, the same group also ran on a treadmill at an average speed of 6.5 mph for 30 minutes. At this relatively higher level of intensity, the subjects used about 15 cal/min for a total caloric expenditure of 450 calories. Of these 450 calories, 76 percent [342 calories] were from carbohydrates and 24 percent [108 calories] were from fats. In other words, exercising at a higher level of intensity resulted in a greater total caloric expenditure than exercising at a lower level of intensity [450 calories versus 240 calories] and also used a greater number of calories from fats in the same length of time [108 calories compared to 96 calories]. Additional

studies have also demonstrated that more calories are expended when running a given distance than walking the same distance (Howley and Glover 1974; Fellingham et al. 1978).

The intent behind advocating low intensity exercise of long duration is to enhance safety and improve compliance in the nonathletic population. However, low intensity exercise is not more effective for fat loss than high intensity exercise (Bryant, Peterson and Hagen 1994; Porcari 1994). In order to lose weight, more calories must be expended than consumed to produce a "negative caloric balance" or a caloric deficit. Whether carbohydrates or fats are used to produce this negative balance is immaterial. A caloric deficit created by the selective use of fat as an energy source doesn't necessarily translate into greater fat loss compared to an equal caloric deficit created by the use of carbohydrate as an energy source.

In short, researchers who perform studies and review the scientific literature in the area of exercise and weight control generally agree that it probably doesn't matter whether you use fats or carbohydrates while exercising in order to lose weight. (Chapter 13 discusses the subject of weight loss in greater detail.) Finally, it should also be noted that low intensity exercise usually doesn't elevate the heart rate enough in healthy adults to produce an aerobic conditioning effect.

13
RECIPE FOR SUCCESS: NUTRITIONAL FACTS AND FICTION

Nutrition is the process by which food is selected, consumed, digested, absorbed and utilized by the body. Unfortunately, this aspect of total fitness is often overlooked and seldom addressed. A person's nutritional habits are a factor in the development of muscular size and strength. Proper nutrition also plays a critical role in a person's capacity to perform at optimal levels and to expedite recovery for future performances. Truly, the ability to fully recuperate after an exhaustive activity directly effects future performance and subsequent intensity in strength training, conditioning activities and skill development.

Nutritional "skills" can be improved by understanding the desirable food sources, the recommended intakes of those food sources and the physiological contributions of the various nutrients. It's also meaningful to examine caloric "needs" along with the principles and procedures for weight management (i.e., gaining or losing weight). A knowledge of what foods to eat before and after vigorous activity is helpful in maximizing performance. Finally, it's important to examine nutritional quackery and fraudulent claims along with the potential dangers of excessive nutritional supplementation.

THE NUTRIENTS

Everything that people do requires energy. Energy is measured in calories and is obtained through the foods — or nutrients — that are eaten. Essentially, the foods that are consumed serve as a fuel for the body. Food is also necessary for the growth, maintenance and repair of the body tissue (such as muscle and bone).

Foods are composed of six nutrients: carbohydrates, proteins, fats, water, vitamins and minerals. These six main constituents of food are divided into the macronutrients and the micronutrients. In order to be considered "nutritious," a person's food intake must contain the recommended percentages of the macronutrients as well as appropriate levels of the micronutrients. No single foodstuff satisfies this requirement. As such, variety is the key to a well-balanced diet.

The Macronutrients

As the name implies, macronutrients are needed in relatively large amounts. Three macronutrients — carbohy-

drates, proteins and fats — provide a person with a supply of energy. Although it has no calories, water is also considered a macronutrient because it is needed in considerable quantities.

Carbohydrates. The primary job of carbohydrates — or "carbs" — is to supply energy, especially during intense exercise. The body breaks down carbohydrates into glucose. Glucose can be used as immediate energy during exercise or stored as glycogen in the liver and the muscles for future use. Highly conditioned muscles can stockpile more glycogen than poorly conditioned muscles. When glycogen stores are depleted, a person feels overwhelmingly exhausted. For this reason, greater glycogen stores provide an individual with a physiological advantage. Therefore, the diet should be carbohydrate-based. In fact,

A person's nutritional habits are a factor in the development of muscular size and strength. (Photo by Rick Phelps)

at least 65 percent of the food intake should be in the form of carbohydrates.

Carbohydrates are found in sugars (such as table sugar and honey), starches (like the starch in bread) and fibers. Carbohydrate-rich foods include potatoes, cereals, pancakes, breads, spaghetti, macaroni, rice, grains, fruits and vegetables.

Proteins. Protein is necessary for the repair, maintenance and growth of biological tissue — particularly muscle tissue. In addition, protein regulates water balance and transports other nutrients. Protein can also be used as an energy source in the event that adequate carbohydrates aren't available. Good sources of protein are beef, pork, fish, chicken, eggs, liver, dried beans and dairy products.

When proteins are ingested as foods, they are broken down into their basic "building blocks": amino acids. Of the 22 known amino acids, the body can manufacture 13 of them. The other 9, however, must be provided in the diet and are termed "essential amino acids" (Guthrie 1983; Sargent 1988; Clark 1990). When a food contains all of the essential amino acids, it is called a "complete protein." All animal proteins — with the exception of gelatin — are complete proteins. The protein found in vegetables and other sources is "incomplete protein" because it doesn't include all of the essential amino acids. Approximately 15 percent of the food intake should be protein (Sargent 1988; Clark 1990).

Fats. It's hard to believe, but fats are essential to a balanced diet. First of all, fats serve as a major source of energy during activities of low intensity such as sleeping, reading and walking. This nutrient also helps in the transportation and the absorption of certain vitamins. Lastly, fats add considerable flavor to foods. This makes food more appetizing — and also explains why fats are craved so much.

Foods high in fat are butter, cheese, margarine, meat, nuts, milk products and cooking oils. Animal fats (such as butter, lard and the fat in meats) are usually termed "saturated" and contribute to heart disease; vegetable fats (such as corn oil and peanut oil) are generally "unsaturated" and less harmful.

There's really no need to add extra "fatty" food to the diet in order to get adequate fat. The fact is that most people consume far too much fat. Fats often accompany carbohydrate and protein choices. In addition, foods are frequently prepared in such a way that fat is never difficult to obtain. For example, a potato is generally an excellent source of carbohydrates. However, preparing a potato as french fries increases the number of fat calories much more than preparing it baked. At most, 20 percent of the diet should be composed of fats. Unfortunately, the quantity of fat consumed by the average American typically exceeds this level — sometimes by twice the recommendation.

Finally, it should be noted that carbohydrates and proteins are converted into fat if not utilized by the body. Any fats that aren't used as energy are also stored as fats.

Water. Although water doesn't have any calories or provide energy, it is sometimes classified as a macronutrient because it is needed in rather large quantities. In fact, almost two thirds of a person's bodyweight is water. Water lubricates the joints and regulates the body temperature. Water also carries nutrients to the cells and waste products away from the cells.

The best sources of water are milk, fruit juices and, of course, water. About 16 ounces of water should be consumed for every pound of weight that is lost during exercise (Lowenthal and Karni 1990; Simmons 1994).

The Micronutrients

Vitamins and minerals are classified as micronutrients because they are needed in rather small amounts. Neither of these nutrients supplies any calories or energy. However, vitamins and minerals have many other important functions.

Vitamins. The term "vitamine" was coined by the Polish chemist Casimir Funk in 1912. Vitamins are potent compounds that are required in very small quantities. As noted, these substances are not a source of energy but perform many different roles. For instance, vitamin A helps maintain vision at night, vitamin C is necessary for wounds to heal, vitamin D is vital for strong bones and teeth, vitamin E protects and maintains cellular membranes and vitamin K is essential for blood clotting. Vitamins occur in a wide variety of foods, especially in fruits and vegetables. An adequate vitamin intake can be obtained from a balanced diet that contains a variety of foods.

Vitamins can be classified as either fat-soluble or water-soluble. The four fat-soluble vitamins — vitamins A, D, E and K — require proper amounts of fat to be present before transportation and absorption can take place. Excessive amounts of fat-soluble vitamins are stored in the body. The eight B vitamins (thiamine, riboflavin, niacin, pantothenic acid, pyridoxine, cobalamin, biotin and folic acid) and vitamin C are considered water-soluble vitamins because they are found in foods that have a naturally high content of water. There is minimal storage of water-soluble vitamins in the body — excess amounts are generally excreted in the urine.

Minerals. Minerals are found in tiny amounts in foods. Like vitamins, nearly all the minerals that are needed can be obtained with an ordinary intake of foods. Calcium, phosphorus, magnesium, potassium, iron and zinc are among the 21 essential minerals that must be provided by the intake of food. Minerals have many functions, such as building strong bones and teeth, helping the muscles work and even enabling the heart to beat.

DAILY SERVINGS

Indulging in a variety of foods ensures that a person obtains a sufficient amount of each type of food with a healthy quantity of essential vitamins and minerals. According to the U. S. Department of Agriculture, a variety of daily foods would include choices from these food groups: 6-11 servings from the Bread, Cereal, Rice and Pasta Group; 3-5 servings from the Vegetable Group; 2-4 servings from the Fruit Group; 2-3 servings from the Milk, Yogurt and Cheese Group; 2-3 servings from the Meat, Poultry, Fish, Dry Beans, Eggs and Nuts Group; and a conservative amount from the Fats, Oils and Sweets Group (Saltos 1993).

CALORIC CONTRIBUTIONS

It's necessary to understand that carbohydrates, proteins and fats provide different amounts of calories. Carbohydrates and proteins yield 4 calories per gram (cal/g). Fats are the most concentrated form of energy, containing 9 cal/g. (Alcohol provides 7 cal/g.) From this information, a person can determine the caloric contributions of each macronutrient in any food.

For example, suppose a nutrition label notes that a certain food has 144 calories per serving and that each serving has 16 grams of carbohydrate, 2 grams of protein and 8 grams of fat. To find the number of calories that are supplied by each macronutrient, simply multiply the quantity of grams per serving by the energy yield. This example is summarized in Table 13.1. Note that even though this food has twice as many grams of carbohydrates as fats, exactly 50 percent of the calories (72 of the 144 calories) are furnished by fats. Incidentally, this food is actually typical of a popular snack food — potato chips.

Knowing the different caloric contributions of the macronutrients is also helpful in understanding food labels

that may contain misleading information about fat content. A food label proclaiming a product as being "95 percent fat-free" means that it is 95 percent fat-free by weight . . . not by calories. Placing 5 grams of fat into 95 grams of water forms a product that, by weight, is 95 percent fat-free. Since water has no calories, however, this particular "95 percent fat-free" product would actually be 100 percent fat in terms of calories.

ESTIMATING CALORIC NEEDS

An individual's need for calories — or energy — is determined by several factors including age, gender, body condition, body composition, metabolic rate and activity level. Caloric needs can be determined precisely by both direct and indirect calorimetry. However, these methods can be costly and impractical for most people. For a quick, reasonably accurate estimate of daily energy needs, the U. S. Department of Agriculture suggests multiplying a person's bodyweight in pounds by a factor that is determined by the level of activity (Guthrie 1983). For females, the value is 14 if the woman is sedentary, 18 if she is moderately active and 22 if she is very active; for males, the factors are 16, 21 and 26 respectively. As an example, a 200-pound male who is very active requires about 5,200 calories per day (cal/day) to meet his energy needs [200 pounds x 26 calories/pound = 5,200 calories].

Once the caloric need is estimated, the next step is to determine how many of these calories should come from carbohydrates, proteins and fats. Table 13.2 shows a range of daily caloric consumptions from 1,400 to 6,000 calories per day in 200 calorie increments. The recommended intake of grams and calories for each of the three energy-providing nutrients are also listed. Simply locate the number of calories needed per day in the far left-hand column and then read across that line to find the suggested daily amount of each nutrient. Using the previous example, some-

MACRONUTRIENT	AMOUNT (g)	ENERGY YIELD (cals/g)	CALORIES
Carbohydrate	16	4	64
Protein	2	4	8
Fat	8	9	72

TOTAL CALORIES: | 144

Table 13.1: Example of caloric content based upon the energy yield of the macronutrients

one who requires about 5,200 cal/day should consume about 845 grams of carbohydrates [3,380 calories], 195 grams of proteins [780 calories] and 116 grams of fat [1,040 calories]. It should be noted that these numbers are based upon a diet that consists of 65 percent carbohydrates, 15 percent proteins and 20 percent fats.

WEIGHT MANAGEMENT

Gaining, losing or maintaining bodyweight is simply a matter of arithmetic. If more calories are consumed than expended, a "positive caloric balance" is produced and weight is gained; if more calories are expended than consumed, a "negative caloric balance" is produced and weight is lost; and lastly, if the same amount of calories are consumed as expended, a "caloric balance" is produced and the bodyweight doesn't change. However, a closer inspection of gaining and losing weight is necessary.

Gaining Weight

The potential to gain weight is determined by several factors, the most important of which is an individual's genetic make-up. A person whose ancestors have ectomorphic tendencies (i.e., slender builds, long limbs) will no doubt have a physique very similar to that as well. This doesn't mean that an ectomorphic person cannot gain weight. However, someone who has a high degree of ectomorphy will have a difficult time increasing bodyweight significantly.

The ultimate goal in gaining weight is to increase lean body mass. One pound of muscle has about 2,500 calories

(Fox and Mathews 1981; Lowenthal and Karni 1990; Wheeler and Cameron 1993). Therefore, if someone consumes 500 cal/day above the caloric needs (i.e., a 500-calorie "profit"), it will take 5 days to add one pound of lean, fat-free weight [2,500 calories divided by 500 cal/day equals 5 days]. So, if the previously mentioned 200-pound individual requires 5,200 cal/day to maintain his bodyweight, he must consume 5,700 cal/day (i.e., 500 calories above the need) to gain one pound of fat-free weight in 5 days. It should be noted that the daily caloric "profit" should not be more than about 1,000-1,500 calories above the normal daily caloric intake (Fox and Mathews 1981). If the weight gain is more than about two pounds per week, it's likely that some excess calories will be stored in the form of fat. However, if the weight gain is less than about two pounds per week and is the result of a demanding strength training program in conjunction with a well-balanced nutritional intake, then it will probably be in the form of muscle tissue.

Proper weight gain relies upon total nutritional dedication for 7 days a week. Additional calories must be consumed daily on a regular basis until the desired weight gain is achieved. The body absorbs food best when it is divided into several regular-sized meals intermingled with a few snacks. One or two large meals aren't absorbed by the body as well — most of these calories are simply jammed through the digestive system. In fact, if a large number of calories is consumed at one time, some calories will be diverted to fat deposits because of the sudden demand on the

The potential to gain weight is determined by several factors, the most important of which is an individual's genetic make-up. (Photo by Kathy Leistner)

Cal/day	CARBOHYDRATES 65%		PROTEINS 15%		FATS 20%	
	cal	g	cal	g	cal	g
1400	910	228	210	53	280	31
1600	1040	260	240	60	320	36
1800	1170	293	270	68	360	40
2000	1300	325	300	75	400	44
2200	1430	358	330	83	440	49
2400	1560	390	360	90	480	53
2600	1690	423	390	98	520	58
2800	1820	455	420	105	560	62
3000	1950	488	450	113	600	67
3200	2080	520	480	120	640	71
3400	2210	553	510	128	680	76
3600	2340	585	540	135	720	80
3800	2470	618	570	143	760	84
4000	2600	650	600	150	800	89
4200	2730	683	630	158	840	93
4400	2860	715	660	165	880	98
4600	2990	748	690	173	920	102
4800	3120	780	720	180	960	107
5000	3250	813	750	188	1000	111
5200	3380	845	780	195	1040	116
5400	3510	878	810	203	1080	120
5600	3640	910	840	210	1120	124
5800	3770	943	870	218	1160	129
6000	3900	975	900	225	1200	133

Table 13.2: Recommended intake of calories and grams for each each of the three energy-providing nutrients based upon daily caloric consumption

After intense exercise or competition, proper nutrition accelerates recovery and better prepares a person for the next bout of exercise.

metabolic pathways. This has been referred to as "nutrient overload."

Losing Weight

The need for weight loss should be determined by body composition rather than bodyweight — especially in the case of an athlete. In general, athletes are larger and more muscular than the rest of the population. For instance, suppose two people were 6 feet tall and weighed 220 pounds. Considering their height and weight without regard for their body composition may result in the conclusion that they're both overweight. However, what if one person had 20 percent body fat and the other had 10 percent body fat? If this were the case, then only one person needed to lose weight — the one with the higher percentage of body fat. As such, the need for weight loss should be based upon body composition. Body fat can be measured in a variety of ways, although using skinfold calipers is generally considered to be the most practical method of assessment. Normal body fats for athletes are lower than the average population, ranging from about 12-22 percent for females and 5-13 percent for males.

The primary goal of a weight loss program is to decrease body fat. One pound of fat has about 3,500 calories. As such, if someone expends 500 cal/day below the caloric needs (i.e., a 500-calorie "deficit"), it will take 7 days to lose one pound of fat [3,500 calories divided by 500 cal/day equals 7 days]. In this instance, if a 200-pound individual needs 5,200 cal/day to maintain bodyweight, 4,700

cal/day (i.e., 500 calories below the need) must be consumed to lose one pound of fat in 7 days. A caloric deficit can be achieved by reducing the caloric intake, increasing the energy expenditure (such as through additional aerobic activity) or a combination of the two. In fact, proper weight loss should be a blend of dieting and exercise. If the weight loss is more than about two pounds per week, it's likely that some of this weight reduction will be the result of lost muscle tissue and/or water.

Weight loss must be a carefully planned activity. Skipping meals — or all-out starvation — isn't a desirable procedure of weight loss, since fuel is still needed for an active lifestyle. Oddly enough, losing weight should be done in a fashion similar to gaining weight. Frequent — but smaller — meals spread out over the course of the day will suppress the appetite. Drinking plenty of water will create a feeling of fullness without providing any calories.

THE PRE-ACTIVITY MEAL

A meal consumed prior to a competition or an exercise session should accomplish several things, such as removing hunger pains, fueling the body for the upcoming activity and settling the person psychologically. No foods will lead directly to a great performance when consumed several hours before an activity. However, certain foods should be avoided prior to competition or exercise. For example, fats and meats are digested slowly. This means that the traditional steak dinner might actually be the worst possible meal to eat before a competition (Lowenthal and Karni

1990). Other foods to omit include those that are greasy, highly seasoned and flatulent (gas-forming), along with any specific foods that an individual may personally find distressful to the digestive system. If anything, the pre-activity meal choices should be almost bland, yet appetizing enough so that the person wants to eat it.

Consumption of large amounts of sugar or sweets — such as candy or soda — less than one hour before an activity or a competition should also be avoided (Clark 1990; Simmons 1994). Sugar consumption causes a sharp increase in the blood glucose levels. The body will respond to this by increasing its blood insulin levels to maintain a stable internal environment. As a result of this chemical balancing, the blood glucose is sharply reduced leading to hypoglycemia (low blood sugar), which decreases the availability of blood glucose as a fuel and causes a feeling of severe fatigue.

The best foods to consume prior to a competition or an exercise session are carbohydrates. Carbohydrates are easily digested and help maintain the blood glucose levels. Water is perhaps the best liquid to drink before competing or exercising. The amount of fluid intake should guarantee optimal hydration during the activity.

The timing of the pre-activity meal is also crucial. To ensure that the digestive process doesn't impair performance, the pre-activity meal should be eaten three hours or more before the activity. In short, the pre-activity meal should include foods that are familiar and well-tolerated — preferably carbohydrates.

RECOVERY FLUIDS/FOODS

After intense exercise or competition, proper nutrition accelerates recovery and better prepares a person for the next bout of exercise. To replenish the depleted glycogen stores and to expedite the recovery process, foods high in carbohydrates should be consumed as soon as possible following exhaustive exercise. Because appetite is suppressed immediately after exercise, it may be more practical to consume a high-carbohydrate beverage rather than solid food or a meal. (A cold beverage will also help cool off the body.) Several commercial exercise beverages are high in carbohydrates, but the label should be read to be sure of its content.

According to Clark (1990), a person should ingest 1/2 gram of carbohydrates per pound of bodyweight within two hours of completing an intense workout. This should be repeated again within the next two hours. For instance, a person weighing 200 pounds needs to consume about 100 grams of carbohydrates (or 400 carbohydrate calories) within two hours after exercising and another 100 grams of carbohydrates during the next two hours [1/2 g/lb x 200 lb = 100 g].

NUTRITIONAL QUACKERY AND FRAUD

The health and fitness industry — perhaps more than any other industry — has been raped and pillaged by hordes of unscrupulous enterprisers who are sometimes severely underqualified to dispense information and seek only to make a quick and easy profit on the naivete of others. Consumers are frequently tempted, teased and seduced by brilliant promises of "losing flab", "gaining muscle" and "getting fit". Because of this, many people give no second thought to spending huge sums of money on nutritional "supplements" that claim to improve overall health, physical appearance and athletic performance. Herbert (1990a) reports that each year, Americans spend more than 25 billion dollars on health quackery about half of which goes for health food pills, powders and potions.

"Snake Oil Salesmen"

Nutritional quackery and outright fraud are nothing new to consumers. During the 1800s, an early form of consumer ripoff flourished in rural America combining free amusement with the sale of "secret" goods supposedly having curative capabilities. These traveling "medicine shows" began innocently enough with complimentary entertainment given by various performers to an unsuspecting audience of people. Soon afterward, "snake oil salesmen" would peddle their magical elixirs and tonics in colored glass bottles as remedies for assorted ills, aches and pains to the gullible and all-to-eager masses using a spellbinding sales pitch. After this climactic appeal, the performers circulated throughout the crowd to sell the "doctor's" product. Quite often, the first bottle was bought by an accomplice who was planted among the spectators.

The cure-alls that were sold included common forms of liniment or laxative, bunion and corn remedies, liver pads, salves, hair growers, electric belts, powdered herbs and, of course, snake oil. The products had alluring names and a variety of purposes. For instance, Dr. Kilmer's Swamp-Root was touted as a "kidney, liver and bladder remedy"; Renne's Magic Oil was promoted for "pain killing"; Dr. McClintock's Dyspeptic Elixir was "effectual for combating dyspepsia" and also cured "heartburn, nervousness, indigestion and all other symptoms arising from want of tone in the stomach"; and McDonald's Cough Annihilator removed "the most fearful cold in a few hours."

Some of the best showmen of that era were actually women — Madame DuBois had a brass band, sold medicine and pulled teeth; Princess Lotus Blossom — a Minnesota farmgirl — sold Vital Sparks, which she described as a "rejuvenator for lost manhood."

The snake oil salesmen of today still target naive consumers with health products that pledge miracles. However, there are some notable distinctions between the two eras. For one thing, the promises of curing heartburn and annihilating coughs has shifted priorities — under the guise of nutritional supplementation — to that of melting fat and building muscle. The covered wagon and touring medicine show has been replaced by huge mail-order businesses and "nutrition" or "health food" stores. Further, the potential profits from this multi-billion dollar industry are far greater for today's charlatans than were for those of yesteryear.

Consumer Protection

Two of the federal government's regulatory arms that protect the public are the Food and Drug Administration (FDA) and the Federal Trade Commission (FTC). Both organizations have been safeguarding consumers since the early 1900s.

The birth of the FDA can be traced back to 1906. In that year, Congress enacted the Federal Food and Drugs Act which authorized the federal government to oversee the safety and quality of food. The responsibility for this act's enforcement was given to the U. S. Department of Agriculture and its Bureau of Chemistry — the forerunner of the FDA. In 1938, the Federal Food, Drug and Cosmetic Act replaced the 1906 Food and Drugs Act. This new act extended the range of commodities coming under federal control and increased penalties for violators. The law also prohibited statements in food labeling that are false or misleading.

The FTC was created by Congress on September 26, 1914. The primary duty of this agency is to protect the public against unfair methods of competition. The FTC is authorized to move against false advertising, mislabeling and misrepresentation of quality, guarantee and terms of sale.

The FTC in Action

In 1985, the FTC flexed its regulatory muscles against Weider Health and Fitness for two products claiming to create muscle: Dynamic Life Essence and Anabolic Mega-Pak. The company was accused of "engaging in deceptive acts and practices" and "disseminating false advertisements" (FTC 1985). In other words, what was claimed to be in the product wasn't really in there and what it was supposed to do didn't really result. Among the company's many untrue or exaggerated claims was that Mega-Pak had been developed by a team of the world's most renowned nutritional biochemists, exercise physiologists and trainers. To avoid a lengthy and highly visible battle, Weider agreed to make up to $400,000 available for consumer redemption to those who had purchased the products — and they received their refund if they were fortunate enough to have "proper evidence of purchase" such as the original receipt or the box. (The money that consumers were actually reimbursed was less than $100,000.)

The Art of the Seduction

Make no mistake about it: The supplement industry is a big business. However, the current medical information about nutritional supplements rarely supports the performance-enhancement claims of the manufacturers (Barron and Vanscoy 1993). The highly sophisticated marketing tactics used to attract consumers are sometimes very aggressive and cunning, while the advertisements for products are often misleading — if not pure fabrication. Here's a sampling of the common practices that manufacturers use to deceive consumers:

Questionable "research." To influence consumers, many companies have falsely claimed that they themselves were involved in recent "breakthroughs" or "scientific research" or had "secret research results." Companies also typically reference studies in their ads that were performed by others. In reality, most of this "research" is so unscientific that it's basically worthless. The research cited is frequently poorly controlled and rarely conducted as "double blind." For these reasons, much of the research noted by manufacturers to endorse their products has never been accepted for publication in reputable professional journals that are peer-reviewed. To persuade consumers, other studies referenced in ads are usually outdated or taken out of context. Lastly, some research references used by manufacturers are often unpublished studies from Eastern European sources that cannot be relied upon.

Patent numbers. Another common deceptive practice is the use of patent numbers to give the false impression that the U. S. Patent Office has approved of the product. The Patent Office is not concerned whether a product is effective or not — their only task is to distinguish one product from another. So, a patent says nothing about the effectiveness of a product — it merely denotes a distinctive difference between one product's claims and another's. Patent numbers can be falsified anyway due to the lack of any verification procedures in advertising.

"Natural" products. Many nutritional supplements claim to improve performance "naturally" or even "legally." Because a product claims to have "natural" ingredients doesn't mean that it's necessarily safe. Several natural substances can cause serious harm including high-potency doses of some vitamins, minerals and certain herbs.

Product labels. Supplement labels rarely contain the false claims found in ads for the same product. Untruthful or misleading information on food labels could cause action by the FDA since only factual data is allowed on labels. As a way around this, some companies place misleading information in their ads — instead of the labels — where they may be ignored by the FTC. For the record, many products purchased from nutrition stores or mail-order companies aren't even subject to inspection by the FDA. Therefore, the exact content of such compounds is unknown and may not be represented accurately on the list of ingredients. Some products may even contain small amounts of banned substances such as testosterone or other anabolic steroids or may actually be anabolic steroids but not labeled as such (NCAA 1991).

Nebulous terminology. Scientific-sounding names can be confusing and, at the same time, appealing — particularly to those who are looking for quick and easy results. Many ads contain ambiguous language and rely upon the inability of consumers to understand complex terms.

Alluring names. Numerous supplements have catchy brand names to bait consumers such as Anabolic Mass, Anabolic Cuts, Anabolic Power, Anabolic Amino Balance, Hi-Test Muscle Octane, Metabolol, Gammaplex, Ammonia Scavengers, Biobolic Power Life, Protein Blast, Carbo Energizer and Carbo Surge. Many of the names combine an image of action (e.g., hi-test, energizer) with bodybuilding lingo (e.g., mass, cuts) and scientific — or pseudoscientific — terminology (e.g., anabolic, biobolic). The idea is to make the product sound unique, irresistible and absolutely essential for a consumer's nutritional needs.

Unknown/unusual ingredients. Philen and her associates (1992) reviewed 311 ads for food supplements and found that only 242 products (77.8 percent) listed ingredients. Their research noted 235 unique ingredients including ecdysterone, an insect hormone with no known use in humans. The authors could not find any reference in the medical literature for numerous other ingredients such as conch grass, muira puama and uva ursi.

No known substance can "burn" fat — the only real method of using fat is exercise. (Photo by Ed Spatola)

Professional endorsements. Some manufacturers have made claims about their products by implying or falsely stating endorsement by professional groups. For instance, some products claim to be "university-tested" which may actually mean that someone inside a university was merely involved. In other cases, university testing may not have even occurred.

Personal testimonials. Scientific nutritionists and reputable physicians are not in the vitamin-selling business (Herbert 1990a). For the right price, however, athletes and other individuals can be quite eager to offer testimonials and anecdotes to promote practically any product. In addition, the popular before-and-after snapshots used as part of testimonials can be easily faked.

Unfamiliar degrees. Advertisements often use credentials or unfamiliar degrees that aren't recognized by responsible scientists and educators such as "C.N." for Certified Nutritionist. According to Herbert (1990a), not even a Ph.D. guarantees that a person is qualified as an authority on nutrition or health. For example, a Ph.D. who dispenses information on nutrition (or exercise) may have the degree in an unrelated field such as sport sociology or endocrinology.

Bodybuilding magazines. Several of the most widely sold "muscle mags" are published by supplements manufacturers and exist mainly to promote their nutritional products. For the most part, these publications are essentially nutritional supplement catalogs that are neatly packaged with some articles on training. A sampling of recent issues of four popular bodybuilding magazines by the City of New York Department of Consumer Affairs (1992) revealed that 56 percent of the full-page ads were for "worthless and possibly even harmful nutritional supplements." Philen and her colleagues (1992) reviewed 12 health and bodybuilding magazines and found 311 ads for food supplements.

The "Loophole"

The FDA and the FTC would like to take more action to protect the public against all the misleading advertising and quack claims, but both agencies have rather limited resources. In a three-year period, the FDA actually took 40 legal actions against dietary supplement manufacturers — mostly on the grounds of fraudulent therapeutic claims or concerns about safety. Nevertheless, the FDA devotes less than one percent of its enforcement resources to dietary supplements. Likewise, the FTC does not have the time, money or manpower to monitor the advertising practices of supplement manufacturers. Moreover, the FDA is somewhat handcuffed by a loophole in the federal law: the 1976 Proxmire Amendment to the Federal Food, Drug and Cosmetic Act. Sponsored by former Senator William Proxmire — a vitamin enthusiast — the amendment permits the FDA to regulate food supplements only when they are inherently dangerous or are marketed with claims that they treat or prevent disease (Pitts 1992).

There is no consistent scientific evidence that indicates a high protein intake or amino acid supplementation improves performance or increases muscle mass.

NUTRITIONAL SUPPLEMENTS

Skillful promoters of nutritional supplements have bestowed protein, amino acids, vitamins, minerals, herbs and other substances with almost supernatural powers having the ability to do practically everything imaginable. However, most of the claims concerning nutritional supplements are purely speculative and anecdotal with little or no scientific basis. In general, dietary supplements do not undergo the same testing as do medications and are not subject to the same quality controls as medications. In addition, the claims of their beneficial effects are not based on scientific evidence (NFL 1994).

Protein and Amino Acids

The need for a high intake of dietary protein and/or amino acid supplements by those who engage in rigorous physical activity has been drastically exaggerated and overrated by health food manufacturers and promoters. The truth is, there are no significant nutritional benefits obtained from the intake of additional dietary protein or amino acid supplements by those consuming adequate diets (Wilmore 1982;

Slavin, Lanners and Engstrom 1988; Benson 1992; Feinberg 1994). Protein is critical to daily existence, but it doesn't produce any superhuman powers. There is no consistent scientific evidence that indicates a high protein intake or amino acid supplementation improves performance (Stone and Kroll 1978; Wilmore 1982; Benson 1992; Williams 1993) or increases muscle mass (Wheeler 1989; Clark 1990; Wheeler and Cameron 1993; Williams 1993). Furthermore, high protein intakes — in excess of 2-3 times the Recommended Dietary Allowance (RDA) — have not been shown to enhance physical endurance or muscle strength (Lemon 1987). An overwhelming number of researchers, scientists, strength and fitness practitioners, scientific nutritionists, registered dieticians and physicians have noted that a high intake of protein or amino acid supplementation is unnecessary for individuals who consume a well-balanced diet (Sharkey 1975; Stone and Kroll 1978; Hatfield 1981; Wilmore 1982; Guthrie 1983; Westcott 1983; Smith 1984b; McArdle, Katch and Katch 1986; Meredith 1988; Sargent 1988; Shils and Young 1988; Slavin, Lanners and Engstrom 1988; Wheeler 1989; Hammock 1990; Lambrinides 1990a; Lowenthal and Karni 1990; Benson 1992; Riley 1992; Wheeler and Cameron 1993; Simmons 1994).

Protein needs. The RDA for protein is .8 grams per kilogram of bodyweight per day (g/kg/day) for adults. RDAs are established by the National Research Council of the National Academy of Sciences. The RDAs are set by first determining the "floor" below which deficiency occurs and then by determining the "ceiling" above which harm occurs (Herbert 1990b). A margin of safety is included in the RDAs to meet the needs of nearly all healthy people (Guthrie 1983; McArdle, Katch and Katch 1986; Fike 1987; Grandjean 1988; Sargent 1988; Clark 1990; Fink and Worthington-Roberts 1992). In fact, the RDAs are designed to cover 97.5 percent of the population (Scrimshaw and Young 1976; Guthrie 1983; Meredith 1988; Clark 1990). In other words, the RDAs exceed what most people require in order to meet the needs of individuals with the highest requirements. The RDAs do not represent minimum requirements and any failure to consume the recommended amounts doesn't necessarily indicate a dietary deficiency (Guthrie 1983; Herbert 1990b).

According to Hammock (1990), most Americans — including those at the bottom of the socioeconomic scale — receive more than enough protein. However, it has been suggested that active individuals require greater amounts of dietary protein. Studies have shown that the protein needs of individuals involved in intense strength training programs may be higher than those of sedentary individuals (Lemon 1991; Lemon et al. 1992; Tarnopolsky et al. 1992). Nevertheless, the protein intakes of highly active individuals are typically well above the RDA for protein and adequately cover any increased need that may be related to strength training and conditioning activities (Fox and Mathews 1981; Hewgley 1984; Burke and Read 1987;

Grandjean 1988; Meredith 1988; Nowak and Knudsen 1988; Kris-Etherton 1989; Lambrinides 1994). In addition, a study by Hickson, Hinkelman and Bredle (1988) suggests that an improved metabolic efficiency allows exercisers to meet enhanced demands for protein without requiring an increased protein intake.

Individuals who consume adequate calories generally obtain sufficient protein (Short and Short 1983; Slavin, Lanners and Engstrom 1988; Kasperek 1989; McCarthy 1989; NCAA 1991). Recall that caloric requirements are determined by several factors including body composition and activity level. Larger, more active individuals require and consume more calories than the average person. With these additional calories come additional protein. In other words, the increased protein need is met by increased caloric intake (McArdle, Katch and Katch 1986; Lowenthal and Karni 1990). Assuming sufficient caloric intake, 1.2-2.0 g/kg/day (about 150-250 percent of the RDA for adults) is present in any mixed diet that contains 12-15 percent of its calories as protein (Lemon 1989; Williams 1993). Recall the previously mentioned 200-pound individual who must consume 5,200 calories to maintain his bodyweight. If 15 percent of these calories came from protein, he would be receiving 780 calories from protein or 195 grams [780 cal divided by 4 cal/g equals 195 g]. Based upon the RDA of .8 g/kg, this individual would be consuming enough protein to meet the needs of a 536-pound man [195 g divided by .8g/kg times 2.2 lb/kg equals 536.25 lbs]. This amount of protein is actually about 2.15 g/kg — or about 2-1/2 times the RDA — without the person making any effort to consume extra dietary protein or using amino acid supplements. Even if the requirement for active individuals may be greater, individuals are already consuming enough protein to ensure proper levels of consumption (Hammock 1990; Bubb 1992a; Fink and Worthington-Roberts 1992). Grandjean (1988) notes that, if anything, an inadequate intake of carbohydrates is more often a problem than an inadequate intake of protein. Interestingly, Layman (1987) suggests that achievement of maximum growth requires only an additional 10 grams of dietary protein per day.

Clearly, there is no need for a high protein intake or for amino acid supplements by individuals who are consuming enough calories. Since amino acid supplementation is very expensive (Guthrie 1983; Meredith 1988; Dunn 1989b; Kris-Etherton 1989; Lambrinides 1990a), purchasing those products is viewed as a waste of money (McArdle, Katch and Katch 1986; Riley 1992). In most cases, amino acid supplements are an expensive form of powdered milk (Guthrie 1983; Lambrinides 1990a). For those who are concerned with getting enough protein in their diet, Hatfield (1981) suggests that sufficient protein can be obtained by simply consuming more foods that are high in protein.

Excessive protein intake. There are no significant nutritional, anabolic or ergogenic benefits obtained from the intake of protein in excess of that provided by a well-balanced diet. However, excessive protein intake does have numerous unwanted side effects — several of which may be physically detrimental (Wilmore 1982; Benson 1992; NFL 1994) and dangerous (Riley 1992).

A high protein intake in excess of the needs for building body tissue and essential body compounds is either stored as fat or excreted in the urine (Applegate 1988; Hickson, Hinkelman and Bredle 1988; Brown 1989). Excreting excessive protein in the urine places a heavy burden on the liver and kidneys (Guthrie 1983; Westcott 1983; McArdle, Katch and Katch 1986; Layman 1987; McCarthy 1989; Clark 1990) and may damage those organs (Slavin, Lanners and Engstrom 1988).

An excessive intake of protein also increases the risk of dehydration (Aronson 1986; Kris-Etherton 1989; McCarthy 1989; Wheeler 1989; Clark 1990; Hammock 1990; Lambrinides 1990a; Fink and Worthington-Roberts 1992; Wheeler and Cameron 1993). According to Hammock (1990), the increased risk of dehydration is the result of extra water being required to rid the body of the by-products of protein metabolism. Wheeler (1989) notes that dehydration increases the risk of developing a heat-related disorder (i.e., heat exhaustion, heat stroke or heat cramps).

Other side effects from excessive protein intake include an excessive loss of calcium in the urine (Aronson 1986; McCarthy 1989), an increased risk of renal disease (Wheeler 1989), diarrhea (McArdle, Katch and Katch 1986; Wheeler 1989; Lambrinides 1990a; Wheeler and Cameron 1993), cramping (McArdle, Katch and Katch 1986; Wheeler 1989; Simmons 1994), gout (Aronson 1986) and gastrointestinal upset (Lambrinides 1990a).

Amino acid mixtures are the largest categories of supplements marketed to bodybuilders (Grunewald and Bailey 1993). The hype-inspired use of amino acid supplements by large numbers of individuals has generated considerable concern for consumer safety. Amino acid supplements taken in large doses are essentially drugs with unknown physical effects (Slavin, Lanners and Engstrom 1988; Hammock 1990). In 1992, the Federation of American Societies for Experimental Biology reviewed the scientific literature on the safety of amino acids and reported that there is insufficient scientific evidence to establish safe levels of intake of the amino acid supplements on the market (Taylor 1993). Additionally, the American Council of Science and Health recommends, "Unless you are participating in a scientific study conducted by reputable researchers, you should not take amino acid supplements since they have not been proven safe." The dangers of amino acid supplementation were tragically illustrated in the late 1980s when the amino acid L-tryptophan was associated with at least 1,500 cases of painful muscle disorder including at least 38 deaths (FDA 1993). Although investigators believe that a contaminated batch may have been the direct cause, closer federal oversight might have prevented the situation.

In short, the effect on the body of the single amino acids contained in many nutritional supplements is still not fully understood and their use in special supplements should be avoided altogether.

Vitamins and Minerals

Vitamins and minerals make up more than 80 percent of the sales in the multi-billion dollar dietary supplement market (Taylor 1993). Vitamins and minerals — like proteins and amino acids — have also been thought to have magical powers. The belief is that if the RDA is good, then more must be better. It's true that a deficiency of vitamins and minerals can make a person unhealthy, but consuming more than needed doesn't necessarily make a person any healthier. The liver is a storehouse for vitamins and minerals. This organ can quickly compensate for a temporary dietary shortfall by releasing its stored nutrients as needed and then replenishing its stores when the opportunity arises (Herbert 1990c). Despite this, millions of Americans believe that their foods do not supply adequate vitamins and minerals and, therefore, they take nutritional supplements — often in potentially dangerous megadoses — and sometimes resulting in actual harm.

Like protein and amino acid supplementation, there is little evidence to suggest that vitamin and mineral supplementation in excess of the RDA is needed by those who consume a well-balanced diet (Hatfield 1981; Wilmore 1982; Westcott 1983; Alhadeff, Gualtieri and Lipton 1984; Smith 1984b; Wells 1985; ADA 1987; Fike 1987; Weight et al. 1988; Fahey 1989; Herbert 1990b; LeLeiko and Rollinson 1990; Benson 1992; Riley 1992; Wheeler and Cameron 1993; Simmons 1994). Research by Weight and others (1988) concluded "multivitamin and mineral supplementation was without any measurable ergogenic effect" and that "supplementation is unnecessary in athletes ingesting a normal diet." There is simply no evidence that increased vitamin consumption improves performance (Sharkey 1975 and 1984; Percy 1978; Stone and Kroll 1978; Fox and Mathews 1981; Hatfield 1981; Wilmore 1982; McArdle, Katch and Katch 1986; ADA 1987; Belko 1987; Fike 1987; Weight et al. 1988; Kris-Etherton 1989; Clark 1990; Benson 1992; Singh, Moses and Deuster 1992; Telford et al. 1992; Sparling, Recker and Lambrinides 1994). Moreover, there doesn't appear to be an increased demand for most vitamins and minerals during periods of increased physical activity (Fox and Mathews 1981; Clark 1990). Recall that active individuals require and consume more calories than the average person. With these additional calories come additional vitamins and minerals (Clark 1990).

According to Herbert (1990c), as a result of the increased knowledge and the availability of a variety of foods rich in vitamins and minerals, deficiency diseases are rare in the United States and other industrialized nations. Fike (1987) adds that there is no risk of a vitamin and mineral deficiency due to the volume of food consumed and even a marginal diet provides adequate vitamins and minerals. In fact, the only commonly documented deficiency in the United States is iron (Fahey 1989; Herbert 1990c; LeLeiko and Rollinson 1990). Other than iron deficiency, physicians rarely encounter any nutrient-deficiency disease except in chronic alcoholics or people with an underlying illness that interferes with their food intake or metabolism (Herbert 1990c).

Whenever possible, it's better to get vitamins from foods rather than pills because the high concentration of a vitamin or a mineral in pill form may interfere with the absorption of some other nutrients. However, vitamin and mineral supplements may be necessary for improving the nutrient intake of those who consume inadequate diets (Nowak and Knudsen 1988; Fahey 1989). For example, a multivitamin and mineral supplement may be warranted for vegetarians (Clark 1990; Herbert 1990b), some infants and pregnant or lactating females (Herbert 1990b). Supplementation may also be appropriate for someone consuming a low number of calories (Sparling, Recker and Lambrinides 1994) such as those restricting their caloric intake to reach a certain weight class to compete in boxing or wrestling. Herbert (1990b) reports that supplements containing more than 150 percent of the RDA are for disease treatment and should never be purchased unless a competent health professional has diagnosed a need for them. Professional advice concerning nutritional supplementation should be sought from a registered dietician (R.D.) or a nutritionist. With few exceptions, vitamin and mineral supplementation is a waste of money (Brown 1989; Fahey 1989; Riley 1992).

Excessive vitamin intake. When sold at reasonable potencies — as most of them are — vitamins (and minerals) pose no health or safety problems. However, megadoses of vitamins (i.e., any dose greater than 10 times the RDA) carry a risk of toxicity (Lowenthal and Karni 1990) which can create adverse side effects and may lead to serious medical complications. The American Dietetic Association (1987) — the largest and best established organization devoted to both practice and research in nutrition — reports that vitamins (and minerals) pose a risk of toxicity. When taken in megadose amounts, the vitamins that are in excess of those needed to saturate the enzyme systems function as free-floating drugs instead of receptor-bound nutrients (McArdle, Katch and Katch 1986; Herbert 1990b). Like all drugs, high doses of vitamins (and minerals) have the potential for adverse side effects (Hatfield 1981; Wilmore 1982; Herbert 1990b; Benson 1992). Though excess amounts of water-soluble vitamins are mainly excreted in the urine, they still may have toxic effects (Alhadeff, Gualtieri and Lipton 1984). Of greatest concern is excessive intake of the fat-soluble vitamins, particularly vitamins A and D (McArdle, Katch and Katch 1986; Fahey 1989; Kris-Etherton 1989) which can be extremely toxic and may have adverse side effects (Fox and Mathews 1981; Wilmore 1982; Hewgley 1984).

Permanent effects of vitamin A toxicity are rare (Guthrie 1983). However, consuming large doses of vitamin A can be dangerous and even lethal (Herbert 1990a). Excessive doses of vitamin A can result in nausea, drowsiness, diarrhea and loss of calcium from the bones (Guthrie 1983; McArdle, Katch and Katch 1986). Additional side effects from vitamin A toxicity include an increased susceptibility to disease (Scrimshaw and Young 1976), muscle and joint soreness (Fike 1987; Herbert 1990b), vomiting (McArdle, Katch and Katch 1986), decalcification of the bones (Sharkey 1984) and cessation of menstruation (amenorrhea) in females (Guthrie 1983). Wilmore (1982) lists undesirable effects from vitamin A toxicity as bone fragility, stunted growth, loss of appetite, coarsening of the hair, scaly skin eruptions, irritability, double vision, skin rashes and enlargements of the liver and the spleen. Guthrie (1983), Fike (1987) and Herbert (1990b) report headaches and dry, itchy skin. A loss of hair has also been documented (Wilmore 1982; Guthrie 1983; McArdle, Katch and Katch 1986; Herbert 1990b). In addition, the toxicity to the nervous system from megadoses of vitamin A is well-demonstrated (Deutsch 1976; Scrimshaw and Young 1976). Finally, Wheeler and Cameron (1993) report that excessive intake of vitamin A may, over time, produce liver cancer.

Consuming large doses of vitamin D can result in nausea, loss of hair, loss of weight, vomiting and decalcification of the bones (McArdle, Katch and Katch 1986). The damaging effects to the kidneys from an excessive intake of vitamin D have also been well-demonstrated (Deutsch 1976; Scrimshaw and Young 1976; McArdle, Katch and Katch 1986; Farley 1993). Wheeler and Cameron (1993) report that excessive intake of vitamin D may, over time, produce liver cancer. Herbert (1990b) lists fragile bones, hypertension, elevated cholesterol, loss of appetite and calcium deposits in the heart, kidneys and blood vessels as side effects from a high intake of Vitamin D. Drowsiness, diarrhea and headaches have also been noted (McArdle, Katch and Katch; Herbert 1990b).

Side effects from megadoses of vitamin E appear to be rare. Wheeler and Cameron (1993) report headaches, fatigue, blurred vision, gastrointestinal disturbances, muscle weakness and hypoglycemia from an excessive intake of vitamin E.

Excess amounts of the B vitamins and vitamin C are generally excreted in the urine (McArdle, Katch and Katch 1986), prompting Wilmore (1982) to suggest that supplementation with water-soluble vitamins leaves a person with nothing more than expensive urine. However, this places an inordinate amount of stress on the liver and kidneys.

Vitamin C supplementation has been controversial since Linus Pauling suggested megadoses of the vitamin be taken as a cure for the common cold. In general, medical research has not supported his claims (Fahey 1989). Vitamin C has been shown to be beneficial to performance but only in subjects who were clearly deficient in vitamin C (Kris-Etherton 1989). As noted previously, most excessive amounts of vitamin C will appear in the urine. While in the body, however, megadoses of vitamin C can be harmful (Sharkey 1984; Lowenthal and Karni 1990). Unwanted side effects include kidney stones (Scrimshaw and Young

1976; Alhadeff, Gualtieri and Lipton 1984; Clark 1990; Herbert 1990a), diarrhea (Guthrie 1983; Alhadeff, Gualtieri and Lipton 1984; McArdle, Katch and Katch 1986; Clark 1990; Herbert 1990b; Farley 1993), bladder irritation (McArdle, Katch and Katch 1986; Herbert 1990a), intestinal problems (Clark 1990) and destruction of red blood cells (Guthrie 1983; Herbert 1990b). In addition, Guthrie (1983) reports nausea, stomach cramps and an increase in plasma cholesterol while Sharkey (1984) notes ulceration of the gastric wall, leaching of calcium from the bones and gout as side effects from an excessive intake of vitamin C. "Rebound scurvy" has also been reported after withdrawal from chronic vitamin C administration (Alhadeff, Gualtieri and Lipton 1984).

Excessive mineral intake. For individuals receiving the RDA of minerals, there is no evidence that mineral supplements benefit exercise performance (Sharkey 1975; Hatfield 1981; Wilmore 1982; McArdle, Katch and Katch 1986; Belko 1987; Weight et al. 1988; Benson 1992; Singh, Moses and Deuster 1992; Telford et al. 1992; Sparling, Recker and Lambrinides 1994).

Excessive intake of minerals has the potential for adverse side effects. It should also be noted that many products contain minerals for which the National Academy of Sciences has not established RDAs. Indeed, there's no evidence that many of the minerals that are frequently listed on product labels are needed in the human body. For instance, one nutritional product claims an abundance of its ingredients "from natural sources of Pacific Ocean mineral-rich seabeds."

Herbs et al. Many herbals and other botanical (i.e., plant-derived) products come with express or implied disease-related claims and are marketed for specific therapeutic purposes for which there may not be valid scientific support. Barron and Vanscoy (1993) reviewed all of the clinical trials published in the biomedical literature between 1966 and 1992 relative to manufacturer's claims regarding their natural products. They found no published scientific evidence to support the promotional claims for 42 percent of the products. Another 32 percent of the products had some scientific documentation to support their claims but were judged to be marketed in a misleading manner. In other words, 74 percent of the natural products reviewed were either marketed in a misleading fashion or had no scientific evidence to substantiate their claims. The products examined included Argentinean bull testes, boron, chromium picolinate, clenbuterol, dibencozide, plant sterols, yohimbe bark, inosine and ma huang.

The truth is that a large number of these substances have no recognized role in nutrition (Taylor 1993). Additionally, the origin and safety of many natural products remains a question (Barron and Vanscoy 1993). For example, Farley (1993) reports five cases of acute toxic hepatitis related to the use of the herb chaparral. The medical literature contains reports of severe liver toxicity linked to the widely used herb germander (Taylor 1993). Between 1985 and

1993, at least 7 cases of liver disease — with one death reported — have been associated with the oral use of products made from the leafy plant comfrey (Farley 1993). Hypertension, rapid heart rate, nerve damage, muscle injury, psychosis, stroke and memory loss have been reported from the use of ma huang (Farley 1993). The City of New York Department of Consumer Affairs (1992) reports that large doses of the natural stimulants found in the herb ginseng can cause hypertension, insomnia, depression and skin blemishes. Products containing yohimbine — a substance which is extracted from the inner bark of the yohimbe tree — has been linked to kidney failure, seizures and death (Farley 1993). There are similar safety concerns with high-potency enzymes and glandular extracts from dried animal organs such as the pituitary gland, the thyroid gland and the testicles. (Chapter 14 discusses the purported ergogenic and anabolic claims of many natural products.)

By the way, no known herb or any other substance can "burn" fat or facilitate its metabolism. The only real method of using fat is exercise.

FOOD FOR THOUGHT

There's no need for supplements provided a person consumes a variety of foods that provide adequate calories and nutrients. Research has concluded that nutritional supplements have little or no positive influence on performance and may even be physiologically damaging. Taking the money used to purchase these expensive supplements and investing it in high-quality foods instead will result in greater success in maximizing potential in a far safer manner. There are no shortcuts to proper nutrition.

14
RISKY BUSINESS: STEROIDS AND STEROID ALTERNATIVES

The development of anabolic steroids essentially began with the early belief that the male sexual fluid had energizing powers. In 1889, a physiologist named Charles-Edouard Brown-Sequard publicly admitted to having injected himself with a liquid extract derived from the testicles of a dog and a guinea pig. Brown-Sequard was the first scientist to associate glandular products with physical strength. Because of his early administration and promotion of these testicular extracts, Brown-Sequard has been referred to as "The Father of Steroids" (Hoberman 1992). In the late 1890s, Oskar Zoth and Fritz Pregl injected themselves with a liquid extract of bulls' testicles and concluded that the extract boosted muscular strength (Hoberman 1992).

It's been widely rumored that anabolic steroids were given to Nazi SS Troops during World War II to make them more aggressive and less fearful of violence (Wade 1972; Haupt and Rovere 1984; Taylor 1985; Fahey 1989; Schrof 1992). However, this rumor has never been confirmed (Hoberman 1992). Athletes of the Eastern Bloc countries were experimenting with steroids (or steroid-like drugs) as early as the 1950s. The first reported use by athletes seems to be by Soviet weightlifters at the 1954 World Weightlifting Championships in Vienna (Wade 1972). In a "patriotic" response to the drug-inspired success of the Soviet athletes at the 1956 Melbourne Olympics, U. S. Team Physician Dr. John Ziegler developed the original anabolic steroid (Dianabol) with Ciba Pharmaceutical Company . . . a move he would later regret. The steroids were given to weightlifters at the York Barbell Club in Pennsylvania who ate the pills "like candy" (Goldman and Klatz 1992). The rampant use of anabolic steroids — along with a new generation of growth-stimulating drugs and "steroid alternatives" — has been rising ever since.

PREVALENCE OF STEROID USE

Initially, steroids were used by competitive athletes who were looking to accelerate their gains in muscular size and strength with the hope that this would improve their performance. This is still true, but steroid use has been reaching other populations as well. Based on data from the 1991 National Household Survey on Drug Abuse, it is estimated that one million Americans are using or have used steroids (Yesalis et al. 1993). From the same study, it is estimated that more than 300,000 Americans had used steroids in 1990.

There is also an astonishing number of teenage steroid users. In a study by Buckley and his associates (1988), 3,403 twelfth-grade male students voluntarily completed a questionnaire concerning steroid use. The results indicate that 6.64 percent of twelfth-grade male students either use or have used steroids and that over two thirds of the user group initiated use when they were 16 years of age or younger. Extrapolating these data suggest that 250,000-500,000 adolescents are using or have used steroids. Approximately 20 percent of the users reported their source of steroids was a health care professional (defined in this study as a physician, a pharmacist or a veterinarian). Moreover, 57 percent of teen users say they were influenced by the bodybuilding magazines they've read (Schrof 1992). Clearly, the use of anabolic steroids is reaching epidemic proportions (Mannie 1991).

WHAT ARE STEROIDS?

Technically referred to as being "anabolic-androgenic," steroids are synthetic derivatives of the powerful male sex hormone testosterone, which was first isolated in Germany in 1935. The "anabolic" or growth-promoting effects of testosterone include increases in skeletal muscle mass, nitrogen retention and protein synthesis while its "androgenic" or masculinizing effects include increases in facial and body hair, a deepening of the voice and a heightened libido. Steroids are derived from testosterone that has been chemically modified — primarily to enhance the anabolic effects and to decrease the androgenic effects (LaBree 1991). Steroids can be broadly categorized as those that are administered by either ingestion or injection. (Chapter 3 presents additional information concerning testosterone.)

Although there is strong anecdotal evidence concerning the efficacy of anabolic steroids for promoting muscular size and strength, the literature is contradictory and controversial (Haupt and Rovere 1984). In general, however, it can be concluded that the use of anabolic steroids can often increase muscular strength beyond that seen with training and diet alone (Haupt and Rover 1984; ACSM 1987). This is particularly true of experienced weightlifters. Anabolic steroids seem to have no positive effect on aerobic capacity (Haupt and Rover 1984; ACSM 1987; Lamb 1989).

POSSIBLE SIDE EFFECTS

Scientific research data appear to be inconclusive regarding the effects of large doses or the long-term administration of anabolic steroids on health. Although the long-term effects are unclear, the use of anabolic steroids poses serious threats to the liver and kidneys as well as the cardiovascular, reproductive and skeletal systems, thereby presenting dangers to overall health and longevity (NSCA 1985; NFL 1993). Mannie (1989) reports that "The list of adverse effects [from steroid use] reads like a Stephen King horror story." It should also be noted that the potential for adverse side effects is a function of the type and amount of steroid being used as well as individual sensitivity. However, the adverse effects associated with the use of anabolic steroids occur quite frequently and many effects undoubtedly are not reported (Kibble and Ross 1987). The following is a list of the dangerous side effects that are well-documented in the medical literature:

Liver

Virtually all of the literature reports liver disorders from the use of anabolic steroids. The American College of Sports Medicine (1987) notes that the most serious liver complications associated with anabolic steroid use are peliosis hepatis (the formation of blood-filled cysts in the liver of unknown etiology) and liver tumors. Taylor (1985) refers to these two conditions as life-threatening. Additionally, both of these conditions are considered irreversible (Kibble and Ross 1987).

A review of the literature by Haupt and Rovere (1984) found 23 reported cases of peliosis hepatis associated with the use of anabolic steroids. All 23 patients were being treated with pharmacologic doses for medical illnesses. The researchers speculate that peliosis hepatis may be a pretumerous lesion that can become malignant with prolonged anabolic steroid treatment. More recently, Cebasso (1994) reports a 27-year-old bodybuilder with peliosis hepatis that developed after chronic intermittent use of anabolic steroids. Rupture of the blood-filled cysts or liver failure resulting from peliosis hepatis has often been fatal (Wright and Stone 1985; ACSM 1987; Maddalo 1992).

Numerous reports have been published linking the use of anabolic steroids with liver tumors in males (Percy 1978; Wright and Stone 1985; Lamb 1989). Moderate to heavy use of anabolic steroids in otherwise healthy individuals will cause liver cancer (Asken 1992) and even death over time (Taylor 1985). The time period for the initial stages of liver cancer on a malignant cellular level to the full-blown clinical expression of this problem may be more than five years. In other words, steroid users may have cancers growing in their livers but the symptoms have yet to reveal themselves (Taylor 1985).

The use of anabolic steroids also impairs the excretory function of the liver and results in jaundice (ACSM 1987). Jaundice — which gives the eyes and the skin a yellowish tint — occurs at relatively low dosages (PDR 1994) and has been reported as an adverse side effect from steroid use (Kibble and Ross 1987; Mannie 1989 and 1991; Asken 1992; Maddalo 1992). Finally, higher doses of anabolic steroids appear to increase the incidence of liver dysfunction (Kibble and Ross 1987).

Kidneys

Another organ of concern is the kidney. The use of anabolic steroids increases the possibility of kidney dysfunction (Mannie 1991; Asken 1992) including an increased risk of kidney stones (Mannie 1991). Wilm's tumor has been associated with steroid use (Goldman and Klatz 1992) and may be fatal.

Cardiovascular System

Long-term or excessive use of anabolic steroids is likely to be detrimental to cardiovascular health (Wright and Stone 1985). Of the five major coronary risk factors noted by the American College of Sports Medicine (1991), two risk factors are increased by the use of anabolic steroids: hypertension and cholesterol levels. Numerous authors have reported increased blood pressure (Percy 1978; Taylor 1985; Wright and Stone 1985; ACSM 1987; Kibble and Ross 1987; Mannie 1989; Pipes 1989; Asken 1992; Goldman and Klatz 1992; Maddalo 1992) and elevated cholesterol levels (ACSM 1987; Kibble and Ross 1987; Lamb 1989; Pipes 1989; Mannie 1991; Goldman and Klatz 1992; PDR 1994) as a result of steroid use. In addition, there is strong evidence that moderate doses of anabolic steroids have the potential to cause a heart attack by "sludging" the arteries that nourish the heart (Taylor 1985).

One of the most graphic examples of the adverse effects of steroid use on the cardiovascular system was experienced by a former professional football player. He encountered many adverse side effects including tachycardia (an accelerated heart rate). In 1984, his resting heart rate was as high as 160 beats per minute (bpm). When he checked himself into a hospital in 1988, his resting heart rate was measured at 200 bpm. His medical problems forced him to seek a heart transplant . . . at the age of 33 (Courson and Schreiber 1991).

In 1989, the Ashtabula County (Ohio) coroner who examined the body of a high school football player officially stated that the 17-year-old's heart attack was in part attributable to the use of anabolic steroids (Goldman and Klatz 1992). This marked the first time that anabolic steroids had been legally linked to a death in the United States.

Male Reproductive System

It appears that anabolic steroids have a profound influence on the male reproductive system (Haupt and Rovere 1984). When a man starts to introduce extra testosterone into his body, his internal regulatory system will reduce its own production in order to maintain a stable internal environment. If too much "foreign" testosterone is added, his body will no longer produce its own supply. In fact, a review of the literature by Haupt and Rover (1984) reports that decreased plasma testosterone was common in athletes who used anabolic steroids. A decreased level of testosterone attributed to the use of anabolic steroids has also been reported by Kibble and Ross (1987).

This chemical balancing results in the increased potential for numerous feminizing side effects that target the male reproductive system. For example, a decreased sperm count and testicular atrophy have been well-documented (Taylor 1985; ACSM 1987; Kibble and Ross 1987; Asanovich 1989; Lamb 1989; Mannie 1989; Pipes 1989; Lowenthal and Karni 1990; Asken 1992; Schrof 1992). Holma (1977) reported that the sperm count of 15 athletes decreased an average of 73 percent over 2 months of anabolic steroid treatment. Another well-documented side effect related to this hormonal irony is gynecomastia, which is the appearance of enlarged, female-like breasts on the male physique (Percy 1978; Taylor 1985; Kibble and Ross 1987; Asanovich 1989; Mannie 1989; Pipes 1989; Asken 1992; Goldman and Klatz 1992; Maddalo 1992; Schrof 1992; PDR 1994). Other possible male-specific side effects include a high-pitched voice (Pipes 1989), prostate enlargement (Asken 1992; Maddalo 1992), sterility (Lamb 1989) and functional impotency (Percy 1978; Asanovich 1989).

Female Reproductive System

When a woman takes anabolic steroids, she is using a substance that has masculinizing effects. In essence, she is a female turning male (Percy 1978; Goldman and Klatz 1992). Females may experience irreversible physical changes including enlargement of the clitoris, decreased breast size, hirsutism (increased facial and body hair) and a deepening of the voice (Taylor 1985; ACSM 1987; Kibble and Ross 1987; Mannie 1989 and 1991; Lowenthal and Karni 1990; Asken 1992; Schrof 1992; PDR 1994). Menstrual irregularities (Taylor 1985; ACSM 1987; Kibble and Ross 1987; Mannie 1991; Asken 1992; Schrof 1992) and amenorrhea (ACSM 1987; Asanovich 1989; Lowenthal and Karni 1990) have also been reported. These and other adverse side effects were noted in a study by Strauss, Liggett and Lanese (1985) involving 10 female steroid users. In this study, all 10 women reported a lowering of the voice and increased facial hair; 8 of them experienced enlargement of the clitoris, increased libido, increased aggressiveness and irritability and acne on the face and the back; and 5 of them noticed a decrease in breast size and menstrual diminution or cessation.

Women who use anabolic steroids also increase their risk of bearing children with birth defects (Goldman and Klatz 1992). When taken by pregnant females, anabolic steroids can cause masculinization of the fetus. The degree of masculinization is related to the amount of anabolic steroid being taken and the age of the fetus during the steroid usage (PDR 1994). Other potential side effects include an increased risk of breast cancer (Goldman and Klatz 1992) and uterine atrophy (Asanovich 1989). Alopecia (a loss of scalp hair) has also been reported in females using anabolic steroids (Taylor 1985; ACSM 1987; Kibble and Ross 1987; Mannie 1989; Lowenthal and Karni 1990; Schrof 1992).

Miscellaneous Adverse Effects

A number of other serious adverse effects are possible from the use of anabolic steroids and deserve a closer inspection.

Psychological side effects. The use of anabolic steroids — even in low doses — potentiates certain psychological behavior patterns (Taylor 1985). Pope and Katz (1988) performed structured interviews of 41 bodybuilders and football players who had used steroids. Five of the subjects (12.2 percent) met the criteria for psychotic symptoms during periods in which they used steroids. None of the subjects had psychotic symptoms when they were not taking steroids. Of the five subjects who had psychotic symptoms, one had auditory hallucinations of voices and the other four developed various delusions. Another five subjects met the criteria for a manic episode during steroid exposure. One of these subjects bought an old car and deliberately drove it into a tree at 40 miles per hour while a friend videotaped him. This research suggests that major psychiatric symptoms may be a common adverse effect of anabolic steroid use.

Additional possible psychological side effects include extreme mood swings (Wright and Stone 1985; ACSM 1987; Mannie 1989), sleeping disturbances (Taylor 1985; Wright and Stone 1985; Asanovich 1989; Mannie 1989), euphoria (Kibble and Ross 1987; Asanovich 1989; Pipes 1989; Mannie 1991), paranoia (Asken 1992; Schrof 1992), irritability (Kibble and Ross 1987; Schrof 1992), an increased or a decreased libido (Taylor 1985; ACSM 1987; Mannie 1991; PDR 1994), anxiety (Mannie 1991; PDR 1994) and delusions (Schrof 1992).

Perhaps the most frequently documented psychological side effect is an increased level of unpredictable hostility and aggression (Taylor 1985; Wright and Stone 1985; ACSM 1987; Kibble and Ross 1987; Mannie 1989; Pipes 1989; Asken 1992; Schrof 1992). This heightened aggressive behavior is commonly referred to as "roid rage." A classic example of roid rage was demonstrated by one individual whose steroid-amplified aggression involved him in numerous brawls and created violent thoughts like "crushing people to death" and "tearing off their limbs" (Chaiken and Telander 1988). According to data from the 1991 National Household Survey on Drug Abuse, more than 80 percent of 12-17 year olds who used anabolic steroids stated that they had acted in an agressive way against people or had committed a crime against property in the previous year (Yesalis et al. 1993).

Steroid users may also experience psychological dependency (Taylor 1985; Wright and Stone 1985; Asanovich

1989). This can lead to depression-related withdrawal when the use of steroids is discontinued (Asken 1992). In the study by Pope and Katz (1988), five subjects developed major depression while withdrawing from anabolic steroids. Linked to the psychological dependency on anabolic steroids is a condition known as "reverse anorexia" (Schrof 1992) or "megarexia" (Asken 1992). As the name implies, reverse anorexia is the opposite of anorexia. In anorexic females, no matter how much weight is lost, the woman stills sees herself as too fat; in megarexic males, no matter how much weight is added, the man still sees himself as too thin. Megarexia would seem to be the male equivalent of anorexia.

Stunted growth. Adolescents who use anabolic steroids may experience a pre-mature fusing of the epiphyseal growth plates located in the ends of the long bones. A pre-mature closure of the epiphyseal plates before completion of the normal growth cycle will result in stunted growth — which is not reversible (Percy 1978; Wilmore 1982; Lamb 1984b and 1989; ACSM 1987; Kibble and Ross 1987; Asanovich 1989; Mannie 1989 and 1991; Lowenthal and Karni 1990; Goldman and Klatz 1992; Schrof 1992).

Weakened connective tissue. Steroid users also have a predisposition to tendon and ligament injuries (Hatfield 1981; Wright and Stone 1985; Pipes 1989; Mannie 1991; Goldman and Klatz 1992). In an extensive review of the literature, Laseter and Russell (1991) recommend that consideration be given to include connective tissue abnormalities among the potential side effects of steroid use. One theory is that anabolic steroids may weaken connective tissue by inhibiting the formation of collagen (Goldman and Klatz 1992). Another theory is that connective tissue does not respond to steroids to the same degree that muscle tissue does. This would create a situation in which the connective tissue cannot keep up with the demands put upon them from using heavier weights, thereby predisposing the user to serious tendon, ligament, fascia and meniscus injuries. Hatfield (1981) likens this to placing a powerful engine into a Volkswagen. Eventually, the tremendous power generated by the engine would tear the chassis to bits.

Injection complications. Users risk blood poisoning and the spread of communicable diseases — including AIDS — from contaminated needles as well as neural dysfunction as a result of improperly placed needles (Asanovich 1989). Additionally, there is a risk of sudden death accompanying injection due to anaphylactic shock (Goldman, Klatz and Bush 1984).

Multiple drug use. Steroid use often leads to multiple drug abuse (Asken 1992; Schrof 1992). Steroid users may start using other drugs in an attempt to control the unwanted side effects of steroid use. For example, amphetamines are taken to combat depression and diuretics are used to avoid fluid retention and to lower the blood pressure. Based on data from the 1991 National Household Survey on Drug Abuse, males who had used anabolic steroids at some time in their lives were about 2-3 times more likely to report current use of illicit drugs (Yesalis et al. 1993).

Dermatologic syndromes. The use of anabolic steroids can cause an increase in oil production by the sebaceous glands of the skin and cause acne to develop anywhere on the body — usually on the back. Acne is a well-documented side effect of anabolic steroid use (Taylor 1985; ACSM 1987; Kibble and Ross 1987; Pope and Katz 1988; Mannie 1989 and 1991; Lowenthal and Karni 1990; Asken 1992; Maddalo 1992; Schrof 1992; PDR 1994).

Other side effects. Many other possible side effects are commonly noted in the literature including fluid retention (Taylor 1985; Kibble and Ross 1987; Mannie 1989; Maddalo 1992; PDR 1994), unprovoked nose bleeds (Taylor 1985; Mannie 1989 and 1991; Maddalo 1992), arthritis (Mannie 1991) and peptic ulcers (Maddalo 1992). Alopecia has also been reported (Taylor 1985; ACSM 1987; Kibble and Ross 1987; Asken 1992; Schrof 1992; PDR 1994).

OVERT SIGNS OF STEROID USE

It's often difficult to identify the use of anabolic steroids. However, there are a few tell-tale signs. Because steroids can be taken orally in tablet/pill form or by direct injection into a muscle, users may have needles, syringes and pill bottles either hidden or in their possession. Steroid users often have puncture marks, bruises, scar tissue or calluses on their upper thighs and buttocks from steroid injections. Many physical indicators of steroid use are related to the adverse side effects. For example, steroid users often have a bloated, puffy look to their faces and skin due to fluid retention (Maddalo 1992). Another physical sign is that the eyes and skin of a steroid user may have a somewhat yellowish tint from jaundice. Several other physical signs of steroid use are an increased incidence of stretch marks (Maddalo 1992), unprovoked nosebleeds, gynecomastia and severe acne (especially on the back). Finally, sudden and significant increases in size, weight and strength can also be signs of steroid use.

In terms of psychological signs, violent and unpredictable rage is a noticeable side effect of steroid use. Other indications of steroid use can be severe depression and an increased or a decreased libido.

Just because one or two of these symptoms are present doesn't necessarily indicate steroid use. However, if more than a few signs are present, the involvement of anabolic steroids is likely.

WINNING AT ALL COSTS

Despite an overwhelming amount of scientific and medical evidence pointing to the dangers to overall health from certain substances, athletes will sometimes do anything — or take anything — to win. Dr. Gabe Mirkin once polled more than 100 top runners with this question: "If I could give you a pill that would make you an Olympic champion

— and also kill you in a year — would you take it?" More than half of the athletes said that they would take the pill (Mirkin and Hoffman 1978). Dr. Robert Goldman asked 198 elite athletes a similar question and again, more than half of those asked (52 percent) said, in effect, that they would give their lives to win (Goldman and Klatz 1992).

A MATTER OF ETHICS

Anabolic steroids do have some legitimate medical applications, such as in treating malnutrition, skeletal disorders, soft tissue injuries, recovery from surgery, osteoporosis and various anemias. However, the use of anabolic steroids in an attempt to improve physical capacity or athletic performance is contrary to the ethical principles and regulations of competitions as established and set down by various athletic foundations and sports-governing bodies. These organizations include the International Amateur Athletic Federation, the International Olympic Committee and the National Collegiate Athletic Association. Strong anti-steroid statements have also been issued by the National Strength and Conditioning Association (1985), the American College of Sports Medicine (1987) and the National Football League (1993).

STEROIDS AND THE LAW

The Anabolic Steroid Control Act of 1990 went into effect at the end of February 1991. Under this act, anabolic steroids are categorized as Schedule III drugs, which makes their use restricted in the same manner as some narcotics, depressants and stimulants (Ropp 1992). Current legislation has penalties that includes a maximum $1,000 fine and a maximum one year sentence for possession (first offense) as well as a $250,000 fine and up to 5 years in prison for trafficking (Goldman and Klatz 1992). The act gives federal drug enforcement officials the authority to regulate manufacturers, wholesalers, doctors and pharmacies. It also allows for the seizure of assets and money earned through the trafficking of steroids.

Aside from the criminal ramifications associated with the provision of anabolic steroids by personnel who are not authorized to prescribe them — as well as direct harm which may come to steroid users — those who provide anabolic steroids to others may face additional civil claims and lawsuits. For example, when anabolic steroids are provided by nonphysicians, lawsuits brought against those providing the steroids may be coupled with additional allegations that the individual provider was illegally engaged in the practice of medicine. Under these circumstances, there is a greater chance of a finding of negligence and liability (Herbert 1990).

Physicians who provide steroids may also be found liable if the steroid user injures a third party. In one instance, a lawsuit was brought against a physician who prescribed steroids to a person who shot two people and killed another. The lawsuit contended that the physician was negligent in providing steroidal medications to the user (Herbert 1990).

STEROID ALTERNATIVES?

The search for increased muscular size and strength has given rise to a number of pharmacological steroid alternatives or "substitutes." Virtually none of these products live up to their billing as being ergogenic (i.e., performance-enhancing) or anabolic and most of these substances carry their own brand of adverse side effects. (Like anabolic steroids, the potential for adverse side effects from these products is a function of the amount being used as well as individual sensitivity.) Many of these substances are also banned by the International Olympic Committee and the National Collegiate Athletic Association.

Boron

This trace mineral has been reported to increase serum testosterone levels and muscular size and strength. A study by Nielson (1992) is frequently cited by the supplement industry as proof of these claims. This study showed that boron supplementation increased serum testosterone concentration up to 300 percent. The truth is that these dramatic increases in testosterone were experienced by boron-deprived postmenopausal women whose testosterone levels were quite low. The 12 women in the study hadn't received adequate boron intake for the previous 119 days prior to the supplementation. A study by Ferrando and Green (1993) concluded that boron supplementation produced no significant increases in serum testosterone, lean body mass or strength in a group of 19 male bodybuilders aged 20-27 years. It should also be noted that overt signs of boron toxicity occur when the intake is 50 milligrams per day or higher (Wheeler and Cameron 1994).

Choline

Choline is purported to increase muscular strength and decrease body fat. There are no valid studies documenting an ergogenic effect from this substance on strength training individuals (Williams 1992; Grunewald and Bailey 1993).

Chromium

This mineral has been marketed as an anabolic aid in the form of chromium picolinate. A study by Hallmark and others (1993) reported no significant effect of chromium supplementation in conjunction with strength training. In this study, chromium supplementation did not increase lean body mass or muscular strength or decrease body fat. Furthermore, claims that this product stimulates the release of human growth hormone are invalidated by the biomedical literature (Barron and Vanscoy 1993).

Clenbuterol

Clenbuterol is a veterinary drug approved for use in animals that aren't intended for food production or human consumption (Black 1992). The drug is used to increase muscle mass in show animals such as cattle, pigs and sheep. The manufacturer's claim that this product enhances anabolism is substantiated by published animal data but has not been documented in humans (Barron and Vanscoy 1993). The Material Safety Data Sheet for clenbuterol describes the drug as extremely potent and capable of causing tachycardia and nausea (Black 1992). In 1990, 135 people were hospitalized in Spain who had eaten beef liver that contained clenbuterol residues (Black 1992; Ropp 1992). Their symptoms included tachycardia, muscle tremors, headaches, dizziness, nausea, fever and chills. Clenbuterol is not approved by the U. S. Food and Drug Administration and isn't legally available in the United States.

Dibencozide

There are no published studies in humans or animals that suggest dibencozide enhances athletic performance or anabolism (Barron and Vanscoy 1993).

Erythropoietin

Simply known as EPO, erythropoietin stimulates the bone marrow to produce more red blood cells and is used for treating anemias. Increasing the number of red blood cells also increases the oxygen-carrying capacity of the blood system. For this reason, it appeals to those hoping to delay fatigue. However, as the body's red blood cell count rises and the blood thickens, the risk of experiencing blood clots, heart attack and stroke increases (Spalding 1991; Ropp 1992). In the late 1980s, EPO may have contributed to the deaths of 18 European cyclists (Spalding 1991).

Gamma Hydroxybutyric Acid

Commonly referred to as GHB, promoters claim that gamma hydroxybutyric acid stimulates the production of human growth hormone and thus produces muscle mass and weight loss. Through November 1990, there were 80 hospitilizations from GHB use (Ropp 1992). Patients reported that within 15-60 minutes of taking 1/2 - 3 teaspoons of GHB, they developed symptoms such as vomiting, drowsiness, dizziness, tremors, seizure-like movements, unconsciousness, bradycardia (a slowed heart rate), lowered blood pressure, breathing difficulty and breathing cessation. Patients recovered in 2-96 hours, usually with emergency room care.

Ginseng

This Chinese herb has been touted as an anabolic agent. Possible side effects from the use of ginseng include gynecomastia, hypertension, nausea, diarrhea and skin rashes (Goldman and Klatz 1992).

Human Growth Hormone

Commonly known as HGH, human growth hormone is produced naturally by the body. It's only approved medical use is in the treatment of pituitary dwarfism. Originally, HGH was extracted from the pituitary glands removed from human cadavers. Later, HGH was produced synthetically in the lab (Taylor 1985). It is believed that HGH promotes muscle growth and muscle strength but this hasn't

The only safe method for increasing muscular size and strength is to combine an intensive strength training program with sensible nutritional practices. (Photo by Rick Phelps)

been confirmed by researchers (Ropp 1992). In a study by Yarasheski and others (1990), HGH supplementation during a strength training program did not increase muscular size, strength or protein synthesis more than the effects produced by strength training alone. Moreover, Saartok (1988) reports that the use of HGH increases the load on the joints and leads to arthritis.

Too much HGH produced by a hyperactive pituitary gland or a tumor — and perhaps by an exogenous intake — is the cause of acromegaly. The term acromegaly was coined by Dr. Pierre Marie in 1886 (Hoberman 1992). Acromegaly is characterized by bony overgrowths in the skull, the hands and the feet and overgrowths of the soft tissue above the eyes (Taylor 1985). There is also a thickening of the skin along with changes in the jawbone size that result in large gaps between the bottom teeth (Taylor 1985). Because of these monstrous appearance-altering side effects, acromegaly is sometimes referred to as "Frankenstein Syndrome." Other side effects include diabetes mellitus, goiter, excessive sweating and cardiovascular disease (Taylor 1985). Acromegaly almost always shortens the life span of the person it afflicts (Taylor 1985) because of the resulting heart disease.

Inosine

Inosine is purported to increase muscular strength. Claims that inosine is beneficial to muscular growth or any form of athletic performance in healthy individuals is purely speculative (Lambrinides 1990b; Barron and Vanscoy 1993). Likewise, there are no valid studies documenting an ergogenic effect on strength training individuals (Williams 1993). Excessive consumption of inosine can lead to gout (Lambrinides 1990b).

Magnesium

Magnesium has been touted as a substance for enhancing muscular growth and strength. McDonald and Keen (1988) did not find any data showing an ergogenic effect of magnesium supplementation in individuals who had normal body magnesium levels. These findings are consistent with a study by Terblance and others (1992). In general, scientific research is not supportive of any ergogenic effect from the use of magnesium (Williams 1993).

Ma Huang

This natural herb contains ephedrine and pseudoephedrine. Large doses of ephedrine can cause insomnia, nervousness, cardiac arrhythmias, vertigo and headaches (PDR 1994). Hypertension has also been noted from the use of ma huang (Barron and Vanscoy 1993).

Smilax

This substance is advertised as a means of increasing serum testosterone, muscle growth and strength. There are no valid studies documenting an ergogenic effect from the use of smilax in strength trained individuals (Williams 1993).

Yohimbine

There are no objective data to support the claim that yohimbine increases muscle mass or strength (Barron and Vanscoy 1993). Potential side effects include tachycardia, migraine headaches, dizziness and tremors (Goldman and Klatz 1992; PDR 1994). Hypertension, irritability and nervousness have also been reported as side effects from the use of yohimbine (PDR 1994).

THE SAFE STEROID ALTERNATIVE

Clearly, the potential risks from using steroids and most steroid alternatives far outweigh any possible benefits. The only safe steroid alternative is to combine an intensive and progressive strength training program with sensible nutritional practices using the guidelines presented throughout the earlier chapters.

15

ACROSS THE AGES: ADOLESCENCE AND ADULTHOOD

The aging process begins the moment after conception and continues until death. No one escapes the effects of the aging process. However, certain activities may delay its effects. Two extremes of the aging process demand additional attention: adolescence and adulthood. With minor adjustments, both the young and the old can achieve excellent results from using the same type of program as is recommended for the general population.

THE ADOLESCENT POPULATION

Adolescents who perform strength and conditioning activities on a regular basis can obtain numerous physical benefits. A safe, practical and productive strength training program facilitates the normal growth and development of the muscles, bones and connective tissue. Strengthening these biological components is also an excellent precautionary measure against injury. In addition, young athletes can perform closer to their potential by increasing their functional strength. Conditioning activities can prepare young athletes for the demands of a particular sport. Proper conditioning will also help youngsters to maintain proper bodyweight and a desirable level of body fat. Furthermore, adolescents who exercise can perform their daily activities without showing signs of undue fatigue. Finally, strength and conditioning activities improve self-discipline, self-confidence and self-esteem during the critical identity-forming years.

The Adolescent Growth Spurt

The strength and body proportions of boys and girls are essentially the same and remain so until the beginning of adolescence. Until girls enter their so-called "adolescent growth spurt," there is little difference in stature between the two genders (Smith 1984a). The adolescent growth spurt is a period of accelerated increases in height and weight that occurs with the onset of adolescence. The age of onset and the duration of the spurt varies considerably from one individual to another. The adolescent growth spurt usually accompanies the onset of sexual maturation (Mussen, Conger and Kagan 1979).

In normal boys, the adolescent growth spurt may begin as early as the age of 10-1/2 or a late as 16 (Mussen, Conger and Kagan 1979). For the average boy, rapid accelera-

tion in growth begins at about 13 years of age (Mussen, Conger and Kagan 1979) and reaches a peak velocity at about 14.06 years of age with a standard deviation of .92 years (Smith 1984a).

In normal girls, the adolescent growth spurt may begin as early as 7-1/2 years of age or as late as 14-1/2 (Mussen, Conger and Kagan 1979). For the average girl, rapid acceleration in growth begins at about 11 years of age (Mussen, Conger and Kagan 1979) and reaches a peak velocity at about 12.14 years of age with a standard deviation of .88 years (Smith 1984a).

Adolescents who perform strength and conditioning activities on a regular basis can obtain numerous physical benefits.

Strength training in the late teenage years has generally been accepted as being safe and productive. (Photo by Mark Asanovich)

Determining the earliest age at which a youngster can safely initiate a strength training program is based upon skeletal development. Chronologically, a youth might be 13 years old but may only be 11 in terms of skeletal maturation; conversely, another 13 year old might possess the skeleton of a 15 year old. These wide individual variations in maturation can create a difficult dilemma for establishing a reasonably safe age at which to begin strength training. Skeletal age can be predicted accurately from the X rays of bones in various parts of the body such as the hand and the wrist. However, physicians sometimes use assessments that are more practical. For example, the Tanner Staging System is used to predict strength, muscle and epiphyseal maturity by using various stages of the development of the secondary sexual characteristics such as the pubic hair, genitalia, breasts (in females) and plasma hormone levels (Goldman, Bush and Klatz 1984).

Unfortunately, there is no clear-cut borderline for determining a safe age at which to begin strength training because each person "ages" at a different rate. Most youngsters are physically mature enough to begin weight training at about the age of 13 or 14. The best advice, however, is to proceed cautiously and carefully.

The Growth Plates

The cartilaginous discs that lie between the diaphysis (central shaft of the bone) and the epiphysis (the end of the long bone) are known as the growth plates. The growth plates are the structures responsible for longitudinal growth of the immature bone. Longitudinal bone growth ceases when the diaphysis and the epiphysis are united or fused and the disc is replaced by bone. Much of the concern in strength training at an early age focuses on the potential risk of damaging the epiphysis. Excessive loads on immature bones, extreme weight bearing activities and various overuse injuries associated with highly repetitive activities may interrupt the normal bone growth patterns or predispose an individual to injury.

The Preadolescent

Strength training in the late teenage years has generally been accepted as being safe and productive. By the late teenage years, most individuals have reached a level of skeletal maturation that greatly reduces the risk of injury. However, strength training activities for preadolescents is controversial. According to Lillegard and Terrio (1994), most studies have shown that preadolescents can attain significant increases in strength with an adequate training stimulus. (Strength gains in preadolescents are more likely to be from neural adaptation rather than muscular hypertrophy. Presumably, this is because the preadolescent lacks an adequate level of testosterone.) Many studies have shown positive results in preadolescents but few have explored injury rates. One of the few studies to examine the injury rates of the preadolescent was performed by Rians and coworkers (1987). In their 14-week study, 18 preadolescent children showed a significant increase in strength from 30 minutes of strength training activities performed 3 times per week. The study showed that a short-term, supervised program for preadolescents results in a low injury rate and does not adversely effect bone, muscle or epiphysis nor does it adversely effect growth, flexibility or development. The study had one injury: a shoulder strain.

According to the American Academy of Pediatrics (1990), preadolescents can increase strength without significant injury if trained and supervised by knowledgeable adults. However, additional studies are needed to examine the potential risk to the growth plates in the preadolescent population. It should also be noted that the preadolescent may not possess the level of emotional maturity necessary to understand age-appropriate goals.

Avoiding Adolescent Injury

Risser (1991) reports that few injuries occur in carefully supervised programs. The need for providing good supervision in order to prevent injuries to adolescents has been echoed by other authors (Brady, Cahill and Bodnar 1982; Risser, Risser and Preston 1990; ACSM 1991; Rice 1993; Tanner 1993).

Young individuals must avoid movements that place an unreasonable amount of stress on the musculoskeletal system so as not to disturb the growth plates. Numerous authors have questioned the potential for injury to adolescents from the competitive lifting movements. The American Academy of Pediatrics (1990) has noted that the competitive lifting movements have a significant potential for injury in adolescents. Potentially dangerous movements that have been identified as being orthopedically unsafe include plyometrics (Horrigan and Shaw 1990), barbell squats and Olympic-style lifting movements such as power cleans and snatches (Jesse 1977; Rice 1993). Risser (1991) noted injuries from the competitive lifts including the clean and jerk, the power clean, the snatch and the barbell squat. Brown and Kimball (1983) investigated the risks to teenagers who perform powerlifting movements. The researchers administered a questionnaire to 71 competitors entered in the 1981 Michigan Teenage Powerlifting Championship. The population sustained 98 injuries relating to powerlifting which caused a discontinuance of training for a total of 1,126 days. The low back region suffered 50 percent of all powerlifting injuries. Risser, Risser and Preston (1990) examined the incidence of injury related to weight training by surveying 354 junior and senior high school football players. The power clean, the clean and jerk and the barbell squat accounted for the majority of the injuries.

The message is clear: The competitive lifting movements are potentially dangerous — particularly to the preadolescent and adolescent populations — and should not be included in a strength training program. (Chapter 1 discusses the orthopedic hazards of the competitive lifts in greater detail.)

THE OLDER POPULATION

A slow but steady increase in life expectancy has resulted in the progressive aging of the general population. As people age, there is a gradual loss in muscular strength. Peak muscular strength is usually attained by the age of 20 in females and between the ages of 20 and 30 in males. Strength appears to remain relatively stable until the ages of about 35 to 45 and then declines gradually with increasing age (Wilmore 1982). The decline in strength may be due to a reduction in muscle mass (Tzankoff and Norris 1977). Indeed, Grimby and Saltin (1983) have suggested that much of this strength loss is due to quantitative rather than qualitative changes in muscles. This has been confirmed by Brown, McCartney and Sale (1990) who found that older men respond to weight training in a qualitatively similar manner as young men. In other words, the muscles of older adults still function basically the same as when they were younger — it's just that they have less muscle mass within their bodies. Between the ages of 25 and 55, people lose muscle mass at the rate of one-half pound per year. In other words, the average 55 year old has 15 pounds less muscle than at age 25. The loss of lean tissue (i.e., muscle, bone, etc.) intensifies after the mid 50s (Westcott 1994). This loss in strength may actually be significant enough to hinder those daily activities that nearly everyone else takes for granted, such as rising from a chair or even walking.

Osteoporosis is a condition of decreased bone density. As a person ages, the risk of osteoporosis increases. The result of a decrease in bone density is a more porous bone that is more apt to break when placed under extreme stress. In addition, a bone that is broken will take longer to heal in an older person. Osteoporosis is a major health concern for women of all ages. Although individuals differ, bone density begins to decrease at around the age of 40 (Wilmore 1982).

Research Findings

Studies have shown that older men and women demonstrate significant and favorable responses to weight training. Early research examining the effects of strength training on older adults found marked improvements in strength but little evidence of muscular hypertrophy. In an 8-week study by Moritani and deVries (1980), young and old men showed similar and significant percentage increases in strength from progressive strength training. Because of the absence of significant hypertrophy, the authors speculated that the effect of the strength increases in the old may

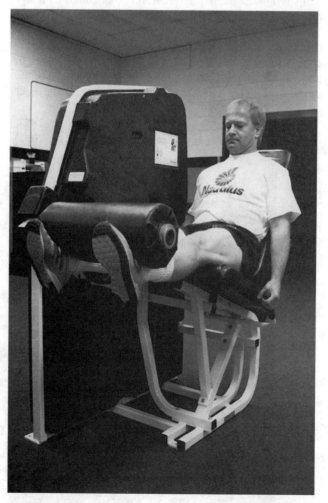

The loss of lean tissue may be delayed for decades through appropriate exercise.

be due to neural adaptation. Other researchers have also demonstrated significant increases in strength in the older population. A 12-week study by Aniansson and Gustafsson (1981) found significant strength gains in the lower extremities of 12 men (aged 69-74) who exercised 3 times per week. In a study by Hurley and others (1984), 13 untrained males (aged 40-55) exercised 3 times per week for 16 weeks. The subjects performed one set of 8-12 repetitions to volitional fatigue on 14 different exercises. The high intensity program in this study produced a 50 percent increase in upper body strength and a 33 percent increase in lower body strength. A 26-week study by Pollock and his associates (1991) involving men and women (aged 70-79) concluded that older men and women can make significant improvements in muscular strength (and maximum oxygen uptake) with appropriate training. In a 13-week study by Koffler and her colleagues (1992), the training program resulted in average increases of 41 percent in the upper body strength and 45 percent in the lower body strength of 7 healthy, untrained men. Significant gains in strength by the older adult have also been reported by Larsson (1982).

Frontera and coworkers (1988) were the first to report that strength gains in older men were associated with significant muscular hypertrophy. Their 12-week study had 12 healthy, untrained men (aged 60-72) perform strength training activities 3 days per week. The subjects experienced a marked and rapid improvement in dynamic strength and a substantial increase in the cross-sectional area of the thigh. Additional studies have since demonstrated that older adults can increase both muscular size and strength. In a 12-week study by Brown, McCartney and Sale (1990), 14 elderly males (aged 60-70) experienced a 17.4 percent increase in maximal cross-sectional area of the elbow flexors. The researchers concluded that elderly individuals retain the potential for significant increases in strength performance and upper limb muscle hypertrophy in response to overload training. A 12-week study by Charette and her associates (1991) reported a significant increase in the lower body strength of 13 elderly women (average age 69.8). The authors also reported that the gains in strength were due — at least in part — to muscle hypertrophy. The researchers concluded that a program of resistance exercise can be safely carried out by elderly women and can significantly increase muscle strength. A 14-week study by Hurley and his associates (1991) reported a 41 percent increase in the lower body strength of 6 healthy, untrained men. The subjects in this particular study also experienced an 8 percent increase in the cross-sectional area of the midthigh. In a 12-week study by Roman and others (1993), five elderly males (average age 67.6) experienced significant increases in muscle mass and isokinetic strength from a strength training program that was performed two times per week. The authors concluded that the skeletal muscles of elderly individuals can adapt to heavy resistance exercise and do so by increases in both muscle size and strength. In a study by Westcott (1994), 116 men and women (aged 55-82) trained 2 or 3 days per week for 8 weeks. Their program consisted of endurance exercise (20-25 minutes) and strength training (20-25 minutes). The strength training exercises were performed for one set of 8-12 repetitions. On the average,

Older individuals demonstrate significant and favorable responses to strength training.

the subjects added 2.5 pounds of muscle, lost 4.5 pounds of fat and increased their overall strength by almost 60 percent.

Gains in muscular size and strength have even been demonstrated by individuals in their tenth decade of life by using standard progressive resistance training techniques. An 8-week study by Fiatarone and others (1990) examined the effects of a high intensity strength training program on frail, institutionalized volunteers. The 10 men and women (average age of 90) performed the program 3 times per week. The authors concluded that high intensity resistance training leads to significant gains in muscle strength, size and functional mobility among individuals of up to 96 years of age.

The Fountain of Youth?

Scientific evidence indicates that the loss of lean tissue may be delayed for decades through appropriate exercise. In addition, regularly scheduled strength training sessions may slow the rate of strength decline that is associated with the aging process. In fact, older individuals have the potential for obtaining substantial increases in muscular strength. Strength training exercises can also have a positive influence on bone density thereby combating the crippling effects of osteoporosis. Is strength training important for older adults? According to Riley (1981b), "It is not how much you lift, but how long you continue to lift." After searching for more than 500 years, perhaps men and women have finally discovered the fountain of youth.

APPLICATIONS FOR THE YOUNG AND THE OLD

With minor adjustments, all of the general guidelines that have been suggested in the previous chapters apply to the younger and the older individual. It's critical to reemphasize several points.

Intensity

A strength training program will produce excellent results if performed with a high level of intensity (i.e., when each exercise is performed to the point of concentric muscular failure). Hurley and his associates (1984) had subjects (aged 40-55) perform one set of 8-12 repetitions to volitional fatigue on 14 different exercises. The high intensity program in this study produced a 50 percent increase in upper body strength and a 33 percent increase in lower body strength. Fiatarone and others (1990) reported that high intensity strength training leads to significant gains in muscle strength, size and functional mobility among individuals of up to 96 years of age. During the first thirteen weeks of a 26-week study by Pollock and his coworkers (1991), moderate weights were used and the subjects (aged 70-79) were not required to work to fatigue; after the thirteenth week, the intensity of training was increased and the subjects were encouraged to complete each exercise to maximum fatigue.

Some younger teenagers and older adults may not tolerate high intensity strength training very well. Those who aren't comfortable with high intensity training can terminate the exercise a few repetitions short of muscular failure. It should be noted that regressions are more appropriate than negatives as post-fatigue repetitions for the younger and the older populations.

Repetitions

It's much safer for the young and the old to perform more repetitions than suggested for the general population in order to reduce orthopedic stress. For example, younger teenagers and older adults should use slightly higher repetition ranges — such as 20-25 repetitions for exercises involving the buttocks, 15-20 repetitions for the legs and 10-15 repetitions for the upper torso. The higher repetition ranges will necessitate using somewhat lighter weights, which will in turn reduce the stress placed upon their bones and joints.

Many individuals will want to "max out" to see how much they can lift for one repetition. There is no need for anyone to perform a one-repetition maximum (1-RM) — particularly a younger person (Rice 1993). Attempting a 1-RM increases the risk of injury. In a study by Pollock and his colleagues (1991), 1-RM strength testing resulted in 11 injuries (19.3 percent of the subjects). Performing a 1-RM also tends to cause an abnormally high increase in blood pressure, which can be dangerous for older adults — particularly those with hypertension. Younger and older individuals should never do less than 10 repetitions of any exercise.

Speed of Movement

To decrease the risk of injury, younger individuals should be required to perform each exercise with a controlled speed of movement (Rice 1993; Tanner 1993). The same is true for older adults (Cress and Colacino 1992). In a study by Fiatarone and coworkers (1990), elderly individuals performed each repetition in 6-9 seconds. Explosive lifting is dangerous. If explosive lifting doesn't cause immediate musculoskeletal damage, it will certainly predispose someone to future injury.

Range of Motion

Both the young and the old should perform each exercise throughout the greatest possible range of motion that safety allows. This will promote or maintain flexibility. Arthritis and painful joints are common problems associated with the aging process. Older individuals who suffer from arthritis or inflamed joints should exercise throughout a range of movement that is pain-free (Cress and Colacino 1992).

Duration of the Workout

A productive workout for a younger or an older person can be performed in 30-40 minutes. The young and the old do not need to spend much more time than that engaged in strength training activities. Both younger and older individuals are highly susceptible to overuse injuries to the muscles and connective tissue. The risk of overuse injuries will be greatly reduced by eliminating marathon strength sessions in the weight room.

The Major Muscle Groups

The major muscle groups (i.e., the hips, the legs and the upper torso) and the neck (if the person is involved in a combative sport) should be emphasized by the young (Tanner 1993) and the old. When selecting exercises, keep in mind that youngsters with relatively small frames may not fit properly on some machines. In the case of preadolescents, calisthenic-type movements that involve their bodyweight as resistance (such as push-ups and sit-ups) are quite effective for building strength without placing an inordinate amount of stress on their bones and joints.

Frequency of the Workout

The strength training sessions for adolescents should be performed 2-3 times per week on nonconsecutive days (Rice 1993; Tanner 1993). This also applies to the older adult. However, older individuals may need to reduce the frequency of their strength training sessions to permit sufficient recovery.

Workout Cards

Workout cards are an extremely valuable tool in making the workouts of the young and the old more meaningful and in providing a guide as to what should be accomplished.

16
FEMALE STRENGTH TRAINING

Females can make substantial gains in strength through weight training activities. However, it is important to understand that there is no need for gender-specific strength training. Even with the use of a high-powered microscope, it is literally impossible for a scientist to differentiate between female muscle tissue and male muscle tissue. In general, females can utilize the same strength training program as males.

DISPELLING THE MISCONCEPTIONS

Prior to the 1980s, strength training for females was not perceived to be socially acceptable primarily because of suspected masculinizing effects. These fears have subsided gradually but slowly. Nevertheless, one of the biggest misconceptions in strength training is the belief that females will lose flexibility and develop large, unsightly muscles.

Flexibility

It was noted in Chapter 6 that a properly conducted strength training program does not reduce flexibility. Exercising throughout a full range of movement against a resistance will maintain or even improve flexibility. Females who have residual fears about losing flexibility can perform a comprehensive stretching routine both before and after the strength training program. As an added measure, the muscles can also be stretched immediately following the completion of each exercise.

Muscle Size

Gains in muscular strength are usually accompanied by an increase in the size of individual muscle fibers. While this is true for both males and females, muscular hypertrophy is much less pronounced in females (Fox and Mathews 1981; Wilmore 1982). Increases in strength without accompanying hypertrophy is thought to be the result of neural adaptation (Ikai and Fukunga 1970; Krotkiewski et al. 1979; Moritani and deVries 1979).

As early as the 1960s, studies have demonstrated that females can achieve significant improvements in muscular strength without concomitant gains in muscle size (Capen, Bright and Line 1961; Wells, Jokl and Bohanen 1963). In a widely referenced study by Wilmore (1974), the largest increase in muscle size experienced by any of the 47 females

in the study was less than one-quarter inch. Substantial improvements in muscular strength have been demonstrated by females in other studies without a significant amount of muscular hypertrophy (Brown and Wilmore 1974; Mayhew and Gross 1974; Oyster 1979; Hakkinen, Pakarinen and Kallinen 1992). Darden (1983) estimates that the number of women who have the genetic potential to significantly increase the size of their muscles is about one in a million.

Clearly, strength training does not lead to excessive muscular bulk or produce masculinizing effects in the majority of females. There are several physiological reasons that prevent or minimize the possibility of a woman significantly increasing the size of her muscles.

Muscle-to-tendon ratio. In Chapter 3, it was noted that the potential for muscular growth is directly related to muscle length. Most women inherit relatively short muscle bellies

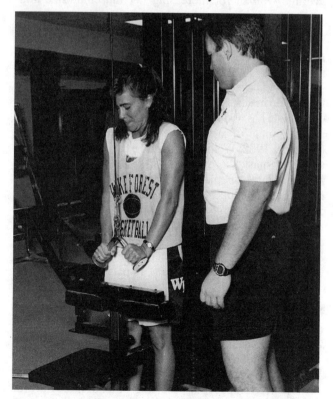

In general, females can utilze the same strength training program as males. (Photo by Wake Forest University)

coupled with long tendinous attachments (Darden 1983). As such, relatively few women possess the capacity for extreme muscular hypertrophy because they are genetically bound by an unfavorable and unchangeable ratio of muscle to tendon.

Testosterone levels. Recall that testosterone is a male sex hormone that has masculinizing effects. Compared to men, most women have low levels of serum testosterone. In fact, the average woman has approximately 100 times less serum testosterone than does the average man (Taylor 1985). The low level of this growth-promoting hormone restricts the degree of muscular hypertrophy in women (Oyster 1979; Fox and Mathews 1981; Wilmore 1982; Darden 1983; Westcott 1983; Wells 1985; Enoka 1988a; Tanner 1993).

The small percentage of females who do develop relatively large muscles may have slightly higher levels of serum testosterone than the average female. In a study by Krahenbuhl, Archer and Pettit (1978), the authors suggested that testosterone may play a role in the "trainability" of women. Hakkinen, Pakarinen and Kallinen (1992) reported a high correlation between the mean serum levels of testosterone and muscular hypertrophy in 10 women who participated in an intense strength training program.

This does not mean that a female who has a higher-than-average level of serum testosterone is any less of a woman. It simply means that she has a greater potential than the average woman for increasing her muscular size and strength.

Body fat. A final physiological factor that prevents or minimizes the possibility of a woman significantly increasing her muscular size is her percentage of body fat. Quite simply, females tend to inherit higher percentages of body fat than do males. For example, the average 18-to 22-year-old female has about 22-26 percent body fat, whereas the average male of similar age has about 12-16 percent (Wilmore 1982; Wells 1985). This extra body fat tends to soften or mask the effects of weight training (Fox and Mathews 1981). Females who possess very little subcutaneous body fat appear more muscular than they actually are because their muscles are more visible. Similarly, the appearance of muscle mass following a strength training program may not be the result of muscular hypertrophy. Rather, a decrease in subcutaneous fat may simply make the same amount of muscle mass more noticeable.

Interestingly, the distribution of fat is gender-specific. Males have a greater amount of their subcutaneous fat located in the abdominal and the upper regions of their bodies while females carry substantially more of their fat in the hips and the lower regions of their bodies (Wilmore 1982; Wells 1985). According to Wilmore (1982) and Wells (1985), the average female somatotype tends more toward endomorphy (fatness) while the average male somatotype tends more toward ectomorphy (leanness) and mesomorphy (muscularity).

Female Bodybuilders

In the case of female bodybuilders, they inherit a greater potential for muscular hypertrophy than the average woman. Highly competitive female bodybuilders have developed large muscles because of their genetic potential. They did not develop large muscles because they were engaged in bodybuilding activities. Wells (1985) notes that anabolic steroids may also have been used by female bodybuilders to enhance their muscular development.

Female bodybuilders often appear to be more muscular while posing on stage than they actually are. Prior to a competition, female bodybuilders have restricted their caloric intake — often severely — thereby reducing their body fat and water. They've also "pumped up" their muscles backstage immediately before the competition. Finally, the stage lighting, the clothing and the oil rubbed on their bodies all contribute to the illusion.

There is a relatively small number of women who have inherited the potential to experience significant muscular hypertrophy from strength training. However, the majority of women can gain considerable strength from a weight training program yet have little or no change in their muscle mass. Clearly, it is physiologically improbable for the average woman to develop large muscles that are unsightly or unfeminine.

GENDER STRENGTH DIFFERENCES

The comparison of strength performance between men and women has been under investigation since the early 1900s (Hettinger 1961). Strength differences between men and women are usually examined from the standpoint of

It is physiologically improbable for the average woman to develop large muscles that are unsightly or unfeminine. (Photo by Nautilus)

absolute strength (i.e., without regard to body size). It is important to also compare gender strength differences relative to bodyweight, body composition and muscle size.

Absolute Strength

In absolute terms, the average male is considerably stronger than the average female. In an early review of the literature, Hettinger (1961) concluded that "general muscle strength in women is about two thirds that of men." Since that time, numerous studies have compared the absolute strength levels of males and females and have reported varying degrees in the amount of the differences. In general, however, studies have consistently shown that males tend to be stronger than females in absolute terms.

It should be noted that the differences in strength between men and women are not consistent for all muscle groups. In comparison to men, women are weaker in the chest, the arms and the shoulders but are strongest in the legs (Wilmore 1974). Laubach (1976) reviewed nine published studies on the strength differences between men and women and found that the absolute upper body strength in women was 35-79 percent (averaging 55.8 percent) that of men while the absolute lower body strength was 57-86 percent (averaging 71.9 percent) that of men. The reason for this is probably related to the fact that both genders use their legs to a similar degree (e.g., standing, walking and running) but females have had less of an opportunity than males to use their upper limb muscles due to previous societal constraints (Fox and Mathews 1981).

Relative Strength

The average male is larger and heavier than the average female. Naturally, the greater bodyweight of males gives them a decided advantage over females in terms of absolute strength. Even more critical than considering differences in bodyweight as a factor in the expression of strength is to examine the difference in the body composition of males and females. Recall that the average female has more body fat than the average male. Having a higher percentage of body fat means that a lower percentage of lean body mass (i.e., fat-free weight such as muscles, bones and connective tissue) is available for use. For example, the average college-age male who weighs 154 pounds with 14 percent body fat would have 21.56 pounds of body fat and about 132.44 pounds of functional tissue [154 pounds times 14 percent equals 21.56 pounds minus 154 pounds equals 132.44 pounds]. On the other hand, the average college-age female who weighs 120 pounds with 24 percent body fat would have 28.8 pounds of body fat and 91.2 pounds of functional tissue [120 pounds times 24 percent equals 28.8 pounds minus 120 pounds equals 91.2 pounds]. So, the average college-age male has 28.3 percent more bodyweight [154 pounds compared to 120 pounds] and 45.22 percent more lean body mass [132.44 pounds compared to 91.2 pounds] than the average college-age female. Therefore, strength must be expressed relative to some measure of size in order to be a better indicator of the strength differences between males and females.

When expressed in relation to muscle size (i.e., the cross-sectional area of the muscle), there is no significant difference between the muscular strength of men and women.

Bodyweight and body composition. When the differences in bodyweight and body composition are taken into consideration, the relative strength differences between males and females are less appreciable. A study by Wilmore (1974) investigated the differences in the strength training response of 26 men and 47 women who used identical testing and training programs. (To minimize the learning effect, a minimum of 4 sessions were completed prior to the initial strength tests.) When leg strength values of the genders were expressed relative to bodyweight, the resulting values were almost identical. Furthermore, the leg strength of females was actually slightly higher than males when expressed relative to lean body mass. (In this study, the upper body measures for men were substantially greater than they were for women regardless of how the values were compared.) Bishop (1983) reported that women's upper body strength measurements averaged 60-70 percent of men's relative to bodyweight and 80-90 percent of men's relative to lean body mass. A study by Heyward, Johannes-Ellis and Romer (1986) involving 55 women and 48 men concluded that the gender differences in strength are a function of lean body mass and body composition (i.e., muscle and fat distribution).

Muscle size. Strength is directly related to muscle size (i.e., the cross-sectional area of the muscle). When expressed in relation to the cross-sectional area of a muscle, there is no significant difference between the muscular strength of men and women (Hettinger 1961; Ikai and Fukunaga 1968; Wilmore 1974; Westcott 1983). As an example, a study by Schantz and others (1983) examined strength per unit of cross-sectional area of muscle tissue of 18 physical education students (7 females and 11 males) and 5 male bodybuilders. The researchers found no significant differences between males and females when strength was expressed in relation to muscle cross-sectional area. Therefore, the differences in strength between males and females appear to be in the volume of muscle fibers not in the makeup of individual fibers. In other words, gender strength differences are quantitative rather than qualitative. This isn't surprising since muscle tissue is essentially the same regardless of gender.

In short, women inherit less muscle mass than men and are, therefore, generally weaker than men with regard to absolute muscle strength. However, the qualitative ability of muscle fibers to generate force is independent of gender (Fox and Mathews 1981; Wilmore 1982; Wells 1985). This means that although the male usually has larger muscles than the female, the force exerted by equal-sized muscles is the same in both genders (Fox and Mathews 1981).

EXERCISE AND PREGNANCY

The fundamental purpose of exercise during pregnancy is to maintain fitness and to prepare the woman for labor and delivery (Bryant and Peterson 1993). There does not appear to be any scientific evidence to suggest that women who perform an exercise program during their pregnancy will shorten or ease their labor and delivery. However, according to the American College of Sports Medicine (1991), it is reasonable to expect that an exercise program will facilitate labor and the recovery from labor.

Potential Benefits

There are numerous other potential benefits associated with exercising during pregnancy. First of all, women who exercise can better meet the progressive physical demands of pregnancy. By strengthening the muscles of the upper torso and the abdominal areas, a woman can compensate for the postural adjustments that typically occur during pregnancy as a result of the forward pull of the growing baby's weight. Women who have stronger muscles can counter fatigue and reduce the severity and the frequency of common pregnancy-related discomforts such as low back pain (Bryant and Peterson 1993). Additionally, pregnant women who develop muscular strength experience minimal biomechanical changes and are better able to maintain their normal activities during pregnancy. Exercising will also help control the amount of weight that a woman gains during pregnancy (Bryant and Peterson 1993). Finally, improving muscular strength can be good preparation for carrying a baby that may weigh 6-10 pounds at birth.

Concerns and Precautions

The safety of an exercise program is the most important consideration for a pregnant woman and her fetus. Proper exercise — including strength training — poses little risk to either the mother or the developing fetus. However, women who have never participated in a strength training program should not initiate one during pregnancy (Bryant and Peterson 1993). In addition, a physician should be consulted before a woman initiates any exercise program.

Although exercise poses little risk during pregnancy, there is the potential for adverse effects to both the mother and the fetus. As such, there are a few areas of concern that must be addressed. With several precautionary measures for added safety, a pregnant female can perform the same type of program that is recommended for the general population. In general, the program variables (e.g., intensity, frequency, volume and duration) should be decreased if a pregnant woman shows signs of exertional intolerance and chronic fatigue. Furthermore, a pregnant female should immediately consult her physician if she experiences any of the following warning signs or complications: abdominal pain or cramping, ruptured membranes, elevated blood pressure or heart rate, vaginal bleeding or a lack of fetal movement (Bryant and Peterson 1993).

Competing needs. During exercise, there is a possibility of competition for various maternal and fetal physiological needs such as blood flow, oxygen delivery and heat dissipation. The prospect of this biological competition is greatest during exercise performed in the third trimester (ACSM 1991).

When a person exercises, there is an increased blood flow to the working skeletal muscles. In fact, the working muscles may receive as much as 85-90 percent of the total blood flow (Fox and Mathews 1981). During pregnancy, the diversion of oxygen-rich blood to the exercising muscles of the mother leads to a transient reduction in blood flow and oxygen to the fetus. This threatens the fetus with the possibility of an inadequate blood and oxygen supply. However, low to moderate intensity exercise of less than 30 minutes does not seem to disturb uterine blood flow.

A potential threat to the safety of the developing baby — especially during the first trimester of pregnancy — is exercise-induced hyperthermia (i.e., an increased core temperature). Exercise is associated with a rise in both maternal and fetal body core temperature. The fetus usually maintains a core temperature slightly above that of the mother. In order to dissipate heat, the fetus must depend entirely on the mother's thermoregulatory abilities. To avoid heat complications, an exercising mother must be adequately hydrated, exercise at a level of intensity that is lower than her prepregnancy state and wear light clothing that permits heat loss. In addition, she must be aware of the existing environmental temperature and humidity. Pregnant females must avoid high ambient temperature and humidity during exercise due to potential problems in thermoregulation. During pregnancy, women should not exercise when the ambient temperature is greater than 90 degrees Fahrenheit and the relative humidity exceeds 50 percent (Bryant and Peterson 1993). Finally, an exercise program should not exceed 30 minutes in duration so as not to expose the fetus to prolonged thermal stress (ACSM 1991).

Increased joint laxity. Females experience an increased laxity in their ligaments and joints during pregnancy. Relaxin is a hormone that is progressively released after con-

traception. Relaxin helps loosen or "relax" the joints and the connective tissue. This allows the ribs and the pelvic cavity to expand in order to encompass the growing baby and to make delivery easier. However, connective tissue softens throughout the entire body and the joints become less stable. The increased joint and connective tissue laxity may make pregnant females more susceptible to back, hip, knee and ankle injuries. Exercise requiring extreme flexion or extension may also be harmful to the joints.

Pregnant females should use slightly higher repetition ranges than suggested for the general population. The higher repetition ranges will require the use of a lighter resistance, which will reduce the orthopedic stress placed upon their vulnerable joint structures. Additionally, pregnant women should not overstretch or perform exercises in a ballistic manner (ACOG 1985). The aim of flexibility programs during pregnancy should be to relieve muscle cramping or soreness and relax the lower back region to alleviate pain. Weightbearing exercises — such as jumping, hopping, twisting, bouncing and running — should be eliminated or minimized.

Supine exercise. The American College of Obstetricians and Gynecologists (1985) recommends that exercise not be performed in the supine (laying face-up) position after the fourth month of pregnancy. When in the supine position, the excess weight of the enlarging fetus may obstruct the flow of blood back to the mother's heart.

Caloric consumption. The intake of calories must be sufficient to meet the extra energy needs of pregnancy and any exercise that is performed. During pregnancy, a woman needs to consume about 300 additional calories per day.

17

STRENGTH TRAINING Q & A

There are some final random topics and issues that should be addressed. This chapter examines 20 of the most frequently asked questions concerning strength and fitness.

1. If explosive training doesn't develop fast twitch muscle fibers, why do studies show that the top Olympic-style weightlifters — who use explosive training methods — have such a high percentage of fast twitch fibers?

If a study shows that the top performers in a certain sport or event possess distinct anatomical traits or specific biochemical characteristics, it doesn't necessarily mean that those biological peculiarities were developed — or even enhanced — by their particular training methods. For example, gathering anthropometric data on elite swimmers may very well reveal that most of them have much wider hands than the average person. Does this mean that swimming increases the width of the hands? Of course not. Having wider hands is an inherited trait and provides a biomechanical advantage that allows swimmers to propel their bodies through the water more efficiently.

Individuals who are highly successful in a sport or activity have polished their skills and technique to perfection. In addition, elite performers possess all the physical, physiological, psychological and neurological qualities that are essential for excelling at the highest levels of competition. Those who are in short supply of the qualities that are necessary to be successful in a particular sport or activity have been systematically weeded out at the lower levels of competition. The sport of Olympic-style weightlifting involves movements that must be executed with great strength, speed and power. Having a high percentage of fast twitch (FT) muscle fibers is a prerequisite for success at Olympic-style weightlifting because these particular muscle fibers generate high levels of force in a relatively short amount of time.

Elite athletes possess all the physical, physiological, psychological and neurological qualities that are essential for excelling at the highest levels of competition. (Photo by Mike Fortenbaugh)

To emphasize correct breathing, exhale when the resistance is raised and inhale when the resistance is lowered.

It may be true that elite Olympic-style weightlifters have a high percentage of FT muscle fibers. However, those athletes are the survivors of a selective weeding out process of which a predominance of FT muscle fibers is a major criterion. Stated in other terms, any athlete with a less-than-favorable fiber type mix for successful weightlifting (i.e., a low percentage of FT fibers) will probably be eliminated well before reaching a world-class level. Finally, the high percentage of FT muscle fibers found in Olympic-style weightlifters was not produced or enriched by performing explosive movements. Rather, this predominant muscle fiber type was an inherited characteristic. (Chapter 3 discusses the role of genetics in greater detail and Chapter 4 presents an in-depth look at explosive training.)

2. What's the correct way to breathe when lifting weights?

It's important to breath properly while performing a strenuous activity such as strength training — especially during maximal efforts. Holding the breath during exertion creates an elevated pressure in the abdominal and thoracic cavities which is referred to as the Valsalva maneuver. The elevated pressure interferes with the return of blood to the heart. This may deprive the brain of blood and can cause a person to lose consciousness.

To emphasize correct breathing, exhale when the resistance is raised and inhale when the resistance is lowered. Or, simply remember EOE — Exhale On Effort. As it turns out, inhaling and exhaling naturally usually results in correct breathing.

3. What precautions should be taken when performing conditioning activities in hot, humid weather?

The importance of safeguarding the body against heat-related injuries cannot be overemphasized. Overweight individuals and those who are unaccustomed to laboring in the heat are most susceptible to thermal disorders which include heat exhaustion, heat stroke and heat cramps.

Under resting conditions, the body's core temperature is 98.6 degrees Fahrenheit (or 37 degrees Celsius) and there is a balance between heat production and heat loss. During exercise, the core temperature increases and triggers several physiological heat-loss mechanisms. The primary mechanism for heat loss during exercise is the evaporation of sweat (Howley and Franks 1992). The blood carries internal body heat to the surface of the skin where sweat is secreted from an estimated 2.5 million sweat glands and evaporation takes place. As the sweat evaporates it cools the skin; this in turn cools the blood. The cooled blood then returns to the warmer core and the cycle is repeated. This process cools the internal body. (To illustrate the effects of evaporation, wet your finger and blow on it. You'll quickly note a cooling sensation as the evaporative process withdraws heat from your skin.)

It's hard to believe, but people are constantly perspiring. In cool, dry weather a relatively small amount of sweat is produced and the rate of evaporation can keep up with the rate of perspiration. In this case, the skin is dry to the touch and the person isn't aware of sweating — even though this alone may involve about a quart of water per day.

However, this cooling mechanism doesn't work well when the heat or humidity is high. When the humidity is high, there's a lot of moisture already in the air. At higher levels of humidity, evaporation of sweat is hindered because the air is virtually saturated with water vapor and, as a result, there's no place for the extra moisture to go. This situation causes the body to overheat and may result in a heat-related injury. In fact, a temperature of only 80 degrees Fahrenheit becomes dangerous if the humidity reaches 90 percent.

Individuals should gradually acclimatize to heat and humidity. This may necessitate initially performing outdoor activities during the cooler parts of the day (i.e., early morning and late evening). Most adverse reactions to heat and humidity occur during the first few days of exercising outdoors. As individuals adapt to hot, humid conditions, they'll be able to exercise at greater levels of intensity while maintaining safe body temperatures. Adequate rest intervals should also be provided.

It's important to rehydrate with cold liquids as needed. The bodyweight should be measured each day before and after a conditioning session. In this way, water loss can be monitored to determine if adequate rehydration is taking place. About 16 ounces of water should be consumed for every pound of weight that is lost during exercise (Lowenthal and Karni 1990; Simmons 1994). Coaches who deny liquids to their athletes under adverse conditions are putting them at risk for a heat disorder.

Lightweight, light-colored clothing that is loose fitting should be worn to promote heat loss. (Lighter colors will reflect the sun's rays; darker colors will absorb them.) Under no circumstances should exercise be performed in rubberized clothing or the so-called "sauna suits" (Fox and Mathews 1981; Wilmore 1982). Exercising with the body covered in this manner can be lethal since these garments trap perspiration and cause the body to overheat rapidly.

4. How much recovery time should be taken between sprints?

It's important to receive sufficient recovery time between sprints. This allows the depleted energy systems to recover so that an all-out effort can be made. The duration of the recovery period is related to the distance of the sprint and the time that it takes to complete it. The rest interval is usually expressed in relation to the work interval. This is known as the "work:rest ratio" and is most often designated as 1:1, 1:2 or 1:3. These ratios state that a person will rest either one, two or three times the duration it takes to perform the sprint. As a general rule, the shorter the sprint time — and the higher the intensity — the greater the work:rest ratio. Because of the high level of intensity, any sprint of less than 30 seconds requires a 1:3 work:rest ratio. As an example, a 20-second sprint should receive a rest interval of about 60 seconds. Sprints from 30-90 seconds have between a 1:3 and 1:2 work:rest ratio. Finally, sprints from 90-180 seconds need between a 1:2 and 1:1 work:rest ratio.

5. Doesn't the eccentric phase of an exercise cause excessive muscle damage and soreness?

Almost everyone who has performed any kind of physical activity will experience some degree of muscular soreness. The two types of muscle soreness are acute and delayed-onset (Fox and Mathews 1981). Acute muscle soreness occurs during and immediately following exercise. A theory advanced by deVries (1974) suggests that this soreness is associated with an occlusion of blood flow to the muscles (ischemia). Because of the lack of adequate blood flow, metabolic waste products (e.g., lactic acid) cannot be removed and accumulate to the point of stimulating the pain receptors in the muscles. On the other hand, delayed-onset muscular soreness (DOMS) refers to the pain and soreness that occurs 24-48 hours after exercise. The exact cause of DOMS is unknown. The most popular theory is that cellular damage occurs to the muscle fibers and/or connective tissue such as tendons.

Perhaps muscular friction is at least partly responsible for muscular soreness. Friction is created anytime the surface of an object contacts and slides over or across another object. The "attach-rotate-detach-rotate" action proposed by the Sliding Filament Theory implies that there is friction within the muscles during a muscular contraction. Friction creates irritation and too much irritation can injure the tissue. For example, if a person were to use a hammer on a regular basis for a short period of time callouses would begin to develop on the palms. Basically, these callouses

are a protective adaptation to frictional heat. However, if the hammer was used for a long enough period of time blisters would develop instead. In this instance, the excessive friction has surpassed the tissue's adaptive ability because it was too much and too frequent. This "blistering" effect may also occur within muscle tissue whenever there is excessive internal muscular friction.

Most research studies investigating eccentric exercise use running downhill, cycling backward, stepping down from heights and lowering weights as ways of loading muscles eccentrically. A number of studies have concluded that eccentric muscle contractions produce greater DOMS and more severe muscle damage than either concentric or isometric contractions. However, many studies of exercise-induced soreness usually loaded the muscle to an excessive degree. For example, a study by Armstrong, Oglivie and Schwane (1983) had untrained rats running down a 16-degree grade "at rapid rates of speed" for 90 minutes. According to the authors, the 16-degree decline was chosen because it was the steepest that could be used before the animals began to slide down the tread surface. At times, electrical stimulation was necessary to encourage the rats to continue running. A study by Schwane and his coworkers (1983) had untrained individuals run 5.25 miles downhill on a treadmill at a 10 percent grade at 7 miles per hour for 45 minutes. In both studies, muscle biopsies showed extreme cellular damage and basically concluded that eccentric exercise causes injury to the muscles. Both of these studies invoked protocols that stressed the muscle eccentrically to such an extreme that there was no doubt that a significant amount of cellular damage would occur. This would be analogous to having someone listen to music played through headphones at an excruciatingly loud decibel level and then concluding that music causes hearing loss. A better conclusion for these studies would have been that the extreme loading of muscle tissue for an extended period of time causes cellular damage.

The truth is that cellular damage and muscle soreness can occur if a muscle is loaded concentrically, isometrically or eccentrically with comparable levels of stress. A study by Carpinelli and Gutin (1991) found that eccentric muscle actions did not induce a greater level of DOMS than did concentric muscle actions. The results of a study by Fitzgerald and others (1991) suggest that exercise intensity — not muscle contraction type — may be the dependent factor in producing exercise-induced muscle soreness. Moreover, the researchers concluded that "there appears to be no difference in the degree of exercise-induced muscle soreness between subjects who perform concentric isokinetic contractions and those who perform eccentric isokinetic contractions at equal levels of power."

The eccentric contractions that are most likely to produce injury are those that occur during the braking of high velocity ballistic movements (Marsden, Obeso and Rothwell 1983). In proper strength training, however, the eccentric loading of a muscle is performed with a controlled speed of movement. Furthermore, the duration of the eccentric loading during proper strength training is for a much shorter period of time than is used in most studies. For instance, if a weight is lowered in about 3-4 seconds per repetition, then the eccentric component for a set of 15 repetitions is about 45-60 seconds. Compare that to the 45-90 minutes of eccentric loading that occurred in the two previously mentioned studies.

Eccentric exercise is safe and productive as long as it's not performed to an extreme. As a person becomes better trained with eccentric-based exercise, muscular soreness and tissue damage are reduced (Clarkson and Tremblay 1988). A gradual progression in the intensity of exercise usually helps in reducing the possibility of excessive muscular soreness.

6. Is it really necessary to warm up in order to maximize physical performance?

The research regarding the need for a warm-up seems to be inconclusive. Some studies have shown that a warm-up facilitates performance; other studies have shown that performances without a prior warm-up are no different than those with a warm-up (Wilmore 1982). Nevertheless, a

The vertical jump can be improved in a safe manner by practicing jumping skills and techniques in the same way they are used in the sport and by strengthening the major muscle groups. (Photo by Larry French)

warm-up has both physiological and psychological importance. In addition, warming up prior to an activity involving rapid muscle contractions — such as sprinting — is advisable to reduce the risk of injury.

Warm-up activities usually consist of low intensity movements such as light jogging or calisthenics. Regardless of the warm-up activity, the idea is to systematically increase the blood circulation and the body temperature. Breaking a light sweat during the warm-up indicates that the body temperature has been raised sufficiently and that the person is ready to begin stretching the muscles. Recall that there's no need to stretch or warm up prior to strength training provided that a relatively high number of repetitions are performed and the weight is lifted in a controlled manner.

7. Will plyometrics improve my vertical jump?

Not necessarily. Since the mid 1960s, plyometrics have been romantically endorsed as a way to "bridge the gap" between strength and speed. The first reference to these types of exercises in American athletic literature appears to have been by the Soviet author Verkhoshansky (1966). However, the term plyometrics seems to have been coined much later by Wilt (1975). Plyometrics apply to any exercise or jumping drill that uses the myotatic or stretch reflex of a muscle. This particular reflex is triggered when a muscle is pre-stretched prior to a muscular contraction, resulting in a more powerful movement than would otherwise be possible. For example, just before jumping vertically — such as for a rebound — a person bends at the hips and the knees. This "countermovement" pre-stretches the hip and the leg muscles allowing the person to generate more force than if the jump were performed without first squatting down. Popular exercises based on this principle include bounding, hopping and various box drills (such as depth jumping). Upper body plyometrics frequently incorporate medicine balls to induce the myotatic reflex.

A study by Kramer, Morrow and Leger (1993) concluded that the "relative value of plyometric training for athletes is unclear." A study by Cook and his colleagues (1993) notes that plyometrics are "controversial." Clearly, most of the support for plyometrics is based upon personal narratives and sketchy research. There is little scientific evidence that definitively proves plyometrics are productive (Duda 1988; Pipes 1988b; Wikgren 1988; Andress 1990). While muscular force is certainly increased by the pre-stretch, it doesn't necessarily follow that a training benefit occurs (Cook et al. 1993). An 8-week study by Scoles (1978) found no significant improvement in vertical jump or long jump performance in 26 college-age subjects who performed depth jumps two times per week. Blattner and Noble (1979) reported no significant difference in the vertical jump between a group training with an isokinetic leg press and a group training with depth jumps. Clutch and others (1983) concluded that plyometric exercises (i.e., depth jumps of varying heights) are no more effective than a regular jumping routine for increasing leg strength and the vertical jump. Ford and his associates (1983) found no significant differences in the 40-yard dash and the vertical jump between one group using weight training and two groups using plyometrics. An 8-week study by Blakey and Southard (1987) found no significant differences in dynamic leg strength and leg power between one group who performed maximum vertical jumps from ground level and two groups who performed depth jumps from different heights. Research by Durak (1987) demonstrated that plyometrics have no effect on power development. A study by Christensen and Melville (1988) concluded that university football players did not derive practical performance benefits from a supplemental 9-week depth jumping program. Kramer, Morrow and Leger (1993) found no significant differences in the vertical jump, the leg press and the peak power of the quadriceps between a group who performed a strength training program and a group who performed a strength training program and plyometrics.

More importantly, the possibility of injury from plyometrics is positively enormous. Blattner and Noble (1979) noted that a disadvantage of plyometrics (i.e., depth jumping) is the potential for injuries. According to Leistner (1987), plyometrics are not safe under any circumstances. In addition to finding no performance benefits from plyometric exercises, Christensen and Melville (1988) also concluded that the relationship found between perceived knee stress and depth jumping warrants more research into the injury potential of this type of training. Hutchins (1992) notes that the use of plyometric exercises is "irresponsible." Cook and his coworkers (1993) noted the risk of injury associated with plyometrics. Additional strength and fitness professionals have questioned the safety of plyometrics (Kennedy 1986b; Duda 1988; Pipes 1988b; Wikgren 1988; Andress 1990; Horrigan and Shaw 1990; Thomas 1994; Watson 1994). When performing plyometrics, the musculoskeletal system is exposed to repetitive trauma and extreme biomechanical loading. Plyometrics place an inordinate amount of strain on the connective tissues of the lower body (Leistner 1987). The most common plyometric-related injuries are patellar tendinitis (Wikgren 1988; Horrigan and Shaw 1990) and stress fractures (Wikgren 1988). Blattner and Noble (1979) note that previous research examining depth jumping has reported shin splints and strains of the ankle and the knee. Leistner (1987) also reports compression fractures related to the use of plyometrics. Other potential injuries include — but aren't limited to — sprains, heel bruises, meniscal damage and ruptured tendons. Young athletes are especially vulnerable (Horrigan and Shaw 1990).

Plyometric exercises involve eccentric muscle contractions that are ballistic, violent, uncontrolled and extreme. According to Faulkner, Clafin and McCully (1986), the high eccentric contractions that occur during the braking of high velocity ballistic movements (Marsden, Obeso and Rothwell 1983), downward stepping (Newham, Jones and Edwards 1983) and downward jumping (Dyhre-Poulsen and Laursen 1984) are most likely to produce injury. A review of the literature by Sale and MacDougall (1981)

notes the possibility of joint injury in cases where the rebound technique involves impact.

Further research is needed to determine if plyometric exercises are safe and effective (Fahey 1989). At this point, plyometrics have not been proven to be productive and carry an unreasonably high risk of injury. The vertical jump can be improved in a much safer manner by simply practicing jumping skills and techniques in the same way that they are used in the sport and by strengthening the major muscle groups, especially the hips and the legs.

8. When I stop lifting weights my muscles will turn to fat, right?

Wrong. It's a common misconception that muscle can be turned into fat. In truth, muscle cannot be changed into fat —or vice versa — any more than lead can be changed into gold. Muscle tissue consists of special contractile proteins that allow movement to occur. The composition of muscle tissue is about 70 percent water, 22 percent protein and 7 percent fat. Conversely, fatty tissue is composed of spherical cells that are specifically designed to store fat. Fatty tissue is about 22 percent water, 6 percent protein and 72 percent fat. Because muscle and fat are two different and distinct types of biological tissue, muscles can't convert to fat when a person stops lifting weights. Similarly, lifting weights — or doing any other rigorous activity — won't cause fat to change into muscle. The fact is that muscles atrophy — or become smaller — from prolonged disuse and muscles hypertrophy — or get larger — as a result of physical exercise.

9. Is it okay to perform sit-ups and leg lifts with straight legs?

Sit-ups and leg lifts should never be performed with straight legs. Laying flat on the back with the hips and the legs in an extended position will exaggerate the arch in the lower back area. When the legs are extended, the iliopsoas muscle of the frontal hip area is stretched out and it tugs the lumbar spine into an exaggerated curve known as lordosis (Lindh 1980; Wirhed 1984). This position creates maximal peak compressive and shear forces in the lumbar region. On the other hand, when the knees and the hips are bent and supported, the iliopsoas muscle is relaxed. This flattens the lumbar curvature and decreases the spinal load (Lindh 1980). Using computer simulation, Johnson and Reid (1991) showed that compressive forces and shear forces were dramatically reduced during the performance of a sit-up exercise with the hips and the knees flexed at 90 degrees. With the hips and the knees flexed at 90 degrees, the iliopsoas generates the least amount of tension. In brief, the compressive and shear forces in the lumbar region are minimized as the degree of hip flexion is maximized.

The abdominals are used primarily during the first 30 degrees of the sit-up. Thereafter, the hip flexors accept most of the workload. For this reason, a partial sit-up — typically referred to as a "crunch" or a "trunk curl" in weight room jargon — can be more effective than a full sit-up.

This limited range movement will target the abdominals and reduce the involvement of the hip flexors. It should also be noted that abdominal activity is greater when the feet are not held or fixed (Johnson and Reid 1991). Stabilizing the feet activates the iliopsoas (Norris 1993).

To perform a trunk curl, lay on the floor and place the backs of the lower legs on a bench or a stool. The angle between the upper and the lower legs should be about 90 degrees. Likewise, the angle between the upper legs and the torso should be about 90 degrees. Fold the arms across the chest and tuck the chin in to the torso so that the head is off the floor. Tucking the chin will help maintain a flat lower back throughout the movement, thereby reducing the amount of stress placed on the lumbar region during the performance of the exercise. To perform the movement, bring the torso up to the legs without snapping the head forward, pause briefly in this position and then return the torso back to the starting position. The next repetition should be performed immediately after the bottom portion of the shoulder blades touches the floor. To maintain tension on the muscles throughout the sit-up movement, the shoulders should not touch the floor between repetitions.

Sit-ups — or any other exercise — should not be performed in a rapid, ballistic manner. Explosive movements create momentum which removes tension from the muscles and makes the exercise less efficient. More importantly, rapid flexion of the spine can place excessive stress on the

The knee-up should be performed instead of leg lifts with straight legs.

posterior structures of the lumbar spine and may ultimately lead to its degeneration (Norris 1993).

Performing leg lifts with straight legs does little to activate the abdominal muscles. Rather, the iliopsoas muscle is most active and tends to pull the lumbar spine into lordosis (Lindh 1980). Because of this, the knee-up described on page 123 should be performed instead of leg lifts with straight legs. Under no circumstances should the so-called "Roman Chair" sit-up be done. This particular movement hyperextends the spine and places undue stress on the low back area (Lindh 1980) which has led to numerous injuries (Brady, Cahill and Bodnar 1982).

10. What guidelines should be used when stretching the muscles?

First of all, it's important to understand that a person's flexibility is effected by several inherited characteristics, particularly the ratio of muscle-to-fat and the insertion points of the tendons. In addition, a person's flexibility has structural limitations including bones, tendons, ligaments and skin. It should also be noted that flexibility is joint-specific — a high degree of flexibility in one joint doesn't necessarily indicate a high level of flexibility in other joints.

Like all other forms of exercise, stretching movements have certain guidelines that must be followed. In order to make stretching safe and effective, each stretch should be performed under control without bouncing, bobbing or jerking movements. Bouncing during the stretch increases the risk of tissue damage. Each stretching movement should be held for about 30-60 seconds. A person should also attempt to stretch a little bit farther than the previous time. Progressively increasing the range of motion will improve flexibility. A person should remain relaxed during each stretch while inhaling and exhaling normally without holding the breath.

Flexibility work should be done on a regular basis and should address the major muscle groups (i.e., the hips, the legs and the upper torso). Stretching should be done prior to a conditioning session or any activity that involves rapid muscular contractions. Muscular soreness will be reduced by stretching after an activity.

11. Does the Strength Shoe really work?

The Strength Shoe is a modified athletic shoe with a four-centimeter thick rubber platform attached to the front half of the sole. This attachment prevents the heel from striking the ground during exercises and drills. The shoe is touted as an effective method of increasing ankle flexibility, calf circumference and "speed, quickness and explosive power" when used in a plyometrics-based training protocol. (Question 7 of this chapter discusses plyometrics in greater detail.)

A study by Pezullo, Whitney and Irrgang (1993) sought to determine if a 10-minute jumping program using the Strength Shoe could improve vertical jump. The 31 test subjects were randomly assigned to one of three groups. One group performed a 10-minute jumping program wearing the Strength Shoe. A second group did the same 10-minute jumping program wearing regular athletic shoes. The third group acted as the control. The study found that subjects who performed a 10-minute jump training program in Strength Shoes (or regular athletic shoes for that matter) did not significantly increase their vertical jump height greater than the subjects who acted as controls.

In an 8-week study by Cook and his colleagues (1993), 12 subjects performed the training protocol recommended by the manufacturers of the Strength Shoe. The subjects were randomly assigned to two groups. One group wore Strength Shoes during the workouts while the other group wore their usual training shoes. The workouts lasted about 45 minutes and were performed 3 times per week. Despite following the suggested protocol of the manufacturers, no enhancement of flexibility, strength or performance was observed for participants wearing the Strength Shoe at the end of the 8-week training program. In this particular study, it's important to note that one third of the subjects who wore the Strength Shoes complained of anterior tibial pain (shin splints) and one subject withdrew from the study because the pain was severe. All of the subjects were previously involved in strenuous activities and none of the subjects reported leg pain prior to the study. Additionally, no subject wearing normal training shoes reported leg pain. As such, the authors felt that "the pain was device-related." In summation, the researchers concluded, "The use of the Strength Shoe cannot be recommended as a safe, effective training method for development of lower leg strength and flexibility."

12. What's the best exercise for getting rid of the "spare tire" around my mid-section?

In exercise physiology parlance, the belief that exercise causes a localized loss of body fat is known as "spot reduction." A litmus test for evaluating the prospect of spot reduction is to examine whether a significantly greater change occurs in an active or exercised bodypart compared to a relatively inactive or unexercised bodypart. Gwinup, Chelvam and Steinberg (1971) compared the circumference and the thickness of subcutaneous fat at specific sites on both arms of a group of tennis players. The use of these particular athletes as subjects in this study is important since tennis players have subjected one side of their bodies to a significantly greater amount of exercise and activity than the other side of their bodies over a number of years. As would be expected, the study noted that both the upper and lower arms on the more active side of the body were significantly more hypertrophied than the upper and lower arms on the less active side of the body. However, there was no significant difference in the thickness of subcutaneous fat over the muscles of the arm receiving more exercise as compared to the arm receiving less exercise. This study provides direct evidence against the notion of spot reduction.

Many people perform countless repetitions of sit-ups, knee-ups and other abdominal exercises every day with the belief that this will give them a highly prized set of "washboard abs." Although such Olympian efforts will certainly work the underlying abdominal muscles, it has little effect on the overlying fatty tissue. The reason a person can't lose fat in one area alone is because during exercise energy stores are being drawn from all over the body as a source of fuel — not just from one specific area. So, a person can do endless abdominal exercises, but that won't automatically trim the mid-section. A study by Katch and his associates (1984) evaluated the effects of a 27-day sit-up exercise training program on the fat cell diameter and body composition of 13 subjects. Over this 4-week period, each subject performed a total of 5,004 sit-ups (with the knees flexed at 90 degrees and no foot support). Fat biopsies from the abdomen, subscapular and gluteal sites revealed that the sit-up exercise regimen reduced the fat cell diameter at all 3 sites to a similar degree. In other words, exercising the underlying abdominal musculature did not preferentially effect the subcutaneous fatty layer in the abdominal region more than the buttocks or the subscapular areas. Quite simply, spot reduction is physiologically impossible (Wilmore 1982; Wells 1985; Clark 1990; Bubb 1992b).

The abdominals should be treated like any other muscle group. Once an activity for the abdominals exceeds about 70 seconds in duration, it becomes a test of endurance rather than strength. The abdominals can be fatigued effectively in a time-efficient manner by exercising them to the point of concentric muscular failure within 8-12 repetitions (or about 40-70 seconds).

13. Why are the Eastern European athletes so much better than American athletes in most sports?

The Eastern European countries — particularly the former Soviet Union and the German Democratic Republic (i.e., East Germany) — went to great lengths and spent enormous amounts of money to identify, select, organize and develop thousands of athletically gifted children for the single-minded purpose of achieving athletic success and concomitant political status. However, the Eastern Europeans are not — and never were — the athletic juggernaut that some organizations and publications make them out to be. The media has also contributed to perpetuating the myth of Eastern European athletic superiority. The truth is that those countries are highly successful in a relatively small number of sports including weightlifting, gymnastics, wrestling, boxing and ice hockey. These sports are as exceedingly popular in the Eastern European culture as are football and basketball in the United States. Athletes in these sports are treated as celebrities and heroes in their particular countries — just as football and basketball players are in America.

Oddly enough, many individuals look to incorporate the latest Eastern European "secret" training methods into their programs. Clearly, the Eastern European athletes certainly win their share of medals, but they certainly do not overpower the rest of the world in athletic competition. For instance, how many Eastern European track and field athletes have dominated events such as the 100-, 200- and 400-meter dashes, the hurdles and the long, triple and high jumps? The answer is very few. Yet, Eastern European methods of conditioning are still espoused as being some sort of miracle breakthrough or advancement. And how much of the athletic success by the Eastern Europeans can be attributed to their well-documented, state-sponsored drug programs? Additionally, all of the research coming out of a country with state-sponsored drug programs for their athletes must be seriously questioned.

14. What strength tests are recommended for checking the progress of my athletes in the weight room?

Strength testing isn't really necessary to monitor progress. If individuals are recording their workout data — and they should — their workout card can simply be checked to evaluate their strength levels. This doesn't mean that strength testing cannot be done — some coaches use it as a motivational tool. That's fine, as long as the strength test doesn't become a weightlifting meet.

The most popular — and traditional — way to assess muscular strength has been to determine how much weight an individual can lift for a one-repetition maximum (1-RM). Unfortunately, attempting a 1-RM is potentially dangerous. Muscular strength can be measured in a safe and practical — yet reasonably accurate — manner without having someone "max out." There is a direct relationship between the percentage of maximal load (strength) and repetitions-to-fatigue (anaerobic endurance): As the percentage of maximal weight increases, the number of repetitions decreases in an almost linear fashion. Unless a person has an injury or other musculoskeletal disorder, the kinship between muscular strength and anaerobic endurance remains constant. Since there is a distinct relationship between these two variables, anaerobic endurance can be determined by measuring strength . . . and strength can also be determined by measuring anaerobic endurance.

This relationship is not exactly linear but it's close enough to determine a reasonably accurate linear approximation for describing the relationship between the two variables. In fact, the following mathematical equation can be used to predict a 1-RM based upon repetitions-to-fatigue:

$$\text{PREDICTED 1-RM} = \frac{\text{Weight Lifted}}{1.0278 - .0278X}$$

where x = the number of repetitions performed

Example: Suppose that a male athlete did 8 repetitions-to-fatigue with 150 pounds. First, multiplying .0278 by the number of repetitions [8] equals .2224. Subtracting .2224 from 1.0278 leaves .8054. Dividing .8054 into the weight lifted [150 pounds] yields a predicted 1-RM of about 186 pounds.

In other words, he can do 8 repetitions with about 80.54 percent (or .8054) of his predicted 1-RM. Regardless of whether his strength increases or decreases, he will always be able to perform exactly 8 repetitions with roughly 80.54 percent of his maximum. Therefore, if he increases his 8-RM (his anaerobic endurance) by 20 percent [from 150 to 180 pounds] then he'll also increase his 1-RM (his muscular strength) by 20 percent [from 186 to 223 pounds]. A study by LeSuer and McCormick (1993) found that the preceding formula was especially accurate for predicting a 1-RM bench press (r=.99).

It appears as if the relationship is not quite as linear beyond about 10 repetitions. So, this formula is only valid for predicting a 1-RM when the number of repetitions-to-fatigue is less than 10. It should also be noted that if the repetitions exceed about 10, then the test becomes less accurate for evaluating anaerobic endurance as well as for estimating a 1-RM. At any rate, a test of anaerobic endurance — though not a direct measure of pure maximal strength — is much safer than a 1-RM lift because it involves a submaximal load. (Because genetic factors — particularly predominant muscle fiber type — play a major role in anaerobic endurance, the aforementioned formula will not be accurate for everyone. However, the formula will still be practical for much of the population.)

The Super Slow Protocol involves 15-second repetitions: The weight is raised in 10 seconds and lowered in 5 seconds.

Finally, the purpose of strength testing should not be to compare the strength of one person to another. It's unfair to make strength comparisons between individuals because each person has a different genetic potential for achieving muscular strength. Strength testing is much more meaningful and fair when an individual's performance is compared to his or her last performance — not to the performance of others.

15. Does the Super Slow Protocol really work?

Sure it does. Any protocol that creates a sufficient level of muscular fatigue and involves progressive resistance is effective for increasing strength. The Super Slow Protocol was developed and refined by Ken Hutchins in the early 1980s. Essentially, Super Slow is performing a set of an exercise using 15-second repetitions: The weight is raised in 10 seconds and lowered in 5 seconds. Because of the elongated duration of each repetition, a set done with the Super Slow Protocol for the upper torso might be composed of 3-5 repetitions. This slow, purposeful speed of movement greatly reduces the effects of momentum. This increases the amount of muscular tension thereby making the exercise more efficient. Further, the controlled speed of movement decreases the stress on the joint structure and reduces the possibility of injury. Because of this, the Super Slow technique seems absolutely ideal for rehabilitation. So, from these standpoints Super Slow is desirable. However, the Super Slow Protocol isn't always practical — especially when training large numbers of people. Generally, the speed of movement must be monitored by either counting cadence or by using a stopwatch. In addition, the slower speed of movement means that a person isn't able to use as much weight as usual. There's nothing wrong with using less weight since the amount of muscular tension is more important than the weight being used. However, some people might find that using a much lighter weight is distressing to their egos. Nevertheless, the Super Slow Protocol is safe and productive and makes a great deal of sense.

16. What exercise(s) work the lower part of the biceps?

Selected parts of an individual muscle cannot be isolated. When a muscle contracts, it shortens across its entire length. However, certain parts of a muscle group can be emphasized. For example, the quadriceps are actually composed of four different muscles: the vastus lateralis, the vastus intermedius, the vastus medialis and the rectus femoris. A different muscle of the quadriceps can be emphasized — but a section of one of those muscles cannot be isolated. The same is true of the biceps as well as all other muscles.

17. What do the two sets of numbers on the weight stack of the Universal Gym leg press mean?

If the leg press incorporates Universal's Dynamic Variable Resistance (DVR), the two numbers correspond to the estimated resistance in the starting and the mid-range positions. As the leg press is performed, the resistance slides up and down the movement arm on rollers thereby changing the length of the resistance arm (RA). In positions of inferior leverage (and inferior strength), the length of the RA is relatively short. This creates a mechanical advantage and a lower level of resistance. As the hips and the legs move into a position of superior leverage (and superior strength), the length of the RA becomes longer. This creates a mechanical disadvantage and a higher level of resistance. The end result is greater muscular effort throughout the range of motion. The lower number on the weight stack indicates the approximate resistance in the starting position and the higher number denotes the approximate resistance in the mid-range position. (Chapter 10 discusses DVR in greater detail.)

Another version of the Universal leg press does not utilize DVR. This variation of the leg press has two foot pedals positioned at different points on the force arm (FA). Figure 17.1 illustrates the dynamics of the lower and the upper foot pedals of the Universal leg press. The force necessary to maintain the 100-pound resistance in a static position using the lower and the upper foot pedals can be calculated using the formula "force times force arm equals resistance times resistance arm" or, more simply, "F x FA = R x RA." The force arm (FA) is defined as the distance from the axis of rotation (i.e., the fulcrum) to the point where the force is applied or exerted. In this example, the length of the FA is 36 inches when using the lower foot pedals and 24 inches when using the upper foot pedals. The resistance arm is defined as the distance from the axis of rotation to the point where the resistance is applied. In this example, the RA is 36 inches regardless of whether the lower or the upper foot pedals are used. Inserting the values of the FA, the RA and the resistance into the previously mentioned formula reveals that a force of 100 pounds is required to maintain the resistance in a static position using the lower foot pedals and a force of 150 pounds is necessary to maintain the resistance in a static position using the upper foot pedals. In other words, the shorter FA of the upper foot pedals produces a mechanical disadvantage and a higher level of resistance. The longer FA of the lower foot pedals produces a mechanical advantage and a lower level of resistance. So, the upper pedals correspond to the heavier weight stack numbers and the lower foot pedals correspond to the lighter numbers.

Finally, recall that the upper foot pedals should be used if available. Using the lower foot pedals tends to create excessive shear forces in the knee joint because of the undesirable biomechanical position of the legs.

18. What determines whether a strength and fitness professional is negligent in causing an injury to someone?

According to Nygaard and Boone (1985), negligence is when an individual fails to act as a reasonable and prudent person would act in a similar situation. If an individual is sued, a judge or a jury determines the appropriateness of the person's actions. Four factors are considered in assessing whether someone is negligent. All four of these factors

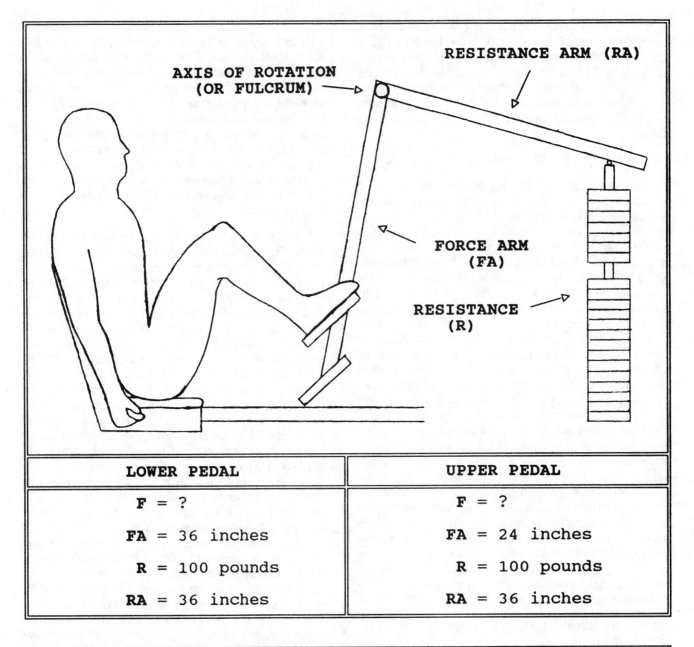

LOWER PEDAL	UPPER PEDAL
F = ?	F = ?
FA = 36 inches	FA = 24 inches
R = 100 pounds	R = 100 pounds
RA = 36 inches	RA = 36 inches

Force x Force Arm = Resistance x Resistance Arm	
(F)(36") = (100 lbs)(36")	(F)(24") = (100 lbs)(36")
F = 100 pounds	F = 150 pounds

Figure 17.1: Universal leg press lower and upper foot pedals

must be present to determine negligence. An individual won't be found negligent if any one of these factors is absent.

The first factor in determining negligence is that there must be a presence of a duty. The strength and fitness professional has a number of responsibilities which include providing adequate supervision and offering a safe environment with good equipment maintained in proper condition. The strength and fitness professional must also warn users of the inherent risks of strength training activities. It is important to understand that an individual can only assume risks that are inherent to strength training. Individuals should not assume the risk of using improper technique or performing potentially dangerous exercises that have been recommended by someone else. The strength and fitness professional must evaluate and determine the limitations of the users based upon age, maturity, experience and previous injuries. In the event of an injury, the strength and fitness professional must provide first aid and reasonable medical assistance as soon as possible.

A second consideration in determining negligence is that one of the aforementioned duties must have been breached. The third factor is whether the breach of duty was responsible for someone's injuries. The breach of the duty and the resulting injury will be examined to determine if the breach of duty was a substantial factor in the injury. Finally, the extent of the damages or injuries is considered.

19. Is the adage "No pain, no gain" really true?

To a degree, yes. The most critical factor in achieving gains in muscular size and strength is the level of intensity or effort. As an exercise becomes more intense, it also becomes more uncomfortable . . . and more painful. The discomfort and pain is related to the high concentration of blood lactic acid (a metabolic byproduct of high intensity, short-duration energy production). However, a person must differentiate between muscular pain and orthopedic pain. Pain throughout a muscle during intense activity is normal and indicates a high degree of effort. Pain throughout a joint during intense activity is abnormal and indicates a possible orthopedic problem.

20. What are the signs of overtraining?

Overtraining is a result of overstressing the body. Excessive stress is produced from performing too many exercises, too many sets and/or too many workouts. Symptoms of overtraining include chronic fatigue, appetite disorders, insomnia, depression, anger, substantial weight loss or gain, muscle soreness, anemia and an elevated resting heart rate (Lambrinides 1990b).

The most obvious indicator of overtraining, however, is a lack of progress in muscular strength. A lack of progress can be identified by keeping accurate records of the resistance that is used and the repetitions that are performed for every exercise done in the weight room. The best cure for overtraining is to provide rest in order to permit the body to recover. This may necessitate reducing the volume of sets, exercises or workouts that are performed. Taking some time off periodically from working out will also help avoid overtraining.

18

DEVELOPING A COURSE IN STRENGTH TRAINING

Courses in strength training have become exceedingly popular at the scholastic and the collegiate levels. This chapter will assist instructors in developing a professional course in strength training that is based upon the material contained in the previous 17 chapters of this book. The focus of this chapter is on teaching strength training to students majoring in physical education and exercise science along with other fitness and rehabilitative curriculums. However, the content can be easily adapted for the so-called Basic Instructional Program in order to meet the needs of the general student population as well.

THE BASIC INSTRUCTIONAL PROGRAM

In a strength training course targeted for the general student population, an instructor should limit the instructional portion of the course to basic anatomy, muscular function, general strength training principles and correct exercise technique for whatever equipment is available. In this case, the students should be supplied with a basic understanding of strength training, instructed in the safe, efficient use of the exercise equipment and permitted to initiate their programs. In other words, lectures should be kept to a minimum so that the students are physically active. After all, that's why they're taking the class. Some students will undoubtedly want more detailed information and seek the instructor out as the "resident expert." Others will simply want to work out on the equipment.

If grades are to be given, an appropriate grading system must be chosen. Grades should not be given on the basis of how much weight someone can lift or how well a student looks in exercise clothing. Such criteria only reward those students who possess favorable genetics for strength training. Additionally, grading on improvement can be unfair since the degree of the training response is also a function of individual genetics (Riley 1983c). Students should be given grades based upon their attendance, attitude, class participation and correct exercise technique. In the Basic Instructional Program, a few simple — but challenging — quizzes concerning strength training fundamentals and exercise technique can also be given to students as part of their grades. Grading in this fashion will place all students on equal ground.

THE PROFESSIONAL MAJOR'S COURSE

Professional strength training courses have also gained widespread popularity for students majoring in the various fitness and rehabilitative curriculums. A large number of universities offer excellent courses in strength training theory and applications. With a course designed exclusively for future strength, fitness and rehabilitative professionals, the instructional content must be far more detailed and technical since these are the men and women who will be instructing others about exercise, fitness and strength training. Naturally, the weight room is an excellent place for the learning of proper lifting technique and the practical applications of strength training. However, much of the professional course should take place in the classroom so that the fundamentals of strength training are firmly established.

WRITTEN EVALUATION OF THE STUDENT

In order to determine how much a student has learned, an instructor must make some type of evaluation. As noted previously, students should not be graded on how much weight they can lift or even on how much they improve on that amount. It has also been noted that evaluations are more fair when based upon attendance, attitude, class participation and correct lifting technique.

Written evaluations are given to students to measure their understanding of the course material and their grasp of the specific instructional objectives. In addition, testing motivates students to learn and provides them with feedback on how well they are learning. The nature — and the degree of difficulty — of these written examinations will differ depending upon the level of comprehension that the students are meant to achieve. For instance, an evaluation of those majoring in exercise science at the collegiate level would be much more detailed and involved than an evaluation of the general student population at the scholastic level.

Regardless of the level of comprehension being tested, it is important to create tests — and test questions — that make valid and reliable assessments of the students' comprehension of the instructional objectives. Writing good test questions is truly an art that demands much time, thought and effort.

TYPES OF TEST QUESTIONS

Essentially, test questions fall into two main categories: subjective and objective. Each type of question has its advantages and disadvantages. However, there are some general guidelines that apply to all types of questions.

Students should be given the directions or "ground rules" for each type of test question. The point values for each question should also be indicated so that the students know how much their answer is worth. In addition, the examination should not contain any optional questions. By using optional questions, an instructor is basically giving students different tests and, therefore, the students can't be compared fairly or accurately. Every question on the test should be important and every student should be expected to respond to it (Owen, Blount and Moscow 1978).

Subjective Test Questions

Traditionally referred to as "essay," subjective questions involve responses that contain the logical organization of written information. Subjective test questions include long-answer, short-answer and completion. These types of questions are very similar in format and only vary in the length of the response that the student needs to write.

Essay questions are good for testing general explanations, interpretations and problem-solving concepts — all of which may be difficult to measure with objective test questions. Additionally, essay questions can be developed faster than other types of questions. On the other hand, essay questions are difficult to grade objectively. If an instructor has a large class, correcting essay questions can also be extremely time-consuming. Finally, the grading of essay questions can be inconsistent and may favor those students who write well.

There are several guidelines for preparing a good essay test question. First of all, an essay question must be written clearly so that all students interpret it the same way. In addition, the requested information should not be too general. Instead, essay questions should ask for specific knowledge. To indicate the exact intent of the question, clear and precise words must be used in the question such as describe, outline, define, compare, contrast, explain, discuss and list.

An instructor should make an answer key listing the major points that are to be contained in each answer. This makes grading much easier and more consistent. Finally, an instructor should grade all of the answers to Question #1, then all of the answers to Question #2 and so on. This also allows for more consistency in grading.

The following is a brief description of long-answer, short-answer and completion test questions. (Figure 18.1 shows several examples of the three types of subjective test questions along with specific directions for answering them.)

Long-Answer. This type of essay question is used for answers that require anywhere from several paragraphs to several pages. The long-answer essay question is useful when a very detailed explanation is desired.

Short-Answer. The format of the short-answer essay question is very similar to that of the long-answer, except that it is used for answers to questions that require only a few sentences. Short-answer essay questions are effective when a brief explanation of some point is desired.

Completion. The completion question is also related to the essay question format. Sometimes referred to as "fill in the blank," completion questions require a response of about three words or less. The answer to a completion question should be a significant word. When writing completion questions, only one or two blanks should be included in any one statement. In addition, the blanks should be located near the end of the sentence.

Objective Test Questions

The two most popular types of objective test questions are multiple-choice and true-false. The biggest advantage of objective test questions is that subjective judgments are not involved in the grading. Furthermore, objective test questions can be graded quickly and efficiently. For these reasons, objective tests are the most widely used type of written evaluation. One of the main criticisms of objective questions, however, has been that they encourage guessing. Indeed, how does an instructor really know if the students actually knew the requested information or simply guessed correctly?

Objective test questions are excellent for evaluating definitions, facts, techniques and terminologies. Additionally, a well-constructed objective test question can measure insight, interpretation and understanding of the subject material. However, such questions are often difficult and time-consuming to prepare.

The following is a brief description of multiple-choice and true-false questions. (Figure 18.2 shows several examples of the two types of objective test questions along with specific directions for answering them.)

Multiple-Choice. The most frequently used form of objective test question is the multiple-choice question. This type of question greatly reduces the likelihood of good guessing. In fact, it's been suggested that in a 10-question test in which each question offers four alternatives, the probability of getting seven right answers by luck is one in a thousand (Payne 1974).

Multiple-choice questions are perhaps the most difficult type of question to construct properly. The multiple-choice question consists of two parts: the stem and several alternatives. The stem is also known as the question or the preliminary statement. It should be simple, concise and in the form of a complete question or a statement. (Testing experts recommend that the stem be in the form of a question.) If any negatively stated questions are used, the negative words (e.g., no, not, none, never and except) should be

PART I - LONG-ANSWER

Directions: Read each statement below and answer it in 1-2 paragraphs. Be concise.

1. Describe the four guidelines that are necessary for developing and improving aerobic fitness. (8 pts)

2. Give three reasons why most women will never significantly increase the size of their muscles. (6 pts)

3. Discuss the two major reasons why momentum should not be used to lift a weight. (4 pts)

PART II - SHORT-ANSWER

Directions: Read each statement below and answer it in 1-2 sentences. Be brief but to the point.

4. Describe the two requirements necessary to increase the efficiency at performing sports skills. (4 pts)

5. Name two advantages of using dumbbells. (4 pts)

6. Define the term "hyperplasia." (2 pts)

PART III - COMPLETION (2 points each)

Directions: Read each statement below and fill in the blank(s) with your response.

7. The horseshoe-shaped muscle that is located on the back of the upper arm is the _____.

8. When the learning of one skill facilitates the learning of a second skill it is called _____ transfer.

9. The muscle that is the antagonistic counterpart of the quadriceps is the _____.

Figure 18.1: Sample subjective test quesitons

PART IV - MULTIPLE-CHOICE (2 points each)

Directions: Read each of the following questions and select the best response from the given alternatives. Place your selection in the blank to the left of the question number.

_____ 10. What portion of the deltoid is exercised during a front raise?

     A. anterior   B. distal   C. middle   D. posterior

_____ 11. What type of muscular contraction occurs when a muscle lengthens against a load?

     A. isotonic   B. isometric   C. eccentric   D. concentric

_____ 12. What somatotype is characterized by long limbs, leanness and a slender physique?

     A. endomorph   B. ectomorph   C. mesomorph   D. pinomorph

PART V - TRUE-FALSE (1 point each)

Directions: Read each statement below and decide whether it is true or false. If the statement is true, put an A in the blank to the left of the question number; if the statement is false, put a B in the blank to the left of the question number.

_____ 13. The body's preferred fuel source during intense exercise is protein.

_____ 14. Hip adduction describes the action of bringing the legs together.

_____ 15. Muscles turn into fat during periods of inactivity.

Figure 18.2: Sample objective test questions

emphasized through underlining, capitalizing or emboldening. Finally, the stem should not give clues to the answers of other questions on the test.

The alternatives are also known as choices; the incorrect alternatives are known as distractors or foils. The number of alternatives usually ranges from three to five. All alternatives should be about the same length and follow a parallel structure that is grammatically correct. In addition, the placement of the correct answer among the distractors should not follow a repeating pattern. In other words, the correct answers should appear sometimes first, sometimes last and sometimes in the middle. Finally, all alternatives should seem plausible and reasonable.

True-False. The other popular type of objective test question is the true-false. The major drawback of a true-false question is that a student has a 50 percent chance of guessing the right answer since there are only two alternatives.

A true-false question should be stated in positive terms unless the negative word is emphasized. When true-false questions are used, there should be the same number of true statements as false statements. Once again, the answers should follow no particular sequence. In answering the true-false question, students sometimes make a "T" that looks very much like an "F." To avoid confusion, the student should use an "A" for a true response and a "B" for a false response or simply write out the words "true" and "false."

EVALUATING TESTS

It's always a good idea for instructors to evaluate their tests. After each written test, all the responses to every question should be examined. If the majority of the class missed a particular question, then it's likely that either the question was written poorly or the material wasn't covered well in class. In any event, it probably wasn't the fault of the students. In the case of poorly written questions, all students should receive the full value of the question since it wasn't fair.

Tests should not be made so difficult that the class average is 50 percent and the students are graded on a curve. A test serves no purpose when the average student only understands half the material. Such a test is far too difficult and needs to be simplified. On the other hand, an instructor shouldn't give a test that is so easy that everyone gets an A. Clearly, instructors must prepare tests and test questions with just the right level of difficulty.

LESSON PLANS

Daily lesson plans can be constructed in a number of different ways. The best form is the one that is most functional for each individual instructor. However, a lesson plan should include the topic or the activity, the instructional objective(s) for the students and an outline of the content.

The following 14 lesson plans are based upon the content of the previous 17 chapters of this book. Each lesson plan includes a general outline and numerous instructional objectives. An instructor can develop more specific outlines and instructional objectives based upon the purpose of the course and the needs of the students. These lesson plans can be modified rather easily in terms of number and design to accommodate differences in class times, course lengths, available equipment, student ages, levels of comprehension and course objectives. If used, written examinations can be scheduled at the discretion of the instructor. (Note that the number enclosed in parentheses under each reading assignment corresponds to the chapter number where the assignment may be found in this book.)

Courses in strength training have become exceedingly popular at the scholastic and the collegiate levels. (Photo by Mark Asanovich)

LESSON #1
Topics for Discussion:
A. Course Introduction
B. Course Objective
    1. To provide students with enough information so that they are capable of developing strength and conditioning programs that are safe, productive, efficient and practical.
C. Course Procedures
    1. Course outline/syllabus and grading policies (attendance, attitude, attire, class participation, exercise technique and written examinations).
Reading Assignment:
A. Strength Training: Past, Present and Future (1)
B. Speed of Movement: An Explosive Issue (4)
C. Developing Athletic Skills (5)

LESSON #2
Instructional Objectives:
The student will be able to
    1. explain how the practice of hiring competitive weightlifters influenced the development of myths and misconceptions about strength training.
    2. discuss the practical problems associated with periodization.
    3. describe the drawbacks and the dangers of attempting a one-repetition maximum.
    4. identify orthopedically unsafe exercises.
    5. discuss the two main areas of orthopedic concern with the barbell squat.
    6. describe the order of muscle fiber recruitment.
    7. describe the "size principle" of motoneuron recruitment.
    8. discuss the belief of explosive "carryover."
    9. discuss the two major reasons why momentum should not be used to lift a weight.
    10. explain why a muscle produces less tension at faster speeds of movement.
    11. explain the difference between skills and abilities.
    12. explain the difference between open and closed skills.
    13. distinguish between the three types of transfer.
    14. give an example of the kinesthetic aftereffect.
    15. discuss four problems that occur when practicing sports skills with weighted objects.
    16. explain how the Principle of Specificity applies to motor learning.
    17. discuss the four elements of specificity.
    18. describe the three stages of motor learning.
    19. describe the two requirements necessary to improve motor skills.
    20. discuss the belief of sport-specific, position-specific and gender-specific exercise.
    21. define ability, motor learning, motor unit, overload training, periodization, Principle of Specificity, skill, spondylolysis and torque.
Topics for Discussion:
A. Strength Training: Past, Present and Future (1)
    1. History of Strength Training
    2. Weightlifter-inspired Programming
        a. Explosive lifting
        b. Specificity
        c. Periodization
        d. One-repetition maximum attempts
        e. Orthopedically unsafe exercises
        f. Free weight superiority
        g. Core exercises
        h. Unnecessary warm-up sets
B. Speed of Movement: An Explosive Issue (4)
    1. The Birth of a Controversy
    2. Scientific Legitimacy
    3. Fiber Recruitment

    4. "Explosive" Specificity
    5. Momentum
      a. Reduced efficiency
      b. Injury potential
    6. Understanding Explosiveness
    7. A Safer Way
C. Developing Athletic Skills (5)
    1. Skills and Abilities
      a. Quickness and balance exercises
      b. Open and closed skills
    2. The Transfer of Learning
      a. Types of transfer
    3. The Use of Weighted Objects
      a. The kinesthetic aftereffect
      b. Problems with using weighted objects
    4. Specificity Versus Generality
      a. Power cleans revisited
      b. Elements of specificity
    5. The Stages of Motor Learning
      a. The cognitive phase
      b. The associative phase
      c. The autonomous phase
    6. Improving Athletic Skills
      a. Practicing the skill
      b. Strengthening the muscles
    7. Sport-specific Exercises

Reading Assignment:
A. Basic Anatomy and Muscular Function (2)
B. The Role of Genetics in Strength Training (3)

LESSON #3

Instructional Objectives:
The student will be able to
    1. name the three different types of muscle.
    2. describe the three different types of muscle contractions.
    3. explain the Sliding Filament Theory.
    4. identify the location and the function of the major muscle groups.
    5. describe how various genetic traits influence the development of muscular size and strength.
    6. explain the differences between fast twitch and slow twitch muscle fibers.
    7. discuss the differences between the three main somatotypes.
    8. define concentric contraction, dorsi flexion, eccentric contraction, ectomorph, endomorph, hip abduction, hip adduction, hip extension, hyperplasia, hypertrophy, isometric contraction, load, mesomorph, pronation, supination and tension.

Topics for Discussion:
A. Basic Anatomy and Muscular Function (2)
    1. Muscle Contractions
    2. The Sliding Filament Theory
    3. The Major Muscles
      a. Hips
      b. Legs
      c. Upper torso
      d. Arms
      e. Neck
      f. Abdominals
      g. Lower back
B. The Role of Genetics in Strength Training (3)
    1. Genetic Factors

a. Predominant muscle fiber type
b. Muscle-to-tendon ratio
c. Testosterone levels
d. Lever lengths
e. Somatotypes
f. Tendon insertion points
g. Neurological efficiency
2. Heritability Versus Trainability

Reading Assignment:
A. The Principles of Strength Development (6)

LESSON #4

Instructional Objectives:
The student will be able to
1. discuss the two main purposes for strength training.
2. name the most important factor — other than genetics — in determining the response from strength training.
3. describe the two types of post-fatigue repetitions.
4. explain the reasoning behind performing negatives after reaching concentric muscular failure at the end of a set.
5. explain how the General Adaptation Syndrome applies to muscular fatigue.
6. discuss the relationship between time and intensity.
7. discuss the importance of using progressive resistance.
8. explain how a favorable level of muscular exhaustion can be produced by performing one set of an exercise.
9. discuss how predominant muscle fiber types effect recommended repetition ranges.
10. explain why the eccentric portion of a repetition should be emphasized.
11. explain why it is necessary to exercise throughout a full range of motion.
12. name the body's preferred fuel source during intense exercise.
13. explain why the order of exercises should be from the largest muscles to the smallest muscles.
14. give two reasons why it is important to keep accurate records of performance in the weight room.
15. define concentric muscular failure, forced rep, hypertension, Overload Principle and split routine.

Topics for Discussion:
A. The Principles of Strength Development (6)
    1. Intensity
        a. The Overload Principle
        b. Post-fatigue reps
        c. The General Adaptation Syndrome
        d. The intensity continuum
        e. Time and intensity
        f. Favorable results
    2. Progression
    3. Sets
        a. Efficient inroads
        b. Utilization
        c. Research findings
        d. Practical and purposeful
    4. Repetitions
        a. Repetition duration
        b. Genetic influences
        c. Range of motion
        d. Orthopedic concerns
    5. Technique
        a. Raising the weight
        b. Pausing in the mid-range
        c. Lowering the weight

            d. Full range of motion
        6. Duration
        7. Volume
        8. Sequence
        9. Frequency
            a. Split routines
        10. Records
Study Assignment:
A. Chapters 1-6

LESSON #5

Exam Topics:
A. Chapters 1-6
Reading Assignment:
A. Free Weight Exercises (8)

LESSON #6

Instructional Objectives:
The student will be able to
    1. discuss two advantages of using dumbbells.
    2. discuss the muscle(s) used, the suggested repetitions, the type of movement and the performance points for selected free weight exercises.
    3. demonstrate proper lifting technique for selected free weight exercises.
Topics for Discussion:
A. Free Weight Exercises (8)
    1. The Use of Dumbbells
    2. The Exercises
        a. Deadlift, calf raise, bench press, incline press, bent arm fly, bent over row, seated press, lateral raise, front raise, internal rotation, external rotation, shoulder shrug, upright row, bicep curl, tricep extension, wrist flexion, wrist extension and side bend
B. Review the First Exam
    1. Questions that were frequently missed
    2. Grade distribution (mean, median, range, etc.)
C. Workout Time
Reading Assignment:
A. Nautilus Exercises (9)
B. Universal Gym Exercises (10)

LESSON #7

Instructional Objectives:
The student will be able to
    1. discuss the muscle(s) used, the suggested repetitions, the type of movement and the performance points for selected Nautilus and Universal Gym exercises.
    2. demonstrate proper lifting technique for selected Nautilus and Universal Gym exercises.
    3. explain how the Nautilus cam and the Universal DVR varies resistance to match the changes in biomechanical leverage.
    4. define cam, Dynamic Variable Resistance, force arm, fulcrum, resistance arm and strength curve.
Topics for Discussion:
A. Nautilus Exercises (9)
    1. The Nautilus Cam

2. The Exercises
   a. Leg press, hip abduction, hip adduction, leg curl, leg extension, calf raise, arm cross, decline press, pullover, torso arm, chin,overhead press, lateral raise, shoulder shrug, bicep curl, tricep extension, wrist flexion, neck flexion, neck extension, lateral flexion, side bend and back extension

B. Universal Gym Exercises (10)
   1. Dynamic Variable Resistance
   2. The Exercises
      a. Leg press, leg curl, leg extension, calf raise, bench press, dip, underhand lat pulldown, overhand lat pulldown, seated row, seated press, shoulder shrug, upright row, bicep curl, tricep extension, wrist flexion, sit-up, knee-up and back extension

C. Workout Time

Reading Assignment:
A. Manual Resistance Exercises (11)

LESSON #8

Instructional Objectives:
The student will be able to
   1. discuss the advantages and the disadvantages of manual resistance exercises.
   2. explain the responsibilities of the lifter and the spotter during a manual resistance exercise.
   3. discuss the muscle(s) used, the suggested repetitions, the type of movement and the performance points for selected manual resistance exercises.
   4. demonstrate proper lifting and spotting techniques for selected manual resistance exercises.

Topics for Discussion:
A. Manual Resistance Exercises (11)
   1. Advantages and Disadvantages
   2. General Technique
      a. The lifter
      b. The spotter
   3. The Exercises
      a. Hip abduction, hip adduction, leg curl, leg extension, dorsi flexion, push-up, bent arm fly, bent over row, seated row, lat pulldown, seated press, lateral raise, front raise, internal rotation, external rotation, bicep curl, tricep extension, neck flexion, neck extension and sit-up

B. Workout Time

Study Assignment:
A. Chapters 8-11

LESSON #9

Exam Topics:
A. Chapters 8-11

Reading Assignment:
A. Designing and Revising the Strength Training Program (7)

LESSON #10

Instructional Objectives:
The student will be able to
   1. design comprehensive strength training programs.
   2. give two reasons why too much emphasis should not be placed on one bodypart.
   3. identify various antagonistic muscle groups.
   4. distinguish between single-joint and multiple-joint movements.

   5. name an advantage of single-joint movements.
   6. discuss the advantages and the disadvantages of multiple-joint movements.
   7. describe four ways in which variety can be provided to a workout.
   8. name an exercise that can be performed in a negative-only manner without assistance from a spotter.
   9. describe three ways to vary a repetition.
   10. describe four different adjustments that can be made in the basic program design that would enable a person to continue strength training an injured bodypart.
   11. define antagonist, bilateral deficit, bilateral transfer, indirect effect, multiple-joint movement and single-joint movement.

Topics for Discussion:
A. Designing and Revising the Strength Training Program (7)
   1. Program Overview
      a. Antagonistic muscles
      b. Types of movements
      c. Sequence
      d. Exercise options
   2. Overcoming the "Strength Plateau"
      a. Rearrange the order
      b. Change the modality
      c. Alternate the exercises
      d. Vary the repetition
   3. Rehabilitative Strength Training
      a. Lighten the resistance
      b. Reduce the speed of movement
      c. Change the exercise angle
      d. Use a different grip
      e. Perform different exercises
      f. Limit the range of motion
      g. Exercise the good limb
      h. Exercise unaffected bodyparts
B. Review the Second Exam
   1. Questions that were frequently missed
   2. Grade distribution (mean, median, range, etc.)

Reading Assignment:
A. Strengthening the Heart (12)
B. Across the Ages: Adolescence and Adulthood (15)
C. Female Strength Training (16)

LESSON #11

Instructional Objectives:
The student will be able to
   1. describe the four guidelines that are necessary for developing and improving aerobic fitness.
   2. determine an age-predicted maximum heart rate.
   3. determine a recommended heart rate training zone.
   4. discuss the different options for scheduling aerobic conditioning and strength training sessions.
   5. discuss the recommended sequence of skill work, conditioning and strength training activities if performed on the same day.
   6. calculate oxygen consumption in absolute and relative terms for an individual running on a level surface.
   7. calculate Functional Aerobic Impairment.
   8. calculate caloric expenditure for an individual running on a level surface.
   9. discuss the notion that low intensity exercise is better than high intensity exercise when it comes to losing weight, "burning" fat and expending calories.
   10. describe the benefits of strength training activities for adolescents.
   11. explain the difficulty associated with determining the earliest age at which a youngster can safely initiate a strength training program.

12. discuss the major concern in strength training at an early age.
13. identify orthopedically unsafe exercises for adolescents.
14. discuss the belief that the strength decline related to the aging process is quantitative rather than qualitative.
15. explain why the young and the old should perform slightly higher repetitions than the general population.
16. discuss the notion that females who engage in strength training activities will lose flexibility.
17. give three physiological reasons that prevent or minimize the possibility of a woman significantly increasing the size of her muscles.
18. explain how bodyweight, body composition and muscle sizeeffect gender strength differences.
19. name three potential benefits associated with exercising during pregnancy.
20. discuss the fetal and maternal concerns when exercising during pregnancy.
21. define adolescent growth spurt, diaphysis, epiphysis, growth plates, hyperthermia, oxygen uptake, relaxin and sternum.

Topics for Discussion:
A. Strengthening the Heart (12)
  1. The Ultimate "Pump"
  2. The Training Effect
  3. Aerobic Guidelines
    a. Frequency
    b. Intensity
    c. Time
    d. Type
  4. Meaningful Exercise
  5. Scheduling Training Sessions
  6. Sequence of Activities
  7. Predicting Oxygen Uptake
    a. Oxygen consumption: Absolute
    b. Oxygen consumption: Relative
    c. Oxygen consumption expectations
  8. Estimating Caloric Expenditure
  9. Exercise: High Intensity Versus Low Intensity
B. Across the Ages: Adolescence and Adulthood (15)
  1. The Adolescent Population
    a. The adolescent growth spurt
    b. The growth plates
    c. The preadolescent
    d. Avoiding adolescent injury
  2. The Older Population
    a. Research findings
    b. The fountain of youth
  3. Applications for the Young and the Old
    a. Intensity
    b. Repetitions
    c. Speed of movement
    d. Range of motion
    e. Duration of the workout
    f. The major muscle groups
    g. Frequency of the workout
    h. Workout cards
C. Female Strength Training (16)
  1. Dispelling the misconceptions
    a. Flexibility
    b. Muscle size
    c. Female bodybuilders
  2. Gender strength differences
    a. Absolute strength
    b. Relative strength
  3. Exercise and pregnancy

    a. Potential benefits
    b. Concerns and precautions

Reading Assignment:
A. Recipe for Success: Nutritional Facts and Fiction (13)
B. Risky Business: Steroids and Steroid Alternatives (14)

LESSON #12

Instructional Objectives:
The student will be able to
    1. name the six nutrients.
    2. name the three macronutrients that supply energy.
    3. name the two micronutrients.
    4. give the primary purpose of carbohydrates.
    5. explain the importance of proteins.
    6. identify food sources for carbohydrates and proteins.
    7. explain why fats are necessary to a balanced diet.
    8. name the two classifications of vitamins.
    9. give the caloric contributions of the four macronutrients.
  10. calculate the number of calories in a food from the amount of macronutrients.
  11. determine the number of calories that must be consumed above the caloric needs to increase lean body mass.
  12. determine the number of calories that must be consumed below the caloric needs to decrease bodyweight.
  13. discuss the guidelines for the pre-activity meal.
  14. explain why large amounts of sugar or sweets should not be consumed less than one hour before activity.
  15. discuss the importance of proper nutrition following intense exercise.
  16. describe the marketing tactics used by supplement manufacturers to attract consumers.
  17. discuss the need for protein and amino acid supplementation by active individuals.
  18. discuss the adverse side effects from an excessive intake of protein.
  19. discuss the need for vitamin and mineral supplementation by active individuals.
  20. discuss the adverse side effects from an excessive intake of vitamins and minerals.
  21. discuss the anabolic effects of testosterone.
  22. discuss the androgenic effects of testosterone.
  23. name two liver disorders that are associated with steroid use.
  24. describe the health risks to the cardiovascular system that are associated with steroid use.
  25. describe the adverse side effects to the male and the female reproductive systems that are associated with steroid use.
  26. describe the psychological side effects that are associated with steroid use.
  27. discuss the overt signs of steroid use.
  28. discuss the adverse side effects that are associated with selected steroid alternatives.
  29. define acromegaly, alopecia, anabolic, androgenic, bradycardia, caloric balance, complete protein, ergogenic, essential amino acid, gynecomastia, hirsutism, hypoglycemia, macronutrient, megarexia, micronutrient, negative caloric balance, nutrient overload, peliosis hepatis, positive caloric balance, roid rage and tachycardia.

Topics for Discussion:
A. Recipe for Success: Nutritional Facts and Fiction (13)
    1. The Nutrients
        a. The macronutrients
        b. The micronutrients
    2. Daily Servings
    3. Caloric Contributions
    4. Estimating Caloric Needs
    5. Weight Management
        a. Gaining weight
        b. Losing weight
    6. The Pre-Activity Meal

7. Recovery Fluids/Foods
8. Nutritional Quackery and Fraud
   a. "Snake oil salesmen"
   b. Consumer protection
   c. The FTC in action
   d. The art of the seduction
   e. The "loophole"
9. Nutritional Supplements
   a. Protein and amino acids
   b. Vitamins and minerals
   c. Herbs et al.
10. Food for Thought
B. Risky Business: Steroids and Steroid Alternatives (14)
  1. History
  2. Prevalence of Steroid Use
  3. What are Steroids?
  4. Possible Side Effects
    a. Liver
    b. Kidneys
    c. Cardiovascular system
    d. Male reproductive system
    e. Female reproductive system
    f. Miscellaneous adverse effects
  5. Overt Signs of Steroid Use
  6. Winning at All Costs
  7. A Matter of Ethics
  8. Steroids and the Law
  9. Steroid Alternatives?
    a. Boron, choline, chromium, clenbuterol, dibencozide, erythropoietin, gamma hydroxybutyric acid, ginseng, human growth hormone, inosine, magnesium, smilax and yohimbine.
10. The Safe Steroid Alternative

Reading Assignment:
A. Strength Training Q&A (17)

LESSON #13

Instructional Objectives:
The student will be able to
1. discuss the notion that the high percentage of fast twitch muscle fibers in highly competitive weightlifters was developed by explosive training methods.
2. explain the correct way to breathe when lifting weights.
3. discuss the precautions that should be taken when exercising in hot, humid weather.
4. name the primary mechanism for heat loss during exercise.
5. discuss the dangers of exercising in rubberized clothing or the so-called "sauna suits."
6. give the recommended work:rest ratios for sprints of different durations.
7. discuss the belief that eccentric exercise causes excessive muscle damage and soreness.
8. discuss the benefit of a warm-up prior to an activity.
9. discuss plyometric exercises in relation to being safe and productive.
10. discuss the notion that muscles turn into fat during periods of inactivity.
11. explain the orthopedic dangers of performing sit-ups and leg lifts with straight legs.
12. describe the guidelines for stretching the muscles.
13. discuss the Strength Shoe in relation to being safe and effective.
14. discuss the notion of spot reduction.
15. explain the myth of Eastern European athletic supremacy.
16. explain the relationship between anaerobic endurance and strength.
17. discuss the Super Slow Protocol in terms of being safe and productive.
18. discuss the belief that selected parts of individual muscles can be isolated during exercise.
19. explain the mechanics of the lower and the upper foot pedals on the Universal leg press.

20. name the four factors that are considered in assessing whether someone is negligent.
21. discuss the notion of "no pain, no gain."
22. describe the signs of overtraining.
23. define acute muscle soreness, atrophy, delayed-onset muscle soreness, ischemia, lactic acid, lordosis, myotatic reflex, negligence, spot reduction and Valsalva maneuver.

Topics for Discussion:
A. Strength Training Q&A (17)
   1. Developing Fast Twitch Muscle Fibers
   2. Correct Breathing During Strength Training Activities
   3. Conditioning in Hot, Humid Weather
   4. Recovery Time Between Sprints
   5. Eccentric Exercise and Excessive Muscular Damage
   6. The Warm-up
   7. Plyometrics
   8. Muscle and Fat
   9. Sit-ups and Leg Lifts
   10. Stretching
   11. The Strength Shoe
   12. Spot Reducing
   13. The Myth of Eastern European Athletic Supremacy
   14. Strength Testing
   15. The Super Slow Protocol
   16. Isolating Parts of Muscles
   17. Universal Leg Press Foot Pedals
   18. Negligence
   19. "No Pain, No Gain"
   20. Signs of Overtraining

Study Assignment:
A. Chapters 1-17

LESSON #14

Exam Topics:
A. Chapters 1-17

REFERENCES

Adams, J. A. 1987. Historical review and appraisal of research on the learning, retention and transfer of human motor skills. *Psychological Bulletin* 101 (1): 41-74.

Adeyanju, K., T. R. Crews and W. J. Meadors. 1983. Effect of two speeds of isokinetic training on muscle strength, power and endurance. *Journal of Sports Medicine* 23: 352-356.

Alexander, M. J. L. 1985. Biomechanical aspects of lumbar spine injuries in athletes: A review. *Canadian Journal of Applied Sport Sciences* 10: 1-20.

Alhadeff, L., C. T. Gualtieri and M. Lipton. 1984. Toxic effects of water-soluble vitamins. *Nutrition Reviews* 42 (2): 33-40.

Allman, F. L. 1976. Prevention of sports injuries. *Athletic Journal* 56 (March): 74.

American Academy of Pediatrics. 1983. Weight training and weight lifting: Information for the pediatrician. *The Physician and Sportsmedicine* 11 (3): 157-161.

———. 1990. Strength training, weight and power lifting and bodybuilding by children and adolescents. *Pediatrics* 86 (5): 801-803.

American College of Obstetricians and Gynecologists [ACOG]. 1985. Exercise during pregnancy and the postnatal period. (ACOG home exercise programs). Washington, D. C.: ACOG.

American College of Sports Medicine [ACSM]. 1987. Position stand on the use of anabolic-androgenic steroids in sports. *Medicine and Science in Sports and Exercise* 19: 534-539.

———. 1990. Position statement on the recommended quantity and quality of exercise for developing and maintaining cardiorespiratory and muscular fitness in healthy adults. *Medicine and Science in Sports and Exercise* 22: 265-274.

———. 1991. *Guidelines for graded exercise testing and exercise prescription.* 4th ed. Philadelphia: Lea & Febiger.

American Dietetic Association [ADA]. 1987. Position of the ADA: Nutrition for physical fitness and athletic performance for adults. *Journal of the American Dietetic Association* 87 (7): 933-939.

Andress, B. 1990. University of Michigan basketball training. *American Fitness Quarterly* 8 (January): 12-15, 22.

Andrews, J. G., J. G. Hay and C. L. Vaughan. 1983. Knee shear forces during a squat exercise using a barbell and a weight machine. In *Biomechanics* VIII-B, ed. H. Matsui and K. Kobayashi, 923-927. Champaign, IL: Human Kinetics Publishers, Inc.

Aniansson, A., and E. Gustafsson. 1981. Physical training in elderly men with special reference to quadriceps muscle strength and morphology. *Clinical Physiology* 1: 87-98.

Applegate, L. 1988. Fad diets and supplement use in athletics. *Sports Science Exchange* 1 (9): 1-4.

Arendt, E. A. 1984. Strength development: A comparison of resistive exercise techniques. *Contemporary Orthopaedics* 9 (3): 67-72.

Armstrong, R. B., R. W. Oglivie and J. A. Schwane. 1983. Eccentric exercise-induced injury to rat skeletal muscle. *Journal of Applied Physiology* 54: 80-93.

Aronson, V. 1986. Protein and miscellaneous ergogenic aids. *The Physician and Sportsmedicine* 14 (5): 199-202.

Asanovich, M. 1989. The coach: Part of the problem or part of the solution? *High Intensity Training Newsletter* 2 (1): 14-17.

———. 1992. What is strength? *Athletic Conditioning Quarterly* 1 (1): 4-5.

———. 1993. Strength training: Women's basketball. *Athletic Conditioning Quarterly* 3 (1): 3.

Ash, D. 1991. Speed of movement while strength training. *High Intensity Training Newsletter* 3 (2): 10-11.

———. 1993. Strength training for sprinters: Questions and answers. *High Intensity Training Newsletter* 4 (3): 4-6.

Ashton, T. E. J., and M. Singh. 1975. Relationship between erectores spinae voltage and back-lift strength for isometric, concentric and eccentric contractions. *Research Quarterly* 46: 282-286.

Asimov, I. 1992. *The human body: Its structure and operation.* Revised ed. New York: Mentor.

Asken, M. J. 1992. Breakfast of champions or fool's gold? *American Fitness Quarterly* 10 (April): 54-56.

Asmussen, E. 1952. Positive and negative muscular work. *Acta Physiologica Scandinavica* 28: 364-382.

Asmussen, E., and K. Heeboll-Nielson. 1955. A dimensional analysis of physical performance and growth in boys. *Journal of Applied Physiology* 7: 593-603.

Astrand, I. 1960. Aerobic work capacity in men and women with special reference to age. *Acta Physiologica Scandinavica* 49 (Supplementum 169): 1-92.

Astrand, P.-O., and K. Rodahl. 1977. *Textbook of work physiology*. 2d ed. New York: McGraw-Hill Book Company.

Bachman, J. C. 1961. Specificity vs. generality in learning and performing two large muscle motor tasks. *Research Quarterly* 32: 3-11.

Barnett, M. L., D. Ross, R. A. Schmidt and B. Todd. 1973. Motor skills learning and the specificity of training principle. *Research Quarterly* 44: 440-447.

Barron, R. L., and G. J. Vanscoy. 1993. Natural products and the athlete: Facts and folklore. *Annals of Pharmacotherapy* 27: 607-615.

Barrow, H. M., and R. McGee. 1979. *A practical approach to measurement in physical education*. 3d ed. Philadelphia: Lea & Febiger.

Bates, B., M. Wolf and J. Blunk. 1990. *Vanderbilt University strength and conditioning manual*. Nashville, TN: Vanderbilt University.

Behm, D. G., and D. G. Sale. 1993. Intended rather than actual movement velocity determines velocity-specific training response. *Journal of Applied Physiology* 74: 359-368.

Belko, A. Z. 1987. Vitamins and exercise — an update. *Medicine and Science in Sports and Exercise* 19 (Supplement): S191-S196.

Bell, G. J., and H. A. Wenger. 1992. Physiological adaptations to velocity-controlled resistance training. *Sports Medicine* 13 (4): 234-244.

Ben-Ezra, V. 1992. Assessing physical fitness. In *The Stairmaster fitness handbook*, ed. J. A. Peterson and C. X. Bryant, 91-108. Indianapolis: Masters Press.

Benson, M. T., ed. 1992. *1992-93 NCAA Sports Medicine Handbook*. 5th ed. Overland Park, KS: National Collegiate Athletic Association.

Berger, R. 1962. Effect of varied weight training programs on strength. *Research Quarterly* 33: 168-181.

Bishop, P. 1983. Biological determinants of the sex differences in muscular strength. Doctoral dissertation. Athens, GA: University of Georgia.

Black, D. 1992. Clenbuterol: Drug of choice for athletes and other show animals. *High Intensity Training Newsletter* 4 (1): 9-10.

Blakey, J. B., and D. Southard. 1987. The combined effects of weight training and plyometrics on dynamic leg strength and leg power. *Journal of Applied Sport Science Research* 1 (1): 14-16.

Blankenship, W. C. 1952. Transfer effects in neuro-muscular responses involving choice. Master of arts dissertation. University of California.

Blattner, S., and L. Noble. 1979. Relative effects of isokinetic and plyometric training on vertical jumping performance. *Research Quarterly* 50 (4): 583-588.

Bobbert, M. F., and A. J. van Soest. 1994. Effects of muscle strengthening on vertical jump height. *Medicine and Science in Sports and Exercise* 26: 1012-1020.

Boileau, R. A., and T. G. Lohman. 1977. The measurement of human physique and its effect on physical performance. *Orthopedic Clinics of North America* 8: 563-580.

Borms, J., W. D. Ross, W. Duquet and J. E. L. Carter. 1986. Somatotypes of world class body builders. In *Perspectives in kinanthropometry*, ed. J. A. P. Day, 81-90. Champaign, IL: Human Kinetics Publishers, Inc.

Boyd, L. P. 1969. A comparative study of the effects of ankle weights on vertical jumping ability. Unpublished master of science thesis. Springfield, MA: Springfield College.

Bradley, M. 1994. Performing a proper repetition. *Coaching Women's Basketball* 8 (Special issue): 31-32, 36.

Brady, T. A., B. R. Cahill and L. M. Bodnar. 1982. Weight training-related injuries in the high school athlete. *The American Journal of Sports Medicine* 10: 1-5.

Braith, R. W., J. E. Graves, M. L. Pollock, S. H. Leggett, D. M. Carpenter and A. B. Colvin. 1989. Comparison of two versus three days per week of variable resistance training during 10 and 18 week programs. *International Journal of Sports Medicine* 10: 450-454.

Brehm, B. A. 1993. The pregnant client: Exercise caution. *Fitness Management* 9 (March): 28-30.

Brose, D. E., and D. L. Hanson. 1967. Effects of overload training on velocity and accuracy of throwing. *Research Quarterly* 38: 528-533.

Brown, A. B., N. McCartney and D. Sale. 1990. Positive adaptations in weight-lifting training in the elderly. *Journal of Applied Physiology* 69: 1725-1733.

Brown, C. H., and J. H. Wilmore. 1974. The effects of maximal resistance training on the strength and body composition of women athletes. *Medicine and Science in Sports and Exercise* 6: 174-177.

Brown, E. W., and R. G. Kimball. 1983. Medical history associated with adolescent powerlifting. *Pediatrics* 72 (5): 636-644.

Brown, S. 1989. *Providence Friars strength & conditioning manual*. Providence, RI: Providence College.

————. 1990. Strength trainer or weightlifter coach? *American Fitness Quarterly* 8 (January): 44-45.

Brown, T., R. Yost and R. F. McCarron. 1990. Lumbar ring apophyseal fracture in an adolescent weightlifter. *The American Journal of Sports Medicine* 18 (5): 533-535.

Bryant, C. X. 1988. *How to develop muscular power*. Indianapolis: Masters Press.

Bryant, C. X., and J. A. Peterson. 1992. Estimating aerobic fitness. *Fitness Management* 9 (August): 36-39.

Bryant, C. X., and J. A. Peterson. 1993. Active pregnancy. *Fitness Management* 10 (October): 36-37, 40-42.

Bryant, C. X., and J. A. Peterson. 1994. Strength training for the heart? *Fitness Management* 10 (February): 32-34.

Bryant, C. X., J. A. Peterson and R. J. Hagen. 1994. Weight loss: Unfolding the truth. *Fitness Management* 10 (May): 42-44.

Brzycki, M. M. 1986. Plyometrics: A giant step backwards. *Athletic Journal* 66 (April): 22-23.

———. 1987. The implications of "Exercise . . . 1986." *American Fitness Quarterly* 6 (October): 11-12.

———. 1988. Special considerations for strength training females. *High Intensity Training Newsletter* 1 (2): 7-9.

———. 1989. Precautions when practicing in heat. *The Home News* 203 (August 13): E10.

———. 1990. Overload: Multiple sets versus "single set to failure." *Scholastic Coach* 60 (November): 84-85.

———. 1992. Strength training an injured bodypart. *Scholastic Coach* 61 (May/June): 70-72.

———. 1993. The five checkpoints of a properly performed strength exercise. *Pennsylvania Journal of Health, Physical Education, Recreation & Dance* 63 (4): 25-26.

———. 1993. Miracle pills, magical powders and mystical potions. *Nautilus* (Winter): 45-48.

———. 1993. Strength testing — predicting a one-rep max from reps-to-fatigue. *The Journal of Physical Education, Recreation & Dance* 64 (1): 88-90.

———. 1993. You can learn a lot from a dumbbell. *Scholastic Coach* 63 (September): 34-35.

———. 1994. Another perspective on explosive lifting. *Bigger Faster Stronger Journal* (Summer): 11-12.

———. 1994. Facts of friction in exercise. *Fitness Management* 10 (June): 48-50.

———. 1994. The case against the one-rep max. *Scholastic Coach* 64 (November): 30-31.

———. 1994. Speed of movement: An explosive issue. *Nautilus* (Spring): 8-11.

———. 1994. Strength training: On the march. *Scholastic Coach* 64 (August): 28-30.

Brzycki, M. M., and S. Brown. 1993. *Conditioning for basketball.* Indianapolis: Masters Press.

Bubb, W. J. 1992a. Nutrition. In *Health fitness instructor's handbook,* 2d ed, by E. T. Howley and B. D. Franks, 95-114. Champaign, IL: Human Kinetics Publishers, Inc.

———. 1992b. Relative leanness. In *Health fitness instructor's handbook,* 2d ed, by E. T. Howley and B. D. Franks, 115-130. Champaign, IL: Human Kinetics Publishers, Inc.

Buckley, W. E., C. E. Yesalis, K. E. Friedl, W. A. Anderson, A. L. Streit and J. E. Wright. 1988. Estimated prevalence of anabolic steroid use among male high school students. *Journal of the American Medical Association* 260 (23): 3441-3445.

Bullock, J. 1994. In-season strength training for basketball. *Coaching Women's Basketball* 8 (Special issue): 19-20, 36.

Burke, L. M., and R. S. D. Read. 1987. Diet patterns of elite Australian male triathletes. *The Physician and Sports Medicine* 15 (2): 140-155.

Caiozzo, V. J., J. J. Perrine and V. R. Edgerton. 1981. Training-induced alterations of the in vivo force-velocity relationship of human muscle. *Journal of Applied Physiology* 51: 750-754.

Cannon, R. J., and E. Cafarelli. 1987. Neuromuscular adaptations to training. *Journal of Applied Physiology* 63: 2396-2402.

Capen, E. K., J. A. Bright and P. A. Line. 1961. The effects of weight training on strength, power, muscular endurance, and anthropometric measurements on a selected group of college women. *Journal of the Association for Physical and Mental Rehabilitation* 15: 169-173, 180.

Cappozzo, A., F. Felici, F. Figura and F. Gazzani. 1985. Lumbar spine loading during half-squat exercises. *Medicine and Science in Sports and Exercise* 17: 613-620.

Carpinelli, R. N., and B. Gutin. 1991. Effect of miometric and pliometric muscle actions on delayed muscle soreness. *Journal of Applied Sport Science Research* 5 (2): 66-70.

Carter, J. E. L. 1970. The somatotypes of athletes - a review. *Human Biology* 42: 535-569.

———. 1974. Physical anthropology of the athletes. In *Genetic and anthropological studies of Olympic athletes,* ed. A. L. deGaray, L. Levine and J. E. L. Carter, 27-82. New York, NY: Academic Press.

Cebasso, A. 1994. Peliosis hepatis in a young adult bodybuilder. *Medicine and Science in Sports and Exercise* 26 (1): 2-4.

Chaiken, T., and R. Telander. 1988. The nightmare of steroids. *Sports Illustrated* 69 (October 24): 83-102.

Charette, S. L., L. McEvoy, G. Pyka, C. Snow-Harter, D. Guido, R. A. Wiswell and R. Marcus. 1991. Muscle hypertrophy response to resistance training in older women. *Journal of Applied Physiology* 70: 1912-1916.

Christenson, D., and S. Melville. 1988. The effects of depth jumps on university football players. *Journal of Applied Sport Science Research* 2 (3): 54.

City of New York Department of Consumer Affairs. 1992. *Magic muscle pills!! Health and fitness quackery in nutrition supplements.* New York, NY: Department of Consumer Affairs.

Clark, N. 1990. *Nancy Clark's sports nutrition guidebook.* Champaign, IL: Leisure Press.

Clarkson, P. M., and I. Tremblay. 1988. Rapid adaptation to exercise induced muscle damage. *Journal of Applied Physiology* 65: 1-6.

Clausen, J. P. 1977. Effect of training on cardiovascular adjustments to exercise in man. *Physiological Reviews* 57: 779-815.

Close, R. I. 1972. Dynamic properties of mammalian skeletal muscles. *Physiological Reviews* 52: 129-197.

Clutch, D., M. Wilton, C. McGown and G. R. Bryce. 1983. The effect of depth jumps and weight training on leg strength and vertical jump. *Research Quarterly* 54: 5-10.

Colliander, E. B., and P. A. Tesch. 1990a. Effects of eccentric and concentric muscle actions in resistance training. *Acta Physiologica Scandinavica* 140: 31-39.

Colliander, E. B., and P. A. Tesch. 1990b. Responses to eccentric and concentric resistance training in females and males. *Acta Physiologica Scandinavica* 141: 149-156.

Cook, S. D., G. Schultz, M. L. Omey, M. W. Wolfe and M. F. Brunet. 1993. Development of lower leg strength and flexibility with the strength shoe. *The American Journal of Sports Medicine* 21: 445-448.

Cook, T. W. 1933. Studies in cross-educational mirror tracing the star-shaped maze. *Journal of Experimental Psychology* 16: 144-160.

Correnti, V., and B. Zauli. 1964. *Olimpionici.* Rome: Marves.

Costill, D. L., J. Daniels, W. Evans, W. F. Fink, G. S. Krahenbuhl and B. Saltin. 1976. Skeletal muscle enzymes and fiber composition in male and female track athletes. *Journal of Applied Physiology* 40: 149-154.

Costill, D. L., E. F. Coyle, W. F. Fink, G. R. Lesmes and F. A. Witzmann. 1979. Adaptations in skeletal muscle following strength training. *Journal of Applied Physiology* 46: 96-99.

Courson, S., and L. R. Schreiber. 1991. *False glory: The Steve Courson story.* Stamford, CT: Longmeadow Press.

Coyle, E. F., D. L. Costill and G. R. Lesmes. 1979. Leg-extension power and muscle fiber composition. *Medicine and Science in Sports* 11: 12-15.

Cress, M. A., and D. Colacino. 1992. Developing exercise prescriptions for older adults. In *The Stairmaster fitness handbook*, ed. J. A. Peterson and C. X. Bryant, 137-150. Indianapolis: Masters Press.

Crouch, J. E. 1978. *Functional human anatomy.* 3d ed. Philadelphia: Lea & Febiger.

Dangles, C. J., and D. L. Spencer. 1987. Spondylolysis in competitive weightlifters. Paper presented at the American Orthopaedic Society for Sports Medicine Annual Meeting. Orlando, FL.

Darden, E. 1975. Frequently asked questions about muscle, fat and exercise. *Athletic Journal* 56 (November): 85-89.

———. 1977. *Strength training principles: How to get the most out of your workouts.* Winter Park, FL: Anna Publishing, Inc.

———. 1979. *Conditioning for football.* Winter Park, FL: Anna Publishing, Inc.

———. 1981. *The Nautilus nutrition book.* Chicago: Contemporary Books.

———. 1982. *The Nautilus bodybuilding book.* Chicago: Contemporary Books.

———. 1983. *The Nautilus woman.* New York, NY: Simon & Schuster.

———. 1985. *The Nautilus book.* Chicago: Contemporary Books.

Davis, W. W. 1898. Researches in cross education. *Studies from the Yale Psychological Laboratory* 6: 6-50.

deGaray, A. L., L. Levine and J. E. L. Carter, eds. 1974. *Genetic and anthropological studies of Olympic athletes.* New York, NY: Academic Press.

DeLateur, B. J., J. F. Lehmann and R. Giaconi. 1976. Mechanical work and fatigue: Their roles in the development of muscle work capacity. *Archives of Physical Medicine and Rehabilitation* 57 (July): 319-324.

DeLorme, T. L. 1945. Restoration of muscle power by heavy resistance exercise. *Journal of Bone and Joint Surgery* 27 (October): 645-667.

DeLorme, T. L., and A. L. Watkins. 1948. Techniques of progressive resistance exercise. *Archives of Physical Medicine* 29: 263-273.

Desmedt, J. E., and E. Godaux. 1977a. Ballistic contractions in man: Characteristic recruitment pattern of single motor units of the tibialis anterior muscle. *Journal of Physiology* (London) 264: 673-693.

Desmedt, J. E., and E. Godaux. 1977b. Fast motor units are not preferentially activated in rapid voluntary contractions in man. *Nature* 267: 717-719.

Desmedt, J. E., and E. Godaux. 1978. Ballistic contractions in fast or slow human muscles: Discharge patterns of single motor units. *Journal of Physiology* 285: 185-196.

Deutsch, R. M. 1976. *Realities of nutrition.* Palo Alto, CA: Bull Publishing Company.

deVries, H. A. 1974. *Physiology of exercise for physical education and athletics.* 2d ed. Dubuque, IA: William C. Brown.

Diange, J. 1984. Football & power cleans: A dangerous mixture. *Scholastic Coach* 53 (January): 22, 74.

Dintiman, G. B. 1984. *How to run faster.* West Point, NY: Leisure Press.

Dons, B., K. Bollerup, F. Bonde-Petersen and S. Hancke. 1979. The effects of weight-lifting exercise related to muscle fiber composition and muscle cross-sectional area in humans. *European Journal of Applied Physiology* 40: 95-106.

Drowatzky, J. N., and F. C. Zuccato. 1967. Interrelationships between selected measures of static and dynamic balance. *Research Quarterly* 38: 509-510.

Duchateau, J., and K. Hainaut. 1984. Isometric or dynamic training: Differential effects on mechanical properties of a human muscle. *Journal of Applied Physiology* 56: 296-301.

Duda, M. 1987. Elite lifters at risk for spondylolysis. *The Physician and Sportsmedicine* 15 (10): 57-59.

———. 1988. Plyometrics: A legitimate form of power training? *The Physician and Sportsmedicine* 16 (3): 213-216, 218.

Dudley, G. A., P. A. Tesch, B. J. Miller and P. Buchanan. 1991. Importance of eccentric actions in performance adaptations to resistance training. *Aviation, Space and Environmental Medicine* 62: 543-550.

Dunn, J. R. 1989a. Developing strength the L. A. Raiders way. *Strength and Fitness Quarterly* 1 (1): 7.

———. 1989b. L. A. Raiders nutrition: Back to the basics. *High Intensity Training Newsletter* 2 (1): 11-12.

Durak, E. 1987. Physical performance responses to muscle lengthening and weight training exercises in young women. *Journal of Applied Sport Science Research* 1 (3): 60.

Dyhre-Poulsen, P., and A. M. Laursen. 1984. Programmed electromyographic activity and negative incremental muscle stiffness in monkeys jumping downward. *Journal of Physiology* (London) 350: 121-136.

Dyson, G. 1973. *The mechanics of athletics.* London: University of London Press LTD.

Enoka, R. M. 1988a. *Neuromechanical basis of kinesiology.* Champaign, IL: Human Kinetics Publishers, Inc.

————. 1988b. Muscle strength and its development. *Sports Medicine* 6: 146-168.

Fahey, T. D. 1989. *Basic weight training.* Mountainview, CA: Mayfield Publishing Company.

Farley, D. 1993. Dietary supplements: Making sure hype doesn't overwhelm science. *FDA Consumer* 27 (November): 8-13.

Faulkner, J. A., D. R. Clafin and K. K. McCully. 1986. Power output of fast and slow fibers from human skeletal muscles. In *Human muscle power*, ed. N. L. Jones, N. McCartney and A. J. McComas, 81-91. Champaign, IL: Human Kinetics Publishers, Inc.

Federal Trade Commission [FTC]. 1985. Weider Health and Fitness, Inc., et al.; proposed consent agreement with analysis to aid public comment. *Federal Register* 50 (162): 33778-33783.

Feinberg, B. 1994. Nutritional strategies for basketball. *Coaching Women's Basketball* 8 (Special issue): 33-35.

Fellingham, G. W., E. S. Roundy, A. G. Fisher and G. R. Bryce. 1978. Caloric cost of walking and running. *Medicine and Science in Sports and Exercise* 10: 132-136.

Ferrando, A., and N. Green. 1993. The effect of boron supplementation on lean body mass, plasma testosterone levels and strength in bodybuilders. *International Journal of Sports Nutrition* 3 (2): 140-149.

Fiatarone, M. A., E. C. Marks, N. D. Ryan, C. N. Meredith, L. A. Lipsitz and W. J. Evans. 1990. High intensity strength training in nonagenarians: Effects on skeletal muscle. *Journal of the American Medical Association* 263 (22): 3029-3034.

Fike, S. 1987. Toxicity of vitamin supplements. *National Strength & Conditioning Association Journal* 9 (5): 32-34.

Fink, K. J., and B. Worthington-Roberts. 1992. Nutritional considerations for exercise. In *The Stairmaster fitness handbook*, ed. J. A. Peterson and C. X. Bryant, 163-186. Indianapolis: Masters Press.

Fitts, P. M. 1964. Perceptual motor skill learning. In *Categories of human learning*, ed. A. W. Melton, 243-285. New York, NY: Academic Press.

Fitzgerald, G. K., J. M. Rothstein, T. P. Mayhew and R. L. Lamb. 1991. Exercise-induced muscle soreness after concentric and eccentric isokinetic contractions. *Physical Therapy* 71: 505-513.

Food and Drug Administration [FDA]. 1993. Health and Human Services press release P93-24. Washington, D. C.: U. S. Department of Health and Human Services.

Ford Jr, H. T., J. R. Puckett, J. P. Drummond, K. Sawyer, K. Gantt and C. Fussell. 1983. Effects of three combinations of plyometric and weight training programs on selected physical fitness test items. *Perceptual and Motor Skills* 56: 919-922.

Fox, E. L., and D. K. Mathews. 1981. *The physiological basis of physical education and athletics.* 3d ed. Philadelphia: Saunders College Publishing.

Fox, E. L. 1984. Physiology of exercise and physical fitness. In *Sports medicine*, ed. R. H. Strauss, 381-456. Philadelphia: W. B. Saunders Company.

Frankel, V. H., and M. Nordin. 1980. *Basic biomechanics of the skeletal system.* Philadelphia: Lea & Febiger.

Freedman, A. 1990. Specificity in exercise training. *Strength and Fitness Quarterly* 1 (3): 9.

Friday, J. 1994. Are the explosive lifts safe and effective? *Coaching Women's Basketball* 8 (Special issue): 23-25.

Frontera, W. R., C. N. Meredith, K. P. O'Reilly, H. G. Knuttgen and W. J. Evans. 1988. Strength conditioning in older men: Skeletal muscle hypertrophy and improved function. *Journal of Applied Physiology* 64: 1038-1044.

Frymoyer, J. 1987. Low back pain, where we are now. Abstract presented at the Challenge of the Lumbar Spine 9th Annual Meeting. New York, NY.

Fuhrman, C. 1987. Integrating a multiple set theory with high-intensity training. *American Fitness Quarterly* 6 (October): 7-9.

Gallon, A. J. 1962. Use of weighted shoes in basketball conditioning. Paper presented at the California Alliance of Health, Physical Education and Recreation Southern District Meeting. Santa Barbara, CA.

Gardner, G. W. 1963. Specificity of strength changes of the exercised and nonexercised limb following isometric training. *Research Quarterly* 34: 98-101.

Garhammer, J. 1989. Weight lifting and training. In *Biomechanics of sport*, ed. C. L. Vaughn, 169-211. Boca Raton, FL: CRC Press.

Garrett Jr, W. E., and T. R. Malone, eds. 1988. *Muscle development: Nutritional alternatives to anabolic steroids.* Columbus, OH: Ross Laboratories.

Gettman, L. R., M. L. Pollock, J. L. Durstine, A. Ward, J. J. Ayres and A. C. Linnerud. 1976. Physiological responses of men to 1, 3, and 5 day per week training programs. *Research Quarterly* 47: 638-646.

Gettman, L. R., P. Ward and R. D. Hagman. 1982. A comparison of combined running and weight training with circuit weight training. *Medicine and Science in Sports and Exercise* 14: 229-234.

Gilbert, B. 1969. Drugs in sports. *Sports Illustrated* 30 (June 22): 64-72.

Gittleson, M. 1984. *Michigan football off-season conditioning.* Ann Arbor, MI: University of Michigan.

Goldberg, A. L., J. D. Etlinger, D. F. Goldspink and C. Jablecki. 1975. Mechanism of work-induced hypertrophy of skeletal muscle. *Medicine and Science in Sports* 7: 248-261.

Goldman, R. M. 1992. Drug use down through the ages. *American Fitness Quarterly* 10 (April): 50-52.

Goldman, R. M., P. Bush and R. Klatz. 1984. *Death in the locker room.* South Bend, IN: Icarus Press.

Goldman, R. M., and R. Klatz. 1992. *Death in the locker room: Drugs & sports.* Chicago: Elite Sports Medicine Publications, Inc.

Gollnick, P. D., K. Piehl, C. W. Saubert IV, R. B. Armstrong and B. Saltin. 1972a. Diet, exercise and glycogen changes in human muscle fibers. *Journal of Applied Physiology* 33: 421-425.

Gollnick, P. D., R. B. Armstrong, C. W. Saubert IV, K. Piehl and B. Saltin. 1972b. Enzyme activities and fiber composition in skeletal muscle of untrained and trained men. *Journal of Applied Physiology* 33: 312-319.

Gollnick, P. D., R. B. Armstrong, B. Saltin, C. W. Saubert, W. Sembrowich and R. Shepherd. 1973a. Effects of training on enzyme activity and fiber composition of human skeletal muscle. *Journal of Applied Physiology* 34: 107-111.

Gollnick, P. D., R. B. Armstrong, W. Sembrowich, R. Shepherd and B. Saltin. 1973b. Glycogen depletion pattern in human skeletal muscle fiber after heavy exercise. *Journal of Applied Physiology* 34: 615-618.

Gonyea, W. J. 1980. The role of exercise in inducing skeletal muscle fiber number. *Journal of Applied Physiology* 48: 421-426.

Grandjean, A. C. 1988. Current nutrition beliefs and practices in athletics for weight/strength gains. In *Muscle development: Nutritional alternatives to anabolic steroids*, ed. W. E. Garrett Jr and T. R. Malone, 56-59. Columbus, OH: Ross Laboratories.

Granhed, H., and B. Morelli. 1988. Low back pain among retired wrestlers and heavyweight lifters. *The American Journal of Sports Medicine* 16: 530-533.

Graves, J. E., and M. L. Pollock. 1992. Understanding the physiological basis of muscular fitness. In *The Stairmaster fitness handbook*, ed. J. A. Peterson and C. X. Bryant, 39-52. Indianapolis: Masters Press.

Graves, J. E., M. L. Pollock, S. H. Leggett, R. W. Braith, D. M. Carpenter and L. E. Bishop. 1988. Effect of reduced training frequency on muscular strength. *International Journal of Sports Medicine* 9: 316-319.

Graves, J. E., M. L. Pollock, A. E. Jones, A. B. Colvin and S. H. Leggett. 1989. Specificity of limited range of motion variable resistance training. *Medicine and Science in Sports and Exercise* 21: 84-89.

Graves, J. E., M. L. Pollock, D. Foster, S. H. Leggett, D. M. Carpenter, R. Vuosso and A. Jones. 1990. Effect of training frequency and specificity on isometric lumbar extension strength. *Spine* 15: 504-509.

Graves, J. E., B. L. Holmes, S. H. Leggett, D. M. Carpenter, M. L. Pollock. 1991. Single versus multiple set dynamic and isometric lumbar extension training. Paper presented at the World Confederation for Physical Therapy 11th International Conference. London, England.

Grimby, G., and B. Saltin. 1983. The aging muscle. *Clinical Physiology* 3: 209-218.

Grunewald, K., and R. Bailey. 1993. Commercially marketed supplements for bodybuilding athletes. *Sports Medicine* 15: 90-103.

Gulch, R. W. 1994. Force-velocity relations in human skeletal muscle. *International Journal of Sports Medicine* 15 (Supplement 1): S2-S10.

Guthrie, H. A. 1983. *Introductory nutrition.* 5th ed. St. Louis: The C. V. Mosby Company.

Gwinup, G., R. Chelvam and T. Steinberg. 1971. Thickness of subcutaneous fat and activity of underlying muscles. *Annals of Internal Medicine* 74: 408-411.

Hafen, B. Q. 1981. *Nutrition, food and weight control.* Expanded ed. Boston: Allyn and Bacon, Inc.

Hakkinen, K., and P. V. Komi. 1981. Effect of different combined concentric and eccentric muscle work regimens on maximal strength development. *Journal of Human Movement Studies* 7: 33-44.

Hakkinen, K., P. V. Komi and M. Alen. 1985. Effect of explosive type strength training on isometric force- and relaxation-time, electromyographic and muscle fiber characteristics of leg extensor muscles. *Acta Physiologica Scandinavica* 125: 587-600.

Hakkinen, K., A. Pakarinen and M. Kallinen. 1992. Neuromuscular adaptations and serum hormones in women during short-term intensive strength training. *European Journal of Applied Physiology* 64: 106-111.

Hall, S. 1985. Effect of attempted lifting speed on forces and torque exerted on the lumbar spine. *Medicine and Science in Sports and Exercise* 17: 440-444.

Hallmark, M. A., T. H. Reynolds, C. A. DeSousa, C. O. Dotson, R. A. Anderson and M. A. Rogers. 1993. Effects of chromium supplementation and resistive training on muscle strength and lean body mass in untrained men. Abstract presented at the American College of Sports Medicine 40th Annual Meeting. Seattle, WA.

Hammock, D. A. 1990. Protein. In *The Mount Sinai school of medicine complete book of nutrition*, ed. V. Herbert and G. J. Subak-Sharpe, 33-45. New York, NY: St. Martin's Press.

Hasue, M., F. Masatushi and S. Kikuch. 1980. A new method of quantitative measurement of abdominal and back muscle strength. *Spine* 5: 143-148.

Hatfield, F. C. 1981. *Powerlifting: A scientific approach.* Chicago: Contemporary Books, Inc.

Hather, B. M., P. A. Tesch, P. Buchanan and G. A. Dudley. 1991. Influence of eccentric actions on skeletal muscle adaptations to resistance training. *Acta Physiologica Scandinavica* 143: 177-185.

Hattin, H. C., M. R. Pierrynowski and K. A. Ball. 1989. Effect of load, cadence and fatigue on tibio-femoral joint force during a half squat. *Medicine and Science in Sports and Exercise* 21: 613-618.

Haupt, H. A., and G. D. Rovere. 1984. Anabolic steroids: A review of the literature. *The American Journal of Sports Medicine* 12: 469-484.

Hellebrandt, F. A., A. M. Parrish and S. J. Houtz. 1947. Cross-education: The effect of unilateral exercise on the contralateral limb. *Archives of Physical Medicine and Rehabilitation* 28: 76-85.

Hellebrandt, F. A., and S. J. Houtz. 1956. Mechanisms of muscle training in man: Experimental demonstration of the overload principle. *Physical Therapy Review* 36: 371-383.

Henneman, E. 1957. Relation between size of neurons and their susceptibility to discharge. *Science* 126: 1345-1347.

Henneman, E., G. Somjen and D. O. Carpenter. 1965. Functional significance of cell size in spinal motoneurons. *Journal of Neurophysiology* 28: 560-580.

Henry, F. M. 1961. Reaction time - movement time correlations. *Perceptual and Motor Skills* 12: 63-66.

———. 1968. Specificity vs. generality in learning motor skill. In *Classical studies on physical activity*, ed. R. C. Brown and G. S. Kenyon. Englewood Cliffs, NJ: Prentice-Hall.

Henry, F. M., and L. E. Smith. 1961. Simultaneous vs. separate bilateral muscular contractions in relation to neural overflow theory and neuromotor specificity. *Research Quarterly* 32: 42-46.

Herbert, D. L. 1990. Steroid provider may be liable for user's actions. *Fitness Management* 7 (October): 22, 24.

Herbert, V. 1990a. Separating food facts and myths. In *The Mount Sinai school of medicine complete book of nutrition*, ed. V. Herbert and G. J. Subak-Sharpe, 21-30. New York, NY: St. Martin's Press.

———. 1990b. Vitamins and minerals. In *The Mount Sinai school of medicine complete book of nutrition*, ed. V. Herbert and G. J. Subak-Sharpe, 89-111. New York, NY: St. Martin's Press.

———. 1990c. What is a healthy diet? In *The Mount Sinai school of medicine complete book of nutrition*, ed. V. Herbert and G. J. Subak-Sharpe, 3-13. New York, NY: St. Martin's Press.

Herbert, V., and G. J. Subak-Sharpe, eds. 1990. *The Mount Sinai school of medicine complete book of nutrition*. New York, NY: St. Martin's Press.

Hettinger, T. 1961. *Physiology of strength.* Springfield, IL: Charles C. Thomas.

Hewgley, C. T. 1984. *Kansas City Chiefs 1984 conditioning manual.* Kansas City, MS: Kansas City Chiefs Football Club.

Heyward, V. H., S. M. Johannes-Ellis and J. F. Romer. 1988. Gender differences in strength. *Research Quarterly* 57: 154-159.

Hickson, J. F., K. Hinkelman and D. L. Bredle. 1988. Protein intake level and introductory weight training exercise on urinary total nitrogen excretions from untrained men. *Nutrition Research* 8: 725-731.

Hickson, R. C., C. Kanakis, J. R. Davis, A. M. Moore and S. Rich. 1982. Reduced training duration effects on aerobic power, endurance and cardiac growth. *Journal of Applied Physiology* 53: 225-229.

Hill, A. V. 1922. The maximum work and mechanical efficiency in human muscles, and their most economical speed. *Journal of Physiology* 56: 19-41.

Hoberman, J. M. 1992. *Mortal engines.* New York, NY: The Free Press.

Hoffman, B. 1939. *Weight lifting.* York, PA: Strength & Health Publishing Co.

Hollering, B. L., and D. Simpson. 1977. The effect of three types of training programs upon skating speed of college ice hockey players. *Journal of Sports Medicine and Physical Fitness* 17 (3): 335-340.

Holma, P. K. 1977. Effects of anabolic steroid on spermatogenesis. *Contraception* 15: 151-162.

Hopek, R. 1967. Effect of overload on the accuracy of throwing a football. Unpublished master's thesis. Charleston, IL: Eastern Illinois University.

Horrigan, J., and D. Shaw. 1990. Plyometrics: The dangers of depth jumps. *High Intensity Training Newsletter* 2 (4): 15-21.

Howley, E. T., and B. D. Franks. 1992. *Health fitness instructor's handbook*. 2d ed. Champaign, IL: Human Kinetics Publishers, Inc.

Howley, E. T., and M. Glover. 1974. The caloric costs of running and walking one mile for men and women. *Medicine and Science in Sports and Exercise* 6: 235-237.

Hurley, B. F., D. R. Seals, A. A. Ehsani, L.-J. Cartier, G. P. Dalsky, J. M. Hagberg and J. O. Holloszy. 1984. Effects of high-intensity strength training on cardiovascular function. *Medicine and Science in Sports and Exercise* 16: 483-488.

Hurley, B. F., R. A. Redmond, K. H. Koffler, A. Menkes, J. M. Hagberg, R. E. Pratley, J. W. R. Young and A. P. Goldberg. 1991. Assessment of strength training effects on leg composition in older men using magnetic resonance imaging (MRI). Abstract presented at the American College of Sports Medicine 38th Annual Meeting. Orlando, FL.

Hutchins, K. 1992. *Super Slow: The ultimate exercise protocol.* 2d ed. Casselberry, FL: Super Slow Systems.

Huxley, H. E. 1958. The contraction of muscle. *Scientific American* 199 (5): 66-82.

———. 1965. The mechanism of muscular contraction. *Scientific American* 213 (6): 18-27.

Ikai, M., and T. Fukunaga. 1968. Calculation of muscle strength per unit cross-sectional area of human muscle by means of ultrasonic measurement. *Internationale Zeitschrift fur angewandte Physiologie einschliessich Arbeitphysiologie* 26: 26-32.

Ikai, M., and T. Fukunaga. 1970. A study on training effect on strength per unit cross-sectional area of human muscle by means of ultrasonic measurement. *Internationale Zeitschrift fur angewandte Physiologie einschliessich Arbeitphysiologie* 28: 173-180.

Ivy, J. L. 1991. Muscle glycogen synthesis before and after exercise. *Sports Medicine* 11 (1): 6-19.

Jacobson, B. 1981. *Conditioning for football the Oklahoma State way.* West Point, NY: Leisure Press.

———. 1986. A comparison of two progressive weight training techniques on knee extensor strength. *Athletic Training* 21: 315-318, 390.

Jesse, J. P. 1977. Olympic lifting movements endanger adolescents. *The Physician and Sports Medicine* 5 (9): 61-67.

———. 1979. Misuse of strength development programs in athletic training. *The Physician and Sports Medicine* 7 (10): 46-50, 52.

Johnson, C., and J. G. Reid. 1991. Lumbar compressive and shear forces during various trunk curl-up exercises. *Clinical Biomechanics* 6: 97-104.

Jokl, E. 1973. Physique and performance. *American Corrective Therapy Journal* 27 (4): 99-111, 114.

Jones, A. 1970. *Nautilus training principles, bulletin #1.* DeLand, FL: Arthur Jones Productions.

————. 1971a. *Nautilus training principles, bulletin #2.* DeLand, FL: Arthur Jones Productions.

————. 1971b. Is it worth the price? *Iron Man* 30 (September): 24-25, 57-58.

————. 1972. Size or strength. *Iron Man* 31 (January): 28-31, 67-68.

————. 1973. The best kind of exercise. *Iron Man* 32 (May): 36-38, 70.

————. 1975a. "Negative accentuated" strength training. *Athletic Journal* 55 (May): 92-93, 100-101.

————. 1975b. The nervous system in sports. *Athletic Journal* 56 (November): 70-72.

————. 1976. The metabolic cost of negative work. *Athletic Journal* 56 (January): 40-41, 80.

————. 1977a. The missing link in athletic performance. *Athletic Journal* 57 (June): 38-40.

————. 1977b. Specificity in strength training . . . the facts and the fables. *Athletic Journal* 57 (May): 70-75.

————. 1977c. Flexibility as a result of exercise. *Athletic Journal* 57 (March): 32, 37-38, 92.

————. 1986. Exercise 1986: The present state of the art. *Athletic Journal* 66 (April): 53-79.

————. 1993. *The lumbar spine, the cervical spine and the knee: Testing and rehabilitation.* Ocala, FL: MedX Corporation.

Jones, A., M. L. Pollock, J. E. Graves, M. Fulton, W. Jones, M. MacMillan. D. D. Baldwin and J. Cirulli. 1988. *Safe, specific testing and rehabilitative exercise of the muscles of the lumbar spine.* Santa Barbara, CA: Sequoia Communications.

Jones, N. L., N. McCartney and A. J. McComas, eds. 1986. *Human muscle power.* Champaign, IL: Human Kinetics Publishers, Inc.

Joseph, A., K. Pomeranz, J. Prince and D. Sacher. 1978. *Physics for engineering technology.* 2d ed. New York, NY: John Wiley & Sons.

Kanehisa, H., and M. Miyashita. 1983. Specificity of velocity in strength training. *European Journal of Physiology* 52: 104-106.

Kaneko, M., P. V. Komi and O. Aura. 1984. Mechanical efficiency of concentric and eccentric exercises performed with medium to fast contraction rates. *Scandinavian Journal of Sport Science* 6: 15-20.

Kaneko, M., T. Fuchimoto, H. Toji and K. Suei. 1983. Training effect of different loads on the force-velocity relationship and mechanical power output in human muscle. *Scandinavian Journal of Sport Science* 5: 50-55.

Karlsson, J., P. V. Komi and J. H. T. Viitasalo. 1979. Muscle strength and muscle characteristics in monozygous and dizygous twins. *Acta Physiologica Scandinavica* 106: 319-325.

Kasper, J. 1990. The effect of slow speed training utilizing free weights on muscular strength. *High Intensity Training Newsletter* 2 (3): 6-8.

Kasperek, G. J. 1989. Amino acid metabolism. *National Strength & Conditioning Association Journal* 10 (6): 23-27.

Katch, F. I., P. M. Clarkson, W.A. Kroll and T. McBride. 1984. Effects of sit up exercise training on adipose cell size and adiposity. *Research Quarterly for Exercise and Sport* 55 (3): 242-247.

Kearns, H. 1990. Safe lifting. *Strength and Fitness Quarterly* 1 (2): 6.

Kelsey, J. L., A. A. White, H. Pastides and G. E. Bisbee Jr. 1979. The impact of musculoskeletal disorders on the population of the United States. *Journal of Bone and Joint Surgery* 61A: 959-964.

Kennedy, P. M. 1986a. Byways & highways in strength training. *Scholastic Coach* 55 (May/June): 30, 32, 100-101.

————. 1986b. Setting the record straight about negative exercise. *Scholastic Coach* 56 (November): 22-23, 69.

————. 1986c. What determines strength potential? *Scholastic Coach* 56 (September): 58-60.

Kibble, M. W., and M. B. Ross. 1987. Adverse effects of anabolic steroids in athletes. *Clinical Pharmacy* 6: 686-692.

Klein, K. K. 1962. Squats right. *Scholastic Coach* 32 (2): 36-38, 70-71.

Klissouras, V. 1971. Heritability of adaptive variation. *Journal of Applied Physiology* 31: 338-344.

Knapik, J. J., R. H. Mawdsley and N. U. Ramos. 1983. Angular specificity and test mode specificity of isometric and isokinetic strength training. *Journal of Orthopaedic and Sports Physical Therapy* 5: 58-65.

Koffler, K. H., A. Menkes, R. A. Redmond, W. E. Whitehead, R. E. Pratley and B. F. Hurley. 1992. Strength training accelerates gastrointestinal transit in middle-aged and older men. *Medicine and Science in Sports and Exercise* 24: 415-419.

Komi, P. V. 1986. Training of muscle strength and power: Interaction of neuromotoric, hypertrophic and mechanical factors. *International Journal of Sports Medicine* 7 (Supplement): 10-15.

Komi, P. V., and E. R. Buskirk. 1972. Effect of eccentric and concentric muscle conditioning on tension and electrical activity of human muscles. *Ergonomics* 15: 417-434.

Komi, P. V., J. H. T. Viitasalo, M. Havu, A. Thorstensson, B. Sjodin and J. Karlsson. 1977. Skeletal muscle fibers and muscle enzyme activities in monozygous and dizygous twins of both sexes. *Acta Physiologica Scandinavica* 100: 385-392.

Komi, P. V., J. H. T. Viitasalo, R. Rauramaa and V. Vihko. 1978. Effect of isometric strength training on mechanical, electrical and metabolic aspects of muscle function. *European Journal of Applied Physiology* 40: 45-55.

Komi, P. V., J. Karlsson. 1979. Physical performance, skeletal muscle enzyme activities and fiber types in monozygous and dizygous twins of both sexes. *Acta Physiologica Scandinavica* (Supplementum 462): 1-28.

Kotani, P. T., N. Ichikawa, W. Wakabayashi, T. Yoshii and M. Koshimune. 1971. Studies of spondylolysis found among weightlifters. *British Journal of Sports Medicine* 6: 4-8.

Kotch, K. R. 1990. Strength training made simple. *High Intensity Training Newsletter* 2 (3): 8-9.

Kraemer, W. J. 1992. Involvement of eccentric muscle action may optimize adaptations to resistance training. *Sports Science Exchange* 4 (6): 1-4.

Krahenbuhl, G. S., P. A. Archer and L. L. Pettit. 1978. Serum testosterone and adult female trainability. *Journal of Sports Medicine and Physical Fitness* 18: 359-364.

Kramer, J. F., A. Morrow and A. Leger. 1993. Changes in rowing ergometer, weight lifting, vertical jump and isokinetic performance in response to standard and standard plus plyometric training programs. *International Journal of Sports Medicine* 14: 449-454.

Kris-Etherton, P. M. 1989. The facts and fallacies of nutritional supplements for athletes. *Sports Science Exchange* 2 (8): 1-4.

Krotkiewski, A., A. Aniansson, G. Grimby, P. Bjorntarp and L. Sjostrom. 1979. The effect of unilateral isokinetic strength training on local adipose and muscle tissue morphology, thickness and enzymes. *European Journal of Physiology* 42: 271-281.

Kulund, D. N., J. B. Dewey, C. E. Brubaker and J. R. Roberts. 1978. Olympic weight-lifting injuries. *The Physician and Sports Medicine* 6 (11): 111-116, 119.

LaBree, M. 1991. A review of anabolic steroids: Uses and effects. *Journal of Sports Medicine and Physical Fitness* 31: 618-626.

Lamb, D. R. 1984a. *Physiology of exercise: Responses & adaptations.* 2d ed. New York, NY: MacMillan Publishing Company.

———. 1984b. Anabolic steroids in athletics: How well do they work and how dangerous are they? *The American Journal of Sports Medicine* 12: 31-38.

———. 1989. Abuse of anabolic steroids in sport. *Sports Science Exchange* 2 (3): 1-4.

Lambrinides, T. 1989. Indirect transfer of strength. *High Intensity Training Newsletter* 1 (4): 5-6.

———. 1990a. Dietary protein: Controversy or confusion? *High Intensity Training Newsletter* 2 (3): 14-15.

———. 1990b. Ergogenic aids and the athlete. *High Intensity Training Newsletter* 2 (4): 13-14.

———. 1990c. High intensity training and overtraining. *High Intensity Training Newsletter* 2 (2): 9-10.

———. 1990d. Playing the percentages: Is it a good or bad idea? *High Intensity Training Newsletter* 2 (4): 12-13.

———. 1994. Protein needs and the strength trained athlete. *High Intensity Training Newsletter* 5 (1 & 2): 10-12.

Landis, D. 1983. Weight training at Princeton University circa 1962: A recollection. *National Strength & Conditioning Association Journal* 5 (2): 40-44.

Lange, L. 1919. *Uber funktionelle Anpassung.* Berlin: Springer Verlag.

Larsson, L. 1982. Physical training effects on muscle morphology in sedentary males at different ages. *Medicine and Science in Sports and Exercise* 14: 203-206.

Laseter, J. T., and J. A. Russell. 1991. Anabolic steroid-induced tendon pathology: A review of the literature. *Medicine and Science in Sports and Exercise* 23: 1-3.

Laubach, L. L. 1976. Comparative muscular strength of men and women: A review of the literature. *Aviation, Space and Environmental Medicine* 47: 534-542.

Laycoe, R., and R. G. Marteniuk. 1971. Learning and tension as factors in static strength gains produced by static and eccentric training. *Research Quarterly* 42: 299-306.

Layman, D. 1987. Dietary protein needs for the athlete. *The Physician and Sportsmedicine* 15 (12): 181-183.

Leggett, S. H., J. E. Graves, M. L. Pollock, M. L. Shank, D. M. Carpenter, B. Holmes and M. N. Fulton. 1991. Quantitative assessment and training of isometric cervical extension strength. *The American Journal of Sports Medicine* 19: 653-659.

Leistner, K. E. 1985. Improper training. *The Steel Tip* 1 (January): 4.

———. 1986a. The quality repetition. *The Steel Tip* 2 (June): 6-7.

———. 1986b. Strength as a general phenomenon. *The Steel Tip* 2 (October): 6-7.

———. 1987a. Coaches' corner: Periodization for football. *The Steel Tip* 3 (August): 1-3.

———. 1987b. More from Ken Leistner. *Powerlifting USA* 10 (April): 17.

———. 1989a. Explosive training: Not necessary. *High Intensity Training Newsletter* 1 (2): 3-5.

———. 1989b. Strength training injuries: On the field but from the weight room. *High Intensity Training Newsletter* 1 (4): 1-2.

———. 1991. The squat part four: What if you can't? *High Intensity Training Newsletter* 3 (3): 1-2.

LeLeiko, N., and D. Rollinson. 1990. Adolescent nutrition. In *The Mount Sinai school of medicine complete book of nutrition*, ed. V. Herbert and G. J. Subak-Sharpe, 222-233. New York, NY: St. Martin's Press.

Lemon, P. W. R. 1987. Protein and exercise: Update 1987. *Medicine and Science in Sports and Exercise* 19 (Supplement): S179-S190.

———. 1989. Influence of dietary protein and total energy intake on strength improvement. *Sports Science Exchange* 2 (4): 1-4.

———. 1991. Protein and amino acid needs of the strength athlete. *International Journal of Sports Nutrition* 1: 127-145.

Lemon, P. W. R., M. A. Tarnopolsky, J. D. MacDougall and S. A. Atkinson. 1992. Protein requirements and muscle mass/strength changes during intensive training in novice bodybuilders. *Journal of Applied Physiology* 73: 767-775.

Lesmes, G. R., D. W. Benham, D. L. Costill and W. J. Fink. 1983. Glycogen utilization in fast and slow twitch muscle fibers during maximal isokinetic exercise. *Annals of Sports Medicine* 1: 105-108.

LeSuer, D. A., and J. H. McCormick. 1993. Prediction of a 1-RM bench press and 1-RM squat from repetitions to fatigue using the Brzycki formula. Abstract presented at the National Strength and Conditioning Association 16th National Conference. Las Vegas, NV.

Lewis, D. 1862. The new gymnastics. *Atlantic Monthly* 10 (August): 129-148.

Lieber, D. C., R. L. Lieber and W. C. Adams. 1989. Effects of run-training and swim-training at similar absolute intensities on treadmill VO_2 max. *Medicine and Science in Sports and Exercise* 21: 655-661.

Lillegard, W. A., and J. D. Terrio. 1994. Appropriate strength training. *Sports Medicine* 78: 457-477.

Lindeburg, F. A. 1949. A study of the degree of transfer between quickening exercises and other movements. *Research Quarterly* 20: 180-189.

Lindh, M. 1979. Increases in muscle strength from isometric quadriceps exercises at different knee angles. *Scandinavian Journal of Medicine* 11: 33-36.

———. 1980. Biomechanics of the lumbar spine. In *Basic biomechanics of the skeletal system*, by V. H. Frankel and M. Nordin, 255-290. Philadelphia: Lea & Febiger.

Londeree, B. R., and M. L. Moeschberger. 1982. Effect of age and other factors on maximal heart rate. *Research Quarterly for Exercise and Sport* 53: 297-304.

Lotter, W. S. 1960. Interrelationships among reaction times and speeds of movement in different limbs. *Research Quarterly* 31: 147-155.

———. 1961. Specificity or generality of speed of systematically related movements. *Research Quarterly* 32: 55-62.

Lowenthal, D. T., and Y. Karni. 1990. The nutritional needs of athletes. In *The Mount Sinai school of medicine complete book of nutrition*, ed. V. Herbert and G. J. Subak-Sharpe, 396-414. New York, NY: St. Martin's Press.

MacDougall, J. D. 1986. Morphological changes in human skeletal muscle following strength training and immobilization. In *Human muscle power*, ed. N. L. Jones, N. McCartney and A. J. McComas, 269-288. Champaign, IL: Human Kinetics Publishers, Inc.

MacDougall, J. D., D. G. Sale, G. C. B Elder and J. R. Sutton. 1976. Ultrastructural properties of human skeletal muscle. Abstract presented at the American College of Sports Medicine 23rd Annual Meeting. Anaheim, CA.

MacDougall, J. D., G. C. B. Elder, D. G. Sale, J. R. Moroz and J. R. Sutton. 1980. Effects of strength training and immobilization on human muscle fibers. *European Journal of Applied Physiology* 43: 25-34.

MacDougall, J. D., D. G. Sale, S. E. Alway and J. R. Sutton. 1984. Muscle fiber number in biceps brachii in bodybuilders and control subjects. *Journal of Applied Physiology* 57: 1399-1403.

Maddalo, A. V. 1992. A self-screening examination for the male athlete taking anabolic steroids. In *Death in the locker room: Drugs & sports*, by R. M. Goldman and R. Klatz, 314-324. Chicago: Elite Sports Medicine Publications, Inc.

Malina, R. M., A. B. Harper, H. H. Avent and D. E. Campbell. 1971. Physique of female track and field athletes. *Medicine and Science in Sports and Exercise* 3: 32-38.

Mannheimer, J. D. 1969. A comparison of strength gains between concentric and eccentric contractions. *Physical Therapy* 49: 1201-1207.

Mannie, K. 1988. Key factors in program organization. *High Intensity Training Newsletter* 1 (1): 4-5.

———. 1989a. Targeting-in on the upper back musculature. *High Intensity Training Newsletter* 1 (3): 13-15.

———. 1989b. What coaches and athletes should know about steroids! *Scholastic Coach* 59 (September): 50-52.

———. 1990. Strength training follies: The All-P.U.B. Team. *High Intensity Training Newsletter* 2 (2): 11-12.

———. 1991. Roid roulette: A dangerous game. Toledo, OH: Media Production Group. Videotape.

———. 1992a. Athletic skill development: An open and closed case. *High Intensity Training Newsletter* 3 (4): 4-6.

———. 1992b. Balancing a weighty issue. *High Intensity Training Newsletter* 4 (2): 6-7.

———. 1993. Lift risks are a weighty matter. *NCAA News* 30 (January 27): 4-5.

———. 1994. Some thoughts on explosive weight training. *High Intensity Training Newsletter* 5 (1 & 2): 13-18.

Marsden, C. D., J. A. Obeso and J. C. Rothwell. 1984. The function of the antagonist muscle during fast limb movements in man. *Journal of Physiology* (London) 335: 1-13.

Marteniuk, R. G. 1969. Generality and specificity of learning and performance on two similar speed tasks. *Research Quarterly* 40: 518-522.

Mathews, D. K., C. T. Shay, F. Godin and R. Hogdon. 1956. Cross transfer effects of training on strength and endurance. *Research Quarterly* 27: 206-212.

Matveyev, L. 1981. *Fundamentals of sports training*. Translated by A. P. Zdornykh. Moscow, USSR: Progress Publishers.

Mayhew, J., and P. Gross. 1974. Body composition changes in young women with high resistance weight training. *Research Quarterly* 45: 433-440.

Mazur, L. J., R. J. Yetman and W. L. Risser. 1993. Weight training injuries: Common injuries and preventative measures. *Sports Medicine* 16: 57-63.

McArdle, W. D., F. I. Katch and V. L. Katch. 1986. *Exercise physiology: Energy, nutrition and human performance*. 2d ed. Philadelphia: Lea & Febiger.

McCafferty, W. B., and S. M. Horvath. 1977. Specificity of exercise and specificity of training: A subcellular review. *Research Quarterly* 48: 358-371.

McCarroll, J. R., J. M. Miller and M. A. Ritter. 1986. Lumbar spondylolysis and spondylolisthesis in college football players. *The American Journal of Sports Medicine* 14: 404-406.

McCarthy, P. 1989. How much protein do athletes really need? *The Physician and Sportsmedicine* 17 (5): 170-175.

McDonagh, M. J. N., and C. T. M. Davies. 1984. Adaptive response of mammalian skeletal muscle to exercise with high loads. *European Journal of Applied Physiology* 52: 139-155.

McDonald, R., and C. Keen. 1988. Iron, zinc and magnesium nutrition and athletic performance. *Sports Medicine* 5: 171-184.

Mendenhall, W. 1979. *Introduction to probability and statistics.* 5th ed. North Scituate, MA: Duxbury Press.

Mentzer, M. 1993. *Heavy duty.* Venice, CA: Mike Mentzer.

Meredith, C. N. 1988. Protein needs and protein supplements in strength-trained men. In *Muscle development: Nutritional alternatives to anabolic steroids,* ed. W. E. Garrett Jr and T. R. Malone, 68-72. Columbus, OH: Ross Laboratories.

Messier, S. P., and M. Dill. 1985. Alterations in strength and maximal oxygen uptake consequent to Nautilus circuit weight training. *Research Quarterly for Exercise and Sport* 56: 345-351.

Mirkin, G., and M. Hoffman. 1978. *The sportsmedicine book.* Boston: Little, Brown and Company.

Moffroid, M. T., and R. H. Whipple. 1970. Specificity of speed exercise. *Journal of the American Physical Therapy Association* 50: 1693-1699.

Moritani, T., and H. A. deVries. 1979. Neural factors vs hypertrophy in the course of muscle strength gain. *American Journal of Physical Medicine and Rehabilitation* 58: 115-130.

Moritani, T., and H. A. deVries. 1980. Potential for gross muscle hypertrophy in older men. *Journal of Gerontology* 35: 672-682.

Morton, C. 1990. The relationship between sprint training and conditioning: A time for quality and a time for quantity. *High Intensity Training Newsletter* 2 (3): 9-11.

Munn, N. L. 1932. Bilateral transfer of learning. *Journal of Experimental Psychology* 15: 343-353.

Mussen, P. H., J. J. Conger and J. Kagan. 1979. *Child development and personality.* 5th ed. New York, NY: Harper & Row, Publishers, Inc.

National Collegiate Athletic Association [NCAA]. 1991. No miracles found in many "natural potions." *NCAA News* 28 (July 17): 7.

NCAA Committee on Competitive Safeguards and Medical Aspects of Sports. 1992. *Ergogenic aids and nutrition.* Overland Park, KS: NCAA memorandum (August 6).

National Football League [NFL]. 1993. *Anabolic steroids and related substances.* New York, NY: NFL.

National Strength and Conditioning Association [NSCA]. 1985. Position paper on anabolic drug use by athletes. *National Strength & Conditioning Association Journal* 7 (5): 44.

Nautilus. 1990. *Nautilus product catalog.* Independence, VA: Nautilus Acquisition Corporation.

Nelson, D. O. 1957. Effect of swimming on the learning of selected gross motor skills. *Research Quarterly* 28: 374-378.

Nelson, R. C., 1979. *Introduction to sport biomechanics.* Revised ed. University Park, PA: Penn State University.

Nelson, R. C. and M.R. Nofsinger. 1965. Effect of overload on speed of elbow flexion and the associated aftereffects. *Research Quarterly* 36: 174-182.

Newham, D. J., D. A. Jones and R. H. T. Edwards. 1983. Large delayed plasma creatine kinase changes after stepping exercise. *Muscle and Nerve* 6: 380-385.

Nielson, F. 1992. Facts and fallacies about boron. *Nutrition Today* 27 (May/June): 6-12.

Nobbs, L., and E. Rhodes. 1986. The effect of electrical stimulation and isokinetic exercise on muscular power of the quadriceps femoris. *Journal of Orthopaedic and Sports Physical Therapy* 8: 260-268.

Norris, C. M. 1993. Abdominal muscle training in sport. *British Journal of Sports Medicine* 27: 19-27.

Nowak, R. K., and K. S. Knudsen. 1988. Body composition and nutrient intakes of college men and women basketball players. *Journal of the American Dietetic Association* 88: 575-578.

Nygaard, G., and T. H. Boone. 1985. *Coaches guide to sport law.* Champaign, IL: Human Kinetics Publishers, Inc.

Ohtsuki, T. 1981. Decrease in grip strength induced by simultaneous bilateral exertion with reference to finger strength. *Ergonomics* 24: 37-48.

Owen, S. V., H. P. Blount and H. Moscow. 1978. *Educational psychology: An introduction.* Boston: Little, Brown and Company.

Oxendine, J. B. 1967. Generality and specificity in the learning of fine and gross motor skills. *Research Quarterly* 38: 86-94.

Oyster, N. 1979. Effects of a heavy-resistance weight training program on college women athletes. *Journal of Sports Medicine and Physical Fitness* 19: 79-83.

Palmieri, G. A. 1983. The principles of muscle fiber recruitment during ballistic movements. *National Strength & Conditioning Association Journal* 5 (5): 22-24, 63.

———. 1987. Weight training and repetition speed. *Journal of Applied Sport Science Research* 1 (2): 36-38.

Payne, D. A. 1974. *The assessment of learning: Cognitive and affective.* Lexington, MA: D. C. Heath.

Pearl, B., and G. T. Moran. 1986. *Getting stronger.* Revised ed. Bolinas, CA: Shelter Publications, Inc.

Percy, E. C. 1978. Ergogenic aids in athletes. *Medicine and Science in Sports and Exercise* 10: 298-303.

Petersen, S. 1988. Functional adaptations to velocity-specific resistance training. Doctoral dissertation. Edmonton, Alberta, Canada: University of Alberta.

Peterson, J. A. 1975. Total conditioning: A case study. *Athletic Journal* 56 (September): 40-55.

———., ed. 1978. *Total fitness: The Nautilus way.* West Point, NY: Leisure Press.

Peterson, J. A., and C. X. Bryant, eds. 1992. *The Stairmaster fitness handbook.* Indianapolis: Masters Press.

Peterson, J. A., and M. B. Horodyski. 1988. *How to jump higher.* Indianapolis: Masters Press.

Peterson, J. A., and W. L. Westcott. 1990. Stronger by the minute. *Fitness Management* 6 (June): 22-24.

Pezullo, D., S. Whitney and J. Irrgang. 1993. A comparison of vertical jump enhancement using plyometrics and strength footwear shoes versus plyometrics alone. *Journal of Orthopaedic and Sports Physical Therapy* 17: 68.

Philen, R. M., D. I. Ortiz, S. B. Auerbach and H. Falk. 1992. Survey of advertising for nutritional supplements in health and bodybuilding magazines. *Journal of the American Medical Association* 268 (8): 1008-1011.

Physician's Desk Reference [PDR]. 1994. 48th ed. Montvale, NJ: Medical Economics Data Production Company.

Piehl, K. 1974. Glycogen storage and depletion in human skeletal muscle fibers. *Acta Physiologica Scandinavica* (Supplementum 402): 1-32.

Pipes, T. V. 1978. Variable resistance versus constant resistance strength training in adult males. *European Journal of Applied Physiology* 39: 27-35.

———. 1979. High intensity, not high speed. *Athletic Journal* 59 (December): 60, 62.

———. 1988a. A.C.T. - The steroid alternative. *Scholastic Coach* 57 (January): 106, 108-109, 112.

———. 1988b. Letter to the author concerning plyometrics (January 18).

———. 1989. *The steroid alternative.* Placerville, CA: Sierra Gold Graphics.

———. 1992. Steroids and overtraining. *Scholastic Coach* 61 (May/June): 52-53.

———. 1994. Strength training & fiber types. *Scholastic Coach* 63 (March): 67-70.

Pitts, E. H. 1992. Pills, powders, potions and persuasions. *Fitness Management* 9 (November): 34-35.

Pollock, M. L. 1973. The quantification of endurance training programs. In *Exercise and sports sciences reviews*, ed. J. H. Wilmore, 155-188. New York, NY: Academic Press.

Pollock, M. L., J. Dimmick, H. S. Miller, Z. Kendrick and A. C. Linnerud. 1975. Effects of mode of training on cardiovascular function and body composition of middle-aged men. *Medicine and Science in Sports and Exercise* 7: 139-145.

Pollock, M. L., S. H. Leggett, J. E. Graves, A. Jones, M. N. Fulton and J. Cirulli. 1989. Effect of resistance training on lumbar extension strength. *The American Journal of Sports Medicine* 17: 624-629.

Pollock, M. L., and J. H. Wilmore. 1990. *Exercise in health and disease: Evaluation and prescription for prevention and rehabilitation.* 2d ed. Philadelphia: W. B. Saunders Company.

Pollock, M. L., J. F. Carroll, J. E. Graves, S. H. Leggett, R. W. Braith, M. Limacher and J. M. Hagberg. 1991. Injuries and adherence to walk/jog and resistance training programs in the elderly. *Medicine and Science in Sports and Exercise* 23: 1194-1200.

Pollock, M. L., J. E. Graves, M. M. Bamman, S. H. Leggett, D. M. Carpenter, C. Carr, J. Cirulli, J. Matkozich and M. N. Fulton. 1993a. Frequency and volume of resistance training: Effect on cervical extension strength. *Archives of Physical Medicine and Rehabilitation* 74: 1080-1086.

Pollock, M. L., J. E. Graves, D. M. Carpenter, D. Foster, S. H. Leggett and M. N. Fulton. 1993b. The lumbar musculature: Testing and conditioning for rehabilitation. In *Rehabilitation of the spine*, ed. S. H. Hochschuler, R. D. Guyer and H. B. Cotler, 263-284. St. Louis: Mosby, Inc.

Pope Jr, H. G., and D. L. Katz. 1988. Affective and psychotic symptoms associated with anabolic steroid use. *American Journal of Psychiatry* 145 (4): 487-490.

Porcari, J. P. 1994. Fat-burning exercise: Fit or farce. *Fitness Management* 10 (July): 40-41.

Poulton, E. C. 1957. On prediction in skilled movements. *Psychological Bulletin* 54:467-478.

Rasch, P. J. 1979. *Introduction to weight training.* 3d ed. Dubuque, IA: William C. Brown Company Publishers.

Rasch, P. J., and C. E. Morehouse. 1957. Effect of static and dynamic exercises on muscular strength and hypertrophy. *Journal of Applied Physiology* 11: 29-34.

Rasch, P. J., and F. L. Allman. 1972. Controversial exercises. *American Corrective Therapy Journal* 26 (4): 95-98.

Reid, C. M., R. A. Yeater and I. H. Ullrich. 1987. Weight training and strength, cardiorespiratory functioning and body composition in men. *British Journal of Sports Medicine* 21: 40-44.

Reinebold, J. 1993. H.I.T. in the CFL British Columbia style. *High Intensity Training Newsletter* 4 (4): 7-8.

Reston, J. 1982. Strength training philosophies come to trial. *Coach & Athlete* (March): 42-43.

Rians, C. B., A. Weltman, B. R. Cahill, C. A. Janney, S. R. Tippett and F. I. Katch. 1987. Strength training for prepubescent males: Is it safe? *The American Journal of Sports Medicine* 15: 483-489.

Rice, S. G. 1993. Strength training in young athletes. In *Sports Medicine Secrets*, ed. M. B. Mellion, 68-71. Philadelphia: Hanley & Belfus, Inc.

Riley, D. P. 1979. Speed of exercise versus speed of movement. *Scholastic Coach* 48 (May/June): 90, 92-93, 97-98.

———. 1980. Time and intensity: Keys to maximum strength gains. *Scholastic Coach* 50 (November): 65-66, 74-75.

———. 1981a. Manual resistance: A productive alternative (part 1). *Scholastic Coach* 51 (September): 80, 82, 85-86.

———. 1981b. Power line. *Scholastic Coach* 51 (August): 74-75, 81.

———. 1982a. *Maximum muscular fitness: How to develop strength without equipment.* West Point, NY: Leisure Press.

———. 1982b. *Strength training by the experts.* 2d ed. West Point, NY: Leisure Press.

———. 1982c. *Strength training for football: The Penn State way.* 2d ed. West Point, NY: Leisure Press.

———. 1982d. Guidelines for strength program. *Scholastic Coach* 51 (May/June): 64-65, 80.

———. 1982e. Power line. *Scholastic Coach* 52 (November): 45, 47, 69, 71.

———. 1982f. Try PPE, the best way! (part 2). *Scholastic Coach* 52 (September): 42, 44, 79.

———. 1983a. Strength training as part of the educational curriculum (part 1). *Scholastic Coach* 52 (January): 74, 76-77.

———. 1983b. Strength training as part of the educational curriculum (part 2). *Scholastic Coach* 52 (February): 48, 50-52, 64.

————. 1983c. Strength training as part of the educational curriculum (part 3). *Scholastic Coach* 52 (March): 72-73.

————. 1983d. Strength training as part of the educational curriculum (part 4). *Scholastic Coach* 52 (April): 69-71.

————. 1992. *Redskin conditioning.* Ashburn, VA: Washington Redskins.

Risch, S. V., N. K. Norvell, M. L. Pollock, E. Risch, H. Langer, M. N. Fulton, J. E. Graves and S. H. Leggett. 1993. Lumbar strengthening in chronic low back patients: Psychological and physiological benefits. *Spine* 18: 232-238.

Risser, W. L. 1991. Weight training injuries in children and adolescents. *American Family Physician* 44 (6): 2104-2110.

Risser, W. L., J. M. H. Risser and D. Preston. 1990. Weight training injuries in adolescents. *The American Journal of Diseases of Children* 144: 1015-1017.

Roberts, D. F. 1984. Genetic determinants of sports performance. In *Sport and human genetics*, ed. R. M. Malina and C. Bouchard, 105-121. Champaign, IL: Human Kinetics Publishers, Inc.

Roman, W. J., J. Fleckenstein, J. Stray-Gundersen, S. E. Alway, R. Peshock and W. J. Gonyea. 1993. Adaptations in the elbow flexors of elderly males after heavy-resistance training. *Journal of Applied Physiology* 74: 750-754.

Ropp, K. L. 1992. Steroid substitutes: No-win situation for athletes. *FDA Consumer* 26 (December): 8-12.

Rosentswieg, J., M. Hinson and M. Ridgway. 1975. An electromyographic comparison of an isokinetic bench press performed at three speeds. *Research Quarterly* 46: 471-475.

Rossi, F. 1978. Spondylolysis, spondylolisthesis and sports. *Journal of Sports Medicine and Physical Fitness* 18: 317-340.

Rossi, F., and S. Dragoni. 1990. Lumbar spondylolysis: Occurrence in competitive athletes. *Journal of Sports Medicine and Physical Fitness* 30: 450-452.

Rowe, G. G., and M. B. Roche. 1953. The etiology of separate neural arch. *Journal of Bone and Joint Surgery* 35A: 102-110.

Rutherford, O. M., and D. A. Jones. 1986. The role of learning and co-ordination in strength training. *European Journal of Applied Physiology* 55: 100-105.

Saartok, T. 1988. Effects of human growth hormone on skeletal muscle. In *Muscle development: Nutritional alternatives to anabolic steroids*, ed. W. E. Garrett Jr and T. R. Malone, 44-49. Columbus, OH: Ross Laboratories.

Sage, G. H. 1977. *Introduction to motor behavior: A neuropsychological approach.* 2d ed. Reading, MA: Addison-Wesley Publishing Company.

Sale, D. G. 1987. Influence of exercise and training on motor unit activation. In *Exercise and sport science reviews* 15, ed. K. B. Pandolf, 95-151. New York: MacMillan.

————. 1988. Neural adaptation to resistance training. *Medicine and Science in Sports and Exercise* 20: 135-145.

Sale, D. G., and D. MacDougall. 1981. Specificity in strength training: A review for the coach and athlete. *Canadian Journal of Applied Sport Sciences* 6: 87-92.

Salmons, S. 1994. Exercise, stimulation and type transformation of skeletal muscle. *International Journal of Sports Medicine* 15 (3): 136-141.

Saltin, B., J. Henriksson, E. Nygaard and P. Andersen. 1977. Fiber types and metabolic potentials of skeletal muscles in sedentary men and endurance runners. In *The marathon*, ed. P. Milvy. New York: New York Academy of Sciences.

Saltos, E. 1993. The food pyramid - food label connection. *FDA Consumer* 27 (June): 17-21.

Sargent, R. 1988. Protein needs for the athlete. *National Strength & Conditioning Association Journal* 10 (4): 53-55.

Schantz, P., E. Randall-Fox, W. Hutchison, A. Tyden and P.-O. Astrand. 1983. Muscle fiber type distribution, muscle cross-sectional area and maximal voluntary strength in humans. *Acta Physiologica Scandinavica* 117: 219-226.

Schmidt, R. A. 1975. *Motor skills.* New York: Harper & Row.

————. 1991. *Motor learning and performance: From principles to practice.* Champaign, IL: Human Kinetics Books.

Schrof, J. M. 1992. Pumped up. *U. S. News and World Report* 112 (21): 54-59, 60-63.

Schwane, J. A., S. R. Johnson, C. B. Vandenakker and R. B. Armstrong. 1983. Delayed-onset muscular soreness and plasma CPK and LDH activities after downhill running. *Medicine and Science in Sports and Exercise* 15: 51-56.

Scoles, G. 1978. Depth jumping! Does it really work? *Athletic Journal* 58 (January): 48-50, 74-76.

Scrimshaw, N.S., and V. R. Young. 1976. The requirements of human nutrition. *Scientific American* 235 (3): 50-64.

Scripture, E. W., T. L. Smith and E. M. Brown. 1894. On the education of muscular control and power. *Studies from the Yale Psychological Laboratory* 2: 114-119.

Seliger, V., L. Dolejs and V. Karas. 1980. Dynamometric comparison of maximum eccentric, concentric and isometric contractions using EMG and energy expenditure measurements. *European Journal of Applied Physiology* 45: 235-244.

Selye, H. 1956. *The stress of life.* New York, NY: McGraw-Hill.

Seminick, D. 1990. *Louisville Cardinals summer conditioning booklet.* 3d ed. Louisville: University of Louisville Graphics.

Sharkey, B. J. 1975. *Physiology and physical activity.* New York: Harper & Row.

————. 1984. *Physiology of fitness.* Champaign, IL: Human Kinetics Publishers, Inc.

Sheldon, W. 1954. *Atlas of men.* New York, NY: Harper and Brothers.

Shils, M. E., and V. R. Young. 1988. *Modern nutrition in health and disease.* Philadelphia: Lea & Febiger.

Short, S. H., and W. R. Short. 1983. Four year study of university athletes' dietary intake. *Journal of the American Dietetic Association* 82: 632-645.

Silvester, L. J., C. Stiggins, C. McGown, and G. R. Bryce. 1982. The effect of variable resistance and free weight training programs on strength and vertical jump. *National Strength & Conditioning Association Journal* 3: 30-33.

Simmons, J. 1994. *Browns' 1994 conditioning*. Cleveland, OH: Cleveland Browns.

Singh, A., F. M. Moses and P. A. Deuster. 1992. Chronic multivitamin-mineral supplementation does not enhance physical performance. *Medicine and Science in Sports and Exercise* 24: 726-732.

Skinner, J. S. 1992. Cardiorespiratory fitness. In *The Stairmaster fitness handbook*, ed. J. A. Peterson and C. X. Bryant, 29-37. Indianapolis: Masters Press.

Skinner, J. S., and T. McLellan. 1980. The transition from aerobic to anaerobic metabolism. *Research Quarterly for Exercise and Sport* 51: 234-248.

Slater-Hammel, A. T. 1950. Bilateral effects of muscle activity. *Research Quarterly* 21: 203-209.

Slavin, J. L., G. Lanners and M. A. Engstrom. 1988. Amino acid supplements: Beneficial or risky? *The Physician and Sportsmedicine* 16 (3): 221-224.

Small, C. L. 1992. Low back problems in young athletes. *High Intensity Training Newsletter* 3 (4): 7-9.

Smith, N. J. 1984a. Children and parents: Growth, development, and sports. In *Sports medicine*, ed. R. H. Strauss, 207-217. Philadelphia: W. B. Saunders Company.

———. 1984b. Nutrition. In *Sports medicine*, ed. R. H. Strauss, 468-480. Philadelphia: W. B. Saunders Company.

Spalding, B. J. 1991. Black-market technology: Athletes abuse EPO and HGH. *Bio/Technology* 9 (November): 1050, 1052-1053.

Sparling, P., R. Recker and T. Lambrinides. 1994. Position statement to football players from Cincinnati Bengals Training Staff and nutrition consultant.

Spassov, A. 1989. Qualities of strength and their application to sports: An introduction. *National Strength & Conditioning Association Journal* 10 (6): 77-79.

Stamford, B. 1986. Leverage and strength. *The Physician and Sportsmedicine* 14 (12): 206.

Starkey, D. B., M. A. Welsch, M. L. Pollock, J. E. Graves, W. F. Brechue and Y. Ishida. 1994. Equivalent improvement in strength following high intensity, low and high volume training. Abstract presented at the American College of Sports Medicine 40th Anniversary Meeting. Indianapolis, IN.

Stockholm, A. J., and R. C. Nelson. 1965. The immediate aftereffects of increased resistance upon physical performance. *Research Quarterly* 36: 337-341.

Stone, M. H., A. C. Fry, M. Ritchie, L. Stoessel-Ross and J. L. Marist. 1994. Injury potential and safety aspects of weightlifting movements. *National Strength & Conditioning Association Journal* 16 (3): 15-21.

Stone, W. J., and W. A. Kroll. 1978. *Sports conditioning and weight training: Programs for athletic competition*. Boston, MA: Allyn and Bacon, Inc.

Stower, T., J. McMillan, D. Scala, V. Davis, D. Wilson and M. Stone. 1983. The short-term effects of three different strength-power training methods. *National Strength & Conditioning Association Journal* 5 (3): 24-27.

Straub, W. F. 1968. Effect of overload training procedures upon velocity and accuracy of the overarm throw. *Research Quarterly* 39: 370-379.

Strauss, R. H., ed. 1984. *Sports medicine*. Philadelphia: W. B. Saunders Company.

Strauss, R. H., M. T. Liggett and R. R. Lanese. 1985. Anabolic steroid use and perceived effects in ten weight-trained women. *Journal of the American Medical Association* 253 (19): 2871-2873.

Stromme, S. B., and H. Skard. 1980. *Physical fitness and fitness testing*. Sandnes, Norway: Jonas Oglaend A.s.

Swift, E. J. 1903. Studies in the psychology and physiology of learning. *American Journal of Psychology* 14: 201-251.

Tanner, J. M. 1964. *The physique of the Olympic athlete*. London: George Allen and Unwin.

Tanner, S. M. 1993. Weighing the risks: Strength training for children and adolescents. *The Physician and Sportsmedicine* 21 (6): 105-106, 109-110, 114-116.

Tarnopolsky, M. A., S. A. Atkinson, J. D. MacDougall, A. Chesley, S. Phillips and H. Schwarcz. 1992. Evaluation of protein requirements for trained strength athletes. *Journal of Applied Physiology* 73: 1986-1995.

Taylor, M. R. 1993. The dietary supplement debate of 1993: An FDA perspective. Presented at the Federation of American Societies for Experimental Biology Annual Meeting. New Orleans, LA.

Taylor, W. N. 1985. *Hormonal manipulation: A new era of monstrous athletes*. Jefferson, NC: McFarland & Company, Inc.

Telford, R., E. Catchpole, V. Deakin, A. Hahn and A. Plank. 1992. The effect of 7 to 8 months of vitamin/mineral supplementation on athletic performance. *International Journal of Sports Nutrition* 2: 135-153.

Terbizan, D. T, and R. L. Bartels. 1985. The effect of set-repetition combinations on strength gains in females age 18-35. Abstract presented at the American College of Sports Medicine Annual Meeting. Nashville, TN.

Terblance, S., T. D. Noakes, S. Dennis, D. Marais and M. Eckert. 1992. Failure of magnesium supplementation to influence marathon running performance or recovery in magnesium-replete subjects. *International Journal of Sports Nutrition* 2: 154-164.

Thomas, J. 1994. *Penn State football strength training summer conditioning manual*. University Park, PA: Penn State University.

Thompson, C. W. 1985. *Manual of structural kinesiology*. 10th ed. St. Louis: Times Mirror/Mosby College Publishing.

Thorndike, E. L. 1903. *Educational Psychology*. New York, NY: Lemke and Buechner.

Thorstensson, A. 1976. Muscle strength, fiber types and enzyme activities in man. *Acta Physiologica Scandinavica* (Supplementum 443): 1-44.

Thorstensson, A., G. Grimby and J. Karlsson. 1976. Force-velocity relationship and fiber composition in human knee extensor muscles. *Journal of Applied Physiology* 40: 12-16.

Thrash, K., and B. Kelly. 1987. Flexibility and strength training. *Journal of Applied Sport Science Research* 1: 74-75.

Todd, T. 1986. A brief history of resistance exercise. In *Getting stronger*, revised ed, by B. Pearl and G. T. Moran, 413-431. Bolinas, CA: Shelter Publications, Inc.

Tzankoff, S. P., and A. H. Norris. 1977. Effect of muscle mass decrease on age related BMR changes. *Journal of Applied Physiology* 43: 1001-1006.

Universal Gym Equipment, Inc. 1994. *Power circuit manual.* Cedar Rapids, IA: Universal Gym Equipment, Inc.

Vander, A. J., J. H. Sherman and D. S. Luciano. 1975. *Human physiology: The mechanisms of body function.* 2d ed. New York, NY: McGraw-Hill, Inc.

Vandervoort, A. A., D. G. Sale and J. R. Moroz. 1987. Strength-velocity relationship and fatiguability of unilateral versus bilateral arm extension. *European Journal of Applied Physiology* 56: 201-205.

Van Oteghen, S. L. 1975. Two speeds of isokinetic exercise as related to the vertical jump performance in women. *Research Quarterly* 46: 78-84.

Verkhoshansky, Y. 1966. Perspectives in the improvement of speed and strength preparation of jumpers. *Track and Field* 9: 11-12.

————. 1991. *Ultra mass manual.* Pleasant Hill, CA: Atletika, Inc.

Vitti, G. J. 1984. The effects of variable training speeds on leg strength and power. *Athletic Training* (Spring): 26-29.

Vorobyev, A. N. 1988. Weightlifting injuries and their prevention. *Tyazhelaya Atletika* 1: 239-242.

Vrbova, G. 1979. Influence of activity on some characteristic properties of slow and fast mammalian muscles. *Exercise and Sport Sciences Reviews* 7: 181-213.

Wade, N. 1972. Anabolic steroids: Doctors denounce them, but athletes aren't listening. *Science* 176: 1399-1403.

Watson, J. 1994. Basketball strength training Q&A. *Coaching Women's Basketball* 8 (Special issue): 40-42.

Weight, L. M., T. D. Noakes, D. Labadorios, J. Graves, D. Haem, P. Jacobs and P. Berman. 1988. Vitamin and mineral status of trained athletes including the effects of supplementation. *American Journal of Clinical Nutrition* 47: 186-191.

Welday, J. 1986. Coming clean on the power clean. *Scholastic Coach* 56 (September): 22-23.

Wells, C. L. 1985. *Women, sport and performance: A physiological perspective.* Champaign, IL: Human Kinetics Publishers, Inc.

Wells, J. B., E. Jokl and J. Bohanen. 1963. The effect of intensive physical training upon body composition of adolescent girls. *Journal of the Association for Physical and Mental Rehabilitation* 17: 68-72.

Wenger, H. A., and G. J. Bell. 1986. The interactions of intensity, frequency and duration of exercise training in altering cardiorespiratory fitness. *Sports Medicine* 3: 346-356.

Wenzel, R. R., and E. M. Perfetto. 1992. The effect of speed versus non-speed training in power development. *Journal of Applied Sport Science Research* 6: 82-87.

Westcott, W. L. 1983. *Strength fitness: Physiological principles and training techniques.* Expanded ed. Boston: Allyn and Bacon, Inc.

————. 1986. Integration of strength, endurance and skill training. *Scholastic Coach* 55 (May/June): 74.

————. 1987. Individualized strength training for girl high school runners. *Scholastic Coach* 57 (December): 71-72.

————. 1989. Strength training research: sets and repetitions. *Scholastic Coach* 58 (May/June): 98-100.

————. 1994. Seniors gain strength. *The Forerunner Newsletter* 1 (7): 2-3.

Wetzel, S. 1994. Letter to the author from the Minnesota Vikings' strength coach. (September 14).

Wheeler, K. B. 1989. Proteins and amino acids. *National Strength & Conditioning Association Journal* 10 (6): 22, 28-29.

Wheeler, K. B., and A. M. Cameron. 1993. Nutrition questions and answers. *American Fitness Quarterly* 12 (July): 24-26.

Wikgren, S. 1988. The plyometrics debate. *Coaching Women's Basketball* 1 (May/June): 10-13.

Williams, M. H. 1992. *Nutrition for fitness and sport.* Dubuque, IA: Brown & Benchmark.

————. 1993. Nutritional supplements for strength trained athletes. *Sports Science Exchange* 6 (6): 1-6.

Wilmore, J.H. 1974. Alterations in strength, body composition and anthropometric measurements consequent to a 10-week weight training program. *Medicine and Science in Sports* 6: 133-138.

————. 1982. *Training for sport and activity: The physiological basis of the conditioning process.* 2d ed. Boston: Allyn and Bacon, Inc.

Wilt, F. 1975. Plyometrics: What it is — how it works. *Athletic Journal* 55 (May): 76, 89-90.

Winningham, S. N. 1966. Effect of training with ankle weights on running skill. Unpublished doctoral dissertation. Los Angeles, CA: University of Southern California.

Winter, D. A. 1990. *The biomechanics of human movement.* New York, NY: Wiley & Sons.

Wirhed, R. 1984. *Athletic ability: The anatomy of winning.* New York: Harmony Books.

Wolf, M. D. 1982. Muscles: Structure, function and control. In *Strength training by the experts*, 2d ed, by D. P. Riley, 27-40. West Point, NY: Leisure Press.

Wood, K. 1991. Cincinnati Bengals' strength training program. *American Fitness Quarterly* 10 (July): 38, 40.

Work, J. A. 1989. Is weight training safe during pregnancy? *The Physician and Sportsmedicine* 17 (3): 257-259.

Wright, J. E., and M. H. Stone. 1985. Anabolic drug use by athletes literature review. *National Strength & Conditioning Association Journal* 7 (5): 45-59.

Yarasheski, K. E., J. A. Campbell, M. J. Rennie, J. O. Holloszy and D. M. Bier. 1990. Effect of strength training and growth hormone administration on whole body and skeletal muscle leucine metabolism. Abstract presented at the American College of Sports Medicine 37th Annual Meeting. Salt Lake City, UT.

Yasuda, Y., and M. Miyamura. 1983. Cross-transfer effects of muscular training on blood flow in the ipsilateral and contralateral forearms. *European Journal of Applied Physiology* 51: 321-329.

Yesalis, C. E., N. J. Kennedy, A. N. Kopstein and M. S. Bahrke. 1993. Anabolic-androgenic steroid use in the United States. *Journal of the American Medical Association* 270 (10): 1217-1221.

Young, A., M. Stokes, J. M. Round and R. H. T. Edwards. 1983. The effect of high-resistance training on the strength and cross-sectional area of the human quadriceps. *European Journal of Clinical Investigation* 13: 411-417.

Zinovieff, A. N. 1951. Heavy-resistance exercise: The "Oxford technique." *British Journal of Physical Medicine* 14: 129-132.

AUTHOR INDEX

SUBJECT INDEX

ABOUT THE AUTHOR

Photo by Audrey Grimaldi

Matt Brzycki was born in Abington (PA) and grew up in Wilkes-Barre (PA). After graduating from James M. Coughlin High School in 1975, he enlisted in the United States Marine Corps. While stationed at the Marine Corps Base in Twentynine Palms (CA), Brzycki won the 1976 Base Powerlifting Championships and the 1977 Base Bench Press Championships in the 165-pound weight class. He attained the rank of sergeant in less than 29 months. Near the end of 1977 — at the age of 20 — Brzycki was approved by the Commandant of the Marine Corps to attend Drill Instructor (DI) School at the Marine Corps Recruit Depot in San Diego. Upon graduation from DI School in 1978, he was one of the youngest drill instructors in the Marine Corps. Among his many responsibilities as a drill instructor was the physical preparedness of Marine recruits.

After completing his four-year enlistment in 1979, Brzycki enrolled at The Pennsylvania State University, where he received his Bachelor of Science degree in Health and Physical Education. He represented the university for two years in the Pennsylvania State Collegiate Powerlifting Championships and was also a place-winner in his first bodybuilding competition.

Following graduation from Penn State in 1983, Brzycki served as a health fitness supervisor at Princeton University (NJ). In 1984, he was named Assistant Strength Coach at Rutgers University (NJ). He remained in that position until 1990, when he returned to Princeton University as the school's Strength Coach and Health Fitness Coordinator. In 1994, he was named the Coordinator of Health Fitness, Strength and Conditioning Programs at Princeton University. His responsibilities at the university include developing classes for the physical education curriculum along with training and evaluating the physical education and Nautilus instructors. Brzycki also teaches strength training classes for the students, faculty and staff at the university. He developed the "Strength Training Theory and Applications" course for exercise science and sports studies majors at Rutgers University and has taught the program since March 1990 as a member of the Faculty of Arts and Sciences.

Brzycki has been a featured speaker at conferences and seminars in New Jersey, New York, Ohio, Pennslyvania, Virginia and Minnesota. He has authored over 140 articles that have been featured in more than two dozen different publications including *Fitness Management*; *High Intensity Training Newsletter*; *Journal of Physical Education and Recreation*; *International Gymnast*; *Nautilus*; *Pennsylvania Journal of Health, Physical Education, Recreation & Dance*; *Powerlifting Canada*; *Scholastic Coach*; *Texas Coach*; *Women's Sports and Fitness*; and *Wrestling USA*. Brzycki has also coauthored the book *Conditioning for Basketball* with Shaun Brown.

He and his wife, Alicia, currently reside in Hamilton Township, New Jersey.